Reconsidering Locali...

'Localism' has been deployed in recent debates over planning law as an anodyne, grassroots way to shape communities into sustainable, human-scale neighborhoods. But 'local' is a moving category, with contradictory, nuanced dimensions. *Reconsidering Localism* brings together new scholarship from leading academics in Europe and North America to develop a theoretically-grounded critique and definition of the new localism, and how it has come to shape urban governance and urban planning.

Moving beyond the UK, this book examines localism and similar shifts in planning policy throughout Europe, and features essays on localism and place-making, sustainability, social cohesion, and citizen participation in community institutions. It explores how debates over localism and citizen control play out at the neighborhood, institutional and city level, and has come to affect the urban landscape throughout Europe. *Reconsidering Localism* is a current, vital addition to planning scholarship.

Simin Davoudi is Professor of Environmental Policy and Planning and Associate Director of the Institute for Sustainability at Newcastle University, UK. She is past President of the Association of the European Schools of Planning, Fellow of the Academy of Social Sciences, expert advisor for the UK Government and EU Commission, and member of national and international research assessment panels. Her research focuses on the interface of society and ecology.

Ali Madanipour is Professor of Urban Design and Director of Global Urban Research Unit (GURU) at the School of Architecture, Planning and Landscape, Newcastle University, UK. His latest books include *Public Space and the Challenges of Urban Transformation in Europe*, and *Urban Design, Space and Society*.

THE RTPI Library Series

Editors: Robert Upton, *Infrastructure Planning Commission in England*
Jill Grant, *Dalhousie University, Canada*
Stephen Ward, *Oxford Brookes University, United Kingdom*

Published by Routledge in conjunction with The Royal Town Planning Institute, this series of leading-edge texts looks at all aspects of spatial planning theory and practice from a comparative and international perspective.

Planning in Postmodern Times
Philip Allmendinger

The Making of the European Spatial Development Perspective
Andreas Faludi and Bas Waterhout

Planning for Crime Prevention
Richard Schneider and Ted Kitchen

The Planning Polity
Mark Tewdwr-Jones

Shadows of Power: An Allegory of Prudence in Land-Use Planning
Jean Hillier

Urban Planning and Cultural Identity
William JV Neill

Place Identity, Participation and Planning
Edited by Cliff Hague and Paul Jenkins

Planning for Diversity
Dory Reeves

Planning the Good Community: New Urbanism in Theory and Practice
Jill Grant

Planning, Law and Economics
Barrie Needham

Indicators for Urban and Regional Planning
Cecilia Wong

Planning at the Landscape Scale
Paul Selman

Urban Structure Matters
Petter Naess

Urban Complexity and Spatial Strategies: Towards a Relational Planning for Our Times
Patsy Healey

The Visual Language of Spatial Planning: Exploring Cartographic Representations for Spatial Planning in Europe
Stefanie Dühr

Planning and Transformation: Learning from the Post-Apartheid Experience
Philip Harrison, Alison Todes & Vanessa Watson

Conceptions of Space and Place in Strategic Spatial Planning
Edited by Simin Davoudi and Ian Strange

Regional Planning for Open Space
Edited by Terry van Dijk and Arnold van der Valk

Crossing Borders: International Exchange and Planning Practices
Edited by Patsy Healey and Robert Upton

Effective Practice in Spatial Planning
Janice Morphet

Transport Matters
Angela Hull

Cohesion, Coherence, Co-operation: European Spatial Planning Coming of Age?
Andreas Faludi

Strategic Spatial Projects: Catalysts for Change
Edited by Stijn Oosterlynck, Jef Van den Broeck, Louis Albrechts, Frank Moulaert and Ann Verhetsel

Implementing Sustainability
Caroline Miller

Land and Limits, second edition
Richard Cowell and Susan Owens

Insurgencies: Essays in Planning Theory
John Friedmann

An Anatomy of Sprawl: Planning and Politics in Britain
Nicholas A Phelps

English Regional Planning 2000–2010: Lessons for the Future
Corrine Swain, Tim Marshall, Tony Baden

Reviving Critical Planning Theory: Dealing with Pressure, Neo-liberalism, and Responsibility in Communicative Planning
Tore Øivin Sager

Planning for Growth: Urban and Regional Planning in China
Fulong Wu

Reconsidering Localism
Edited by Simin Davoudi and Ali Madanipour

Planning/Conflict: Critical Perspectives on Contentious Urban Developments
Edited by Enrico Gualini

"The UK Government embracing localism has created much discussion. In their own contributions, Davoudi and Madanipour cast light on its many facets and ambivalences and they have brought together readings showing the historical depth and the breath of the concept. This gives the work value well beyond the UK planning context."

– *Andreas Faludi, Professor Emeritus, Delft University of Technology, the Netherlands*

"The topicality of this book can hardly be overestimated. If crisis learned the planning community one thing it is that we have to reconsider the pivotal role of social interaction at the local scale in drawing up the potential of planning and spatial intervention. The challenge is to root the planning issues of knowledge and action but also the meaning of institution and societal power in the civic reciprocity of local practices without being trapped in a grassroots type of local particularism. New localism is not static and place bounded in a time of globalization, it is highly dynamic and its meaning has to be conquered and reconquered in macro- and micro level sociological processes of rescaling. Urbanism today considers the phenomenon of localism as an open process of discovery reflecting on the permanently changing meaning of place. The editors authoritatively managed to connect the planning discourse with this new local reflexivity and selected a fine collection of papers with experiences in different disciplines."

– *Willem Salet, Professor Urban Planning, University of Amsterdam*

"This important and timely collection has been well crafted by its editors, both leading thinkers in the field of planning studies. The essays point to the possibilities but also the paradoxes inherent in the contemporary emphasis on localism in many national settings. In a context of seemingly intractable global environmental and economic crises the book's critical emphasis on sustainability is especially pertinent and powerful."

– *Professor Brendan Gleeson, Director, Melbourne Sustainable Society Institute, University of Melbourne*

Reconsidering Localism

Edited by
Simin Davoudi and Ali Madanipour

NEW YORK AND LONDON

First published 2015
by Routledge
711 Third Avenue, New York, NY 10017

and by Routledge
2 Park Square, Milton Park, Abingdon, Oxon OX14 4RN

Routledge is an imprint of the Taylor & Francis Group, an informa business

Library of Congress Cataloguing in Publication data
Reconsidering localism / [edited by] Simin Davoudi and Ali Madanipour.
pages cm. – (RTPI library series)
1. Local government–Europe–Citizen participation. 2. Urban planning–Europe.
I. Davoudi, Simin. II. Madanipour, Ali.
JS3000.R426 2015
307.1′16094–dc23
2014026109

ISBN: 978-0-415-73561-2 (hbk)
ISBN: 978-0-415-73562-9 (pbk)
ISBN: 978-1-315-81886-3 (ebk)

Typeset in Goudy Old Style
by Out of House Publishing

Printed and bound by CPI Group (UK) Ltd, Croydon, CR0 4YY

Contents

Illustrations

Figures

Tables

Contributors

Elizabeth Brooks is a Post-Doctoral Research Fellow at the Crichton Institute, Glasgow University. Liz's doctoral research study took place in the North East and focused on the sustainability of rural areas as places to grow older; she currently works on community resilience and rural sustainability in southern Scotland.

Susan E. Clarke is Professor in the Department of Political Science, University of Colorado, Boulder, USA. She is co-author of *The Work of Cities* (1998) and *Multiethnic Moments: The Politics of Urban Education Reform* (2006) and co-editor of *The Oxford Handbook on Urban Politics* (2012). Her current research centres on politics and policies in Denver, CO.

Richard Cowell is Reader in Environmental Planning at the School of Planning and Geography, Cardiff University, and Course Director for the MSc in Sustainability, Planning and Environmental Policy. He has researched and published widely on land use planning and sustainable development, scale and environmental governance, and planning for renewable energy.

Paul Cowie is a Research Associate at Newcastle University, UK. His main research focus is on the relationship between representatives and those being represented in a range of governance situations. Dr Cowie has published a number of papers in relation to governance and legitimacy in relation to both terrestrial and marine spatial planning.

Simin Davoudi is Professor of Environmental Policy and Planning and Associate Director of the Institute for Sustainability at Newcastle University. She is past President of the Association of the European Schools of Planning, Fellow of the Academy of Social Sciences, expert advisor for the UK Government and EU Commission and member of national and international research assessment panels. Her research focuses on the interface of society and ecology.

Frank Gaffikin is Professor and Director of the Institute of Spatial & Environmental Planning, at Queen's University, Belfast. His research focus has been on urban policy and regeneration, and he has acted as a government advisor on this issue for many decades in Northern Ireland. He has written widely on the issue of planning in contested societies, and his most recent book on this topic is: *Planning in Divided Cities* (2011).

Susannah Gunn is a Senior Lecturer in Planning at Newcastle University. Dr Gunn's research interests relate to the changing arrangements to planning, focusing on the UK, and its implications for those involved in planning activities.

Patsy Healey is Professor Emeritus in the School of Architecture, Planning and Landscape at Newcastle University, UK. She is a specialist in planning theory and the practice of strategic planning and urban regeneration policies. Her most recent books are *Urban Complexity and Spatial Strategies* (2007) and *Making Better Places* (2010).

Andrew Hoolachan received his MA in Geography from the University of St Andrews and his MSc in International Town Planning from UCL. He is currently a PhD student in the Department of Architecture, University of Cambridge. He has previously worked as a Civil Servant in the Cabinet Office.

Ali Madanipour is Professor of Urban Design and Director of Global Urban Research Unit (GURU) at the School of Architecture, Planning and Landscape, Newcastle University. His latest books include *Public Space and the Challenges of Urban Transformation in Europe* (2014) and *Urban Design, Space and Society* (2014).

William E. Rees is Professor Emeritus at the University of British Columbia and former director of the School of Community and Regional Planning (SCARP) at UBC. His primary interest is in public policy and planning relating to global environmental trends and the ecological conditions for sustainable socio-economic development. He is the originator of the 'ecological footprint' concept and co-developer of the method.

Mark Shucksmith is Director of the Newcastle Institute for Social Renewal and Professor of Planning at Newcastle University. Mark's main areas of research include social exclusion in rural areas, rural housing, rural development, agricultural change and rural policy. Mark served on the Boards of the Countryside Agency and Commission for Rural Communities, on the Affordable Rural Housing Commission, chaired the Scottish Government's Committee of Inquiry into Crofting and led the Joseph Rowntree Foundation's rural programme.

Hilary Talbot has been a researcher in the Centre for Rural Economy at Newcastle University since 2006. Her focus is on rurality, and in particular on how people living in rural places band together to provide themselves with services, typically those that the public and private sector are unable or unwilling to provide to sparsely populated areas.

Mark Tewdwr-Jones is Professor of Town Planning at Newcastle University and a specialist in land use, spatial planning, governance and place representation. He often works as a boundary spanner across disciplines and sectors, and is interested in repositioning social science between and within science and humanities perspectives.

Jurgen van der Heijden works as a private consultant for AT Osborne Comp. The past five years he has helped over 20 groups of citizens establish their own energy or care cooperatives. As a volunteer he is member of the board of the energy cooperative in his home town. Jurgen is (co-)author of a range of publications (in Dutch) about the civic economy. In English he recently wrote a paper titled: 'Acceleration of the energy transition with the local energy cooperative'.

Geoff Vigar is Professor of Urban Planning at Newcastle University. His research focuses on: institutional design for spatial plan-making with a focus on inclusion and participation; ideas of professionalism in planning; and the politics of planning and transport policy-making.

Hendrik Wagenaar is Professor of Town and Regional Planning at the University of Sheffield. He publishes in the areas of urban governance, citizen participation, prostitution policy, practice theory and interpretive policy analysis. His publications include: *Deliberative Policy Analysis: Understanding Governance in the Network Society* (2003), *Meaning in Action: Interpretation and Dialogue in Policy Analysis* (2011) and *Practices of Freedom: Decentred Governance, Conflict and Democratic Participation* (2014).

Acknowledgement

We are grateful to Newcastle University's Social Renewal Societal Challenge for sponsoring the symposium held on 28–29 March 2012 in which the contributors to this book presented and discussed their papers.

1
Introduction

Simin Davoudi and Ali Madanipour

> I have three very clear priorities: localism, and we'll weave that into everything we do from parks to finance to policy. My second priority is localism, and my third is … localism. (Eric Pickles, Minister for Communities and Local Government, June 2010)

The above statement is an indication of how localism was propelled into the limelight of British politics after the 2010 election when a coalition of Conservatives and Liberal Democrats came into office and made it their mantra. Their emphasis on localism reflects what has become a zeitgeist where 'we are all localist now' (Walker, 2002). The popularity of the term is shared across the political spectrum. Indeed, it was the newfound salience of localism in British politics that provided the original impetus for this book because, despite its 'feel good' factor, localism evokes multiple and contested meanings. Localism is seen as: a re-ordering and liberalisation of political spaces, a site of empowerment, a locus of knowledge generation, a framework for social integration and community-building, a localisation of economic activities and a site of resistance and environmental activism. The motivations for localism range from communitarian intents to liberal and libertarian agendas and are riddled with tensions between progressive and regressive potentials.

Localism also means different things in different domains. From an *economic* perspective, it is seen as a localisation process, reversing 'the trend of globalisation by discriminating in favour of the local' (Hines, 2000: 27); a process that nurtures locally owned businesses, using local resources, employing local workers and serving local consumers (Shuman, 2000: 6). Its normative focus is on how to enable tighter, more visible and proximate relationships between producers and consumers as a way of strengthening endogenous growth. Thus, in the age of globalisation, localism can be seen as signifying the opposite of the global.

From a *political* perspective, localism denotes the decentralised and grassroots forms of power. It is often used in the context of subsidiarity, devolution and decentralisation of the state's powers, activities and responsibilities downwards to local governments and sideways to the market and civil society. Localism is often equated with democratisation and as such is one of the most frequently rehearsed rationales for decentralisation and for making the state accountable to people. The local is, therefore, portrayed as the site of resistance and empowerment of civil societies. It is the political perspective that underpins the elevation of localism in the British political landscape, as is reflected in the following statement:

> There's the efficiency argument that in huge hierarchies, money gets spent on bureaucracy instead of the frontline. There is the fairness argument that centralised national blueprints don't allow for local solutions to major social problems. And there is the political argument that centralisation creates a distance in our democracy between the government and the governed. (HM Government, 2010: 4)

From a *social* perspective, localism conjures up images of the community, which itself is a contested concept with multiple meanings. Some see the community as an object, while others consider it as a process. The structural functionalist approaches of the 1960s (as in the Chicago School) conceptualised the community as an 'organic whole' contained in a small geographical unit; a kind of a refuge from anonymity and alienation. The more recent post-structural approaches conceptualise the community as being diverse and fragmented with no necessary ties to location. Instead, emphasis is put on symbolic and discursive meanings of the community, and on values and interests as the bases for its formation (Walkerdine and Studdert, n.d.). Does localism challenge this shift of emphasis from place-based to interest-based communities? Or is it premised on the assumption that there is a close affinity between the bonds of culture and the ties of locality and that both are necessary conditions of a collective life?

From a *spatial* perspective, localism often refers to small geographical scales down to neighbourhoods. Some see it as a lower tier of a neatly nested hierarchy of global, national, regional levels; what Marston (2000) calls a Russian-doll view of scale. Others consider the local not as a fixed spatial unit but as a fluid, relational space that is socially (re)produced. They argue that to consider any one scale as a priori preferable to another is to fall into a scale trap (Purcell, 2006). From an *environmental* perspective, localism is seen as a path to sustainability. Some argue that downscaling activities and local self-sufficiency is seen as necessary for reversing the ecological crisis. Others question the ability of local sustainability actions in bringing about systemic change; that environmental problems are global problems requiring global action.

The book examines the notion of localism and its multiple meanings in the economic, social, political and environmental domains and highlights the tensions that arise from the localism agenda. It brings together contributions from leading academics in Europe and North America to provide an expansive understanding of 'localism'. The aim is to develop a theoretically grounded critique of the concept of localism and its articulation in the debates about: governance, democracy, citizen participation, place-making, social cohesion, civic capacity and sustainability transition. Attention is paid to both progressive and regressive potentials of localism and how these are played out in different contexts ranging from small neighbourhoods to contested cities and global ecologies, with examples from Britain as well as North America and Europe.

The book is organised in three parts and 14 chapters. After this introduction, Part I engages with different meanings of localism and its contested interpretations in diverse political contexts. Part II focuses on the relationship between localism and democracy and investigates whether localism can offer a promising prospect for the renewal of progressive politics. Part III addresses the relationship between localism and sustainability, raising the question as to whether and how the shift of attention to the local can address the global environmental crisis.

The four chapters in Part I critically engage with the theory and practice of localism and how it is understood in the context of political and social theories and played out in different contexts ranging from small neighbourhoods to divided cities and in the wider European debate on social cohesion. Chapter 2 analyses the concept of localism and its multiple meanings, with the aim of providing a theoretical understanding of the concept. It argues that the meaning of localism lies at an institutional–territorial–representational nexus with its own contested and continually changing ontologies, identities and boundaries. This nexus is formed by the different territorial and institutional arrangements that shape localities and by continually shifting intersection of different perspectives about the specificity and autonomy of a locality. From one perspective, which may be characterised as the view from within, localism is interpreted as a bid for autonomy, a form of resistance to the pressures from the outside, against the forces that try to integrate a locality into larger political units, economic processes and cultural identities. From another perspective, the view from the outside and from a more general standpoint, localism is seen as an attempt at efficiency exerted and encouraged by the higher levels of authority, which may demand openness and integration, while interpreting any form of resistance as fragmentary and regressive. The chapter argues for going beyond this dichotomy and analyses the local and localism at the intersection of institutions, territories and representations.

In Chapter 3, Frank Gaffikin engages with the paradox of localism in contested societies, drawing on the experiences of Northern Ireland. Localism proclaims the virtue of subsidiarity, and extols the ingenuity generated by home-grown resilience. However, he argues that whatever its democratic and entrepreneurial credentials in 'normal' urban conditions, the policy has less traction in 'contested' cities, where community is a much more exclusive concept. The chapter shows that in a context of deep division and pronounced spatial segregation, the primary objective of much neighbourhood activism can be to protect territory against the incursion of the alien 'other'. Thus, localism amid such separatist politics contains a central paradox: though professing a restorative potential, it can inadvertently accentuate rather than ameliorate the contest. Since contested cities are often crucibles for the bigger issue that they reflect (such as race, or ethno-nationalist belonging), when focus is placed on micro-spaces within them, the imprint of the macro quarrel is often acutely visible. Gaffikin, therefore, explores the ramification of this paradox for creating shared space, and for the capacity to twin the processes of regeneration and reconciliation that is crucial to the creation of peaceful and sustainable places. He concludes with an outline of how agonistic forms of collaboration that embrace wider socio-spatial constituencies can overcome the deficiencies of a narrow localism.

Through the example of Denver, Colorado, in Chapter 4 Susan Clarke analyses the political opportunities that localism may bring about. She argues that the recent entrepreneurial leveraging strategy in the city has retained a place-based focus, although one targeting the economic fabric at the neighbourhood level rather than a more holistic regeneration approach. As a result, leveraged investments are targeted in a smaller number of neighbourhoods than in traditional distribution strategies: neighbourhoods are being systematically carved up into districts that better serve the policy emphasis on their roles as investment sites. She argues that Denver's trajectory illustrates a shift from the 'politics of distribution' centred on distribution of public resources to the 'politics of construction' where assembling rather than directing resources is the key public role. Drawing on the post-political cities concept Clarke analyses the trajectory of neighbourhood regeneration policies in Denver between 1980 and 2012 and examines whether there is an emergent post-political landscape in Denver, one in which neighbourhood regeneration is de-politicised and removed from political debate. The chapter puts the Denver case in the context of neighbourhood policies in other American cities and considers the ways in which neighbourhood policies reflect a particular understanding of localism in the American context.

Chapter 5 presents a Foucauldian interpretation of localism, arguing that the emerging top-down localism in the UK is the spatial manifestation of 'post-social' technologies of neoliberal governmentality that began with the introduction of 'the community' a few decades ago. It suggests that localism re-imagines the local as 'the natural' geography of 'the community', which itself is seen as the 'natural' articulation of collective life. Governing through 'the local' involves freeing localities to become responsible for their own fates and bear the consequences of their own conducts, yet in such a way that their action is aligned with governmental ends. The chapter aims to demonstrate how the local is made both the target of governmental action and the voluntary partner of government, through a complex process of identification and responsibilisation, and how this process is enabled and regulated at a distance through technocratic and calculative technologies of agency and performance.

Part II of the book focuses on the progressive potentials of localism for developing civic capacity, shaping places and enhancing local knowledge exchanges. In Chapter 6, drawing on her engagement with practices of local planning and neighbourhood regeneration in the UK, Patsy Healey positions the concept of localism within the wider context of a search for more progressive approaches to place governance in complex, pluralistic and conflicted Western democracies. She centres the discussion on developing a civic capacity to promote integrated, richly informed and pluralistic conceptions of place qualities and connectivities, as these are evolving into the future. Healey argues that this requires recognition of the often deep conflicts that divide communities over current issues and future pathways, and that the challenge of place governance provides one of the key arenas within which the qualities of democratic systems are being tested at the present time. In this context, she discusses the hopes and dangers of the 'localist' agenda, and identifies its more progressive directions that can be cultivated in the micro-practices at multiple levels.

In Chapter 7, Hendrik Wagenaar and Jurgen van der Heijden draw on the experience of the Netherlands to describe a new generation of social economy initiatives that they call civic enterprises. They suggest that civic enterprise is distinguishable from the social economy as it has been practised, studied, made the object of government policies and invested with hope, by government officials and academic promoters for over two decades. This is because civic enterprises contain considerable economic and democratic potential that rests on the close association of the economic and democratic benefits of civic enterprise because social production and civic enterprise produce social goods in a democratic non-hierarchical, non-profit way that form an alternative to the traditional social production system of democratic capitalism, in which large centralised firms provide mass-produced goods to consumers with little or no voice in the production system. They also argue that since the early 1970s the market economy has eroded the quality of representative democracy in Western nations and threatens basic civic freedoms and social values. Social production and civic enterprise both operate on different principles that include associative democracy and informality. They suggest, therefore, that social economy and civic enterprise open up a perspective on economic, social and democratic governance that forms a real alternative to the inherent shortcomings of democratic capitalism.

Chapter 8 is developed from a case study of the emerging practices of neighbourhood planning in England and its latent assumption that communities have the capacity to develop a plan that can gain statutory status. Susannah Gunn, Elizabeth Brooks and Geoff Vigar review the trajectory of English planning's attempts to engage with communities and reflect on whether increased opportunity for empowerment is accompanied by communities' capacity to take advantage of it. They introduce the idea of community capacity as an analytical tool and use it to reflect on a case study of one of the vanguard Neighbourhood Planning processes (Allendale) and the plan it produced. They conclude that a community as rich as Allendale, in terms of community capacity and a relatively straightforward well-protected planning context, is able to complete such a task with considerable help from a highly engaged local authority, but raise important questions as to whether other communities with more limited assets, more complex and pressured development contexts and less local authority support are likely to find it harder.

In Chapter 9, Paul Cowie and Simin Davoudi question the democratic legitimacy of neighbourhood planning, which is the most visible manifestation of localism in England. Following a review of the type and sources of legitimacy, they suggest that in order to judge the legitimacy of a given political authority (such as neighbourhood forums) the analysts need to move beyond both normative–descriptive dualism and procedural–substantive dualism and consider a broader framework that allows for a situated and contextualised assessment. Their proposed framework, therefore, considers both procedural/democratic and substantive/outcome sources of legitimacy. As regards the former, the framework broadens the concept of representation to include its multiple forms. As regards the latter, it focuses not on ideal notions of outcomes, but rather on the premises upon which outcomes are considered as beneficial or otherwise. They use this framework, of contextualised and relational understanding of legitimacy, to examine the democratic legitimacy of English neighbourhood forums in general and the North Shields Fish Quay Neighbourhood Forum in particular, where the authors followed the process of plan making.

Part III of the book compares and contrasts the processes that are involved in promoting global environmental sustainability and actions undertaken at the local level, such as dealing with localisation of the production and consumption of goods and services in order to combat climate change. In Chapter 10, William Rees opens a global perspective on localisation and sustainability. The overarching premise of his argument is that global change represents new contexts for local planning that cannot be ignored. He advocates that both ecological and socio-economic trends at the global scale should be a major consideration in reframing local development policy. He draws a compelling picture of how the world may be in ecological overshoot and warns against human-induced climate change. He argues that the 'localism' agenda ignores the global context of local development and the increasingly pressing concerns raised by such issues as climate change. Arguing against 'business as usual', Rees advocates a deliberate planning and execution of prosperity without constant growth. Rees argues that this would restore and maintain the ecosphere while ensuring reasonable economic security and social order for all. He emphasises that such an agenda requires a complete transformation of national and global development paradigms where the world would abandon its myths of perpetual progress and material growth and focus instead on de-growth toward a sustainable steady-state with greater equity.

In Chapter 11, Richard Cowell investigates the effects of localism on sustainability. After reviewing the main criticisms of localist agendas within eco-political thinking, he identifies ways in which local arenas may possess positive qualities for transitions to sustainability but insists that these are contingent on other relations, and are potential rather than necessary qualities. He suggests that rather than viewing localities as arenas for promoting environmental sustainability, they should be viewed as one set of arenas in which struggles about the reconciliation of economy and environment are played out. By focusing on renewable energy policy and land use planning in England, Cowell assesses how the UK localism agenda intersects with potential qualities of local environmental action. His conclusion follows a similar line to that of Chapter 5 as he argues that in practice, localism is scarcely seen by the Coalition as a motor for environmental protection. Instead it is introduced to discipline local action, to ensure that local environmental actions do not unduly restrict economic growth. When it comes to society–environment relations, Cowell argues that the Coalition's promotion of localism is based on a desire to encourage economic development rather than environmental protection.

In Chapter 12, Andrew Hoolachan and Mark Tewdwr-Jones also attempt to deconstruct the meaning and contestation over the word 'local' and discuss how places and localities manifest themselves through planning processes. Making reference to observations and discussions of contemporary events that have been occurring in localities in England, they identify elements of local activism in place contention and sustainability and planning disputes. These are seen as a wider shift in participatory processes that are divergent, unique and often centred on different issues. They argue that localism and neighbourhood planning will refocus mindsets on the importance of what is local, what is distinctive, and how change may assist or threaten that. Furthermore, they foresee a degree of fuzziness emerging between how communities see the locale and local places, with contention over what counts for important and relevant.

Mark Shucksmith and Hilary Talbot, in Chapter 13, look at localism in the rural context. They introduce the main conceptualisations, policies and practices of rural development in the UK that resonate with a 'localism' agenda. These include not only those initiated by the state but also those of local people working collectively to address local needs and problems. More specifically, they discuss how these depart from many mainstream themes in the localism literature. The chapter outlines how rural localism is being damaged by government austerity measures, and how even fully resourced localism is not sufficient to address all rural problems in the UK, arguing that some can only be addressed by larger-scale structural adjustments at national or supranational scales.

Chapter 14 concludes the book by bringing together some of the key themes from across the contributions. It offers an overview of the subject to pave the way for a reconsideration of localism.

References

Hines, C. (2000) *Localisation: A global manifesto*, London: Earthscan.

HM Government. (2010) *The Localism Bill*, London: Stationery Office.

Marston, S. (2000) The social construction of scale, *Progress in Human Geography*, 24: 219–242.

Pickles, E. (2010) *Speech by Communities Secretary Eric Pickles at the Queen's Speech Forum*, 11 June 2010. Available at: www.gov.uk/government/speeches/queens-speech-forum (accessed 8 January 2014).

Purcell, M. (2006) Urban democracy and the local trap, *Urban Studies*, 43(11): 1921–1941.

Shuman, M. (2000) *Going Local: Creating self-reliant communities in a global age*, New York: Routledge.

Walker, D. (2002) *In Praise of Centralism: A critique of new localism*, London: Catalyst Forum.

Walkerdine, V. and Studdert, D. (n.d.) *Concepts and Meanings of Community in the Social Sciences*, discussion paper for AHRC Connected Communities Programme. Available at: www.ahrc.ac.uk/Funding-Opportunities/Research-funding/Connected-Communities/Scoping-studies-and-reviews/Pages/Scoping-Studies-first-round.aspx (accessed 2 May 2014).

PART I
THE LOCAL IN LOCALISM

2

Localism: Institutions, Territories, Representations

Ali Madanipour and Simin Davoudi

This chapter analyses the concept of localism and its multiple and contested meanings, with the aim of providing a theoretical understanding of the 'local' and of 'localism'. It argues that the meaning of localism lies at an institutional–representational–territorial nexus with its own contested and continually changing ontologies, identities and boundaries. This nexus is formed by the different territorial and institutional arrangements that shape localities overlaid by a continually shifting intersection of different perspectives and interpretations about the specificity and autonomy of a locality. The chapter is organised in three sections. First, it briefly engages with the meaning of localism. Second, it presents a critical examination of its dichotomous interpretations. Third, it argues for going beyond this dichotomy and analysing the local and localism according to ontologies, identities and boundaries; in other words, an investigation into what constitutes a locality, how it is represented and how it is delineated.

Localism as favouring the local

The word local, which stems from the Latin *locus* and appears in more or less similar forms in several European languages, means relating to or concerned with a particular place. The word localism is a much more recent word, first appearing in English in the early nineteenth century. According to the *Oxford English Dictionary*, its earliest application in 1823 indicates the characteristics of a particular place, such as local idioms, customs and expressions that are specific to an area. Authors, therefore, have written about the 'lingual localism' or 'architectural localism' to describe features that distinguish one area from another. Since the middle of the nineteenth century, the word has also found a political and normative character that by now has become its primary meaning.

In this latter meaning, localism indicates attachment to a locality in which individuals or groups live, with all the ideas, sympathies and interests associated with such attachment, amounting to an outlook that favours what is local. The earliest example given by the *Oxford English Dictionary* is from the English traveller George Borrow in his 1843 book, *The Bible in Spain*, who refers to a strong 'spirit of localism, which is so prevalent throughout Spain'. The people of Santiago di Compostella, as Borrow wrote, 'seemed to care but little if all others in Galicia perished'; and in the impoverished town of Ferrol, people boasted about their town's public walk being better than Madrid's Prado. Therefore, while the 'local' may offer a descriptive relationship between a phenomenon and a place, 'localism' refers to an attitude, a disposition that centres on a place. It sets up an emotional attachment, a normative link between phenomena and places, and in doing so it becomes an ingredient in the development of an ideology.

While the use of the term localism may only go back to the nineteenth century, the concepts of local features or the attitude of favouring what is local go farther back in history. As long as human communities have existed, we may safely assume that some sort of preference for the local has been the glue used for binding people together. The question that needs exploring, therefore, is the contemporary significance and use of the concept. What is new in the current discussions of localism and what is meant by the term in these narratives? If we define localism as favouring the local, new questions emerge about how to delineate and represent the locality and what it means to privilege the local.

The anatomy of a dichotomy

The conceptualisation of the local tends to be dichotomous, defining the local in contradistinction from extra-local. Alongside, and in the context of centralised forms of power, localism may be described as the demand for autonomy from below, as distinctive from decentralization from above. From one perspective, which may be characterised as the view from within, localism is interpreted as a struggle for self-determination, a bid for local autonomy, a form of resistance to the pressures from the outside, against the forces that try to integrate a locality into larger political units, economic processes and cultural identities, even to the extent of being enclosed, parochial and regressive. From another perspective, which may be characterised as the view from the outside and from a more general standpoint, localism is seen as an attempt at decentralisation, control, efficiency and legitimacy exerted and encouraged by the higher levels of authority, which may demand openness and integration, while interpreting any form of resistance as fragmentary and parochial. It is argued here, however, that this dichotomous interpretation may simplify a more complex phenomenon, as an analysis of the changing ontologies, identities and boundaries in the next section will show.

Localism as autonomy: resistance and self-determination

The idea of localism as preferring the local is often a view from within a locality, as an expression of the desire for self-determination and/or resistance against outside forces. It is frequently expressed as the desire by the smaller and weaker social groups and forms of political power to argue for and assert their control over their own affairs; a bid for autonomy in the face of larger and more powerful extra-local forces that may attempt to rule over them. At the core of this meaning of localism lies the desire for territorialisation. This is the desire to maintain or assert control over a territory, often from within that territory and in contradistinction to other territories. Such localism may be the result of a local elite's bid to continue their hold on power, or the expression of a local community's desire for self-determination or for some control over the processes that affect their lives. However, it is a desire that may generate a spectrum of outcomes from an inward-looking attitude and extreme mistrust of others to openness and management of relations between different places.

Whereas local pride and regional rivalry may go far back into feudal times, the emergence of the political meaning of the word localism in the mid nineteenth century was not accidental. It coincided with the rise of the nation state and nationalism in which regional forces were resisting the establishment of national sovereignty or disagreeing with its configuration. In that context, the term localism was used to distinguish the local from the national. This is reflected in an 1852 statement from the American senator Daniel Webster, which is also one of the earliest uses of the term given by the *Oxford English Dictionary*. Uttered on the eve of the American Civil War that tore the nation into two parts, he stated: 'I am one of those who believe that our government is not to be destroyed by localisms, North or South.'

Enabled by absolute monarchies, the nation state emerged in Europe as a unifying force against medieval factionalism (Potter, 1995; Smith, 1984). It was a long process in which local and regional sources of power were suppressed in favour of central control. In time, modern democracies have replaced absolute monarchies and limited the size and scope of the state. The nation state and the modern notion of the individual were the dual outcomes of this historical process that had started as early as the fourteenth century in Europe (Coleman, 1996). The primary force to limit the power of the state in liberal democracies has been the protection of the individual with the emphasis put on finding a balance between maintaining individual liberties and governing it through democratic government. The tense coexistence between the two has consistently pulled the political communities into different directions (Bobbio, 1990). In yet another turn, the emphasis on individual freedom has been seen to threaten the coherence of the political fabric (Bobbio, 1990: 43).

The liberal solution to this challenge has centred on the development of political institutions aimed at binding these individuals together. John Locke (1980 [1689]: 8) envisaged a state of nature in which individuals were free and equal:

> a state of perfect freedom to order their actions, and dispose of their possessions and persons, as they think fit, within the bounds of the law of nature, without asking leave, or depending upon the will of any other man.

This concept of the state of nature was meant to provide a basis for individuals to resist the tyranny of the state. The powerful nation state could be seen as a threat to such freedoms. This is why, in his desire for frugal government, Thomas Jefferson famously believed in 'ward republics' (Jefferson *et al.*, 1999: 214), whereby the counties were to be divided into 'wards of such size as that every citizen can attend, when called on, and act in person' (Jefferson *et al.*, 1999: 213). As he noted, this form of government had already existed in New England under the name of townships and had 'proved themselves the wisest invention ever devised by the wit of man for the perfect exercise of self-government, and for its preservation' (Jefferson *et al.*, 1999: 214). These early forms of localism have gone through many variations, and the tension between liberalism and democracy has shaped the liberal democratic systems of governance (Bobbio, 1990). The primary concern of liberal thought, however, has remained the freedom of individual, as argued by Hayek (1944: 52): 'Democracy is essentially a means, a utilitarian device for safeguarding internal peace and individual freedom.'

As a critique of the liberal argument, communitarians have advocated the creation of communities out of the atomised individuals. They argue that although resistance by the individual is the foundation of liberal politics, it is also the path to excessive atomisation and individualisation that tears the social fabric into pieces. Communitarians suggest that 'the pendulum has swung too far towards the individualistic pole, and it is time to hurry its return' (Etzioni, 1995: 26). They argue that the rights of individuals have been the focus of too much attention and need to be balanced by a focus on the responsibilities of individuals to the community. The lost sense of community should be rebuilt 'not only because community life is a major source of satisfaction of our deeper personal needs, but because the social pressures community brings to bear are a mainstay of our moral values' (Etzioni, 1995: 40). Society is therefore envisaged as a community of communities in which communal bonds can be re-established. Localism, in this view, becomes the spatial and institutional expression of such social imagination whereby localities are expected to frame the reconstruction of a sense of community in fragmented and atomised societies.

With globalisation, the scale and strength of extra-local forces are far beyond the nation state. Localism therefore takes yet another form: as the expression of resistance against the forces of globalisation (Castells, 1997). The global flows of capital and labour, products and ideas, are seen as a threat to local sovereignty and distinctiveness, urging the localities to adopt a localist agenda and resist the crushing forces that are altering localities. Alternatively, these flows are seen as the inevitable processes of a global marketplace, in which localities have to compete with distinctive products to offer, branding themselves as commodities for sale. In either perspective, localism becomes a way of distinguishing localities from one another and responding to extra-local pressures.

Meanwhile, localism as a response to environmental degradation and climate change is the other side of the coin. It has been seen as the practical embodiment of sustainable development and a way of reducing the use of energy and materials and advocating the use of products and services that are locally produced. Through technological changes in information, communication and transportation, globalisation has accelerated the movement of goods and services across the world. Localism is projected as a key solution to this heightened mobility. The care for the environment has become one of the most vocal advocates of localism as resistance to global forces. The spatial manifestation of this form of localism can be found in the approaches to urban development that are changing, for example, from a preference for car-based planning and design of cities sprawling outwards, to one focusing on compact urban form and walkable neighbourhoods.

Localism as resistance and self-determination, therefore, can take different forms: resistance by individuals, communities or localities against the power of the state and the forces of globalisation, and expression of the desire for self-rule, cultural distinction and environmental care. However, the fear of individual atomisation or a return to medieval factionalism and charges of parochialism and provincialism are never far away. According to a liberal egalitarian critic, 'The spectre that now haunts Europe is one of strident nationalism, ethnic self-assertion, and the exaltation of what divides people at the expense of what unites them' (Barry, 2001: 3). This critique of localism is also expressed from the other end of the political spectrum, which looks critically at the social fragmentation that localism brings about (Hobsbawm, 1990). The term parochialism, which originated in the spatial subdivision of the Church into ecclesiastical parishes, is often used pejoratively to refer to limited local interests resulting in narrow-mindedness and the absence of a global perspective.

Localism as decentralisation: efficiency, legitimacy and control

The political question of localism is about the spatial distribution of power, which may be conceptualised from two different directions: a subdivision of power by the higher authority, or a bid for autonomy by the lower ones; each constituting one end of a political spectrum. While localism as resistance characterises the bid for autonomy, localism as efficiency may be the view from above.

If seen from a higher position of authority, localism may mean the subdivision of tasks into smaller units. It becomes the functional and territorial division of responsibilities and powers, as in the formation of the regional and local levels of management in a large organisation, or the subdivision of a large city into districts. The criteria for such a subdivision may be based on a set of calculations about the efficient distribution and use of resources, and ensuring an effective reach of the central powers into the entirety of the territory they control. The subdivision may be an integral part of a process of division of labour and bureaucratisation, in which complex tasks are split into smaller parts and complex organisations are formed out of a network of lower-level agents. This may amount to no more than a hierarchical and managerial organisation of functions for improved efficiency and smooth operation of complex institutions (Weber, 1948). Theoretically, this approach is based on a number of related ideas such as: the rationalist analytical method of splitting complex phenomena into smaller parts to make them easier to understand (Descartes, 1968), the long-established practices of the division of labour for undertaking complex tasks (Smith, 1993) and making the society transparent with no hidden corners left unseen (Foucault, 1980). While the division of labour may not be simply equated with localism, it is an essential component in debates about localism. Rather than relying entirely on a single source of authority, the division of labour recognises the need for distribution of tasks, knowledge, skills and power, stages of operations and levels of authority. Sometimes these functional subdivisions are associated with a push for decentralisation and devolution based on the idea that the local-level agents are better placed to make certain decisions. As Hayek (1945: 524) argues:

> If we can agree that the economic problem of society is mainly one of rapid adaptation to changes in the particular circumstances of time and place, it would seem to follow that the ultimate decisions must be left to the people who are familiar with these circumstances, who know directly of the relevant changes and of the resources immediately available to meet them. We cannot expect that this problem will be solved by first communicating all this knowledge to a central board which, after integrating all knowledge, issues its orders. We must solve it by some form of decentralization. But this answers only part of our problem. We need decentralization because only thus can we ensure that the knowledge of the particular circumstances of time and place will be promptly used.

For him, however, this decentralisation inevitably leads to a reliance on the market and its price mechanism as the most efficient way of accessing relevant information produced by individual decisions.

An alternative model of decentralisation is the principle of subsidiarity, which has been embedded in the organisation of the Catholic Church and embraced by the European Union in its Maastricht Treaty (Cass, 1992). It is seen as opening up space for manoeuvre for the lower levels of authority. According to the principle of subsidiarity, 'a larger and higher ranking body should not exercise functions which could be efficiently carried out by a smaller and lesser body' (Melé, 2005: 293). Subsidiarity paves the way for a system of governance in which different levels of power can work together on a functional basis, each playing a role in a hierarchical organisation. A degree of autonomy is therefore offered to the lower levels of authority while maintaining the control exerted by the higher levels. The concept is developed as an alternative to an authoritarian and bureaucratic mode of organisation in which people are treated as cogs in a machine rather than intelligent actors with the ability to make decisions based on their own judgement.

Subsidiarity offers a form of decentralisation based on the belief that the devolution of power and decision-making may contribute to higher productivity, better working practices and political relations. The principle has been used both in the functional organisation of multinational entities such as the EU, the restructuring of the nation states into federal or quasi-federal arrangements, and in the development of regional and sub-regional forms of political institutions. It has also been used in restructuring private corporations and changing them from a highly integrated hierarchy to a network of semi-independent units, in which the workers find a degree of control over their working practices (Melé, 2005). In all these forms, from the functional subdivision to decentralised structures, the urge for localism is often generated from the top, in which the centre reshapes the complex organisation and its workings for improved efficiency. It is a technical interpretation of political control, a spectrum of localism as seen from the perspective of a higher-ranking authority.

From this perspective, however, there should be a limit to decentralisation as localism bears the danger of fragmentation and parochialism. In its institutional form, the problem of parochialism is well exemplified in metropolitan governance, where a degree of coordination of multiple local authorities, each pursuing its own needs and agendas, is required. Parochialism, however, is not limited to spatial arrangements. It can also be manifested in sectoral or institutional parochialism, in which one sector, one institution, one discipline or one profession becomes an expression of the desire for exclusivity in the face of large-scale complex processes, without being open to wider views of the range of issues involved. Sometimes this institutional parochialism is merely the result of habit and history, which solidifies thinking and behaviour in a narrow and rigid way, and its bid for autonomy is an expression of a conservative attitude that detests change. The term 'silo-mentality' has repeatedly been used to criticise this institutional parochialism. The parochial places and institutions are urged to leave aside their limited outlook, work together, integrate within a larger framework and look at the world from a holistic perspective.

In this perspective, elements of democratisation and legitimation may be present, as seen in the pressure for public participation. In both public and private sectors, the idea of involving citizens or employees in the process of decision-making has been advocated as good practice (Barnes *et al.*, 2007; Perotin and Robinson, 2004; Plummer, 2000). As an experienced practitioner notes, 'Public participation applies to administrative decisions – that is, those typically made by agencies (and sometimes by private organizations), not elected officials or judges', with the overall goal of 'better decisions that are supported by the public' (Creighton, 2005: 7). While the range and extent of citizen involvement varies significantly (Arnstein, 1969), the benefits of such involvement are widely accepted, to the extent that public participation is now a legal requirement in many countries, based on the principle that citizens who are affected by government decisions should have a say in those decisions and be able to influence them. Although it may be a response to democratic demands, participation can be seen as a form of localism that is initiated from the global perspective, the view from the higher authorities attempting to engage the perceived less powerful agents in the process of decision-making while maintaining their authority to have the final say.

Localism as an institutional–representational–territorial nexus

There is no guarantee that the above two perspectives, from the higher and lower levels of political power, meet halfway or overlap in a meaningful way, and in many cases both of these meanings may tensely coincide. Furthermore, the two perspectives are not neatly separable, as they may coexist in the ideas and actions of both local and extra-local agents. The ambiguity created by their overlap and coincidence, or the multiple uses that may be made of each meaning, is a source of potential tensions. The view from the higher authorities may be used to suggest that localism is indeed a response to a local desire for autonomy and participation, rather than a managerial attempt for higher efficiency and reduced costs. Moreover, the higher authorities are themselves based in specific localities with implicit or explicit preferences for those places. This may create a sense of inequality and marginalisation, as evidenced in regional disparities within national space, and local disparities within the urban and regional space. The view from the locality, meanwhile, may portray localism as a democratic reaction to the pressures from the outside rather than maintaining the status quo in favour of the local elite unwilling to share their privileges. The view from the locality may also look at the locality from the outside, judging itself on the basis of standards set by others, or reflecting on the image it may have in the eyes of the outsiders. The local, therefore, may mean many things at the same time with agencies using it in its multiple meanings to think about themselves and justify their own positions, intentions and actions.

The political question, therefore, goes beyond a neatly drawn, dichotomous relationship. Instead, it revolves around an ambivalent institutional–representational–territorial nexus: what political powers are or should be at work and at what spatial level; how political institutions operate with what range of powers and competences and for what territorial coverage. Localism as the spatial distribution of power is therefore a nexus of political struggle between different forces over the control of processes and territories. It can be at once a functional subdivision of territories and tasks, a positive assertion of the local forces and a negative reaction to the external ones; at once an ordering exercise from above, an emancipatory force from below and a parochial narrow-mindedness towards others. It is at this intersection that localism is located and can be interpreted according to the different views that analyse it: bidding for autonomy and rejecting the role that is assigned to a place in the national and international division of labour; an expression of resistance and the desire for self-rule; seeing the bigger picture and criticising parochialism; or, remaining open to various forces and playing a complementary role in the national and global space and its global division of labour. The multiple meanings that localism takes at the intersection of these perspectives, and its institutional–representational–territorial nexus, generate a permanent state of flux and ambivalence that is open for contradictory interpretations and applications.

The tension between an instrumental and a cultural concept of the local, and between managerial and emancipatory ways of seeing it, has been used to frame the way the concept of localism is developed and used. This tension is played out in the context of the diverse and changing nature of localities, which leads to a continually evolving reconfiguration of the idea of the local. In this context, a series of tensions emerge around the representations of the locality, in which different groups offer differing readings of a place, each trying to produce a stable representation. The parameters that define this nexus may be identified around three concepts: ontologies, identities and boundaries. The questions that we ask are: what makes up a locality and how consistent are the local agents? Are they as local as they are assumed in the discussions? How are their identities shaped, for what purpose and by whom? Do they have stable and unchanging identities, or are they subject to flux? And finally, do localities have fixed boundaries? These three sets of questions indicate the difficulties of defining and maintaining a stable and coherent sense of localities and thus the challenges facing localism.

Institutions: consistent ontologies?

Localism may use the idea of the local as a banner for resistance or an efficient form of organisation, but a locality is a social world composed of diverse local and extra-local agencies. What constitutes a locality, therefore, is not consistent.

By imagining space as universal and homogeneous, rationalists have assumed a consistent ontology for a locality. The Cartesian idea of space, which was a revival of Euclid's concepts, saw space as 'a continuous body, or a space extended indefinitely in length, width and height or depth, divisible into various parts, which could have various figures and sizes and be moved or transposed in all sorts of ways' (Descartes, 1968: 58). This idea was used in Newtonian physics and modern science as well as in modernist architecture and planning (Davoudi, 2012). Le Corbusier thought about space as 'mass' and 'surface', shaped through the tool of the 'plan' (Le Corbusier, 1986: 2–3). A complex ontology was reduced to these abstractions through a rationalist epistemology, giving it an idealised functional order and shape. It assumed the existence of space as a neutral substance that could be shaped.

The reaction to the metaphysical idea of abstract and homogeneous space was captured in the concept of relational space mentioned first by Leibniz (1979: 89), who considered

> space to be something merely relative, as time is … an order of coexistences, as time is an order of successions. For space denotes, in terms of possibility, an order of things which exist at the same time, considered as existing together.

With the arrival of non-Euclidean geometry and Einstein's relativity in physics, the idea of abstract space as a distinctive entity was almost completely discarded. In the social sciences, space was located in social processes and contexts. As Lefebvre argued (1991: 12), space, 'in isolation, is an empty abstraction'; it is not detached from social processes, and so human space is relational and social. Similarly, Bourdieu (2000: 134–135) suggests that social space is 'a structure of juxtaposition of social positions', which tends to be translated into physical space, so space becomes 'correspondence between a certain order of coexistence (or distribution) of agents and a certain order of coexistence (or distribution) of properties'. At the urban level, a process of social sorting is always at work to separate the social groups located in different places; a process that has intensified with the rise in social inequalities. Land and property markets solidify and institutionalise these differences, shaping the social geography of an area on the basis of access to resources laid on top of the natural and historical configuration of the area.

The social differences at all levels, therefore, are reflected in and influenced by space, turning the local into a mosaic of difference, even when 'purified' through social sorting. A further complication is the extent of non-local actors and connections within a locality, which may lead to hollowing out the concept of a stable locality altogether. In the increasingly global relations between localities, agents based in one place may have links and relations with many others in various locations. The parameters of the political questions about defining localities, therefore, are no longer the same as the eighteenth century, in which the pioneers of liberalism made their case, when stakeholders were almost all local and localities relied on their own resources to live and thrive. The rise of globalisation has introduced heightened levels of mobility and connectivity, in which localities now face the challenges of globalisation, in addition to their relation to the nation state (Castells, 1997). The integration of local, national and global markets, the multiplication of extra-local agencies and the ease of movement for capital, goods, services and labour have fundamentally transformed the basic conditions for the spatial distribution of power. Technological innovations in transport, information and communication have transformed the way localities are organised. Stakeholders are no longer necessarily small and local, but there are also large corporations operating at national and global scales that have a significant impact on local processes.

This is illustrated by, for example, the Clone Town Britain campaign, which argues that British towns and cities are losing their local identity. It reports that only one-third of British high streets have retained their distinctive character, measured as having more than two-thirds of their shops being independents. In two-thirds of the towns, the multiple chain outlets dominate the high street, with Cambridge announced to be the most cloned town (NEF, 2010). Therefore, while a city like Cambridge may be regarded as a highly distinctive place, owing to its history, architecture and the university, its distinctiveness may be hollowed out when seen through the lens of its retail sector. The prevalent presence in the localities of national and international retail companies is paralleled in other sectors in British cities such as housing and banking, whereby a small number of large companies dominate the national space. The dominance of large-volume house-builders and their impact on localities have been noted for a long time (Whitehand, 1992), but their role in local and regional affairs is ever more far-reaching.

The significance of these large private-sector players in the local scene is reflected in the governance of places and the complexity of stakeholder involvements when the state opens up new spaces for private actors to become involved in urban and regional transformation (Madanipour *et al.*, 2001).

When the state retreats, the gap is not always filled with civil society players. Instead, it is the large private-sector players who found it easier to manoeuvre and to occupy the emptied space. In the UK, the abolition of the regional tier of government and the long-standing pressures on local government have opened up the spaces of possibility for private corporations in localities. Competition from larger companies and the impact of the economic crisis have undermined the ability and viability of smaller businesses, while civil society organisations and groups have also lost out on many of their sources of funding as a result of cuts in public spending. The locality may become the playground of the large corporations, who will now decide which localities to choose for higher rewards and which ones to abandon to under-investment and impoverishment.

The diversity of a locality, both in the local make-up and in its connections with outside forces, therefore, tends to undermine the idea of a consistent locality as a basis for localism. In a cultural framework, such diversity may contribute to the richness of a locality, but in a technical or regressive political framework, disgruntled voices may be seen as inconvenience or bad publicity, an anomaly that needs to be treated according to the principles of marketing and public relations.

Representations: stable identities?

To deal with the actual diversity of a place, a stable and homogeneous identity may be presented for a locality. As the local and extra-local actors may no longer be neatly separable, and the views from inside or outside may not be easily distinguishable, the question that emerges is about the existence and extent of homogeneity. In the simplified perspectives discussed above, the representations of a locality tend to assume a certain degree of homogeneity for it. Local identities are thought to be original, rooted in a place, somewhat unchanging through time, and creating an imagined community with authentic and stable features (Anderson, 1991). Indeed, the same dynamics that apply to the question of nationalism and its perceived unified features (Hobsbawm, 1990) also apply to subnational localities that are endowed with unified meaning and identity. This process of identity construction is also at work at the sub-metropolitan level where neighbourhoods and districts are imbued with particular identities. It is a key ingredient in the cultural processes through which various social pressures are handled. As Castells (1997: 1) argues, the global space of flows is contradicted by the local processes of constructing meaning: 'Our world, and our lives, are being shaped by the conflicting trends of globalization and identity.' The question is: how and by whom is the local identity constructed? Is it an existing condition in need of discovery and mobilisation, a normative goal to be met or a mythology to be created?

In this process, the actual differences within localities may be suppressed in order to produce a unified and coherent representation. The construction of such an image is often closely intertwined with the power relations at work within a locality, so that the more powerful actors and processes find their ideas and practices in the main narratives about a place, whereas the weaker and more marginal players are left out of this narrative. The stable narrative about the identity of a place may reflect the existing power relations in that locality. Diversity of experience and the material conditions of a locality, therefore, may be narrowed down in the construction of an overarching narrative into which the locality is introduced. In the democratic struggle for local identity, therefore, what is on offer may be the representation of the local elites rather than a nuanced and diverse story that recounts the various aspects of a place.

In politics and economics, the question of local identity is increasingly driven by branding and competition. Following the logic of private corporations working in a competitive market, local authorities have increasingly embraced the idea of global competition, in which localities compete for financial and human capital. Competition and markets have become the driving force of the economy (Aglietta, 2000). This in turn encourages the competitors to rely on quality and differentiation to stand out (Simmie, 2003). Branding is one of the main vehicles for such differentiation, used to advertise distinctive features and 'unique selling points' in a crowded global marketplace. Whether the competition is real or imaginary is beside the point because the perception of competition shapes much of the representation of the local. Establishing a presentable image of a locality, therefore, becomes a vehicle of local economic development. A prime example of this approach can be found in the deindustrialising regions where the image and memory of the manufacturing past is replaced by new images, some of which rarely resemble the reality of the place. Furthermore, erasing the memories with which many identify becomes a source of tension and contestation. The instrumental perspective prevails in redefining the representations of a locality, a view that is also embraced by the local actors who now look at themselves through external eyes and an instrumental rationale.

Branding is also a significant part of the urban development processes. The growing size of construction industry developers indicates the growth of productive capacities that can produce an entire urban neighbourhood or district in a short period of time (Whitehand, 1992). At the same time, through public-sector regeneration or market dynamics, the processes of gentrification change the character of some urban areas (Atkinson and Bridge, 2005; Lees *et al.*, 2008). In both cases, place branding becomes a selling point. Localism, both as defining the local characteristics and as showing preference for a locality, becomes an integral part of commercial operations. The reductive processes of money economy that Georg Simmel (1978) wrote about come into play to reduce the locality to a commodity. In this reductive process, any divergences are suppressed to achieve the main mission of increasing profitability. A locality is portrayed through a narrow lens so as to present a marketable image.

While the suppliers attempt to shape the image of their product, the consumers expect and desire to find access to an exclusive product. To escape social atomisation and the sense of alienation in large urban societies, individuals seek reliable forms of identification. For individuals, identity is a narrative told about the self (Jenkins, 1996; Madanipour, 2013), and that narrative is closely related to the development of a symbolic capital and a sense of social status (Bourdieu, 2000). In consumerist societies, the source of identification has become the patterns of consumption, whereby individuals think of themselves through the lens of the goods and services they consume, or through the image of this consumption (Debord, 1994). Distinctive local identities, therefore, would offer the possibility of such identification, taking refuge from the unknown and impersonal metropolitan world, and being able to tell secure stories about the self. Social identity is a process of similarity and difference (Jenkins, 1996) in which security comes from knowing whom a person is similar to and different from. The significance of localism for the consuming individuals becomes the security of knowing their place in the world. Inside the narrative of a locality, produced by powerful agents or participating individuals, diversity and digression from the message are carefully edited out to create a polished and desirable message.

In parallel with the political and economic significance of branding, the importance of social cohesion and integration is emphasised through localism. In large urban areas, the diversity of the population in terms of age, ethnicity, culture and lifestyle, as well as income and education, is addressed through efforts for social cohesion and integration. Localism provides a way of mobilising efforts to address the problems of disadvantage in particular areas, or bringing the disparate people together under the banner of cohesion and integration. A stable and consistent identity is therefore sought out of a multiplicity of social agents and procedures. If successful, however, the integrative promise of localism runs the risk of generating factional fragmentation and parochialism, as discussed earlier. If unsuccessful, it may be at the risk of remaining at the level of rhetoric.

The tension between the top-down and bottom-up perspectives, and between the views from inside and outside a locality, as mentioned above, may also be interpreted as a tension between instrumental and expressive concerns. The drive for efficiency may be seen as an instrumental approach to localism, using the locality as a vehicle of shaping and regulating the performance of others. The drive for self-determination, therefore, may be interpreted as a reaction to this instrumental approach, seeing localism as an expression of the local identity and culture. However, the instrumental and expressive views are neither pure nor necessarily dichotomous, and they can be as overlapping and ambiguous as the two views from inside and outside a locality. The locals and extra-locals may equally have instrumental designs on a locality. They may share the idea of creating and offering a stable representation for a place, a representation that could bridge the gap between reality and presentable images. This identity, however, cannot remain stable, owing to the diversity of what constitutes the locality and the inevitable reductionism of the outward-oriented representation created.

Territories: fixed boundaries?

The process of editing and polishing the representation of a place always involves defining and tightening clear boundaries. The views from above and from below (or from the outside and from the inside of a locality) may attempt to draw boundaries around the locality, defining it in a way that may fit their perspective and expectations. The existence of the boundary, the extent of its reach and coverage and the degree of its fixity or porosity, become the subjects of political struggle.

A bounded space may emerge as a result of administrative processes that define an area for the delivery of services and management of the territory, which may be the result of long historical processes or the outcome of an administrator's stroke of a pen. In both cases, the boundary finds a functional purpose, with which the responsibilities are determined and division of labour decided upon. It can also become a contested line around which claims are made over territory between warring parties, as evidenced by many territorial struggles in history. The lines on the map, however, do not reflect the actual processes on the ground, which may cut through these boundaries, or merely become frustrated and aborted by these lines. One of these attempts at delimiting space has been the concept of neighbourhood.

For generations, the idea of the neighbourhood unit was a framework for analysing and planning the urban society. For the Chicago sociologists, the neighbourhood was the way in which the urban society was formed, segregated into different racial and socio-economic areas. For planners and designers, the neighbourhood was an expression of community and a basis on which to reshape the city (Mumford, 1954). Kevin Lynch (1960) aimed to show how people's memories depend on clear edges and identifiable districts. He argued for the legibility of the urban environment, in which clear boundaries were set between places. The subdivision of urban society into such groups, or reshaping the urban space on that basis, was criticised for ignoring the structural processes at work, the mobility of the population (Webber, 1964), the absence of an urban perspective and the adoption of social engineering attitudes (Keller, 1968). These criticisms ruled out the use of neighbourhood units in planning and design, but not the idea of neighbourhood as a distinctive locality, an idea that was subsequently revived through the market-driven urban development (Duany and Plater-Zyberk, 1994).

The notion of a locality with a clear, identifiable identity offers a sense of order for planners and designers, and also a sense of security for those who wish to take refuge from the perceived alienating and impersonal conditions of life in metropolitan societies. The extreme example is the gated neighbourhoods that have the sharpest and hardest of the boundaries. The rise in crime, the growth of social inequality and the offer of a life in an exclusive gated neighbourhood come together to justify the gated neighbourhoods (Blakely and Snyder, 1999). These are small localities that affirm a social status for their residents, protect their property value and give them a sense of identity associated with the consumption of space. The narrative of identity created for a neighbourhood of this kind is therefore at once a reflection of the supply of and demand for space and a medium through which production, branding and consumption of space come together. However, as this narrative and its spatial manifestations marginalise some people, the effect can be exclusionary (Madanipour, 2011) with considerable implications for the society at large (Landman, 2006).

The impact of localism on the urban society, which is already divided along the lines of social inequality, may be fragmentary. Urban space is subdivided into public and private spaces, social enclaves and functional areas (Madanipour, 2003). Rather than sharpening the boundaries and furthering the subdivisions, the challenge is to cross the barriers and establish linkages. Localism may enhance the local sense of identity, but it also fuels social fragmentation and may act as an obstacle to democratic governance. Porosity of the boundary is at once a reality and a normative goal.

Localities, therefore, are not homogeneous entities and their identities, often defined by their boundaries, are contested. The pressure to distinguish one place from another may find economic, political and cultural significance at the same time, a pressure that seeks stable and presentable identities either as commercial commodities or cultural self-expressions. The question, however, is about whether the resulting representation is open and inclusive or closed and exclusive. Is the identity of a locality the effort to create a bounded and stable account reflecting the interests of a minority, or of taking into account the diversity of the local actors, the actual porosity of its boundaries and the possibility of retelling the local stories in new and diverse ways? Under the conditions of diverse contexts, multi-locational actors, porous boundaries and contested representation, the meanings and implications of localism are multiple and ambivalent. In other words, the local may not be as fixed and stable as may be assumed, and the conditions in a locality not as free to the local actors as sometimes suggested.

Conclusion

Localism is an institutional–representational–territorial nexus with multiple and contested meanings. It has often been portrayed through a dichotomous sketch. If viewed from the perspective of a locality, it may be seen as resistance to outside forces. Individuals, communities or localities resist the power of the state and the forces of globalisation, demonstrating a desire for self-rule, cultural distinction and environmental care. If viewed from a larger, extra-local perspective, it is at best an efficient method of organisation through decentralisation and democratic management. Each perspective runs its own risk of pushing the intersection in a different direction: the global view is in danger of instrumentalising the locality and falling into managerial dismissal of local needs and wishes, and the local view is in danger of falling into parochialism and narrow-mindedness. In the absence of democratic accountability, localism may merely disarm the weak localities before the strong national and international players, or display parochial and factional interests that are at odds with the neighbouring localities and with the wider society. The meaning of localism, however, goes beyond the dichotomy of two overlapping perspectives.

The challenge for making sense of this shifting intersection lies in the local ontology, identity and boundary. While the practices of localism are based on assuming a consistent ontology, the composition of a locality, or the forces in action within a locality, are diverse, formed by different local and extra-local agencies with very different needs, interests, roots and loyalties. This diverse reality may be managed through an attempt to create a stable and coherent representation, offering an identity that is branded and competitive, but which has a large gap with the local reality and need. It may also be managed through the creation of fixed and rigid boundaries without recognising the actual porosity of these boundaries. The boundaries are blurred and the representation unstable, capable of both undermining and frustrating the local processes. Local democratic processes are needed to be continually engaged with this nexus, negotiating these ambiguities and making sense of where the locals stand and what the future trajectories are.

References

Aglietta, Michel. (2000) *A Theory of Capitalist Regulation: The US experience*, new edn, London: Verso.

Anderson, Benedict. (1991) *Imagined Communities*, London: Verso.

Arnstein, Sherry. (1969) A ladder of citizen participation, *Journal of the American Institute of Planners*, 35(4): 216–224.

Atkinson, Rowland and Bridge, Gary (eds) (2005) *Gentrification in a Global Context: The new urban colonialism*, London: Routledge.

Barnes, Marian, Newman, Janet and Sullivan, Helen (2007) *Power, Participation and Political Renewal: Case studies in public participation*, Bristol: The Policy Press.
Barry, Brian. (2001) *Culture and Equality*, Cambridge: Polity.
Blakely, E.J. and Snyder, M.G. (1999) *Fortress America: Gated communities in the United States*, Washington, DC: Brookings Institution Press.
Bobbio, Norberto. (1990) *Liberalism and Democracy*, London: Verso.
Borrow, George. (1908 [1843]) *The Bible in Spain*, London: Cassell and Co. Ltd. Available at: www.gutenberg.org/files/415/415-h/415-h.htm (accessed 2 December 2013).
Bourdieu, Pierre. (2000) *Pascalian Meditations*, Cambridge: Polity Press.
Cass, Deborah. (1992) The word that saves Maastricht? The principle of subsidiarity and the division of powers within the European Community, *Common Market Law Review*, 29(6): 1107–1136.
Castells, Manuel. (1997) *The Power of Identity*, Oxford: Blackwell.
Coleman, Janet. (ed.) (1996) *The Individual in Political Theory and Practice*, Oxford: Clarendon Press.
Creighton, James. (2005) *The Public Participation Handbook: Making better decisions through citizen involvement*, Hoboken, NJ: John Wiley & Sons.
Davoudi, S. (2012) The legacy of positivism and the emergence of interpretive tradition in spatial planning, *Regional Studies*, 46(4): 429–441.
Debord, Guy. (1994) *The Society of the Spectacle*, New York: Zone Books.
Descartes, René. (1968) *Discourse on Method and The Meditations*, London: Penguin.
Duany, Andres and Plater-Zyberk, Elizabeth. (1994) The neighbourhood, the district, and the corridor, in P. Katz (ed.), *The New Urbanism: Toward an architecture of community*, New York: McGraw Hill, pp. xvii–xx.
Etzioni, Amitai. (1995) *The Spirit of Community: Rights, responsibilities and the communitarian agenda*, London: Fontana Press.
Foucault, Michel. (1980) The eye of power, in Colin Gordon (ed.), *Power/Knowledge*, Harlow: Pearson Education Limited, pp. 146–165.
Hayek, F.A. (1944) *The Road to Serfdom*, London: Routledge.
Hayek, F.A. (1945) The use of knowledge in society, *The American Economic Review*, 35(4): 519–530.
Hobsbawm, E.J. (1990) *Nations and Nationalism since 1780*, Cambridge: Cambridge University Press.
Jefferson, Thomas, Appleby, Joyce, Ball, Terence, Geuss, Raymond and Skinner, Quentin (eds) (1999) *Jefferson: Political writings*, Cambridge: Cambridge University Press.
Jenkins, Richard. (1996) *Social Identity*, London: Routledge.
Keller, Suzanne. (1968) *The Urban Neighbourhood: A sociological perspective*, New York: Random House.
Landman, Karina. (2006) *An Exploration of Urban Transformation in Post-Apartheid South Africa*, unpublished PhD thesis, Newcastle-upon-Tyne: Newcastle University.
Le Corbusier. (1986) *Towards a New Architecture*, New York: Dover Publications.
Lees, L., Slater, T. and Wyly, E. (eds) (2008) *Gentrification*, London: Routledge.
Lefebvre, Henri. (1991) *The Production of Space*, Oxford: Blackwell.
Leibniz, G. (1979) The relational theory of space and time, in J.J.C. Smart (ed.), *Problems of Space and Time*, New York: Macmillan, pp. 89–98.
Locke, John. (1980 [1689]) *Second Treatise of Government*, Indianapolis, IN: Hackett.
Lynch, Kevin. (1960) *The Image of the City*, Cambridge, MA: MIT Press.
Madanipour, A. (2003) *Public and Private Spaces of the City*, London: Routledge.
Madanipour, A. (2011) Social exclusion and space, in R. LeGates and F. Stout (eds), *The City Reader*, 5th edn, London: Routledge, pp. 186–194.

Madanipour, A. (2013) The identity of the city, in Silvia Serreli (ed.), *City Project and Public Space*, Dordrecht: Springer, pp. 49–63.
Madanipour, A., Hull, A. and Healey, P. (2001) *The Governance of Place*, Aldershot: Ashgate.
Melé, Domènec. (2005) Exploring the principle of subsidiarity in organisational forms, *Journal of Business Ethics*, 60(3): 293–305.
Mumford, Lewis. (1954) The neighbourhood and the neighbourhood unit, *Town Planning Review*, 24: 256–270.
NEF. (2010) *Clone Town Britain 2010: High street diversity still on endangered list*. Available at: www.neweconomics.org/press/entry/clone-town-britain-2010-high-street-diversity-still-on-endangered-list (accessed 13 December 2013).
Perotin, V. and Robinson, A. (2004) *Employee Participation, Firm Performance and Survival*, Burlington, VT: Elsevier Science.
Plummer, Janelle. (2000) *Municipalities and Community Participation: A sourcebook for capacity building*, London: Earthscan.
Potter, David. (1995) *A History of France, 1460–1560: The emergence of a nation state*, Basingstoke: Macmillan.
Simmel, Georg. (1978) *The Philosophy of Money*, London: Routledge & Kegan Paul.
Simmie, James. (2003) Innovation and urban regions as national and international nodes for the transfer and sharing of knowledge, *Regional Studies*, 37(6–7): 607–620.
Smith, Adam. (1993) *An Inquiry into the Nature and Cause of the Wealth of Nations*, Oxford: Oxford University Press.
Smith, Alan G.R. (1984 [1776]) *The Emergence of a Nation State: The commonwealth of England 1529–1660*, London: Longman.
Webber, Melvin. (1964) The urban place and the nonplace urban realm, in M. Webber, J. Dyckman, D. Foley, A. Guttenberg, W. Wheaton and C. Bauer Wurster (eds), *Explorations into Urban Structure*, Philadelphia: University of Pennsylvania Press, pp. 79–153.
Weber, Max. (1948) Technical advantages of bureaucratic organizations, in H.H. Gerth and C. Wright Mills (eds), *From Max Weber: Essays in sociology*, London: Routledge & Kegan Paul, pp. 214–216.
Whitehand, J.W.R. (1992) *The Making of the Urban Landscape*, Oxford: Blackwell.

3

Paradoxes on Local Planning in Contested Societies

Frank Gaffikin

Current debates about the limits and potential of localism to respond to the challenges of contemporary society have tended to neglect the particular context of those places marked by deep division. In such circumstances, the relationship of the local to the central can be very distinctive and problematic. Beginning with a reminder of how old and vexed the issue of localism is, this chapter proceeds to address the nature of contested societies, and the paradoxes of localism they generate, before finally considering an alternative paradigm that might offer a means to tap into the best of local civic governance within a more global and transcultural framework. Reference is made to Northern Ireland as illustrative of the contingencies that shape localism in a conflictive society.

Localism: an old debate

Traceable to Durkheim and Weber, a long-standing conceptual ambiguity has prevailed in social science around terms such as 'community', 'neighbourhood', 'district' and 'locality'. An ambitious, if ultimately futile, attempt to surmount this inexactness was undertaken by Hillery (1955). But, his analysis of 94 definitions of 'community' reaches the facile conclusion that beyond dealing with people, the various classifications share little substantial in common. Correspondingly, Stacey (1969) disputes whether the word 'community' refers to a useful socio-spatial abstraction. In her view, a central confusion derives from its variable scale to describe anything from a small neighbourhood to a whole society, or indeed, it may be added, more recently to a transnational entity such as the European Community. Likewise, Halsey (1974: 130) comments that the term has 'so many meanings as to be meaningless … All attempts to give this concept a precise empirical meaning have failed'. Others, such as Bell and Newby (1971), endorse this verdict about an elusive sociological definition, while such resignation has led some, like Pahl (1970), to suggest the alternative concept of 'social network', or Stacey (1969), to reference the 'local social system', in their take on the reciprocities between spatial and social structure.

Nevertheless, some have braved a comprehensive explanation fundamentally in terms of local attachment, as in that by Sutton and Kolaja (1960: 197), who describe community as:

> a number of families residing in a relatively small area within which they have developed a more or less complete socio-cultural definition imbued with collective identification and by means of which they solve problems arising from the sharing of an area.

This social organisation goes beyond the idea of 'the geography of local living and working situation' (Minar and Greer, 1969: 47), of bounded territory, in which people stably settle in close proximity (Arensberg and Kimball, 1965). It acknowledges that dimensions such as locality, social coherence and interaction are pivotal in constructing a collective and cognitive *sense of being* a community. In a scale bigger than family, but still familiar and personal, 'community' is seen as a process of belonging and bonding, underpinned by some consensual common identity (Clark, 1973). This spatial-temporal framework is not to imply that community inevitably evolves from people sharing a relatively confined locality over a sustained period of time, an assumption that led some post-war planners to posit that communities could be physically engineered in an expert-driven environmental determinism. An eminent ecological variation of this view asserts that 'all the evidence suggests that there are certain fairly well defined limits of size, population, and density within which neighbourliness is easily fostered and outside which the community tends to disintegrate' (White, 1950: 41). In a cogent rebuttal (Pahl, 1968: 293), such a mechanistic formulation is resisted from the standpoint that 'any attempt to tie patterns of social relationships to specific geographic milieu is a singularly fruitless exercise'. Bell and Newby (1971: 101) similarly insist that it is untenable to associate particular ways of life with particular settlement patterns, though they concede that ecology can 'give some indication of the spatial constraints within which choices are made'. The problem remains that, in practice, few areas, however physically distinct or relatively isolated, can be demarcated exactly as separate communities that do not blend or overlap with others.

Of course, it is argued that in a modern mobile society, community as a socio-spatial category has been overtaken by 'community of interest', which arises not from residential proximity, but from shared values and concerns, so that community is 'no longer the community of place ... but an interest community which within a freely communicating society need not be spatially concentrated, for we are increasingly able to interact with each other wherever we may be located' (Webber, 1963: 29).

Despite the greater potential of this 'placelessness' attending the erosion of traditional collectivities and the advance of social media and other features of globalisation, the dominant characteristics recurring in the literature concern the binding solidarities of customary daily life that induces interdependence, loyalty and quality sociability. As summarised by Simpson (1937: 71), 'it is to human beings and their feelings, sentiments, reactions that all look for the fundamental roots of community'. In understanding this relational emphasis, Cohen (1985) adopts an interpretative and cultural appreciation of the symbols, values, codes and norms that make and remake communal togetherness. As expressed by Hamilton, in his introduction to Cohen's book (1985: 8):

> The study of community will continue to be necessary as long as local relationships play an important part in people's lives, for we have a long way to go until we are all part of a McLuhanesque 'global village', or feel that the only determining feature of our social lives is our relationship to the means of production and membership of a social class.

From such perspectives, it can be suggested that primal human imperatives for meaning, attachment and continuity find time-honoured expression in habitual communal settings, marked by intimate relationships. Here, it is argued, the vital personal sense of significance and recognition can best flourish. In this regard, Park (1952: 176–177) contends that

> every individual finds himself in a struggle for status: a struggle to preserve his personal prestige, his point of view, and his self-respect. He is able to maintain them, however, only to the extent that he can gain for himself the recognition of everyone who is in his set or society.

Yet, despite the persistent connotation that 'community' is an intrinsically good feature of an otherwise uncongenial urbanism, there is, at the same time, an enduring claim that it is in irreversible decline. Examples of this pessimistic prognosis, going back over half a century, can be found in Stein's work (1964) on the 'eclipse' of community in a more 'disorganized' society, in which ties to people and place are loosening, and in Nisbett's exploration (1953) of the 'quest' for community, a rediscovery of roots and rapport amid the impoverishment consequent upon the dehumanising rationality of mass corporate society. But, these ideas of 'community' assume a definition similar to that of Redfield's *folk society* (1947) and Tönnies's *Gemeinschaft* (1957) – a place where culture was relatively homogeneous; where human relations were primary; where status was largely ascriptive; and where the population was mostly immobile. In other words, a tradition of shared culture made for intimate and enduring loyalties to the locality and its people. Commenting on these idealistic notions of 'community', Halsey (1974: 130) claims that they contain 'the persistent residue of a romantic protest against the complexity of modern urban society – the idea of a decentralized world in which neighbours could and should corporately satisfy each other's needs and legitimate demands for health, wealth and happiness'. So, the idealised representation of 'community' is of primary group relations, personal and cooperative, arising spontaneously and valued intrinsically, stable and integrated yet permissive of dissent. Dissolution of these close social bonds is seen to inevitably attend the greater anonymity and specialisation that accompany the twin processes of industrialisation and urbanisation. Increasing complexity and differentiation of advanced industrial societies are thought to make rationalised, bureaucratic controls imperative, bringing with it greater formality in many kinds of social interaction. By contrast, the favourable features of urban community life are defended by Jane Jacobs (1961: 73):

> it is possible in a city street neighbourhood to know all kinds of people without unwelcome entanglements, without boredom, necessity for excuses, explanations, fears of giving offence, embarrassments ... and all such paraphernalia of obligations which can accompany less limited relationships.

At core, Jacob's argument was against the regimentation and idiocy of centralist modernist city planning, in favour of respecting the urban as a multifaceted organic entity, best understood at the local level of 'ordinary' spectacle and episodes. From such perspective, a 'community' has no clear-cut boundary. It is very much interdependent, and identity to it is ambivalent. Nevertheless, some question whether such hankering after 'community' is a reactionary quest that may denote a wistful craving for a lost sense of attachment, based mostly on tenuous nostalgia (Bloomberg, 1969); and whether this fostering of local affinities can inadvertently become a constriction on the deprived, a penalising myth that succeeds in excluding the poorest from wider societal opportunity. In this regard, it is interesting that one set of synonyms for 'local' is: restricted, limited, confined and narrow. Nevertheless, the appeal of the term as signifying 'homely', 'familiar' and 'genial' endures.

New localism

While praise for this assumed virtue of the local scale has been recurrent, echoing centuries-old theological social teaching about the primacy of subsidiarity, this enduring debate about the efficacy of local social connection and administration has been reawakened in the UK and US in recent decades (Clarke, 1993). For instance, in the 1980s, the transformative potential of municipal socialism as an antidote to Thatcherism, and the proliferation of 'locality studies' concentrating on the changing geography of production and related reshaping of the spatial division of labour, were trailed the following decade by deliberations about the 'reinvention' of government. As elaborated by Osborne and Gaebler (1992), this was a call for a flatter, more dynamic and decentralised government, that would steer rather than row; be concerned about results rather than inputs; be more preventative rather than curative; deploy more innovative mixes of competitive market and collaborative community to problem-solve; and enable and empower rather than directly provide. The argument seemed at once simple and irrefutable. Not only was old-style centralist, hierarchical, rigid bureaucracy no longer nimble enough to respond flexibly to a complex, rapidly changing world, but also an enterprising public sector could operate more effectively on tap rather than on top, availing of the dormant potential of overlooked social productivity in the public.

In the US, which had already come through the New Federalism of both Nixon and Reagan, as a device to de-politicise central government responsibility for cities and states impaired by post-industrialism, this reconceptualisation presented a convenient rationale for Clinton's New Democratic administration in the 1990s to take this re-scaling of the state further. By the same token, such a putative shift from government to governance offers elements of the political left opportunity to propose progressive models of a revitalised participative democracy (Fung and Wright, 2001), underpinned by active, even subversive, citizenship (Barnes and Prior, 2009; Durose *et al.*, 2009), in a 'conversing' rather than 'consulting' polity (Burns *et al.*, 1994). So while some, like Harvey (2010), see, in this focus on localism, a regressive politics in the face of resurgent market capitalism and its logic of accumulation, others acknowledge the need for a 'glocalist' perspective that identifies how universal processes of macro socio-economic change come to ground in the layered histories and contingencies of particular micro places (Massey, 2005; Soja, 2000). For them, such a 'global village' perspective provides the best means of understanding how local markets integrate into an increasingly transnational economy.

Specifically in the UK, since 2000, this New Localism became bound up in the search for a Third Way between the market and state, and developed a notion of 'double devolution' – first from central to regional and local government, and subsequently from the latter to drill down further to neighbourhoods and families (Davies, 2009; Morphet, 2008; Stoker, 2004). Under New Labour, this agenda found expression in proposals for sustainable, resilient and empowered communities (DCLG, 2006, 2008), a policy landscape cultivated further by the Coalition government with its Localism and Decentralisation Bill (2010), contextualised in the Conservatives' Big Society. While these processes are examined at length elsewhere in this volume, the concern here is to underline how they still generate a contested politics around their purpose and promise.

Has emphasis on social capital and networking partnerships in recent decades been an inevitable recognition of an increasingly complex society that traditional government has neither the legitimacy nor competence alone to command? Does this localism represent an authentic instrument for greater policy agility and deeper democracy, or is the rhetoric of community empowerment largely a tokenistic ruse to mitigate the impact of more centrally driven state intervention? Is it part of a genuine move to animate civil society and build community capacity, or is it an expedient means of privatising societal responsibilities in a period of fiscal stress and welfare cuts? Does it capture the zeitgeist, in recognising that, in both private and public realms, the Fordist era of mass production and standardisation has given way to one of flexible specialisation and personalisation that can best be customised in the singularities and idiosyncrasies of the decentralised level? But, can such 'personalised provision' still be operated within the protective framework of common social rights, guaranteed by the state? In terms of radical politics, does it offer novel forms of self-actualisation and autonomy as preferable to the dependencies generated by paternalistic welfare? Further, can it create new political spaces to mobilise sites of resistance, both formal and informal, to the unaccountable determinations of global finance and investment? Or, does it present a political cul-de-sac of communitarianism that fails to appreciate that while many social problems are most manifest at the local level, they are increasingly generated and resolved at more comprehensive global levels? In other words, is it a delusionary refuge for progressives who have seen the terrain for socialist transformation diminish markedly since the late 1980s? Is 'community', as Herbert (2005) insists, a 'trapdoor' that locks vulnerable populations under ambiguous collectivisms, like 'deprived areas'? Such argument and ambivalence are rooted in four central paradoxes behind this decentralising agenda that will be problematic to reconcile.

First, the 'local' seems to offer a platform that is at once simple, human-scale, accessible and operable, compared to its more remote alternative. Yet, as a term, it continues to confound with respect to both scale and dimension. For instance, in a recent attempt to capture the essence of neighbourhood and locality as an organically formed social agglomeration, Galster (2001) identifies a very 'composite commodity', with ten categories interwoven into the concept: structural; infrastructural; demographic; class status; public services; environmental; proximity; political; social-interactive; and sentimental. Not much better are Kallus and Law-Yone (2000), who specify three facets: the *humanistic* (relating to perception of social needs and bonds circumscribed in a physical setting); *instrumental* (concerning the functional planning/administrative system); and *phenomenological* (addressing the continuous collective memory that binds people to place over time and events). In other words, what seems at first to be straightforward, knowable and applicable is far more complicated and political (Massey, 1991), as indicated by earlier attempts at concise definition.

Second, some argue (Naisbitt, 1994) that as the world economy expands, so does the significance of its smallest parts – such as local areas – as power shifts from the vertical to the horizontal, and attributes of the small, such as adaptability, attain higher premium. Small can not only be beautiful, but also smart. In this new technological wave, related paradoxes emerge. For instance, as the world increasingly integrates, there is escalating appreciation for that which differentiates, and it is at the local that this distinctiveness can be drawn and disseminated through place branding and similar promotion. But, selling the local to a global audience can inadvertently cause local leaderships to neglect the priorities of their native populations, particularly the poorest.

Third, there is a tension between a shift to localism, designed in part to redress political disaffection and declining electoral participation, and the ambition of contemporary nation states to amplify their levers of influence in a world that, in the final analysis, respects power. For instance, Blair's impulse for devolution and decentralism in the UK was compromised by his recognition that his core project of modernisation in the face of new global competition demanded a far-reaching reformist agenda that could only be secured by clear, consistent and determined central direction. So, for instance, it was good for Londoners to select their own mayor, as long as they didn't choose Ken Livingstone. Behind all the Assemblies, Mayors, Local Strategic Partnerships, Local Area Agreements, City Deals, etc., central targets and audits were to prevail.

Finally, this relates to the over-riding friction between a modern *politics*, in which many publics seem to want to partake in proximate and intimate enough jurisdictions, in which they feel that they can share cultural bonds and shape key decisions that affect their lives, and a modern *economics*, that pressures countries to form into larger blocs, like the European Union, alliances designed to afford scale and protection for material prosperity. While, as earlier indicated, this assumption about the virtues of economies of scale rather than scope may prove to be misconceived, politics is presently pulling to the small local, while economics is pulling to the large centre. Meanwhile, democratic mandates are becoming buffeted in between. One obvious reflection of this dilemma lies in current controversies around immigration. The economic imperative is to facilitate movement of people as well as finance to optimise efficient use of labour, land and capital, while the political challenge is how to accommodate the increasing diversity such mobility brings. Not only is the global becoming more urban, but also the urban everywhere is becoming more global (Soja, 2000). Many cities are now hosting multi-ethnicities, and urban politics will become increasingly concerned about how to deal with such difference in ways that address both social inclusion and community cohesion (Gaffikin and Morrissey, 2011b).

Another potential outcome can be seen in the recent travails of the Republic of Ireland. There, the political culture has long held that 'all politics is local'. Indeed, the long-standing patronage system is rooted in 'pork-barrel' spending, which brings largesse to local constituencies for electoral dividend. Such practice militated against regulatory and strategic spatial planning, and in the property boom that accompanied the Celtic Tiger years, great clusters of over-development were sanctioned in particular locales. When the subsequent private debt of the profligate banks and developers was transferred as sovereign debt to burden the whole country in late 2008, Ireland had to supplicate itself to the financial support and political direction of international institutions like the European Bank if it was to avoid insolvency. Having indulged in a series of local 'parties', the country woke up, after its hangover, to the erosion of its very national sovereignty.

But, if these patterns and paradoxes about '"negotiated self-governance" in communities, cities and regions' (Newman, 2001: 24) are germane to the general experience of reconfigured local–central relations, how much more thorny is localism in the context of a deeply contested society like Northern Ireland? Superimposed on conventional considerations about the appropriate spatial unit of analysis, the rhetoric and reality of new governance, or whether community action bridges democratic deficits or domesticates radicalism by co-option, and such like, are other formidable quandaries. In such places, these become most discernible in the urban arena.

Contested societies and divided cities

Cities are intrinsically centres of conflict and contest. In that sense, all cities are 'divided' (Amin, 2005, 2008). Indeed, 'difference in the city is as old as the city itself' (Madanipour, 1996: 78), and consequently, urban contestedness has a long, troubled history (Gunn, 2001; Johnson, 1985). But, a voluminous literature distinguishes types and degrees of division. So, for instance, we have Hepburn's (2004) distinction between 'divided' cities, which may be marked by hostilities between ethnic or religious groups, and 'contested' cities, in which the conflict concerns ownership and control. Following Kotek's (1999) term of 'frontier' city for those places caught up in a macro nationalist dispute, Pullan (2011) refers similarly to 'frontier urbanism'. Benvenisti (1986) likewise insists that when urban contest is contextualised within a wider national conflict, the city is not merely 'divided', but 'polarised'. Bollens (1996, 1999, 2000) refers to the contested city as one in which identity and nationalism interact and impact on all aspects of urbanism. Essentially then, there are two main forms of urban contested space: one concerning disputes about *pluralist* issues of class, status and power, and the other where these perennial antagonisms are interlocked with ethno-nationalist conflict about *sovereignty* and the legitimacy of the state itself. In other words, in cities like Belfast, Jerusalem and Nicosia, traditional quarrels about 'whose city' get tangled with the wider clash about 'whose country'.

As Castells (1997) reminds us, the influence of identity in the contemporary world, and 'the need to belong' in a more mobile and rootless time (Maalouf, 2003), are potent determinants of social affiliation, particularly since the economic restructuring of advanced capitalism has tended to be accompanied by a bifurcation of labour markets, a related debilitation of traditional working-class communities and greater socio-spatial segmentation. In such a fragmented process, the identity politics around race and ethnicity (Giannakos, 2002; Ratcliffe, 2004) has sharpened in many places. But, while five key components of standard urban conflict can be specified – identity, equity, security, territory and the proprietary – it is the last of these issues, that of ownership, that marks the sovereignty-based contest. In many parts, over the last half-century, such ethno-nationalist ruptures have been burgeoning in the context of sovereignty re-alignments attending both the post-colonial experience and the end of the Cold War. Given the critical role of space in such territorial rivalry (Boal, 2002; Purbrick *et al.*, 2007), and planning's competency in the social shaping of space, planning is inextricably implicated in the conflict's resolution. By the same token, the ancestral and visceral character of these disputes makes for intractable conflict, whose very duration then deepens the animosity (Pullan, 2011), and with it, the territorial demarcations and partitions (Bose, 2007; Crocker *et al.*, 2004). In turn, such barriers that localise and insulate, though offering protection from the 'Other' in the immediate emergencies of acute violence, 'typically become a self-fulfilling prophesy of exclusion and resentment in the long term' (Calame and Charlesworth, 2009: 15).

Moreover, such discord about national identity and territorial tenure, and the related macro contest around ethno-nationalism, telescope right down into small neighbourhoods, where the relationship between space and identity constructs its own conflict zones of borders, boundaries and interfaces (Anderson and O'Dowd, 1999; Anderson and Shuttleworth, 1998). But, peace-building in conflict cities cannot only happen at the big formal political table, without also finding root in the formalities and informalities of such difficult localities (Brewer, 2010). Yet, it is at this foundational level that the incongruities and ambiguities of contested space are at their most acute.

As noted by Massey (2005), the concept of *space* here is seen not as a static entity, a passive theatre of social life, but rather as a dynamic agent in itself. Its lack of social fixity is attributable to its unremitting social construction and reconstruction. In that regard, it has little inherent or immutable meaning or representation. Rather, these alter with its designation and application.

Conflict societies, marked by frequent occurrences of claimed space for exclusive ownership and use tied to select forms of identity, tend to have four main types of space: *ethnic* (signified and dominated by one or other main clan); *neutral* (offering some degree of security for universal use, but not substantial cross-community interaction); *shared* (the relatively rare safe dialogic space that actively encourages engagement across the divide); and *cosmopolitan* space (which is not legible within the contours of local contest, but rather transcends it with more global references and associations) (Gaffikin and Morrissey, 2011a).

It is when the predominance of ethnic space corrals many people into 'local lives' inextricably linked to indivisible identities that persistent conflict is likely (Sen, 2006). The solution is seen to lie in the dilution of exceptionalism and absolutist identities into more unique hybridities and multiplicities of being and becoming. In these terms, Sandercock (2003: 98) talks about the conversion of a 'politics of pure identity' into a 'politics of difference' that affirms the right of recognition and inclusion, an approach that can at once 'embrace cultural autonomy and, at the same time, work to strengthen intercultural solidarity'. This is the search for what I would call '*diversity without disconnection*'. But, such planning for recognition also entails a strategy for redistribution, since identity operates within unequal power relations (Fincher and Iveson, 2008). In this respect, it is not an issue that can be tackled mainly at the local level. For one thing, it has to be framed in macro choices about policy direction. To take one example: do we accept that multiculturalism ultimately is an enemy of liberalism insofar as it encourages parallel lives in segregated congregations that fragment rather than cohere the social fabric (Baber, 2008)? If so, what is the prospect for an interculturalism that combines both bonding and bridging social capital (Bloomfield and Bianchini, 2004; James, 2008), and the fluidity of identity that follows? These critical debates demand a national and international perspective and arena, which capture the way we are all formed from permutations of global and local cultures that both tie us to particular origins and community attachments, while liberating us for the wider embrace of cosmopolitanism, shared with most of our contemporaries (Maalouf, 2003; Parekh, 2000).

Notwithstanding this wider lens, some insist that cities and localities can play a significant role in peace-building in contested societies (Bollens, 2007: 8):

> Challenges regarding identity, citizenship, and belonging in a globalizing world will need to be addressed most immediately at the local level; our degree of progress at this grassroots level will either fortify or confine our ability to address these issues at broader geographies both within and between states.

Elevating *demos* over *ethnos*, fostering civic spirit over partisan sensibility, appreciating and accepting people of all cultural origin, while providing equitable access to pathways of difference and dissent – such values are extolled in societies at ease with non-conformity, eccentricity, authenticity and pluralism. This urban challenge of accommodating deep diversity is relevant to many parts of the contemporary world, from Belfast to Nicosia, to Jerusalem, to Kiev (Charalambous and Hadjichristos, 2011). Indeed, it used to be thought that Northern Ireland was a place apart, whose divisions were a leftover from some obscurantist seventeenth-century struggle over religious and national identity. But more recently, far from being anachronistic, we have witnessed the proliferation of such ethno-nationalist conflict as a global phenomenon. As expressed by O'Doherty (2008: 184):

> What we didn't realise until the Cold War was over, was that the global stand-off had been dampening down ethnic tensions. It was replaced not by diverse wars over class and capital, as might have been predicted, but by wars over ethnic rights to nationhood, in which religion was nearly always a definer of ethnic allegiance. Suddenly there were Northern Irelands all over the place and that type of war seemed standard rather than eccentric.

But in embracing the opportunity for cultural cross-pollination and more cosmopolitan futures, it is crucial to pay heed to the contradictions that can confound such commendable intent.

Paradoxes in localist planning in contested space

A set of paradoxes beset 'localist' planning in deeply contested places. The following eight examples illustrate the conundrums involved:

1 The genesis and nature of modernist planning are embedded in a conviction about the rationality, knowability and predictability of society, and in the ultimate capacity for ordering and patterning social space. Specifically, it extols the virtues of connectivity, permeability and of mediating processes to determine consensual concepts of the public good. Yet, in deeply contested places, marked by disorder, instability and discord, the force of argument is often trumped by the argument of force. Passion, and indeed mercurial expressions of fear, loathing and bitterness, compete on an uneven playing field with dispassionate objectivity (Bridge, 2005). Instead of 'the public', it is apparent that there are rival 'publics', each with its own vernacular of what constitutes mutuality. Also, assumptions about the predictability and controllability of trends are often humiliated by the actual

volatilities ingrained in a disturbed society. While post-modernist critiques of conventional planning would insist that its vaulting ambitions are universally misplaced in a relativist world, this gap between the pretensions of professional planning, and the real mayhem that can shape daily life in the streets and neighbourhoods of contested cities, is particularly striking. In such a contentious context, reconciling conflicting perspectives on local advancement with wider strategic perspectives on societal enrichment can be distinctly problematic.

2 In deeply divided societies, 'community', in the sense of local area, can be an exclusive concept, whereby the solidarities within an area can be nurtured in part by hostility to, and rivalry with, those outside it. A planning process that responds mainly to the preferences of such local segregated areas risks reinforcing the division and ghettoisation. So, what in 'normal' circumstances may be considered a democratic and decentralised form of planning – working in partnership with neighbourhood – may unintentionally buttress patterns of separation and diseconomies of duplicated services. To circumvent this tendency, planning processes would have to proactively engage discursively and agonistically across the adversarial communities (Pløger, 2004), making for a very resource- and time-intensive participatory exercise. Yet, such investment runs counter to the increasingly proceduralist and managerialist forms of urban governance, which privilege economy and efficiency over equity and empowerment. Indeed, while the efficacy of local participation is formally endorsed, currently planning is under pressure to expedite decision-making, without any explanation of how the inclusiveness and distributive justice implied in the former are compatible with emphasis on cost-effectiveness and competence associated with the latter.

3 Taking this problem with 'community' further, if communalism is elevated above the civic as a core urban value, as it often is in conflict societies, additional difficulties about the marking of territory and ownership of 'turf' can arise, confounding attempts to create open and inclusive place (Knox, 2011). In cities like Belfast, it is common practice to paint kerbstones and wall murals with colours and symbols of tribal loyalty to designate belonging and welcome. Since such behaviour is usually acclaimed as expression of 'community culture', police tend to argue that it is a matter for political arbitration, and they are powerless to intervene. Yet, the reality is that there are no community plebiscites taken to test the residents' consent for such partisan displays, which are instead the strategic outcome of paramilitary initiative. So, while an average citizen attempting to paint on a public path or wall could be arrested for criminal damage, these acts of defacement, in the name of 'community' identity, are executed with impunity. Even though their effect is to exacerbate inter-communal enmity and

malice, their imprimatur as valid local articulations goes unchallenged by the planning system. In response, some suggest a robust legal approach to the problem, one that deals with people as citizens bound by the rule of law, rather than as members of an ethno-nationalist clan with a collective right to parade sectarian adherence. Certainly, 'citizenship' can be presented as a more inclusive framework than 'community' (Wallace, 2010). But, the dilemma in a society conflicted about sovereignty is that the very concept of 'citizenship' lies at the heart of the contest (Gaffikin and Morrissey, 2006).

4 Efficient urban land and resource use has been increasingly judged to demand compact form, involving the need to avail of brownfield sites before the possible exploitation of greenfield. Such sequential development is taken to at once help regenerate urban dereliction, while minimising the ecological detriment of urban sprawl. But, in cities torn by civil disturbance, available brownfield land is not just that left behind from deindustrialisation, but also that generated by the exodus of populations 'pushed' to the sub- and ex-urbs by the insecurities of the violence and intimidation that tend to spatially concentrate in the urban core. Moreover, these population migrations become a very significant factor in conflicts where demographic weights are a crucial part of the political calculation. Given such demographic shifts, supply of brownfield land may become more available in or near one community, while housing demand may become more acute in the other. In such circumstances, local housing strategies that may properly seek to meet housing need on unused land may be perceived to be legitimating the incursion of one community into the 'territory' of another, a spatial re-designing of electoral influence in a sensitive local 'geo-politics' that will be cast as trespass.

5 In deeply divided cities, it is common for there to be an equivalence between those areas of acute deprivation and those where the argument around identity and affiliation is most ruthlessly contested. Accordingly, combined programmes of regeneration and reconciliation are imperative (Beall *et al.*, 2002; Forrest and Kearns, 2001). Yet, if these are locally focused, they may highlight local rivalries, since policies designed to promote both social inclusion and community cohesion at the same time may themselves generate friction between the two objectives (Gaffikin and Morrissey, 2011b; Robinson, 2005). The redistributive intentions of social inclusion may alert inter-communal controversy about the relative allocation of public resources to each side. Thereby, reconciliation objectives are threatened. It may be thought that the solution here rests in transparent and indisputable data giving objective ranking of deprivation. But, this is to ignore the complex relationship among ontology, epistemology, ideology and methodology in such conflictive local circumstance. Basically, it

discounts: (a) the way the *reality* of the stance and substance of the conflict is itself part of the quarrel; (b) the disputed validation of *knowledge* deployed to offer causal insight into the feuds; (c) the mutually exclusive *values* that make for incompatible perspectives between both sides; and (d) argument about the *methods* that generate the data to justify the 'evidence'.

6 In many contested societies, disputed cultural identities can problematise interventions around the built environment and heritage (Ragab, 2011). Accordingly, there can be attempts to de-politicise planning, housing and development, passing these sensitive provisions as much as possible over to centralised professionals to negotiate with local community interests, largely removed from partisan politics (Neill, 2004). For instance, in Belfast, at the start of the Troubles, planning and housing were removed from local political control and given over to 'independent' quangos and central government civil servants. Such a mix of bureaucratic and participatory approaches may be seen to prudently professionalise and neutralise the testing provision of such social commodities. But, criticism can be made that this produces a 'democratic deficit' with problematic accountability. So, it is unsurprising that one of the reforms in a post-violent conflict Northern Ireland has been to restore planning powers to local government, as part of a general strategy to reanimate local politics. Yet, the contradiction here is that re-politicisation of spatial planning assumes that politicians who mostly rely on sectarian demographies for their electoral arithmetic will be the very same people who can lead society out of the sectarian geographies that facilitate such constituency calculation.

7 In contested societies, the relationship between market and state works in perplexing ways for local input and benefit. Public policy designed for the general good can be interpreted very differently in different locales. For some, it can be seen as partisan social engineering favouring 'the other side', or as promoting values of equality and diversity that threaten the position of the previously dominant interest. In other words, it is difficult to present highly visible planning and policy as impartial in the uneven arena that usually marks such conflicts, and, as such, its interventions can provoke resistance from particular local areas. By contrast, the hidden hand of the market can be thought to be colour-blind and neutral, motivated by dispassionate profit, and thereby it can 'get away' with developments, whose delivery the public sector might find controversial. So, in Belfast, there has been significant market-driven transformation of the waterfront. To many, this has helped create new cosmopolitan spaces that are above and beyond the local conflict, and offer new residential and recreational opportunities to those residents who seek to escape the more traditional sectarian terrains. This can be seen to pre-figure an alternative Belfast, in which market

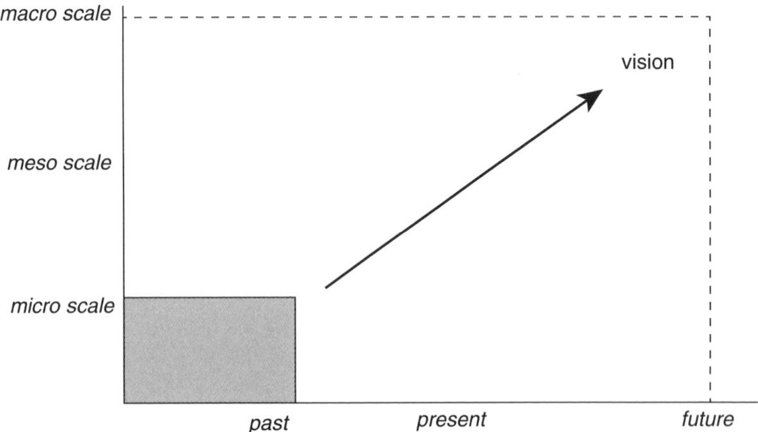

Figure 3.1 Time–space matrix

status matters more than ethno-national affiliation. But, these transformations have happened with little local participation, and concern has been expressed by some critics about how speculative development has taken priority over more balanced forms, which include affordable housing. So, the contradiction here is that in these instances of attempting to privatise the reshaping of the city away from its sectarian pattern and image, market-based demand has been favoured over needs-based development, and local voices have been muted in the process (Murtagh, 2002).

8 Taking 'local' to refer to micro spaces such as neighbourhoods and districts, with meso spaces being city–region and macro scale covering the national–global, there is a tendency for those areas enduring greatest deprivation and violent conflict to operate mostly within the narrow territory of the micro. Within a temporal–spatial matrix, the 'localism' of the most segregated and deprived communities not only involves much of their social interaction and regeneration being enclaved within a restricted spatial framework. It tends also to involve perspectives being pulled persistently to the past, as their conflict narrative is continuously traced and replenished through blinkered versions of an aggrieved history. Yet, if such ghettoised areas are ever to escape the rotation of victimhood and reprisal, they have to be opened to wider vistas, networked into broader socio-spatial opportunities, and focused on visionary scenarios that travel from dismal present to more promising future.

For instance, for the past four decades in Belfast, various locally-based urban programmes have been targeted to such areas: from Belfast Areas of Need, through to Belfast Action Teams, to Making Belfast Work, to Neighbourhood Renewal. These have been complemented by European-funded local initiatives, such as the Poverty programmes, and URBAN, and all this regeneration effort has been augmented by community relations schemes, such as the PEACE programmes, and myriad support from Foundations. All of this investment has generated a cadre of community workers and 'gatekeepers', and a proliferation of local partnerships that overlap in a confusing labyrinth. But yet, taking the indices of multiple deprivation back 40 years, it is the same wards, almost exactly in the same ranking, that persistently come out as the most disadvantaged, segregated and conflict-ridden, with related indicators of poor health and educational attainment. In other words, this local drive has failed to make a significant impression on the problem. It is not so much that a war was fought against poverty, and poverty won. Rather, the 'war' proved to be more a local skirmish, with the battlefield entrapping the poorest, as the more socially mobile over time deserted that particular local combat zone.

Indeed, the long-standing dispute between structural and cultural causes of poverty mirrors this local/global dichotomy. Some emphasise that problems of deprivation may be manifest locally, but that their roots lie in more global structures and patterns, such as the distribution of wealth and allocation of investment. By contrast, those focusing on cultural causality stress the responsibility of specific communities and families for behaviour and attitudes that contribute significantly to their disadvantage, with the implication that they are largely the authors of their own misfortune. While the latter suggests the efficacy of local intervention, the former posits its limited impact in the face of primary macro influence.

These paradoxes, particularly those associated with sovereignty-based conflict, intersect with the central paradoxes mentioned earlier. For instance, definition of 'community' is even more elusive in deeply divided societies. Does it refer to the racial or ethno-nationalist 'communities' in contest, or to local neighbourhood affiliation? Similarly, the premium of local uniqueness in a global age becomes problematic if the main thing for which a place is distinguished is its violent division, a distinction that brings notoriety rather than acclaim. Moreover, the argument that the pull between more globalism on the one hand and devolution on the other is 'crowding out' the nation state has particular relevance to those conflicts centred on the contesting sovereignty of particular nation states, such as Britain and Ireland in the case of Northern Ireland. For one thing, should Scotland achieve greater autonomy from the rest of Britain, the configuration of 'national identity' in the 'British Isles' will become ever more complicated, confounding the solidarities currently felt by Unionists in Northern Ireland. Finally, here, the paradox that, in the contemporary world, politics is becoming more local, while economics is becoming more global, is often presented to combatants in contested societies as a stark choice – you can indulge in your local dispute all you want, but there will be a price to pay in terms of international confidence and investment. In short, the central paradoxes of devolution have particular pertinence in places where space and identity form the criss-crossing fault lines of political quarrel.

So, what can be learned from these patterns and paradoxes, and the role of locally focused action in addressing the challenge of moving from a contested to a shared society? Perhaps, a central lesson is that planning in a contested society can inadvertently accentuate rather than ameliorate the problems of division (Dumper, 1997). But, what is the prospect of a different planning paradigm?

Planning a shared society: the scope of localism?

The traditional land use planning model has struggled to deliver a more shared society in places like Northern Ireland, tending to 'airbrush' out the pertinence of division and segregation to the planning process, as if such issues are beyond the remit and competence of planners (Gaffikin and Morrissey, 2011a). It has shown limited capacity to challenge the 'diseconomies of conflict' that often see the duplication of services and amenities within each sectarian bloc. Because of concentration on 'land use planning' – a technical concern about zoning and regulating particular development activity – and its emphasis on the *physical* aspects of infrastructure and development, it has shown restricted scope for considering the wider social fabric. Within this partial framework, potential has been granted to major sectarian blocs to exploit planning to carve up 'spheres of influence', thereby inhibiting the creation of a more integrated and shared society. Moreover, its reluctance to recognise openly the differences among ethnic, neutral, shared and cosmopolitan spaces in a conflict-ridden society does not afford it the perspective to craft plausible common visions that appeal to the mutuality of both combatant sides. Given the close correspondence between the areas of greatest deprivation and the areas that have endured the greatest violent conflict, the traditional approach has failed to twin the processes of regeneration and reconciliation. In particular, it has struggled to relate the fortification, disconnection and barriers that proliferate at such local levels to wider city–region planning. This is, in part, attributable to its limited facility for nesting neighbourhood planning and regeneration strategies within an overall statutory and strategic planning framework, without which such local planning lacks legal authority.

The question arises as to whether the introduction of *community planning* and *spatial planning* brings the prospect of an innovative approach that gets beyond this old-style, physically dominated 'land use planning', to a more comprehensive and holistic model, linking the physical with the social, economic, environmental and cultural aspects of development. Can this planning approach facilitate clearer insight into the spatial *needs* and *impact* of all other policy sectors, such as health, education and social services, thereby allowing for a clearer picture of the spatial needs and impact of policies designed to promote good relations across the divided communities, throughout the whole of governance?

For one thing, this approach may help deal with the awkward issue of 'community'. As explained earlier, in Northern Ireland at present, there are two main uses of the term: first, 'community' as in '*local neighbourhood*'; and second, 'community' as in '*the two main communities: Protestant and Catholic*'. By contrast, the idea of 'community' in the concept of *community planning* is much broader and civic rather than ethnic. Under this rubric, 'community' is not understood in terms of the district geographies critiqued earlier as restricted, limited, confined and narrow, fragmenting and factionalising into contesting enclaves. Rather, this notion of 'community' encourages all residents to consider the wider city as their 'neighbourhood', and to look to the mutual benefits involved in its city-wide development. This overall need to get beyond narrow definitions of the 'local' and to adopt the core principle of connectivity – linking areas, services, opportunities and people – is critical to the formation of more shared physical and social spaces in deeply divided societies.

It involves an iterative process of building a city vision and strategy from a critical *engagement* between 'top-down' macro priorities and major development investments, on the one hand, and the series of 'local' planning processes designed to address the regeneration of vicinity, on the other. Such exchanges are more likely to be controversial and combative than to be conciliatory or consensual, more agonistic than deliberative and collaborative, since in addressing socio-spatial inequality and separatism, relations of domination and subjugation produce encounters of differential power characterised more by clash than concord. But, in this perpetual contest, the adversarial collisions inherent in this 'stitching' of the city into a coherent formation – whereby the whole is greater than the sum of the parts – may offer prospect of a more candid and transparent urban polity. If so, it can provide a planning framework for challenging the segregated political and physical spaces shaped by sectarianism. Similarly, if fully realised, the comprehensive and inclusive perspective of *spatial planning* carries potential for rethinking space as an active agent, whose meaning and use are understood in relational terms. Accordingly, it cannot avoid the pertinence of all aspects of societal conflict to the shaping of social space, and thus addressing the conflict has to be considered as a central feature of the planning process.

However, this is not to suggest that such agonistic engagement across difference offers a ready panacea. An example of the intractable discourse typically encountered comes from some action-research we conducted with community agencies involved in the difficult interface areas in Belfast. We asked them to consider the efficacy of the following ten principles for good planning practice in a deeply divided city.

1. No particular grouping has a right to claim any territory on behalf of a communal identity. All of the city should be considered as commonwealth – as shared space.
2. Since the city as a whole is every resident's neighbourhood, urban policy and planning should be concerned to create a pluralist city for a pluralist people – open, connected and interdependent.
3. Civic values of equity, diversity, mutuality and social cohesion should take precedence over those ethnic or community values, rooted in tribal partisanship.
4. Capacity for such interlocking networks and good relations should be cultivated as a central mark of genuine community development.
5. Initiatives concerning interfaces and contested spaces should be considered within the regeneration of their wider environments.
6. Development of disadvantaged areas requires a collaborative and coordinated approach involving cross-community local groups working with multi-agency teams to achieve deliverable outcomes, tied to the overall development of the city–region.
7. Poor physical connectivity among neighbourhoods, and from those neighbourhoods to key sites of employment, education and other services, should be addressed as a planning and regeneration priority.
8. New housing developments need to avoid the replication of single-identity social and/or religious or ethnic communities, and should aim to create mixed neighbourhoods, well linked to wider city opportunities.
9. Such mixed developments, designed to create high-quality diverse communities, should become the model to help break down the social, ethnic and sectarian divisions of existing city neighbourhoods.
10. Location of key public services is crucial to their accessibility and perception as a common civic asset. Public services should be sited in areas that are securely accessible to all communities.

While the principles as generalised statements attracted wide support, reservations emerged. Some felt that they were too imprecise, and thus prone to operational ambiguity and ambivalence. But, as their implications were interrogated more forensically, their challenge became clearer. For instance, the first one suggests that no identity community can determine conditions of access to its locality by people of a different persuasion. In other words, in a context of a city like Belfast that there is no valid 'jurisdiction' such as a Catholic area or a Protestant area, through which the 'other side' has to seek permission to march. All areas are to be regarded as part of an open pluralist city. In a very territorialised city, demarcated very definitely in terms of divergent political allegiance, such a porous and permeable approach to planning and mobility would constitute a radical departure in dealing with traditional boundary and border. In the immediate term at least, it would demote the role of 'community' and locality within the primary objective of improving the city for all residents and users. Similarly, reference to concepts such as 'civic values' invites discussion about what such values are, by whom they are determined and in what way they have intrinsic virtue over ethnic values. Similarly, it is facile to say that you favour a 'shared city'. Who is going to admit to wanting a 'divided city'? Thus, peace-building in divided societies demands the deconstruction of such 'empty signifiers' (Oberschall, 2007) to permit specific interrogation of what exactly is meant by 'shared'. Who pays for, and who benefits from, pursuit of this objective?

In short, such principles are unlikely to command ready consensus. Rather, their purpose lies in offering the basis for detailed engagement across deep socio-spatial divides about how best to accord everyone 'the right to the city'. Such discourse helps draw in a wider set of stakeholders, and it helps clarify the disagreement and dissent. Or, to mix metaphors, it can provide scope for a new choreography, that in reshaping the dance, it reshapes the relationship among the dancers. But urban policy and planning, based on such considerations, is inevitably drawn into the links between identity formation and recognition on the one hand, and power relations on the other. It cannot avoid being overtly political.

There is a role for local action in shaping this transformative politics. But, it is a 'connected localism' (Somerville, 2011; Taylor, 2003), one that links various forms of local governance with appropriate wider networks that can scale up responses proportionate to the issue being addressed (Ross, 2013). At the same time, it is not just about changing systems and structures. It is very much about changing culture, including imaginative 'ways of living at home abroad, or abroad at home' (Pollock *et al.*, 2002: 11). In such transcultural engagement, the candid and robust dialogue that underlies agonistic planning is preferable to the consensual assumptions implicit in collaborative planning, a difficult process for deeply divergent publics that need to acknowledge the fragilities of governance in societies seeking to move out of conflict (Brinkerhoff, 2007). In an ever less collaborative world, in which power seems ever more remote and intangible, and in which the social realm is being de-politicised and marketised, these approaches avow the politics of smart pluralism – that is, an approach that acknowledges that to achieve my objectives, I may have to win support from at least some of the opposing constituency, and, to do so, I have to be ready to concede at least some of what they want. In this sense, urban democracy, comprising diverse and divergent publics, has to be wary of 'local traps' that insulate such publics into separatist rivalry, rather than opening them to mutually beneficial networks (Purcell, 2006).

Given the planning and regeneration powers that operate at local level – such as local government – it is important to appreciate that, in a deeply contested society, the knowledge and skills required for this more comprehensive and inclusive planning need to be nurtured rather than assumed. This demands major investment in enhancing local government competencies and civic literacy and aptitude in general, a capacity-building programme designed to:

a develop the institutional capacities to re-think and reorganise planning to make it fit for purpose in building a more inclusive, equitable, sustainable and peaceful society;
b specifically, help to make the building of a shared society a central feature of the new community planning and spatial planning; and
c promote the linkage between local neighbourhood planning, particularly in the most isolated, disadvantaged and conflict-ridden communities, and the broader planning process, since a sustainable peace depends on the connection of such troubled areas into wider society.

References

Amin, A. (2005) Local community on trial, *Economy and Society*, 34(4): 612–633.

Amin, A. (2008) *Thinking Past Integration and Community Cohesion*, paper presented at 'Integration and Community Cohesion' seminar, Belfast Castle, 5 February 2008, Belfast: Belfast City Council's Conflict Transformation Project.

Anderson, J. and O'Dowd, L. (1999) Contested borders: Globalisation and ethno-national conflict in Ireland, *Regional Studies*, 33(7): 681–696.

Anderson, J. and Shuttleworth, I. (1998) Sectarian demography, territoriality and political development in Northern Ireland, *Political Geography*, 17(2): 187–208.

Arensberg, C. and Kimball, S. (1965) *Culture and Community*, New York: Harcourt, Brace & World, Inc.

Baber, H.E. (2008) *The Multicultural Mystique: The liberal case against diversity*, New York: Prometheus Books.

Barnes, M. and Prior, D. (eds) (2009) *Subversive Citizens: Power, agency and resistance in public services*, Bristol: Policy Press.

Beall, J., Crankshaw, O. and Parnell, S. (2002) *Uniting a Divided City: Governance and social exclusion in Johannesburg*, London: Earthscan.

Bell, C. and Newby, H. (1971) *Community Studies*, London: Allen & Unwin.

Benvenisti, M. (1986) *Conflicts and Contradictions*, New York: Villard Books.

Bloomberg, W., Jr. (1969) Community organization, in R.M. Kramer and H. Specht (eds), *Readings in Community Organization Practice*, Englewood Cliffs, NJ: Prentice-Hall Inc., pp. 91–127.

Bloomfield, J. and Bianchini, F. (2004) *Intercultural City: Planning for the intercultural city*, Basildon: Comedia.

Boal, F.W. (2002) Belfast: Walls within, *Political Geography*, 21: 687–694.

Bollens, S.A. (1996) On narrow ground: Planning in ethnically polarised cities, *Journal of Architectural and Planning Research*, 13(2): 120–136.

Bollens, S.A. (1999) *Urban Peace Building in Divided Societies: Belfast and Johannesburg*, Boulder, CO: Westview Press.

Bollens, S.A. (2000) *On Narrow Ground: Urban policy and ethnic conflict in Jerusalem and Belfast*, Albany: State of University of New York Press.

Bollens, S.A. (2007) *Cities, Nationalism, and Democratization*, Abingdon: Routledge.

Bose, S. (2007) *Contested Lands: Israel–Palestine, Kashmir, Bosnia, Cyprus and Sri Lanka*, Cambridge, MA: Harvard University Press.

Brewer, J.D. (2010) *Peace Processes: A sociological approach*, Cambridge: Polity Press.

Bridge, G. (2005) *Reason in the City of Difference: Pragmatism, communicative action and contemporary urbanism*, London: Routledge.

Brinkerhoff, D.W. (2007) Introduction: Governance challenges in fragile states – re-establishing security, rebuilding effectiveness, and reconstituting legitimacy, in D.W. Brinkerhoff (ed.), *Governance in Post-Conflict Societies: Rebuilding fragile states*, Abingdon: Routledge, pp. 1–22.

Burns, D., Hambleton, R. and Hoggett, P. (1994) *The Politics of Decentralisation: Revitalising local democracy*, London: Macmillan.

Cabinet Office. (2010) *The Coalition: Our programme for government*, London: Cabinet Office.

Calame, J. and Charlesworth, E.R. (2009) *Divided Cities: Belfast, Beirut, Jerusalem, Mostar, and Nicosia*, Philadelphia: University of Pennsylvania Press.

Castells, M. (1997) *The Power of Identity*, Oxford: Blackwell.

Charalambous, N. and Hadjichristos, C. (2011) Overcoming division in Nicosia's public space, *Built Environment*, 37(2): 170–182.

Clark, D.B. (1973) The concept of community: A re-examination, *The Sociological Review*, 21(3): 397–416.

Clarke, S.E. (1993) The new localism: Local politics in a global era, in G.E. Goetz and S.E. Clarke (eds), *The New Localism: Comparative urban politics in a global era*, Newbury Park, CA: Sage Publications.

Cohen, A. (1985) *Symbolic Construction of Community*, London: Routledge.

Crocker, C.A., Hampson, F.O. and Aall, P. (2004) *Taming Intractable Conflicts: Mediation in the hardest cases*, Washington, DC: United States Institute of Peace.

Davies, J. (2009) The new localism, in M. Flinders, A. Gamble, C. Hay and M. Kenny (eds), *The Oxford Handbook of British Politics*, Oxford: Oxford University Press.

DCLG. (2006) *Strong and Prosperous Communities: The Local Government White Paper*, London: Department for Communities and Local Government.

DCLG. (2008) *Communities in Control: Real people, real power*, London: Department for Communities and Local Government.

DCLG. (2010) *The Decentralisation and Localism Bill: An essential guide*, London: Department for Communities and Local Government.

Dumper, M. (1997) *The Politics of Jerusalem since 1967*, New York: University of Columbia Press.

Durose, C., Greasley, S. and Richardson, L.E. (eds) (2009) *Changing Local Governance, Changing Citizens*, Bristol: Bristol University Press.

Fincher, R. and Iveson, K. (2008) *Planning and Diversity in the City: Redistribution, recognition and encounter*, Basingstoke: Palgrave Macmillan.

Forrest, R. and Kearns, A. (2001) Social cohesion, social capital and the neighbourhood, *Urban Studies*, 38(12): 2125–2143.

Fung, A. and Wright, E.O. (2001) Deepening democracy: Innovations in empowered participatory governance, *Politics and Society*, 29(1): 5–41.

Gaffikin, F. and Morrissey, M. (2006) Planning for peace in contested space: Inclusion through engagement and sanction, *International Journal of Urban and Regional Research*, 30(4): 873–889.

Gaffikin, F. and Morrissey, M. (2011a) *Planning in Divided Cities: Collaborative shaping of contested space*, Oxford: Wiley-Blackwell.

Gaffikin, F. and Morrissey, M. (2011b) Community cohesion and social inclusion: Unravelling a complex relationship, *Urban Studies*, 48(6): 1089–1118.

Galster, G. (2001) On the nature of neighbourhood, *Urban Studies*, 38(12): 2111–2124.

Giannakos, S.A. (2002) *Ethnic Conflict: Religion, identity and politics*, Athens: Ohio University Press.

Gunn, S. (2001) The spatial turn: changing histories of space and place, in S. Gunn and R.J. Morris (eds), *Identities in Space: Contested terrains in the Western city since 1850*, Aldershot: Ashgate, pp. 1–18.

Halsey, A.H. (1974) Government against poverty in school and community, in D. Wedderburn (ed.), *Poverty, Inequality and Class Structure*, London: Cambridge University Press, pp. 123–140.

Harvey, D. (2010) *The Enigma of Capital and the Crises of Capitalism*, New York: Oxford University Press.

Hepburn, A.C. (2004) *Contested Cities in the Modern West*, London: Palgrave.

Herbert, S. (2005) The trapdoor of community, *Annals of the Association of American Geographers*, 95(4): 850–865.

Hillery, G.A. (1955) Definitions of community: Areas of agreement, *Rural Sociology*, 20(2): 111–123.

Jacobs, J. (1961) *The Death and Life of Great American Cities*, New York: Random House.

James, M. (2008) *Interculturalism: Theory and policy*, London: The Baring Foundation.

Johnson, C. (ed.) (1985) *The City in Conflict*, London: Mansell Publishing Limited.

Kallus, R. and Law-Yone, H. (2000) What is a neighbourhood? The structure and function of an idea, *Environment and Planning B*, 27(6): 815–826.

Knox, C. (2011) Cohesion, sharing, and integration in Northern Ireland, *Environment and Planning C: Government and Policy*, 29(3): 548–566.

Kotek, J. (1999) Divided cities in the European cultural context, *Progress in Planning*, 52(3): 227–239.

Maalouf, A. (2003) *In the Name of Identity: Violence and the need to belong*, New York: Penguin Books.

Madanipour, A. (1996) *Design of Urban Space: An inquiry into a socio-spatial process*, Chichester: Wiley.

Massey, D. (1991) The political place of locality studies, *Environment and Planning A*, 23(2): 267–281.

Massey, D. (2005) *For Space*, London: Sage.

Minar, D. and Greer, S. (eds) (1969) *The Concept of Community: Readings with interpretations*, Chicago: Aldine.

Morphet, J. (2008) *Modern Local Government*, London: Sage.

Murtagh, B. (2002) *The Politics of Territory: Policy and segregation in Northern Ireland*, New York: Palgrave.

Nagle, J. and Clancy, M.A. (2010) *Shared Society or Benign Apartheid? Understanding peace-building in divided societies*, Basingstoke: Palgrave Macmillan.

Naisbitt, J. (1994) *Global Paradox: The bigger the world economy, the more powerful its smallest players*, London: Nicholas Brealey Publishing.

Neill, W.J.V. (2004) *Urban Planning and Cultural Identity*, London: Routledge.

Newman, J. (2001) *Modernising Governance: New Labour, policy and society*, London: Sage.

Nisbett, R. (1953) *The Quest for Community*, New York: Oxford University Press.

Oberschall, A. (2007) *Conflict and Peace Building in Divided Societies*, London: Routledge.

O'Doherty, M. (2008) *Empty Pulpits: Ireland's retreat from religion*, Dublin: Gill & Macmillan.

Osborne, D. and Gaebler, T. (1992) *Reinventing Government: How the entrepreneurial spirit is transforming the public sector*, Reading, MA: Addison-Wesley.

Pahl, R.E. (1970) *Patterns of Urban Life*, London: Longmans.

Pahl, R.E. (ed.) (1968) *Readings in Urban Sociology*, New York: Pergamon Press.

Parekh, B. (2000) *Rethinking Multiculturalism*, Palgrave: Basingstoke.

Park, R.E. (1952) *Human Communities: The city and human ecology*, New York: Free Press.

Pløger, J. (2004) Strife: Urban planning and agonism, *Planning Theory*, 3(1): 71.

Pollock, S., Bhaba, H.K., Brekenridge, C.A. and Chakrabarty, D. (2002) Cosmopolitanisms, in C.A. Breckenridge, S. Pollock, H. Bhabha and D. Chakrabarty (eds), *Cosmopolitanism*, Durham, NC: Duke University Press, pp. 1–14.

Pullan, W. (2011) Frontier urbanism: The periphery at the centre of contested cities, *The Journal of Architecture*, 16(1): 15–35.

Purbrick, L., Aulich, J. and Dawson, G. (eds) (2007) *Contested Spaces: Sites, representations and histories of conflict*, Basingstoke: Palgrave Macmillan.

Purcell, M. (2006) Urban democracy and the local trap, *Urban Studies*, 43(11): 1921–1941.

Ragab, T.S. (2011) The crisis of cultural identity in rehabilitating historic Beirut-downtown, *Cities*, 28(1): 107–114.

Ratcliffe, P. (2004) *Race, Ethnicity and Difference*, Buckingham: Open University Press.

Redfield, R. (1947) The folk society, *American Journal of Sociology*, 52(4): 293–308.

Robinson, D. (2005) The search for community cohesion: Key themes and dominant concepts for the public policy agenda, *Urban Studies*, 42(8): 1411–1427.

Ross, A. (2013) *Policy in Practice: Neighbourhood Planning*, LGiU Essential Policy Briefing, August, London: LGiU.

Sandercock, L. (2003) *Cosmopolis II: Mongrel cities in the 21st Century*, London: Continuum.

Sen, A. (2006) *Identity and Violence: The illusion of destiny*, London: Penguin Books.

Simpson, G. (1937) *Conflict and Community: A study theory*, New York: T.S. Simpson.

Soja, E. (2000) *Postmetropolis: Critical studies of cities and regions*, Malden, MA: Blackwell.

Somerville, P. (2011) *Understanding Community: Politics, policy and practice*, Bristol: Policy Press.

Stacey, M. (1969) The myth of community studies, *British Journal of Sociology*, 20(2): 134–147.

Stein, M. (1964) *The Eclipse of Community*, New York: Harper & Row.

Stoker, G. (2004) New localism, progressive politics and democracy, *The Political Quarterly*, 75(1): 117–129.

Sutton, W.A., Jnr. and Kolaja, J. (1960) The concept of community, *Rural Sociology*, 25: 197–203.

Taylor, M. (2003) *Public Policy in the Community*, London: Palgrave.

Tönnies, F. (1957) *Community and Society*, Michigan: Michigan State University Press.

Wallace, A. (2010) New neighbourhoods, new citizens? Challenging 'community' as a framework for social and moral regeneration under New Labour in the UK, *International Journal of Urban and Regional Research*, 34(4): 805–819.

Webber, M. (1963) Order in diversity: Community without propinquity, in L. Wingo (ed.), *Cities and Space*, Baltimore, MD: Johns Hopkins University Press, pp. 25–54.

White, L.E. (1950) *Community or Chaos: Housing estates and social problems*, London: National Council of Social Service.

4

Localism Agendas and Post-political Trends: Neighbourhood Policy Trajectories in Denver

Susan E. Clarke

The post-political cities concept developed in the context of British and European cities is used here to analyse neighbourhood regeneration policies in Denver, Colorado (USA), 1980–2012. The post-political cities concept provides a critical view on the links of localism to governance and democracy.[1] It anticipates the re-ordering of political spaces through policy changes that move political agency outside democratic channels. In contrast to research analysing these trends at larger scales such as the metropolitan region, my focus is on neighbourhoods as contested sites for place-making and democratic renewal (see also Farrelly and Sullivan, 2010). This allows a critical perspective on the strategic use of localist rhetoric in American cities and introduces the prospect that the localism agenda potentially can disrupt or destabilize post-political forces.

Viewing Denver politics through a post-political lens portends an emergent landscape in which neighbourhood regeneration is 'de-politicized' and removed from political debate. This landscape is constructed through processes of 'post-democratic institutional formation' (MacLeod, 2011), particularly initiatives that carve up neighbourhoods into Business Improvement Districts and other forms of 'mobilized policies'. The post-political concept anticipates a blend of neoliberal ideas and localist trends encompassing a more extensive arena of policy actors. After a brief comment on localism in the American context, this chapter analyses the adequacy of the post-politics schema for understanding policy change in Denver, and indirectly in other American cities. It introduces an understanding of policy change that emphasizes periods of flux and uneven transitions to new political orders. This addresses an underspecified element of the post-political framework – the mechanisms by which post-political elements become embedded in local political orders and their stability over time.

Overall, the Denver case appears to corroborate McCarthy's (2013) argument that the post-democratic city concept is less relevant for the US since localities are more autonomous and political dynamics more volatile than in the UK and European cities. But it also raises several caveats regarding the conceptualization of the post-political city: the partial and incomplete nature of de-politicization trends, the possibilities of new political spaces and the emergence of multiple pathways. These also are evident in cities outside the US, suggesting comparative empirical research is essential for theory development.

Localism, governance and democracy in American cities

The meaning of 'localism' in the American context is dynamic and complex (Clarke and Goetz, 1993). Localities are embedded in a decentralized federal structure but have no constitutional standing. The formal, historical status of local governments in the US is that they are 'creatures of the state' and have no powers other than those granted by their state governments. Although there are significant variations by state, local governments have attained substantial authority and autonomy over time in the US. The failure to acquire concomitant elastic revenue sources and the constraints of an outdated tax code are more often cited as limiting local autonomy than the legal structure itself. As a result of subnational boundary-setting powers and inelastic local revenue sources, the local landscape in the US consists of multiple, relatively autonomous governments competing with each other for households and businesses able to provide tax revenues needed to support city services.

So localism is built into the American governmental system but 'localism' more commonly refers to trends towards decentralizing authority and power to subnational governments. These are powerful sentiments in American political culture and history; advocacy of localism cuts across partisan and ideological divides even when adjoined to more nuanced analyses of federal responsibilities. It often encompasses strategies to broaden the participatory base as well, sometimes as a means to enhance local political practice and leverage institutional change. Localism strategies increasingly are justified as means to build social capital and civic capacity by extending power, responsibility and authority to governance arrangements including non-elected groups. Although often cloaked in the rhetoric of 'empowerment', these localizing strategies too often founder on the socio-economic and political inequities that hamper broad and meaningful political engagement at the community level.

Analysing localism and governance in such a localistic setting would seem a golden opportunity. But the complexity and dynamic nature of the meaning of localism in the decentralized US system requires some attention to the multiple ways in which localism can be constructed (Fraser *et al.*, 2003; Jun and Musso, 2013). Considering the formal and legal standing of local communities, for example, is insufficient for understanding their actual capabilities and autonomy. Assuming a cultural preference for decentralized responsibility and choice overlooks the political use of the concept of localism and the many ways in which groups can be disadvantaged by localist strategies. Given the plasticity of the localism concept, any analysis of localism and governance in the American context necessarily begins from a critical perspective on its strategic use by multiple actors and interests seeking local advantage.

Why Denver?

Denver is a promising case for this exploration. As a western city, the political culture emphasizes a 'sagebrush' mentality treasuring local autonomy and initiative and is resistant to the priorities of national politicians thousands of miles away. Founded in 1859, Denver mostly skipped over the decades of political machines and industrial economies hampering older cities in the northeast and Midwest. Like many western cities, Denver's political structure is relatively 'reformed' and professionalized. It also is one of the creative and entrepreneurial cities Swyngedouw (2010: 8) posits as likely 'arenas' for the construction of a post-political consensus. Since the 1980s, a series of Latino, African-American and White mayors have provided relatively strong leadership in a still White-majority, but increasingly multi-ethnic, city. Local electoral bodies are paralleled by a growing suite of non-elected agencies, many with independent taxing authority. Severe cuts in federal funds, along with a state ballot initiative capping revenue and expenditures for the last three decades, constrain local choices. Over this period, local neighbourhood regeneration policies turned away from a distributional orientation towards a new policy paradigm emphasizing growth, risk and opportunity at the neighbourhood level.

Denver courted immigrants early on, as did the state of Colorado. Given its inland location, many immigrants arrived in Denver after trekking from gateway cities in the east and the west. This sequenced immigration continues today, but there is a marked increase in immigration directly to Denver. The 1990s were a boom decade for the city, with many 'previously poor' neighbourhoods showing signs of population growth and prosperity. In many cases, immigration and Latino population growth fed this neighbourhood change. By 2010, 16.6 per cent of the city's population was foreign-born. While Denver's population growth and foreign-born population appear to be stabilizing, the inner suburbs are becoming much more diverse, with some (e.g. Adams County) having greater shares of Latino residents than Denver. Overall, the city of Denver now is becoming 'whiter' while the suburbs are becoming more diverse (Hubbard, 2009). This is hailed as 'the new metropolitan reality' by some urban analysts (Hanlon *et al.*, 2009) but the reality for Denverites is more problematic, particularly at the neighbourhood level. In 2010, 52.2 per cent of the city's residents were White, 31.8 per cent were of Hispanic origin and 9.7 per cent were African American (Piton, 2011a).

Denver considers itself a 'neighbourhood-oriented' city; it is also characterized as such in much of the scholarly literature (Galster *et al.*, 2003; Judd, 1983; Leonard and Noel, 1990). The economic boom in the 1990s and volatile growth in the early 2000s brought rapid transformation in many neighbourhoods, including a growing Hispanic presence in many formerly Black neighbourhoods and growing White presence in many previously poor neighbourhoods. One of the most notable features of Denver's neighbourhoods is this dynamic racial and ethnic change and the consequent variation in neighbourhood capacity and organization. By 2010, 'all but 10 of Denver's 77 neighborhoods had a racial/ethnic majority: 47 were majority White, 19 were majority Hispanic, and one was majority African American' (Piton, 2011a: 4). The poorest neighbourhoods are Latino and African American: most of the Latino population is settled in neighbourhoods north and west of the city, where the greatest concentrations of poverty also exist.

As many of Denver's neighbourhoods experience substantial demographic change, the city's strategy towards neighbourhood regeneration is shifting. The question here is whether this emergent landscape is one in which neighbourhood regeneration is 'de-politicized' and removed from political debate.

Is Denver becoming a post-political city?

Under what conditions might this post-political landscape emerge? To counter the tendency to see these trends as 'universalizing' (McCarthy, 2013), drawing on the post-political literature, six key trends signifying the post-political city are highlighted here.[2] A seventh consideration focuses on distinguishing the 'turning points' in which these trends begin to shape local settings.

1 *Prior condition: national austerity policies and cuts in local funding.* These measures bring shifts in the 'strategic priorities of city government and coalitions' (MacLeod and Jones, 2011: 2444).
2 *Widespread agreement over conditions that exist and what needs to be done.* Despite conflicts of interest and opinion, there is widespread agreement over conditions that exist and what needs to be done (Rancière, 2003a).
3 *Growth in managerial approaches to government.* Government is reconceived as a managerial function, deprived of its proper political dimension (Žižek in Swyngedouw, 2011).
4 *Expert opinions called on to legitimize decisions.* Options presented as complex and in need of expert opinions to legitimize decisions (Sloterdijk, 2005).
5 *Politics as distribution of spaces.* Importance of activities that create order by distributing places, names, functions (Rancière in Swyngedouw, 2011).

6 *Gradual de-politicization and de-democratization of significant institutional forms.* Urban institutions 'streamlined' to foreclose debate and respond to market; now less accountable to public (MacLeod, 2011).
7 *Distinguishing the 'turning points' in which post-political elements emerge.* Debates on the temporal and spatial nature of post-political forces.

The following discussion is organized in terms of these features. While this may resemble a 'checklist' approach, it allows us to analyse the particular ways in which the Denver case may fit and challenge the post-political concept.

1. National austerity policies and cuts in local funding as a prior condition

Constraints on local resources from state tax and expenditure limits,[3] outdated local tax structures and declining federal aid are a constant backdrop for Denver's policy-makers. State support of local government is modest. Property taxes are a declining source of local revenue. Sales taxes and user fees are significant and growing revenue sources; the city is adept at turning to debt to facilitate major local initiatives.[4] The city revenue base relies on sales tax; over 50 per cent of the general fund is generated by sales taxes from small businesses. Many new economic development initiatives aim at redressing this vulnerable tax base and continual budget shortfalls.

Most of Denver's neighbourhood strategy is funded by federal grants and external foundation grants. The different federal entitlement grants received by the City and County of Denver with potential impacts on neighbourhood development totalled $15,944,710 in 2010. By 2012, the total had sunk to $11.5 million, with Community Development Block Grant (CDBG) funds at $6,957,695. Overall external funding continued to decline in 2013, to $11,072,526, with a slight gain in CDBG funds to $7,170,263. The unrelenting pressure of resource uncertainty and scarcity increasingly compels local officials in many American cities to fold neighbourhood regeneration concerns into other policies such as poverty reduction or sustainability (Stone and Stoker, 2014).

2. Consensus on 'the problem' and what needs to be done: tracing continuity and change

Given these conditions, the post-political city argument anticipates that, despite conflicts of interest and opinion, there is widespread agreement over conditions that exist and what needs to be done (Rancière, 2003a: 2). Overall, neighbourhood regeneration issues are generally present on Denver's policy agenda but the priority varies over time, with policy shifts in orientation often demarcated by mayoral administrations. Neighbourhood regeneration remains on the agenda for many reasons: as a bounded city, Denver's growth depends on continual redevelopment of existing space. The city political structures reflect a hybrid arrangement of at-large and district representation. The consolidated City and County of Denver comprises 77 (officially recognized) neighbourhoods along with more than 250 neighbourhood organizations registered with the city. Despite periods of significant economic growth, a substantial number of neighbourhoods remain 'persistently poor'. Many federal programmes continue to demand spatial targeting and the city responds accordingly. A symbolic discourse of 'the city of neighborhoods' is nurtured by city officials.

But in Denver, consensus on 'the problem with neighbourhoods' and the consequent different sets of policy solutions is fleeting. Historically, community development policy in Denver centres on infrastructure investment. Infrastructure is a public good that brings business to the table in a city where business interests historically have been erratic actors in city politics. While infrastructure investment empowers a relatively strong city planning staff, leadership is often exercised by non-elected special authorities.

Spatially, the city consciously sought neighbourhood revitalization for over three decades in a U-shaped belt of neighbourhoods around the western and northern edge of the downtown district. City policy consistently targeted these neighbourhoods from urban renewal to the Downtown Agenda, as 'Areas of Change' in the Blueprint Denver plans, and now as stations on FasTracks, Denver's transit-oriented development strategy (TOD).

Temporally, the most substantive priority for neighbourhood regeneration occurred during the Peña administration in the 1980s; since then the commitment has become increasingly symbolic and shifted from a programmatic distributional orientation to a market-oriented paradigm. These framing shifts reflect mayoral goals and constituencies as well as changing local conditions. Several factors refract this tenuous ability to sustain and carry out a neighbourhood commitment: changing paradigms or ideas about how best to support neighbourhood regeneration; restrictive state-wide limitation on taxes and expenditures; the sense that there may be less need for neighbourhood policy as the poor and recent immigrants increasingly settle in suburbs; and shrinking federal aid for neighbourhood (vs. regional) initiatives.

Substantively, from 1983 to 2003, Peña's neighbourhood planners and Webb's Focus Neighborhood Initiative (FNI) constituted the heart of the neighbourhood policy agenda in Denver. In 2003, this policy trajectory was punctuated with the election of John Hickenlooper as mayor.[5]

Peña's neighbourhood strategy: change the rules of the game

In consolidating his governing coalition after his 1983 upset electoral victory as the first minority mayor in a majority White city in the US, Federico Peña did not directly target Latinos or neighbourhoods as programme beneficiaries. Instead, he sought to bring minorities and neighbourhoods to the table so their voices would be heard in city decision processes. These indirect strategies entailed strategic use of his appointive powers and contracting authorities, bringing neighbourhood representation into planning processes and broadening opportunities for participation in public hearings and meetings (Saiz, 1993). More directly, the Peña administration opened up revolving loan and neighbourhood business programmes, along with CDBG funds, to residents of lower-income neighbourhoods. In addition, eight new planners were hired by the City Planning Department to work with the low- and moderate-income neighbourhoods surrounding downtown. By the end of Peña's first term, eight neighbourhood plans were completed and adopted by ordinance by the Denver City Council as amendments to the city's comprehensive plan. While Peña's legacy includes the launch of a new international airport and dramatic plans to revitalize the city, his long-lasting accomplishments may be less obvious. Overall, Peña changed the rules of the game to increase neighbourhood voice in city policy discussions. In doing so, Latino groups gained some visibility and increased access to city resources. While these resources were modest, distributing them to lower-income neighbourhoods and marginalized groups signalled a power shift in Denver politics.

Wellington Webb's neighbourhood strategy: target neighbourhoods

Wellington Webb succeeded Peña in office (1991–2003), becoming the first African American mayor in Denver and winning office with the support of a multi-racial electorate. While Peña was perceived as a neighbourhood advocate, Webb suffered in comparison (Hodges, 1994). Although both Peña and Webb necessarily relied on 'deracialization' electoral strategies to reach diverse constituencies, Peña's administration is credited with giving neighbourhoods a real voice in decision processes while Webb's overall record features mega-projects and infrastructure development, although he also initiated numerous programmatic neighbourhood initiatives (George, 2004).

Webb's signature move was the 1992 appointment of Jennifer Moulton, former Executive Director of Historic Denver Inc., as the first woman to serve as Denver Planning Director. Moulton set the tone for the Webb administration's emphasis on implementation during the 1990s,[6] in contrast to the 'planning' view ascribed to Peña's administration (Vasquez, 1999). In further contrast to Peña, the Webb administration put a priority on bringing the middle and upper class back to the city. This was not an uncommon policy priority in American cities during this period, but to the Webb administration it could only be accomplished by making the downtown area more attractive to investors and tourists.

This not only reversed Peña's strategy, it actually framed neighbourhoods as part of the problem: neighbourhood revitalization became a necessary if not sufficient condition for downtown regeneration and Denver's overall economic growth. As articulated in Moulton's 'Downtown Agenda', Denver government's role was as 'an efficient economic machine' able to transform lower-income areas into 'investor quality downtown residential neighborhoods', and to attract 'people with money to spend on housing' (Moulton, 1999). As a result, in many core-city neighbourhoods, low-income housing disappeared and 'bleached barrios' emerged – more White and fewer Latino and African-American residents (Robinson, 2005: 29).

Overall, Wellington Webb's administration emphasized enhancing the investment climate for upper- and middle-class investors in downtown areas. Webb also left a legacy of mega-projects such as the new Denver International Airport and new sports stadiums. Yet Webb also continued the distributional orientation of the Peña administration through programmatic initiatives supporting neighbourhood revitalization with federal funds. Webb's FNI in 1998 responded to the stark realities that several areas of the city were not doing as well as others and needed extra attention.[7]

Hickenlooper's neighbourhood strategy: an entrepreneurial approach

John Hickenlooper brought his business experience to city issues, including the need to recognize and respond not only to need but to opportunity. Following his 2003 election, Hickenlooper brought in many outsiders to direct his new entrepreneurial approaches to city government and economic development. Many of these were from the East Coast and Midwest; the cities they worked in previously had much more complex and sophisticated policy and financial infrastructures and professional expertise in neighbourhood revitalization and economic development. The new policy-makers frequently compared Denver to other cities and appeared to be focused on bringing Denver 'up to speed'. Not only was the distributional paradigm outdated, in their eyes, it also prevented Denver from becoming the 'Great City' it aspired to be.

In the words of a newly arrived Hickenlooper adviser in 2003, Denver appeared 'stuck' in a CDBG world.[8] Neighbourhood policy and community development in general were shaped and funded by federal programmes, with regular forays by the Denver Urban Renewal Authority (DURA). As a result, the city relied on HUD's definitions of neighbourhood distress and the policy solutions offered by CDBG programme funds. These modest resources were targeted to neighbourhoods in need, shaped by City Council preferences and generally spread among multiple small-scale efforts. This distributional CDBG focus prevailed during the Peña and Webb administrations, complemented by the city's penchant for public investment in large-scale mega-projects and public works that operated at a much different policy level.

Under Hickenlooper, ShoreBank Advisory Services was brought in for consultation, a role it has played in many other American cities. ShoreBank's

(2005) market analysis underscored Denver's outdated and underdeveloped approaches to community development and justified Hickenlooper's turn to a new market-oriented paradigm for neighbourhood revitalization. Mayor Hickenlooper's new definition of neighbourhood problems as deficits in the financial infrastructure disrupted – or 'punctuated' – the CDBG policy subsystem in 2003. It shifted power from city line agencies, particularly the Community Planning and Development Agency and its Housing and Neighborhood Development Services division, to the Mayor's Office and new off-budget institutions. The Mayor's Office of Economic Development (OED) became the locus of neighbourhood policy formulation and implementation. In the face of high-powered financing and strategic investment strategies needed to address this newly defined problem, the City Council lost ground to the experts brought in by the new mayor.

3. *Growth in managerial approach to government*

The post-political city framework includes an assumption that managerial approaches to government will grow: government is reconceived as a managerial function, deprived of its proper political dimensions (Žižek, quoted in Swyngedouw, 2011: 373; Davidson and Wyly, 2012). In Crouch's (2004) terms, this focus on organizational and managerial functions leads to a 'trivialisation of politics', weakening the role of civic society while amplifying the roles of non-state actors. In American cities, the city government's authority and power to ameliorate transaction costs associated with reorganizing land use and physical infrastructure changes is critical. It provides local governments with the means and 'infrastructural power' (Horan, 1997) to leverage negotiations with private actors. And, as MacLeod (2013: 2216) notes, landownership and property relations are at the heart of 'the global circulation of localist projects'. In Denver, many of Hickenlooper's paradigmatic changes stem from this recognition of the importance of developing and using the city's 'infrastructural power' to influence private investment decisions and assemble critical institutional configurations. Deploying this infrastructural power leads to a seemingly paradoxical increase in both managerial and entrepreneurial approaches.

Hickenlooper created the Office of Economic Development (OED) by Executive Order in 2004. It consolidated several line agencies into the mayor's office and became the lead agency for neighbourhood revitalization. OED characterizes neighbourhoods as the key to a vibrant city economy but its budget and programme emphasis primarily focuses on business investment and gap financing. A neighbourhood orientation emerged in 2006 when OED introduced its Neighborhood Revitalization Strategy (NRS) and established a Division of Neighborhood and Housing Development to spearhead neighbourhood revitalization. The NRS promoted poverty deconcentration with the explicit goal of mixed-income communities (Newman and Ashton, 2004). In this framework, locating affordable housing sites and business investment became strategies for poverty deconcentration. By 2008, the rationale for OED's Neighborhood Marketplace Initiative (NMI) articulated a view of neighbourhoods as important sites for small businesses, a significant element in Denver's economy.

Hickenlooper's 2003 election led to the merging, if not the subordination, of neighbourhood policies with economic development priorities, the restructuring of institutional arrangements to focus on the city's competitiveness, the ongoing transformation of neighbourhoods into 'districts' and the effort to adapt to a 'post-CDBG' funding era by reframing neighbourhood distress as lack of investment capital. It also shifted power over neighbourhood priorities from the City Council to the Mayor's Office, although this shift remains contested. Clearly the City Council's role in neighbourhood revitalization is eroded by the market-oriented policy paradigm. In the CDBG era, the City Council played a strong role in directing allocations across the board; in this entrepreneurial era, there are fewer funds to allocate overall and the emphasis is on leveraging investments. This diminishes the role that the council can play in making policy decisions; its role is reduced in many cases to questioning OED policy-makers and others making presentations and recommendations.[9]

In many ways, these policy shifts also appeared to weaken the volunteer activist traditions that distinguish Denver politics and played such an important role in Peña and Webb's elections. The symbols and discourse of the market tend to trump conventional modes of participation. Hickenlooper's re-election in May 2007 with 86.3 per cent of the vote accelerated the move towards entrepreneurial initiatives.

4. *Options presented as complex and in need of expert opinions to legitimize decisions*

While any type of local economic revitalization strategy is complex, this complexity is intensified when it involves spatial targeting and gap financing by the public sector. The continued erosion of federal funds exacerbates the uncertainty and risk in using public funds. Given his entrepreneurial business background, Hickenlooper turned to outside experts rather than the in-house capacity available in the city government. The local capacity was seen as outdated and Hickenlooper's office openly described the city as 'lagging behind' other cities in adopting the tools necessary for this new policy era.

In defining 'the problem with neighborhoods' as the lack of gap financing, the introduction of Community Development Financial Institutions (CDFIs) became the obvious policy solution. While CDFIs are in place in many

American cities, their introduction to Denver shifted the city away from its distributional focus to emphasize the use of city CDBG funds to leverage private investment in distressed neighbourhoods. To launch the new CDFI, Denver needed state approval. More significantly, the CDFI required reallocation of a portion of CDBG funds from their traditional neighbourhood programmes to create an equity investment pool. This set the stage for shifting from CDBG distribution of federal funds to a targeted but large set of neighbourhoods, to a more strategic emphasis on using CDBG funds to leverage private funds targeting a smaller set of core neighbourhoods.

Not surprisingly, the technical and strategic tactics attendant on this new orientation created a demand for expert opinion. Council deliberation and neighbourhood participation seemed beside the point. This diminished voice was exacerbated by the relative inexperience of the council at this critical point. When Hickenlooper was elected in 2003, 10 of the 13 City Council representatives were also newly elected; term limit provisions removed many of the council members most familiar with neighbourhood programmes. One neighbourhood activist describes this as 'unfortunate' since there was very little institutional memory and recognition of the 'mutual understandings' that had characterized the informal and long-standing ties between neighbourhood groups and city agencies in the past. As a result, the council was dependent on the information and analyses presented to them on new projects, with little precedent or experience to build on or refer to. The City Council traditionally was the champion of distributional programmes but the entrepreneurial discourse left them in a defensive, dispirited stance.[10]

5. *Politics as distribution of spaces: small is the new big as 'districts' trump neighbourhoods*

In the post-political city, Rancière (1994: 173, as cited in Swyngedouw, 2011: 375) emphasizes 'all the activities which create order by distributing places, names, functions'. In Denver this is reflected in the carving out of neighbourhood business 'districts' and the renaming of neighbourhood spaces. Politics becomes the distribution of different spaces as 'it is always a matter of knowing who is qualified to say what a particular place is and what is done to it' (Rancière, 2003b: 201, in Swyngedouw, 2011: 376). In Denver we see this authority moving from the neighbourhood itself and beyond the elected City Council representatives to the mayor's office and off-budget entities.

In Colorado, Business Improvement Districts (BIDs) must be created through a state statute and council approval of the governing board of directors (NCBR 2008: 3).[11] BIDs have taken on an iconic status as an exemplar of policy mobilization. To Peck and Theodore (2010) these mobilized policies allow for new forms of globalizing neoliberal urban governance practices. While Denver is similar to other cities in its increased regulation and securitization of downtown areas through privatized agencies such as BIDs (MacLeod, 2011; Schwedes and Michel, 2014; Ward, 2006), it is distinctive for moving these same definitional processes to the neighbourhood scale. Increasingly, historical neighbourhood identities are being obscured as they are systematically carved up into districts that better serve their economic potential and identity. The elasticity and resilience of the BID concept underscores the localization of modes of urban governance.

According to OED's Neighborhood Marketplace Initiative, 'small is the new big': creating neighbourhood business districts, community improvement districts and other specialized territorial agents able to work directly with the city is an emerging trend. The NMI exemplifies an entrepreneurial place-based economic strategy. Launched by the mayor's Office of Economic Development in 2008, the NMI identifies neighbourhoods as the locus for small business and promotes an inter-departmental strategy for neighbourhood development. The NMI emphasizes 'the alignment of powerful influences such as land use, infrastructure, access to transit corridors or options to strengthen and enhance Denver's diverse neighborhood districts', and aims at strengthening neighborhood revitalization through creation of neighborhood business districts and combining 'local collaboration with citywide support' (OED, n.d.). Locally created 'District Development Plans' (covering three to seven years) are developed for the five neighbourhoods selected as initial pilot projects: each neighbourhood is considered unique and at different stages of market potential.

OED's role in establishing Special Districts such as Business Improvements Districts or Community Improvement Districts (CID) is critical. Each of the five pilot neighbourhoods worked with OED and PUMA (Progressive Urban Management Associates) to develop their strategic District Development Plan. In every case, the Plan recommended transforming existing neighbourhood organizations into 501 (c) (3) non-profit organizations capable of raising fees and revenues, establishing Community Development Corporations and/or eventual (within 2–3 years) formation of a CID or BID as the organizational structure for the neighbourhood's development.[12]

Along with the neighbourhood market focus, these district transformations threaten the council's role as neighbourhood representative while dampening the prospects for citizen mobilization. The promotion of these new institutions and territorial arrangements is often challenged in the council's NCBR committee but the council also approves these new districts: to date, nearly all proposed districts have been approved.

6. *Post-political institutional formation processes*

The institutional formation process attendant on this new policy paradigm in Denver exemplifies a key element of the post-political city argument: the gradual de-politicization and de-democratization of significant institutional forms (MacLeod, 2011: 2652; Swyngedouw, 2011). Much of the literature on governance processes recognizes widespread trends towards 'governance-beyond-the-state' in which various forms of public authority are extended to non-elected actors. (Swyngedouw 1995, 11). While the elected public institutions continue to operate, the argument is that new 'stake-holder' arrangements share economic and politic power in ways that trump the capacities of traditional elected offices (Swyngedouw, 2005, 2011). Again, this is not a new argument. But the post-political city contribution is the emphasis on the ways in which these new 'instituted forms of governing' (Swyngedouw, 2009) shrink the space for political dissent and debate. As a result, new institutions become less accountable to the public in order to be more responsive to the market (MacLeod, 2011: 2649).

The introduction of a CDFI in Denver signalled a dramatic departure from the city's conventional regeneration strategies – and it failed within two years. In a competitive bid process, the city selected Seedco as its new CDFI to meet the gaps identified by the ShoreBank study.[13] Seedco was a private, non-profit CDFI operated through Seedco Financial Services of New York City. The contract between the city and Seedco centred on community economic development, including neighbourhood commercial revitalization, affordable housing and small business expansion. Referred to locally as a 'city-financed non-profit', Seedco's ambitious plans centred on workforce development and revitalization in distressed and underserved neighbourhoods. While these neighbourhoods were primarily ones identified by earlier administrations, they were a much smaller set. According to the contract, Seedco would leverage at least $17 million in Denver to create jobs and stabilize distressed neighbourhoods but this was contingent on the City Council's approval of granting Seedco $15 million of CDBG funds in 2007 over a five-year period. Each Seedco project required council approval but the most controversial aspect of the partnership was the initial investment of $15 million of CDBG funds no longer available for neighbourhood projects. After some debate, the City Council gave their approval to Seedco in February 2007.

Seedco anticipated increasing the assets under management to $300 million by 2009 (NCBR, 2007: 4).[14] But a very slow rollout and continuing concerns about invoicing practices, record-keeping and the handling of CDBG funds brought repeated attention from the City Council. Seedco's yearly contract renewal stirred vigorous debates and split votes in the council until the city finally ended the Seedco contract in November 2009.[15] The lack of job creation and the failure to build local capacity brought Seedco down. This conspicuous failure undermined any efforts to institutionalize this new de-politicized entrepreneurial subsystem. These challenges to CDFI performance meant a consequent drift to more fragmented, less focused neighbourhood policies.

7. Turning points

While we may identify evidence of post-political trends and institutional configurations, distinguishing the 'turning points' where these trends begin to shape local political dynamics is problematic. Many typologies describe substantive differences in neighbourhood policy trajectories over time (e.g. see Chaskin, 2001; Newman and Ashton, 2004; Rohe, 2009; Saegert, 2006). The post-political cities concept differs in its emphasis on the consequences of these policy changes for democratic practice. As articulated by a number of scholars (e.g. MacLeod and Jones, 2011; Swyngedouw, 2011), late neoliberal regimes are characterized by an extension of governance arrangements that encompass diverse actors but a shrinkage of government channels that allow dissent and democratic voice. The implicit characterization of previous periods as 'more' democratic or 'more' political invites challenge (MacLeod, 2011) but offers a distinctive perspective on urban policy change.

Many analyses founder on this question of delineating and defining 'turning points'. The 'punctuated equilibrium' concept (Baumgartner and Jones, 1993; Jones *et al.*, 2003) is increasingly used in American and European research as a powerful way to describe changes over time in issue frames and agenda priorities. But it is less useful (Givel, 2010) in explaining contingent choices over time. Indeed, Horak (2007) argues that no single decision can 'usher in the rapid and wholesale "seismic shift" of punctuated equilibrium' since institutional change is asynchronous and layered: multiple eras of political institutions coexist and operate in parallel fashion rather than the wholesale replacement of one institutional configuration by another.

Horak (2007) contends that to be empirically useful, a more 'fine-grained' understanding of critical junctures is necessary. As he points out, the notion of critical juncture fails to specify a clear dividing line between a period of critical juncture and the subsequent consolidation of a new institutional order. He contends that there is rarely a clear dividing line and that we need to reconceptualize critical junctures as characterizing a 'period of flux marked by a series of non-simultaneous critical decision points, whose cumulative resolution results in the construction of a new political order' (Horak, 2007: 24). Horak's view of junctures as clusters of decision points and 'flux' provides a more dynamic understanding of the potential emergence of de-politicized spaces; it also allows for the potential emergence of new, or 'more' political, spaces. This emphasizes the multi-stage and potentially ambiguous dimension of institutional change and is critical to identifying a post-political landscape.

In assessing the trajectories of neighbourhood regeneration policies in Denver, I argue that a 'turning point' can be identified with the election of Mayor John Hickenlooper in 2003. Policy shifts often mark US mayoral administration turnovers. In this sense, mayoral transitions provide an opportunity to 'punctuate' institutional policy equilibriums and to change the direction of neighbourhood policy. But not all mayoral elections lead to 'punctuated equilibriums'. Hickenlooper's did: relative to previous mayors' approaches, the actors, institutions, resources, policy mobilities, discourse and strategic priorities attendant on Hickenlooper's election introduced a more entrepreneurial policy orientation and, potentially, the de-politicization of neighbourhood regeneration policies in Denver. The trajectory of neighbourhood regeneration policies turned away from a distributional orientation towards a new policy paradigm emphasizing growth, risk and opportunity at the neighbourhood level.

Yet this was a contested and uneven process, featuring some successes and stunning failures. The critical junctures approach offers a broad view of the consequences of the destabilization of existing arrangements – particularly multiple layers of institutional arrangements and the halting transition to a new political order. The latter is especially important in understanding the Denver case since the punctuation is clear but the asynchronous nature of the change is yet to be resolved. In other words, the Hickenlooper administration 'punctuated' or destabilized the dominant neighbourhood revitalization paradigm but a new policy equilibrium is not yet established. While the market-oriented entrepreneurial paradigm resonates with some elements of the post-political city framework, its partial and incomplete status raises questions about the post-political landscape.

Discussion

The Denver case appears to corroborate McCarthy's (2013) argument that the post-political city concept may be less relevant for the US since localities are more autonomous and political dynamics more volatile than in the UK and European cities. It also reflects McCarthy's concern with the 'potentially analytically flat, totalizing' nature of the concept. Using the post-political city framework to analyse Denver's neighbourhood regeneration policy trajectories proved useful in highlighting important dimensions of these changes over time. But it also raised several caveats regarding the conceptualization of the post-political city.

The partial and incomplete nature of de-politicization trends

As Jacobs (2012: 418) astutely notes, recognizing the coexistence of success, 'failure, absence, and mutation are significant empirical examples of differentiation in policy implementation that counter the tendency to assume universal and ever expanding processes such as neoliberalism and post-political dynamics'. The standout theme in the Denver case is the partial and incomplete nature of any post-political city trends: the existing CDBG policy subsystem was destabilized with Hickenlooper's election but the form and content of a new policy subsystem remains in doubt. The entrepreneurial Seedco venture failed. It is at least likely that more policy reforms will be tried and will continue to 'churn' through the system.

The new regional TOD projects could inject some of the distributional elements of Denver's earlier policy orientation: council representatives must approve these transit projects and, not surprisingly, there are transit stations in each council district. Such a turn would reflect Denver's traditional infrastructure orientation and respond to the realities of a less needy city population. Or some version of an entrepreneurial neighbourhood strategy framed in terms of small business support, as in OED's 2008 declaration, may persist. At a minimum, the continuing resource crisis in Denver makes a return to the previous CDBG policy equilibrium unlikely. This situation corresponds to Jones *et al.*'s argument that there are more punctuations involved in entering a new policy domain than exiting an old one (2003: 166). Or as Horak puts it, the critical decision points following a critical junction prove the most telling. The consequent uncertainty, volatility and instability encourage the competition of ideas in Denver – debates about how to define the problem of neighbourhood revitalization and how to become a more entrepreneurial, competitive city.

These contingencies are not unique to the fragmented American case. As Beveridge *et al.* (2014) note, seeming consensus can be disrupted and new alternatives or pathways considered. In analysing the Berlin Water Company, they argue for 'the politics of possibility' in which 'local contingencies in urban governance problematize sweeping notions of a post-political condition' (2014: 64). This is the implication of the Denver case, in which possibilities of new political spaces and multiple pathways are evident. As Beveridge *et al.* put it, this 'tempers' the broad-brush claims of a post-political future and encourages more empirical and comparative research of variations within a neoliberal urban governance paradigm. Whether these variations are considered as 'a variegated neoliberalism, in which different elements of public policy are characterized by differing forms and degrees of neo-liberalization' (Deas, 2013: 74) or as persuasive evidence of the continuing importance of political agency remains open to debate. Recall, however, as Allmendinger and Haughton (2012) remind us, that Rancière argues that 'post-politics is bound to fail – politics will always re-emerge'. Whether this new political order is another version of the post-political condition is at the heart of the research agenda on localism.

Possibilities of new political spaces

These re-alignments and the halting construction of a de-politicized entrepreneurial policy path during recessionary times may have opened new policy spaces. In 2004, Denver metro area voters approved a 0.4 per cent increase in the sales tax (4 cents on every $10) to support the build out of a regional transportation system, known as FasTracks. Transit-oriented development, particularly the FasTracks system, is touted (OED, 2010) as 'a neighborhood economic development opportunity' absent the impacts of auto-centric development. Although initially a locally funded project, the FasTracks plans attracted federal and foundation funding that promoted more social and equity considerations in the implementation of the transit system. As CDBG funding declines in importance, transportation funding increasingly shapes neighbourhood regeneration in Denver. Given the scale and regional scope of the transit project, neighbourhoods are not meaningful actors. But each corridor and transit mode is organized around 'stations' in mostly poor areas with clear neighbourhood referents – and council representatives.

The FasTracks initiative opened new fault lines in Denver politics that bring into question the apparent 'turn' to market-oriented neighbourhood policies. It is unlikely there will be a return to the strong public-sector role in neighbourhood regeneration evident in Peña's and even Webb's administrations. But the disequilibrium attendant on Hickenlooper's stalled market-oriented initiatives created a window for collaborative foundation and non-profit initiatives. For example, the implementation of the FasTracks system prompted the formation of Mile High Connects (formerly the Mile High Transit Opportunity Collaborative), a non-profit collaborative, to mitigate gentrification around transit stations in poor neighbourhoods.[16] This model of collective impact collaboration is a growing trend in the non-profit sector in the US; its emergence in Denver addresses the absence of equity considerations in many city initiatives, including FastTracks and the entrepreneurial policies dominating the agenda.[17]

Denver is also characterized by many agendas and institutions less obviously fitting neoliberal/post-political city frameworks: a school board consumed by ethnic/racial competition, a recent state-wide voter initiative approving legalizing the recreational use of marijuana, transit-oriented development, community benefits agreements, and other fissures where non-governmental organizations and local movements resist categorization. This is a more fluid and fragmented process than anticipated by the post-political framework: these clearly are not the 'ultra-politics' anticipated by the post-political city argument but they do pose potential disruptions to a city agenda featuring entrepreneurial initiatives. This more differentiated and nuanced understanding of a post-political landscape is necessary in order to understand where, when and under what conditions new governance possibilities and the prospect for 're-politicization' emerge.

Emergence of multiple pathways

Two turning points are of special significance for Denver's neighbourhood policy orientations: Peña's upset election in 1983 raising neighbourhood policy priorities and Hickenlooper's 2003 election introducing market-oriented policy paradigms emphasizing assets, leveraging and entrepreneurship. On their own, neither crisis nor ideas nor new mayoral administrations would have been sufficient to change the policy-making process – the 'punctuation' required the convergence of these factors. Both junctures introduced new ideas, new actors and new institutional arrangements for neighbourhood regeneration, often layered on top of earlier ones.

But the new pathways following these junctures remain incomplete. The entrepreneurial ideas and institutions brought in by the Hickenlooper administration meant an incomplete and uneven destabilization of Peña's CBDG-dominated neighbourhood policy strategy. Hickenlooper's new institutional arrangements and market discourse reduced the public-sector role prominent in neighbourhood regeneration during the Peña and Webb administrations in favour of market-oriented policy orientations created and carried out by the mayor's Office of Economic Development.

The seeming entrenchment of market orientations in discourse and local institutions and the dominance of managerial norms signalled a post-political future. But the difficulties in establishing a new policy orientation were exacerbated by Mayor Hickenlooper's 2010 election as Governor of Colorado, intermittent challenges to these new orientations from the City Council and the growing importance of TOD. As argued here, the fragmentation and fractures in American cities create too many fault lines to anticipate a smooth transition to a post-political landscape. And particularly in the American context, debates 'for' and 'against' localism elide the diverse meanings of this concept and policy agenda that change over time.

While McCarthy (2013) argues for a more modest approach to the post-political city conceptualization, the exercise here also suggests the need for more comparative analyses. Rather than the 'totalizing' and sweeping aspects of some initial presentations of the post-political framework, a recognition of multiple pathways potentially leading to more or less politicized local landscapes would invite a more nuanced understanding of the conditions under which these variations might occur or alternatives might emerge. This underscores the spatial dimension of local governance contestations: it emphasizes differing structural and political conditions as well as variations by policy arena, scale and over time.[18] As other authors in this volume detail, Deas's (2013: 79) contention that 'the localism agenda potentially introduces a significant dissonance to the stability of local political control of regeneration in which local state actors (from quangos as well as local authorities) have worked harmoniously alongside the private sector' underscores the disruptive potential of the localism agenda. Determining whether these 'post-political' concepts are adequate and useful in explaining these changes across different political, cultural and economic structures and localism agendas is a basic and important question for theory development.[19]

Notes

1 Both 'post-democratic' and 'post-political' labels are used to characterize these conditions. Here I use 'post-democratic' given my focus on the institutional landscape (see Swyngedouw, 2011).

2 A seventh – 'Ultra-politics' is seen as a challenge to the circumspect city – emphasizes an implicit consensus to control and police anything that might disrupt consumerist citizenship (MacLeod, 2011). It is especially salient in light of the Occupy Now movements and other local protest activities but requires an analytic focus on political rather than policy decisions. Surely Denver has escalated its attempts to manage public space, cut down on panhandling and the homeless presence in downtown, and normalize disruptive events such as anti-abortion protests and the Occupy Denver movement.

3 In 1992 Colorado voters approved a constitutional amendment (TABOR) limiting both revenue and expenditure choices for local governments. Any state or local tax change that could result in increased tax revenue (after allowing for inflation and population growth) must be approved by voters. In 2005, state voters approved a 'waiver' of TABOR until 2015 if local voters approved. Denver voters approved this waiver by a 2 to 1 ratio, allowing the city to retain surplus tax revenues for basic city services.

4 In contrast to British and European cities, the City of Denver and certain special authorities gain access to the private bond market through a variety of debt mechanisms. Denver retains excellent credit ratings in the municipal bond market and remarkably strong voter support for debt obligations. Resorting to the municipal bond market is necessary in the face of state tax and expenditure limits, weak external resources, and a tax base insufficient to support major infrastructure initiatives. Denver pioneered the creation of single-issue multi-county tax districts in which multi-county voter approval of bond issues allowed the construction of large cultural, infrastructure, and athletic facilities usually located in Denver but serving a regional population (Clarke and Saiz, 2002).

5 The discussion of Denver politics draws on Clarke (2014).

6 This encompassed several mega-projects such as the redevelopment of Lowry Air Force Base and the old Stapleton Airport site, the new Denver International Airport, the new sports stadiums, the Union Station restoration, and Central Platte Valley redevelopment expanding the downtown core.

7 Significant CDBG funds were allocated to the 16 FNI 'target' neighbourhoods, with substantial citizen participation planned.

8 See further detail in Clarke (2014).

9 In 2006, the council established the Neighborhood, Community, and Business Revitalization (NCBR) committee to address issues associated with neighbourhood revitalization, especially approval of ordinances for the new districts and investment strategies being set up by the Mayor's Office. On occasion, the council will vote against a project only to find it is being implemented anyway.

10 This draws on Clarke (2014).

11 In addition to Business Improvement Districts (BIDs), Denver is promoting Community Improvement Districts (CID): private-sector (residential, commercial, and mixed-use) actors voluntarily tax themselves in a specific geographic area for improvements and services augmenting the basic-level services provided by the city in that area. The CID brings together Local Improvement Districts (LIDs) and Local Maintenance Districts (LMDs) in a special district with streamlined processes for constructing and maintaining improvements. This addresses the fragmentation

among special districts common to many American cities (BIDs, LIDs, LMDs, General Improvement Districts, Metro Districts, etc.) and provides a mechanism for use in mixed-use neighbourhoods.

12 While a CID allows for resident as well as business involvement, both involve earmarked assessments that would be redirected into the business district development.

13 CDFIs leverage external capital to provide equity and debt financing to projects that will benefit low-income people and/or projects unable to secure conventional lending.

14 The funding criteria emphasized substitution: projects were only funded if no other revenue streams/resources were available.

15 According to OED, Seedco had generated 16 loans since inception, 11 with CDBG funding; created total loan capital $5.24 million, $2.03 million from CDBG; brought in new outside capital invested in Denver – $3.2 million; operated with a match ratio of 1:5:1, leveraged ratio (capital growth) of 14:1; and created 40 jobs. Since 93 jobs were promised in Seedco's last contract, the lack of job creation and the failure to build local capacity brought Seedco down.

16 Mile High Connects (MHC), founded in 2010, is a Denver-based coalition of more than 20 local and national non-profits that also supports affordable housing, jobs, and workforce development initiatives for TOD. MHC's goal is to develop low-income communities within walking distance of transit centres. With support from the Ford Foundation's Metropolitan Opportunity Initiative, MHC plays a major role in providing data and analysis on the equity and access of area transportation through its Regional Equity Atlas. See: www.milehighconnects.org/main.html.

17 Similarly, the Piton Foundation launched the Children's Corridor to target investment to children living in the most disadvantaged neighbourhoods.

18 Many of the initial post-democratic city arguments were developed regarding environmental policies and politics. In Denver, it is likely that the post-democratic conditions are more clearly present in the environmental policy arena than in the neighbourhood policy arena.

19 Not surprisingly, this is an underdeveloped enterprise. There is no 'US Neighborhood Policy' as a referent. Asking about neighbourhood policies in the US means looking at individual cities, possibly states, but the sheer number of cities in the US, each with multiple neighbourhoods, defies a comprehensive effort. Most neighbourhood analyses are case studies. Efforts at comparative neighbourhood analyses are rare. The most recent compared neighbourhoods in North America, Europe, and the UK with a standard research protocol attempting to delineate neighbourhood policy agenda status (Stone and Stoker, 2013). This research focus precludes tracing markers of 'post-political' landscapes but does characterize neighbourhood policy trajectories across cities.

References

Allmendinger, Phil and Haughton, Graham. (2012) Post-political spatial planning in England: A crisis of consensus?, *Transactions of the Institute of British Geographers*, 37: 89–103.

Baumgartner, Frank A. and Jones, Bryan D. (1993) *Agendas and Instability in American Politics*, Chicago: University of Chicago Press.

Beveridge, Ross, Hüesker, Frank and Naumann, Matthias. (2014) From post-politics to a politics of possibility? Unravelling the privatization of the Berlin Water Company, *Geoforum*, 51: 66–74.

Chaskin, Robert. (2001) A definitional framework and case studies from a comprehensive community initiative, *Urban Affairs Review*, 35: 291–323.
Clarke, Susan E. (2014) Intersecting policies and power shifts shaping Denver's neighborhood agenda, in Clarence N. Stone and Robert Stoker (eds), *In a New Era*, Chicago: University of Chicago Press, pp. 139–173.
Clarke, Susan E. and Goetz, Edward G. (1993) *The New Localism: Comparative urban politics in a global era*, Newbury Park, CA: Sage.
Clarke, Susan E. and Saiz, Martin. (2002) From waterhole to world city: Place luck and public agendas in Denver, in Dennis Judd and Alan Artibise (eds), *The Infrastructure of Urban Tourism*, New York: M.E. Sharpe, pp. 168–201.
Crouch, C. (2004) *Post-Democracy*, Cambridge: Polity Press.
Davidson, Mark and Wyly, Elvin. (2012) Class-ifying London, *City*, 16(4): 395–421.
Deas, Iain. (2013) Towards post-political consensus in urban policy? Localism and the emerging agenda for regeneration under the Cameron Government, *Planning Practice & Research*, 28: 65–82.
Farrelly, Michael and Sullivan, Helen (2010) Discourses of democracy in neighborhood governance, *Critical Policy Studies*, 4: 234–249.
Fraser, J.C., Lepofsky, Jonathan, Kick, Edward L. and Williams, J. Patrick (2003) The construction of the local and the limits of contemporary community building in the United States, *Urban Affairs Review*, 38: 417–445.
Galster, George C., Tatian, Peter A., Santiago, Anna M., Pettit, Kathryn L.S. and Smith, Robin E. (2003) *Why Not in My Backyard? Neighborhood impacts of deconcentrating assisted housing*, New Brunswick, NJ: Center for Urban Policy Research.
George, Hermon. (2004) Community development and the politics of deracialization: The case of Denver, Colorado, 1991–2003, *Annals of the American Academy of Political and Social Science*, 594: 143–157.
Givel, Michael. (2010) The evolution of the theoretical foundations of punctuated equilibrium theory in public policy, *Review of Policy Research*, 27: 187–198.
Hanlon, Bernadette, Short, John Rennie and Vicino, Thomas J. (2009) *Cities and Suburbs: New metropolitan realities in the US*, New York: Routledge.
Hodges, Arthur. (1994) Denver's planning department is accused of planning obsolescence, *Westword*: 11 May.
Horak, Martin. (2007) *Governing the Post-communist City*, Toronto: University of Toronto Press.
Horan, Cynthia. (1997) Coalition, market, and state: Postwar development politics in Boston, in Mickey Lauria (ed.), *Reconstructing Urban Regime Theory: Regulating urban politics in a global economy*, Thousand Oaks, CA: Sage, pp. 149–170.
Hubbard, Burt. (2009) Denver gets whiter; Suburbs more diverse, *Denver Post*, 29 March.
Jacobs, Jane M. (2012) Urban geographies I: Still thinking cities relationally, *Progress in Human Geography*, 36(3): 412–422.
Jones, Bryan D., Sulkin, Tracy and Larsen, Heather A. (2003) Policy punctuations in American political institutions, *American Political Science Review*, 97: 151–169.
Judd, Dennis. (1983) From Cowtown to Sunbelt City, in Susan S. Fainstein, Norman I. Fainstein, Richard Child Hill, Dennis Judd and Michael Peter Smith (eds), *Restructuring the City: The political economy of urban redevelopment*, New York: Longman Publishing Co. (rev. edn 1986).
Jun, Kyu-Nahm and Musso, Juliet. (2013) Participatory governance and the spatial representation of neighborhood issues, *Urban Affairs Review*, 49: 71–101.

Leonard, Stephen J. and Noel, Thomas J. (1990) *Denver: Mining camp to metropolis*, Niwot, CO: University Press of Colorado.
MacLeod, Gordon. (2011) Urban politics reconsidered: Growth machine to post-democratic city?, *Urban Studies*, 48(12): 2629–2660.
MacLeod, Gordon. (2013) Post-politics in local development planning new urbanism/smart growth in the Scottish Highlands: Mobile policies and post-politics in local development planning, *Urban Studies*, 50: 2196–2221.
MacLeod, Gordon and Jones, Martin (2011) Renewing urban politics, *Urban Studies*, 48(12): 2443–2472.
McCarthy, James M. (2013) We have never been 'post-political', *Capitalism Nature Socialism*, 24: 19–25.
Mile High Connects. (n.d.) www.milehighconnects.org/main.html.
Mile High Transit Opportunity Collaborative (MHTOC). (2011) http://urbanlandc.org/collaboratives.
Mouffe, Chantal. (2005) *On the Political*, London: Routledge.
Moulton, Jennifer. (1999) Ten steps to a living downtown, Discussion Paper, Washington DC: Brookings Institution, Center on Urban and Metropolitan Policy.
NCBR committee, Denver City Council. (2007) Minutes, 27 February, p. 4.
NCBR committee, Denver City Council. (2007) Minutes, 11 December, p. 4.
NCBR committee, Denver City Council. (2008) Minutes, 24 June, p. 3.
NCBR committee, Denver City Council. (2008) Minutes, 14 October.
Newman, Kathe and Ashton, Philip. (2004) Neoliberal urban policy and new paths of neighborhood change in the American inner city, *Environment and Planning A*, 36: 1151–1172.
OED (Office of Economic Development). (2007) *City and County of Denver Action Plan 2007*. Available at: www.denvergov.org.
OED. (2010) *Neighborhood Development*. Available at: www.denvergov.org.
OED. (n.d.) *Denver's Neighborhood Marketplace Initiative*. Available at: www.denvergov.org/Portals/690/documents/Neighborhoods/GrowDenver%20Brochure%20rev.pdf.
Peck, J. and Theodore, N. (2010) Mobilizing policy: Models, methods, and mutations, *Geoforum*, 41: 169–174.
Piton Foundation. (2004) *Neighborhood Data Book*, Denver: Piton.
Piton Foundation. (2011a) *Neighborhood Focus: Denver's growth slows, diversity unchanged*, The Piton Foundation's 2010 Census Project. Available at: www.piton.org/census2010.
Piton Foundation. (2011b) *Denver Children's Corridor*. Available at: www.denverchildrenscorridor.org.
Rancière, Jacques. (2003a) *The Philosopher and His Poor*, Durham, NC: Duke University Press.
Rancière, J. (2003b) Politics and aesthetics: An interview, *Angelaki*, 8: 194–211.
Robinson, Tony. (2005) *Missing the Target: How Denver's inclusionary housing ordinance and urban renewal policy could better meet Denver's housing needs*, Denver: FRESC. Available at: http://fresc.org/wp-content/uploads/2013/12/Denver-Housing-Study.pdf.
Rohe, W.M. (2009) From local to global: One hundred years of neighborhood planning, *Journal of the American Planning Association*, 75: 209–230.
Saegert, S. (2006) Building civic capacity in urban neighborhoods: An empirically grounded anatomy, *Journal of Urban Affairs*, 28: 275–294.
Saiz, Martin. (1993) Transforming growth politics: Denver during the Peña Administration, paper prepared for delivery at the Annual Meeting of the Western Political Science Association, Pasadena, California.

Schwedes, Christian and Michel, Boris. (2014) Reclaiming the European city and lobbying for Privilege: Business improvement districts in Germany, *Urban Affairs Review* (forthcoming).

ShoreBank Advisory Services. (2005) *Denver Market Analysis*, Chicago: ShoreBank.

Sloterdijk, P. (2005) *Damned to Expertocracy*. Available at: www.signandsight.com/features/238.html.

Stone, Clarence and Stoker, Robert (eds) (2015) *Urban neighborhoods in a new era: Revitalization Politics in the Post-Industrial City*, Chicago: University of Chicago Press.

Swyngedouw, Eric. (2005) Governance innovation and the citizen: The Janus face of governance-beyond-the-state, *Urban Studies*, 42: 1–16.

Swyngedouw, Eric. (2009) The zero-ground of politics: Musings on the post-political city, *NewGeographies*, 1: 52–61.

Swyngedouw, Eric. (2010) Post-democratic cities: For whom and for what?, presented to Regional Studies Association (RSA) Annual Conference, Pécs, Hungary.

Swyngedouw, Eric. (2011) Interrogating post-democratization: Reclaiming egalitarian spaces, *Political Geography*, 370–380.

Vasquez, Beverly. (1999) Moulton molds Denver, *Denver Business Journal*, 11 July. Available at: www.bizjournals.com/denver/stories/1999/07/12/story3.html?s=print.

Ward, Kevin. (2006) 'Policies in motion', urban management and state restructuring: The trans-local expansion of business improvement districts, *International Journal of Urban and Regional Research*, 30: 54–75.

5

Localism and the 'Post-social' Governmentality

Simin Davoudi and Ali Madanipour

> If there is such a thing as Cameronism, it is giving power away.[1]
> (*The Economist*, 2009: 39)

The failure of the 2010 general election in the United Kingdom (UK) to produce a parliamentary majority for any single political party led to the formation of the first (in 60 years) Coalition Government made up of the Liberal Democrats and the Conservatives. On taking office, they made 'localism' and 'Big Society' the central theme of their government, promising to: enable 'a fundamental shift of power from Westminster to people', 'promote decentralisation and democratic engagement' and 'end the era of top-down government by giving new powers to local councils, communities, neighbourhoods and individuals' (HM Government, 2010a: 11). In December 2010, this agenda appeared in the Localism Bill as the linchpin of the government's 'Big Society' policy. The Bill, which a year later became the Localism Act 2011, confirmed the government's intention to 'devolve power, money, and knowledge to … elected local representatives, frontline public service professionals, social enterprises, charities, co-ops, community groups, neighbourhoods, and individuals' who are seen as 'those best placed to find the best solutions to local needs' (HM Government, 2010b: 4).

While the Coalition Government has given localism a strong political salience, it is wrong to assume that localism is their invention. On the contrary, localism in its various forms has been a long-standing feature of British politics and public policy (Painter *et al.*, 2011) and can be traced back to Edmund Burke (a founder of British conservatism), 'who extolled the small platoons as the pillars of the state' (Crick, 2002: 497). The more recent calls for decentralisation surfaced during the administration of the former Labour government (1997–2010). What was then called 'the New Localist' agenda (Stoker, 2004: 117) was captured in a speech by Alan Milburn, who became its champion in Tony Blair's government. He stated that

> We have reached the high water mark of the post-1997 centrally-driven target-based approach … Reforms to enhance choice, diversify supply and devolve control are all now taking hold as the Government moves from

> a centralised command and control model to what has been called new localism ... Public services cannot be run by diktat from the top down ... accountability needs to move downwards and outwards to consumers and communities. (Milburn, 2004: n.p.)

As Gerry Stoker (himself a keen supporter of what he calls progressive localism) suggests, beyond this enthusiasm for localism lay an attempt to pre-empt the Conservatives from using the term to attack 'the control freakery, state paternalism and big spending plans' that characterised the Labour government (Stoker, 2004: 117). Despite this observation, there is much continuity in government mentalities between the two administrations in advocating localism, and between governing through 'the local' and governing through 'the community'. The latter became particularly pronounced in the 1990s and featured prominently in the Labour government's policies and programmes. It is, therefore, not surprising that Labour shadow ministers have fully embraced localism and want 'to look at how local communities can be incentivised to think about development in their areas' and 'feel that they're being given the tools to shape what's happening in their communities, including where housing would go' (*Planning*, 2013: 14).

This continuity may be due to the populist appeal and the 'warm glow' of terms such as community and localism that tend to conjure up romantic images of small groups bound together through cultural and geographical ties and collaborate reciprocally and voluntarily to find local solutions for local problems; an image akin to Tönnies's (1957 [1887]) *Gemeinschaft*. But, there is more to localism than mere populist rhetoric. Drawing on a Foucauldian perspective we argue that this form of localism, which is introduced from the top by the national government, is the spatial manifestation of 'post-social' technologies of neoliberal governmentality, which began with 'the birth of the community' a few decades ago (Rose, 1996). Localism complements the fragmentation of 'the social' into multiple communities with the fragmentation of 'the national' into multiple localities. It re-imagines the local as the 'natural' geography of 'the community', which itself is seen as the 'natural' articulation of collective life. We argue that, as the language of 'the community' weakens 'the hold of "the social" in our socio-political imagination' (Rose, 1996: 353), so the language of 'the local' weakens the hold of 'the national' in our socio-spatial imagination. Governing through 'the local' involves freeing localities to become responsible for their own fates and bear the consequences of their own conducts, yet in such a way that their action is aligned with governmental ends. Through a complex process of identification and responsibilisation, the local becomes both the *target* of governmental action and the voluntary *partner* of government (Burchell, 1993). Furthermore, the local provides a new space through which the subjectivity and identification of individuals are reconstituted. The process is enabled and regulated *at a distance* through technocratic and calculative technologies of agency and performance.

The chapter is organised in five sections. In the next section, we describe Foucault's concept of governmentality and its two inter-related dimensions of political rationality and governmental technologies. In the third section, we discuss liberalism and its contemporary manifestation in two distinct modes of government that emerged in the twentieth century: welfarism and neoliberalism. Here, we pay particular attention to the ways in which neoliberal rationality understands, accounts for and articulates the subjects of government and their freedom and responsibility. Then we focus on 'post-social' government to discuss the emergence of the community and localism, arguing that the government of 'big society' is not a social government. In conclusion, in the final section we present a normative critique of neoliberal localism that, we argue, risks social Darwinism and technicisation of political space.

Governmentality

> It would not be going too far to say that today we are creatures of the state. (Miller, 2003: 19)

A key contribution of Foucault's concept of governmentality is its departure from the kind of state-centred analyses of political authority that is reflected in the above statement and has preoccupied many social theorists and political philosophers. There has been an over-emphasis on the place of the state in political authority and its portrayal as a unified, all-powerful entity that is separated from two other unified and seemingly 'non-political' entities, the market and civil society (Rose and Miller, 1992). This perceived separation is in fact a legacy of liberalism itself, whose emergence as an 'art of governing' (Rose *et al.*, 2009: 3) was based on a critique of state intervention in individual freedoms. The critique of the state was not limited to classical liberals. For example, Nietzsche considered the state as 'the coldest of all cold monsters' that imposed its power on free and autonomous individuals; 'when the state ceases, does the man who is not superfluous begin' (Nietzsche, 1969: 75). The suggested alternatives to the state span across a spectrum ranging from communitarianism at the one end and libertarianism at the other. For the former, governing is best left to the good will of 'communities'. For the latter, it is best left to the invisible hand of the market. One romanticises a civil society based on reciprocity and voluntary cooperation; the other idealises a free market based on economic transactions. Both suggest that only in these state-free utopias can life worthy of emancipated individuals be made possible. Both assume that the absence of *the state* translates into the absence of *government*.

Foucault's notion of governmentality challenges the view that the state is a separate entity from society and is 'the origin, animator, beneficiary, or terminal point of power' (Rose *et al.*, 2009: 5). Referring to state-centric approaches, he famously suggested that despite the overthrow of absolute monarchies, 'in the field of political thought we haven't yet cut off the king's head' (Foucault, 1979a: 88–89). By positioning the state *within* the wider field of government Foucault points to the existence of diverse forms of power in everyday life and its diffusion across multiple political and 'non-political' authorities. Defining government as 'the conduct of conducts' implies a continuum of power relations ranging from governing *the self* to governing *others* within which self-discipline is intertwined with the wider governmental regulation. It also implies that 'most individuals are not merely the subjects of power but play a part in its operations' (Rose and Miller 1992: 174) simply through mundane practices of everyday lives. Thus, when Foucault speaks of the 'governmentalization of the state' (Foucault, 1991a: 103) he refers to the state as 'a powerful, metaphysical effect' of distinctive governmental practices (Painter, 2010: 1116).[2] In this chapter, we adopt this Foucauldian, non-essentialised understanding of the state as a specific, dynamic and historic way in which societal power relations are now discursively codified (Lemke, 2000: 11; Rose and Miller, 1992: 177).

Rationalities and technologies of government

Making sense of the multiple ways in which our lives are connected to the aspirations of authorities requires an understanding of the act of governing (*gouverner*) and its rationalities (*mentalite*). It requires understanding the *art* of government, or 'governmentality' as Foucault puts it. He coined the concept in his lecture on 'genealogy of modern state' (on 5 April 1978, quoted in Lemke, 2000: 2) to draw attention to the purpose of governmental action and the means by which it is achieved (Dean, 1999: 11; Lemke, 2000: 5). He argued that governmentality is an 'ensemble formed by the institutions, procedures, analyses and reflections, the calculations and tactics, that allow the exercise of [this] very specific albeit complex form of power' (Foucault, 1979b: 20). Governmentality focuses the attention on political rationalities (ends) and technologies of government (means) and the intricate interdependencies between them as they are played out in specific places and times.

Foucault uses the term *rationality* not as a form of absolute or transcendental reason but rather to refer to its pragmatic, 'instrumental and relative meaning' (Foucault, 1991b: 79). It is about rationalisation of particular practices. The focus is not on how practices conform to particular rationalities, but which kind of rationality they use and 'how forms of rationality inscribe themselves in practices' (Foucault, 1991b: 79). For example, the move towards localism is justified by the liberal rationalities of freedom, choice and responsibility. As

Rose and Miller (1992: 179) argue, political rationalities 'are morally coloured, grounded upon knowledge, and made thinkable through language'. It is these characteristics that underpin the distinctions between different forms of liberalism, as discussed below.

The term *technology* refers to the bundle of strategies, techniques, procedures, mechanisms and practices through which authorities seek to make government programmes operable (Dean, 1999; Foucault and Gordon, 1980). Thus, while rationalities are about knowing, constructing and signifying the objects, subjects and goals of government, technologies are about the mechanisms by which these goals are achieved. However, the relation between rationalities and technologies is not a simple application of the former by the latter; it constitutes complex interdependencies between the two. Technologies are complex assemblages with their own characteristics and dynamics. They are enrolled, mobilised and pragmatically adjusted to enable authorities to exercise political power even if they may not present a perfect fit. We argue that 'community' and 'localism' are just that. They are complex assemblages that constitute and are constitutive of a particular mentality of government, namely liberalism. In the following section we briefly discuss *liberalism* and its emergence in the eighteenth century in the West. We then focus on two specific forms of liberalism that became the dominant modes of government in the twentieth century, particularly in the UK and US, while acknowledging its wider political heterogeneity. These are: post-war *welfarism* and post-1970s *neoliberalism*. We pay particular attention to the ways in which liberal mentalities of government conceive of the nature, obligations and responsibilities of the subjects of government (i.e. the governed) and how such conceptions differ between welfarist and neoliberal modes of government.

Liberalism

> We will be strong in defence of freedom. The Government believes that the British state has become too authoritarian, and that over the past decade it has abused and eroded fundamental human freedoms and historic civil liberties. We need to restore the rights of individuals in the face of encroaching state power, in keeping with Britain's tradition of freedom and fairness. (HM Government, 2010a: 11)

Liberalism fractures into multiple interpretations as soon as one begins to examine it. One major fault line in political philosophy is the concept of *liberty* itself. While the principle is sacrosanct to all liberals, there is much variation in how liberty is understood in relation to society and market, and what is seen as the legitimate exercise of power by political authorities. Central to

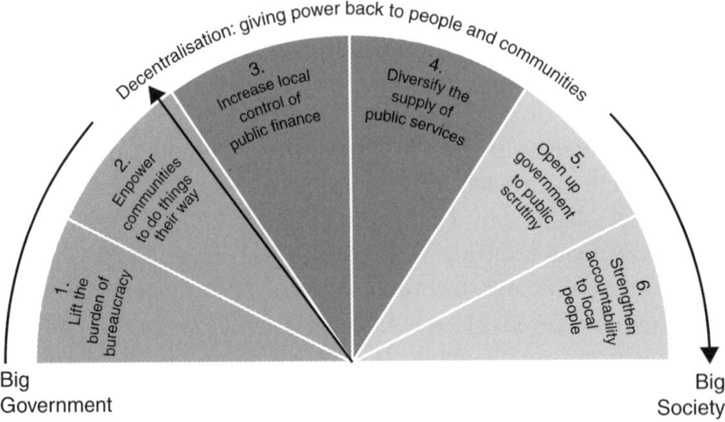

Figure 5.1 From 'Big Government' to 'Big Society' (source: HM Government, 2010c: 2)

the latter are the perennial questions of how much government is enough government, and how the complex relationship between freedom and domination should be managed. Or, in the language of contemporary debate, what is the 'right' balance between 'big society' and 'big government', as depicted in Figure 5.1. However, as mentioned earlier, from the governmentality perspective, the real questions are not about *how much* government but *what type* of government, *for what* ends (rationality) and *by what* means (technology). In the last three centuries or so, different forms of liberalism have offered different responses to these questions. Based on the above it is possible to distinguish between: classical liberalism of the eighteenth and nineteenth centuries, welfarism of the mid-twentieth century and the post-1970s neoliberalism, as outlined below.

Classical liberalism

For *classical* liberals, liberty and private property were intimately connected and even considered as the same thing to the extent that free markets were seen as 'the embodiment of freedom' (Robbins, 1961: 104). For them, liberty was not simply defined by the freedom to obtain private property; it was also seen as best protected by it. In the words of Friedrich Hayek (1978: 149): 'There can be … no freedom of movement if the means of transport are a government monopoly.' For classical liberals, social (individual freedom) and economic (market freedom) liberalism went hand in hand and only a minimal 'nightwatchman state' (as John Stuart Mill (1963) put it) whose primary task was to protect individual liberties could be considered as legitimate. The rise of liberal political philosophy in the eighteenth century was based on the normative critique of excessive and authoritarian government. A new way of governing emerged whose objective was not simply to maintain the power of absolute rulers over their territories and sovereign subjects, but to govern the *civil society* that was construed as a 'non-political' and 'private' realm and endowed with freedoms and rights. To govern was no longer simply about making juridical subjects obey laws issued by 'the king' and imposed directly on them. It was also about shaping the conduct of the subjects by acting upon 'the possible fields of their action' (Foucault, 1982: 221), their network of relations and the environment within which they operate (Dean, 1999; Lemke, 2000; Rose *et al.*, 2009). The focus was less on players and more on the rules of the game. New technologies, which were not limited to mechanisms of direct control and coercion, were invented to shape, steer and modify the imagined private sphere of civil society towards desired directions. This change of technologies should not be seen as the exercise of coercion and control from the back door, but rather as new ways of governing civil society 'without destroying its existence and its autonomy' (Rose and Miller, 1992: 180). This required embedding the state within an ensemble of rules, institutions and procedures, and connecting it to other forces that shaped the networks of civil society relations.

To govern, in liberal mentalities, was to align the aspirations of the individuals, communities and institutions with those of government in such a way that their self-fulfilments coincide with the fulfilment of government goals. Government in this sense is 'a contact point' where governing of the self is integrated in the structures of coercion.

> Governing people in the broad meaning of the word … is not a way to force people to do what the governor wants; it is always a versatile equilibrium, with complementarity and conflicts between techniques which assure coercion and processes through which the self is constructed or modified by himself. (Foucault, 1993: 204)

Central to the operation of 'the contact point' is how freedom is understood. Liberalism considers freedom not as the opposite of coercion or the site of struggle for utopian emancipation and resistance to authorities, but as an instrument or, as Hayek (1976: 163; original emphasis) put it, '*an artefact*' that can be utilised for governing. Technologies of the self are considered as complementing rather than contradicting technologies of domination. Instead of being merely obedient subjects governed from the top, people fulfil the ends of government by freely and responsibly fulfilling themselves. Far from being an ethical critique of social control, liberal governmentality considers 'the very ethic of freedom itself' as 'part of a particular formula for governing free societies' (Rose *et al.*, 2009: 12). We are ethically *obliged to be free* (not to be dependent) and to conduct ourselves freely yet in a responsible way (Foucault, 1982). *Responsibilisation*, therefore, is at the heart of the liberal way of governing the self. It is used to steer individual freedom towards desired outcomes and governmental goals. In the liberal mentality, freedom brings about choice and choice brings about responsibility and obligation regardless of the structural constraints that are imposed upon the actors. We will elaborate on the limitations of this perspective in the fourth section. Here it suffices to note that to speak of responsibilisation as a technology is not to speak of it as a neutral process. On the contrary, it is politically charged and entangled with moral questions of: *responsible to whom and for what.* As will be shown below, what differentiates welfare liberalism from neoliberalism is based largely on how they respond to these normative questions.

Welfarism

The first half of the twentieth century saw the rise of a 'revisionist' approach to liberalism. This, in contrast to classical liberalism, did not see an intimate or necessary connection between liberty and a private-property-based market (Paul *et al.*, 2007). Central to this revisionist approach were the emerging ideas in the German schools of Freiburg and Frankfurt whose *Ordo*-liberals were promoting the creation of a 'social market economy' (Lemke, 2010: 192).[3] They considered no juxtaposition between the state and the market and instead argued that 'one mutually presumes the existence of the other' (Lemke, 2010: 193). Economy was defined as 'a social field of regulated practices' and an object of government that is constituted and maintained through socio-political interventions, rather than being a separate, autonomous domain with its own internal logics (Lemke, 2010: 194, drawing on Foucault's lecture of 20 February 1979).

As suggested by Gaus and Courtland (2010), these revisionist ideas were based on a number of powerful criticisms. First, the ability of free markets to maintain a 'prosperous equilibrium' (Beveridge, 1944: 96) with full employment was being questioned, notably by John Maynard Keynes. Drawing attention to the experience of the 1930s Great Depression, he challenged the assumptions of neo-classical economics, arguing that private markets could become stuck in equilibrium with high levels of unemployment. Second, the diminishing faith in markets as the guarantor of all freedoms was coupled with a growing faith in the legitimacy of the state to supervise economic life. Keynes advocated the need for government intervention to moderate the boom and bust cycles of the economy and the use of fiscal measures to mitigate the adverse effects of recessions. This change of heart towards the role of government was reinforced by the democratisation of the Western states whose elected members were seen as representing the population. Third, it became clear that far 'from being the guardian of every other rights', property rights generate inequitable power relations and an uneven realisation of liberty (Ely, 1992: 26). Concerns about equity were heightened by the development of liberal theories of social justice through the work of John Rawls (1971) and other advocates of egalitarian liberalism.

The revisionist ideas underpinned the rationalities of a new mode of government in many Western societies after the Second World War, one that we know as the welfare state (or the 'New Deal' in the US). Welfarism considered a set of appropriate goals for the government that included: the pursuit of national economic growth and its redistribution across the national territory and social groups as well as the management of social risks across individuals' life cycle. To these ends, responsibilities were shared by the growing bureaucratic apparatus of the state and citizens (civil society). In the UK, this rationality was reflected in the social contract that was formulated in William Beveridge's 1942 Report. His pledge of war on five 'giant evils' of squalor, ignorance, want, idleness and disease underpinned the Labour government's welfare programme. On the one hand, the state was made responsible for providing full employment through Keynesian demand management, free health care through a nationalised health service, lifelong free education and lifetime social security through a system of social insurance and pensions. On the other hand, citizens had to play their part by becoming 'thrifty, industrious, and socially responsible' (Rose and Miller, 1992: 192). In line with the liberal understanding of freedom and choice, welfarism conceived of the subjects of government as *responsible* citizens. However, in contrast to neoliberalism it ensured that citizens' responsibility was directed primarily towards *the society*, which itself, as will be discussed in the fourth section, was a construct of welfarism (Burchell, 1993).

Citizens were seen as free and autonomous individuals yet firmly 'bound into a system of solidarity and mutual inter-dependency' (Rose and Miller, 1992: 196) through various governmental technologies. Key among these technologies was the social insurance system. Although it was motivated by moral and political aspirations, it had the paradoxical effect of de-politicisation: decisions became dominated by technical calculations of risk and security by expert professionals whose concentration in the states' institutions endowed them with a growing influence (Davoudi, 2014; Rose and Miller, 1992: 196). Beneficiaries of social security were (and still are) given new 'identities' or, as Maffesoli (1991) puts it, were 'identified' with certain categories of risks such as unemployed, job-seeker, school-leaver, carer, homeless and disadvantaged. Thus, despite their egalitarian motivations, these technocratic processes of identification created social stigmatisation (Fraser, 2000).

Neoliberalism

The post-war welfare states and their social contracts became the subject of much criticism, particularly in the second half of the twentieth century.

Marxist analysts and communitarians criticised it for its paternalistic mechanisms of social control, hierarchical structures, undifferentiated responses to individual needs, over-confidence in experts and professionals, and command and control planning under whose weight civil society was fading away (Davoudi and Madanipour, 2013). These criticisms paralleled and, inadvertently, echoed a neoliberal critique of welfarism, which was gathering pace and strength particularly through the work of a few Viennese economists and their Mont Pelerin Society (MPS).[4] The Society, founded by Hayek in 1942, along with its offspring think-tanks,[5] combined the classical liberal's moral critique of big government with the economic critique of Keynesianism to embark on a sustained criticism of welfare states for their ineffective fiscal interventions and their *dirigiste*, excessive and centralised power (Stedman Jones, 2012).

Karl Popper, a philosopher, played a major part in the critique of Hegelian and Marxist theory and its collectivist (as opposed to individualistic) understanding of society. Ludwig von Mises, an economist, attacked the growing bureaucracy and its lack of ability to restrain itself. It is interesting to note that the Coalition Government used a similar argument in defence of its localism agenda, claiming that 'There's the efficiency argument – that in huge hierarchies, money gets spent on bureaucracy instead of the frontline' (HM Government, 2010b: 4). Friedrich Hayek pointed to the impossibility of central planning on the ground that no one is capable of knowing what people want no matter how clever they are and how much expertise is available to them. Another related wave of criticism came from Milton Friedman, an economist in the Chicago School. Like classical liberals, he 'saw economic liberty as the safeguard of all other freedoms; and a swelling state as the road to tyranny' (*The Economist*, 2012: 93). Although he considered himself as the heir to Adam Smith, a founder of classical liberalism, unlike him Friedman argued in favour of a greater role for the private sector and competition in the provision of public services such as schools, infrastructure, utilities and health (Stedman Jones, 2012) and, hence, advocated for privatisation to become the core strategy of neoliberal governments. The rise of neoliberal governmentality was premised on and fed by these ideas.

As a mode of government, neoliberal political mentality differs from welfarism at several levels: 'moralities, explanations and vocabularies' (Rose and Miller, 1992: 198). One key difference is its understanding of the relationship between *society and the state*. The centrality of this relationship in defining the form of liberalism is reflected in the UK Coalition Agreement, which attempts 'to completely recast the relationship between people and the state' (HM Government, 2010a: 8). Whereas welfarist liberals consider the state as the necessary regulator and keeper of the social order – albeit for the sake of the market economy – neoliberals consider big government to be not only inefficient and ineffective in regulating the economy, but also morally dangerous for society. They argue that the state institutions are: first, self-serving, because vote-seeking political parties tend to make lavish promises that can only be met with large amounts of borrowing; and second, immoral, because the provision of welfare by the state cultivates 'a culture of dependency' which is morally damaging to individual freedom (Rose and Miller, 1992: 198). They suggest that the alternative to the state is the market, private insurance and self-reliance. The emphasis on self-reliance brings about a different morality of responsibilisation because it plays down the welfarist ideals of a reciprocal relationship between individuals and society, as will be elaborated in the following section.

In neoliberal mentality, what was previously seen as the 'political' responsibilities of government is reconfigured as commodities to be supplied by private providers and exchanged in the free market. This leads to the second difference between welfarism and neoliberalism, namely their understanding of the relationship between *society and economy*. Whereas the former advocates 'the idea of governing society in the name of the economy', the latter redefines society as a form of economic domain (Lemke, 2010: 197) and conducive to market principles of competition, supply and demand equilibrium and enterprise. These principles have increasingly become 'a kind of permanent economic tribunal' (Foucault's lecture of 21 March 1979, quoted in Lemke, 2010: 198) or a court of appeal before which the performance of all other activities by individuals, society and even the state are calculated, measured and assessed. The social is increasingly colonised by the economic criteria of efficiency, competition and productivity, and measured by cost–benefit analyses. These criteria have come to define the rules of the game and shape the conduct of all conducts. The reconfiguration of the political into techno-economic moves beyond classical liberalism's view of economic liberty and extends the scope of free markets from being the *safeguard* of all freedoms to being *the organiser and regulator* of the state and society. In neoliberal mentality it is the market that governs the state and society and not vice versa.

The emergence of 'neoliberal states' in the 1970s was rooted in these rationalities and their scepticism of the capacity and legitimacy of any forms of political authority to govern for the best. They used the social and economic storms of the 1970s as the evidence of the failure of welfarism. Two heads of state became widely known as champions of neoliberalism: Margaret Thatcher, Britain's Conservative Prime Minister (1979–1990), and Ronald Reagan, the US Republican President (1981–1989). Despite the considerable contextual and historical differences in which they were operating, both drew on neoliberal ideas to embark on a major restructuring of government and put in place a series of policies and programmes aimed at privatisation and creation of markets for areas that were previously seen as belonging to the 'political' domain of government. The list is far too long and familiar to justify its reiteration here, but one point is worth stressing. Contrary to its rhetoric and its critique, the 'rolling back' of state intervention was not so much about less intervention as it was about *different* forms of intervention. It is true that both administrations radically changed the size, shape and role of the state, but they simultaneously created other, indirect forms of intervention.

The outcome was, therefore, not less government but a *different* form of government; one that foregrounded 'governing at a distance'. The term, inspired by Latour's 'action at a distance' and coined by Miller and Rose (1990), means complementing and sometimes replacing *direct* regulation of formal institutions of the state with *indirect* mechanisms of control, located in multiple centres of calculations that are spatially and organisationally separate and distant from the subjects of government. Dean (1999) refers to these indirect mechanisms as *technologies of agency* (such as responsibilizing, empowering, mobilising) and *technologies of performance* (such as auditing, monitoring, setting standards and targets). If technologies of agency are 'deployed from below', technologies of performance are 'utilized from above' (Dean, 1999: 167). The former obliges us to be free yet self-responsible while the latter seeks to align the outcome of our free choices with governmental goals of enhancing competition and enterprise. Such an alignment is sought through a complex assemblage of technologies that make our choices and actions calculable, comparable and controllable indirectly (and if necessary directly) and governable from a distance. Neoliberal technologies focus less on players and more on the rules of the game. By changing the parameters of the environment in which people operate, they seek to shape their conduct. As Dean (1999: 171) suggests, under neoliberalism 'the national state takes on less a directive and distributive role, and more a coordinative, arbitrary and preventive one'. So, 'the retraction of the welfare state may lead to less *state* intervention and provisions, but it does not necessarily lead to less *government* and discipline in Foucault's sense of the word' (Davoudi and Madanipour, 2013: 559). In fact, the possibility of governing increases through government at a distance because it provides a better fit between the neoliberal mentalities and neoliberal technologies of government to which we now turn our attention.

The 'post-social' government: community and localism

> There is no such thing as society. (Thatcher, 1987: 10)

The above infamous remark by Mrs Thatcher has come to epitomise the neoliberal individualist view of the world. She subsequently clarified her remark by suggesting that her 'meaning … was that society was not an abstraction, separate from men and women who composed it, but a living structure of individuals, families, neighbours and voluntary associations' (Thatcher, 1993: 626). The clarification brought her even closer to the liberalist view of society as simply a sum of individuals. This kind of seeing 'human beings *in* society' (Mill, 1963: 879; emphasis added) is rooted in the classical liberalism of philosophers such as Herbert Spencer (1995 [1851]: 1), who claimed that 'the property of the mass are dependent upon the attributes of its component parts'. Mrs Thatcher's remark was in keeping with the resurgence of liberal principles in the second half of the twentieth century (mentioned above) and the growing criticism of the collectivist views of society. Increasingly, the supremacy of individuals as autonomous, free, self-interested and economically rational beings was being centre-staged as the focus of government. However, what rarely features in this narrative is that there is no such thing as 'pure choice' and that individuals' choices and responsibilities are shaped and sometimes determined by factors beyond their control or even consciousness.

The re-emphasis on individuals should not be seen as 'the end of the social' (Baudrillard, 1983). On the contrary, it is misleading 'to speak of "the death of social"' (Rose, 1996: 330) because, far from being unified, the social has always been a hybrid zone of multiple affiliations related to race, religion, culture, space and place. Deleuze (1979: xi) refers to the social as 'a sector' that groups together a diverse set of problems, institutions and interventions. Instead, the emphasis on individualism indicated the fading away of the construction of 'the social' as an essential, eternal and organic entity. For decades, a particular perception of the social prevailed that imagined society as the primary articulation of collective life and the welfare state as the *social* government. As Rose and Miller (1992: 192) suggest, 'the key innovation of welfarism lays in the attempts to link the fiscal, calculative and bureaucratic capacities of the apparatus of the state to the government of social life'. The social was imagined as the dominant articulation of collectivity and its cohesion was seen as a pre-requisite for a well-functioning 'national' economy. It was this particular construction of the social that began to lose its appeal and relevance in the 1970s when the neoliberal mentality began to take hold. New rationalities and technologies emerged that sought 'to govern without governing society' (Rose, 1996: 328).

One reason was the perceived irrelevance of the 'national' in the globalising economy and the diminishing ability of national authorities in controlling borderless and footloose capital. A nationally cohesive society was no longer seen as necessary in the pursuit of economic competitiveness. A de-nationalised economy did not need a nationalised society in order to sustain its growth. Competition was encouraged not just between the nations, but also between localities (regions and cities) and *within* the national space. Another reason was that 'the social', as the primary target of government, was being criticised from across the political spectrum by those who contingently coalesced around concerns over the homogenising, universalising, alienating and disempowering tendencies of the social forms of government (Rose, 1996). The result was the colonisation of politics by 'an unguarded faith in the individual and free market as deliverer of freedom' (Stedman Jones, 2012: 19). This was reflected in the opposition to a range of perceived collectivism including Fabian socialism and the One Nation group in Britain, and the New Deal and Great Society in the US (Stedman Jones, 2012).

The supremacy of free individuals in political debate was coupled with a shift in the moral underpinning of responsibilisation in terms of responsible to whom and for what. First, while post-war welfarism considered individuals to be citizens made responsible towards their society and reciprocally to be looked after by social provisions, post-1970s' neoliberalism sees them responsible to and crucially *for* themselves first, and only then, and in a strict moral order, responsible for their families, neighbours and associations. Mrs Thatcher (1987: 10) said it all: 'people must look to themselves first. It is our duty to look after ourselves, and then to look after our neighbour.' Second, post-war welfarism considered citizens to be responsible for economic growth and its equitable distribution. Neoliberalism considers the self-reliant individuals to be responsible *for* economic growth and enterprise. Responsibilisation as a government strategy remained but its targeted beneficiaries and its purpose have been radically transformed. Furthermore, while the welfare state assumed the role of maintaining social order through technologies of regulations and mediation, neoliberalism considers such a role as almost redundant and best left to another regulating entity: the market. Hayek's (1996 [1949]) theory of 'spontaneous order' advocates that social order emerges from the interaction of self-serving individuals and not as a result of deliberate planning by the state; that individuals, seen as rational-economic beings, gradually use the price systems to adjust their plans with each order and create a spontaneous social order, making the role of the state as the keeper and guarantor of social order almost redundant.

Community as a 'new social'

On coming to office in 1997, the Labour government softened the hard edges of the neoliberal dismissal of the social as a mere heap of individuals by reconstructing a 'new social'; one that was not imagined as a totalising, organic whole, but as a sum of associations of free and responsible individuals. The Labour Party's long-standing *associational* traditions of unionism, cooperatives, mutuals and friendly societies provided the discursive field for the construction of a new collectivity in political imagination; one that was not made from the top down but built from the bottom up. The language of associations made the reconfiguration of 'the social' politically palatable and helped mask the perceived amoral language of the free market and its dogged, atomised individualism. The term that captured and somewhat eternalised the idea of associational society was 'the community'. In 1996 Tony Blair declared that 'the search is on to reinvent community for a modern age, true to core values of fairness, co-operation and responsibility' (Blair, 1996). Since then, there has been an avalanche of legislation, policies and programmes whose titles begin or end with the term 'community'. Indeed, it became 'a key unit in the repackaging of the economy and society associated with the Third Way' and a means of segregating and localising socio-economic problems (Amin, 2005: 614).

Today, 'the community' has become a hegemonic signifier of imagined collectivity and the terrain through which a growing number of societal concerns are problematised and acted upon. Unlike the social, which was construed as a single collective being, communities are imagined as infinitely diverse, heterogeneous and overlapping with multiple allegiances that do not necessarily map on national territory, economy or society. Communities have come to represent the post-social collective life. As such they are perceived as the locus of unique and shared sets of values and moralities (e.g. religion, gender), commitments (e.g. to environment, places), lifestyles (e.g. vegetarianism, dress codes), fears and concerns (e.g. crime), and/or nostalgia (e.g. diaspora) (Rose, 1996: 333). David Cameron appears to have remained faithful to this associational view of society. Therefore, rather than questioning the idea of the society and reshaping the state in the name of the market, as Mrs Thatcher did, he has made 'the Big Society' his 'passion' (Cameron, 2010) and aims to reshape the state in the name of civil society. His understanding of society appears to follow New Labour's *democratic* individualism rather than Mrs Thatcher's *liberal* individualism. Norberto Bobbio (1990: 43) describes the difference between the two:

> Liberal individualism amputates the individual from the organic body … plunges him into the unknown and perilous world of the struggle for survival; … democratic individualism joins the individual together once more with others like himself, so that society can be built up again from their union, no longer as an organic whole but as an association of free individuals.

Thus, the government of the 'Big Society' is not a *social* government; it is a government of splintered communities.

Localism as a 'new national'

There is much continuity between the emergence of 'the community' and the birth of localism, at least in the UK. Both represent post-social technologies of government, with localism rendering 'the community' a spatial characteristic. As the community is imagined and articulated as the 'natural' embodiment of collective life, so is the locale imagined and articulated as the 'natural' spatial scale within and through which collective life is experienced, enacted and performed. This is clearly reflected in the statement by the UK Secretary of State for Communities and Local Government, who justified the abolition of the regional tier of government by referring to 'the region' as an 'arbitrary' political geography based on 'unnatural blocks' (Pickles and Cable, 2010: n.p.). By contrast, the local is portrayed as the 'natural block' in which place-based allegiances are valued beyond and above the calculations of self-interests, and where communities are 'best placed to find the best solutions to local needs' (HM Government, 2010b: 2).

As discussed above, the widespread support for governing through 'the community' was made possible because of the critiques of 'the social' from across the political spectrum. The same can be said about the political attraction of 'the local', because this too was based on the critique of 'the global' by a range of political dispositions including those in 'leftist academia and activism' (Purcell, 2006: 1924). The local has long been romanticised and essentialised as a force for 'the good'. It is romanticised on the basis of 'a Tocquevillean vision of locally based collective action and a belief in neighbourhoods as real and potential units of such action' (Chaskin and Ambunimah, 1999: 60, in Purcell, 2006). The local is also essentialised as *a priori* democratic scale (Purcell, 2006) and the site of civic empowerment and resistance to global capitalism, colonialism and state-centrism (Mohan and Stokke, 2000).

Defending localism, Cameron also equates decentralisation with democratisation and argues that 'there is the fairness argument – that centralised national blueprints don't allow for local solutions to major social problems. And, there is the political argument – that centralisation creates a distance in our democracy between the government and the governed' (HM Government, 2010b: 4). It appears that 'we are all localist now' (Walker, 2002) and risk falling into what has come to be known as the 'localist trap' (Mohan and Stokke, 2000) where the local, as a well-defined geographic unit, is equated with 'the good' (Purcell, 2006) and a natural scale for doing 'good'. Built into the localist trap is a Euclidean and hierarchically nested (like a Russian doll) conceptualisation of scale. Not recognising the fluid and relational quality of scale (Davoudi, 2012a; Davoudi and Strange, 2009; Healey, 2007) and its construction through social and political struggle (Marston, 2000) underpins the localist trap and its assumption that the local is more democratic than other scales. On the contrary, the politics of the local is neither unified nor confined to a perceived locality; they are inseparably and relationally intertwined in a web of political and social actions within and beyond the localities.

The governmentality perspective avoids the localist trap and considers localism not as the antidote of globalisation and centralisation or the site of empowerment and resistance, but as 'a different way of governing' (Cameron, 2011). It is governing *through* localities. It offers a new site through which government is enacted. This does not mean the death of 'the national'. Rather, it means the emergence of a particular construction of 'the national', one that is imagined as an archipelago of diverse localities that are home to a bundle of communities who make up 'the social'. Localism has been mobilised as a government strategy for creating new ways of mapping and defining the conduct of individuals and communities. Through a complex process of identification and subjectivity the local becomes both the subject of government and the technologies through which the subjectivity of individuals could be reconstituted. They become the site where new links are forged between governing others and governing the self, with the latter being extended from individuals to communities within their imagined 'natural' scale. It is a post-social technology used to inscribe liberal rationality in the practice of governing. That is why we concur with Clarke and Cochrane (2013) that localism should not be measured against an ideal notion of decentralisation and self-government. Instead, the governmentality perspective raises a different set of questions related not to *how much* freedom and choice, but *what type* and to what ends. It focuses on the nature (not extent) and purpose of responsibilisation, raising questions such as: to whom is the local responsible and for what?

Freedom and responsibility

Localism extends the liberal conceptions of freedom, choice and responsibility that are associated with individuals and communities to localities. Its language is peppered with the liberal advocacy of responsibility and self-reliance. Consider Cameron's statement below:

> What is my mission? It is actually social recovery … to mend the broken society. That's what the Big Society is all about … *responsibility* is the absolute key, giving people more control to improve their lives and their communities, so people can actually do more and take more power … But above all, it's *entrepreneurship* that is going to make this agenda work. (Cameron, 2011; emphasis added)

In the welfarist liberalism of the first half of the twentieth century, the social was invoked as a collective responsibility, spatialised across the national territory (Rose, 1996). Individuals were held responsible for their conduct in and towards the society, but the society and its 'external' structuring forces were taken into account in the consequences of their (mis)conduct. The emergence of the community has shifted the responsibilisation from being directed to the society as a whole, towards the self-selected, imagined communities to which the responsible individuals are seen to belong. The social determinants of individual conducts are largely replaced by the specific moral codes of their specific communities. The focus on the communities appears to have fragmented, pluralised and cosmopolitanised the field of morality. As Rose (1996: 334) suggests, 'the subjects are addressed as moral individuals' and 'atomised actors' whose conducts are determined by their own morality and that of their imagined and real communities. The influence of social structures is increasingly played down. Individuals in communities are expected to be self-reliant and masters of their own destiny.

As the discourse of the community retrieves individual conduct from the social order and locates it in the moral pluralism of communities, so the discourse of localism retrieves it from 'the national' order and places it in the pluralism of localities. Individuals' ethical responsibilities towards the 'national' interest are played down, while their responsibilities towards their own localities are played up. Localities, as the new imagined collectivity, are expected to be responsible for their own conduct and their own fates. Localities are responsibilised *to* and *for* themselves. In some ways, this can be seen as the heightening of a trend that began a few decades ago, albeit not always in the name of localism. One example is the shift in regional policy of the 1960s and 1970s away from the regional redistribution of resources to 'regions for themselves'. Indeed, post-1970s governments in the UK, and several other Western countries, have long been localists, in the sense that 'the national' has increasingly resisted being held responsible for the fate of 'the local'. Tackling the divide between the rich south and the poor north in England, for example, has ceased to be cast in the language of and policies for regional distribution, social solidarity or 'territorial cohesion'. Rather, it is about making the north stand on its own feet and act as an autonomous, self-reliant and responsible locale. The emphasis has shifted from public investment in places that are most *in need of* growth to those that show the greatest *potential for* growth. Thus, while it is accepted that an infrastructure investment of £2,600 per head in London compared with only £5 per person in the North East 'is not fair', the neoliberal mentality does not consider fairness as 'the right measure by which to judge an urban policy', because 'Scarce resources should go where they will generate the greatest returns' (*The Economist*, 2013a: 15). This is reflected in the 2010 Comprehensive Spending Review that cut the local governments' budget by an average of 4.4 per cent, but some of the most deprived local authorities received cuts of 8.9 per cent while some of the most affluent ones received cuts of only 1 per cent or less (Clarke and Cochrane, 2013).

Thus, although localism is portrayed as an emancipatory process of self-government, in practice it is conditional and calculative and works by utilising the self-governing potentials of 'the local' to align their goals to the neoliberal values of free market, enterprise and self-reliance. The locals are freed to 'become entrepreneurs of themselves' (Rose *et al.*, 2009: 11), yet within the framework of 'the national' governmental priorities such as deficit reduction, competitiveness and growth. As Cruikshank (1999: 60) argues, the 'will to empower may be well intentioned, but it is a strategy for constituting and regulating the political subjectivities of the empowered. Whether inspired by the promise of self-government and autonomy ... empowerment is itself a power relationship'.

Resilience and self-reliance

Neoliberal responsibilisation involves the offloading of responsibility from the formal institutions of the state to individuals, communities and localities in the name of self-reliance and resilience. Although the latter is an ecological concept, promoted by Buzz Holling and his fellow ecologists in the Resilience Alliance, it has now colonised multiple arenas of public policy (Davoudi, 2012b). The speed with which resilience is taking hold in public discourses and government agenda is largely due to its intuitive ideological fit with the neoliberal mentality. In short, evolutionary resilience suggests that all social and ecological system dynamics can be seen as a non-linear iteration of an adaptive cycle (Gunderson and Holling, 2002). It is, therefore, advocated not only as a property of ecosystems, but also as a general systems theory that integrates society, economy and ecology. At the heart of resilience thinking lies the principle that systems are non-linear, complex and *self-organising*; that they are endowed with forms of 'capital' defined as 'the inherent potential of a system that is available for change, since that potential determines the range of future options possible' (Holling, 2001: 393).

The principle of self-organisation also defined Hayek's theory of spontaneous order (mentioned above) and his call for a reform of 'all social institutions in accordance with the self-organising dynamic of the market' (Walker and Cooper, 2011: 150). He was working on his theory at the same time as Holling was working on his pioneering paper on resilience (Holling, 1973). Like Holling, Hayek also drew on complexity and non-equilibristic systems theories to embark on a sustained criticism of 'the state-engineered equilibria of Keynesian demand management' (Walker and Cooper, 2011:150). He argued that 'social systems are like biological systems newly defined by scientists as complex, adaptive and non-linear' (Hayek, 1974).

When resilience is used in the social context, the principle of self-organisation is translated into self-reliance, implying that individuals, communities and localities should 'pull themselves up by their bootstraps and reinvent themselves in the face of external challenges' (Swanstrom, 2008: 10). It is this ideological fit that has turned resilience and self-reliance into a key government mantra. Self-reliance justifies the retreat of public support and social security from vulnerable individuals and localities in the name of resilience, as shown in the following statement from a government-funded report on community resilience: 'if the Government takes greater responsibility for risks in the community, it may feel under pressure to take increasingly more responsibility, thereby eroding community resilience' (RRAC, 2009: 6). The neoliberal insistence on free and self-reliant individuals and localities comes close to social Darwinism and the survival of the fittest (Davoudi, 2012b). It resonates with the Darwinian law of natural selection with resilience being the measure of the ability of people and places to survive in a turbulent world.

Furthermore, self-organisation and spontaneous order carry anti-political motifs (Clarke and Cochrane 2013; Rose, 1996; Schedler, 1997) in the sense that they replace political authority with other forms of maintaining social order and coordinating collective affairs. As mentioned in the second section, neoliberals' preferred alternative to political authority is the self-regulating dynamics of the market. Clarke and Cochrane (2013: 16) distinguish between the anti-politics of New Labour and that of the Coalition Government, arguing that the former 'recognised the pre-conditions for politics' which is about recognizing the plurality of society, but 'replaced the content of politics ... with expertise and technology'; while the latter 'denies even the preconditions for politics. It imagines a nation of autonomous and internally homogenous localities. Then it replaces the content of politics ... with two things: markets ... and technologies of direct democracy such as referenda'.

We would argue that the distinction is not so pronounced. If acknowledging pluralism is the differentiating criterion, as they suggest, then New Labour's elevation of 'the community' is as much a denial of the preconditions for politics as the Coalition's elevation of localism. If the local is perceived as uniform and homogeneous by the latter, so was the community by the former. Both used various technologies of government to de-politicise and techno-economise politics. Both represented communities and localities as sites in which 'the apparent opposites of enterprise and community, of efficiency and welfare, of economic means and local ends' (Brenner and Theodore, 2002: 341–342) could be reconciled. The rise of evidence-based policy in the 1990s is a profound example of the pursuit of anti-political technology (Davoudi, 2006). Although performance targets are largely replaced with market incentives as a way of regulating and governing from a distance, the goal has remained intact: 'to construct prudent subjects whose moral quality is based on the fact that they rationally assess the costs and benefits of a certain act as opposed to other alternative acts' (Lemke, 2010: 201) and hence bear the consequences of their action. Both have used neoliberal indirect technologies of government that tend to control, regulate and steer the conduct of communities and localities without being held responsible for their actions and fates (Lemke, 2010: 201).

Conclusion

> We should not assume that all is for the worst in this 'post-social' age. (Rose, 1996: 353)

There is a degree of truth in this statement and many commentators in this volume have shown the progressive potentials of localism. Indeed, if there is one lesson to be learned from resilience thinking it is that uncertainty and complexity open windows of opportunity and possibilities for alternative actions. Localism may well be such a window through which new spaces of contestation and new ways of breaking away from the undesirable 'normal' (Davoudi, 2012b) may emerge. Whether there is sufficient appetite for ceasing such transformative opportunities depends to a large extent on societal preferences that, in England, appear to be shifting towards neoliberal values. The 2012 British Social Attitudes Survey, for example, showed a move to the right. During the early 1990s' recession less than a third of Britons thought unemployment benefits discouraged work; this figure rose to two-thirds in 2011 (*The Economist*, 2012: 36). The trend is stronger among the young who appear to be becoming 'classical liberals: as well as prizing social freedom, they believe in low taxes, limited welfare and personal responsibility' (*The Economist*, 2013b: 29). An Ipsos MORI poll indicates that 'every successive generation is less collectivist than the last' (*The Economist*, 2013b: 29), and while 'all age groups are becoming more socially and economically liberal, the young are ahead of the general trend'. Another poll, by YouGov, confirms that 'those aged 18–24 are more likely to consider social problems the responsibility of individuals rather than government' (*The Economist*, 2013b: 29). The right-wing think tanks are of course celebrating and consider the high level of 'libertarianism' among the politically active young as the 'visible tip of an iceberg of passive libertarian sentiment among the disengaged' and a sign of 'the emergence of a mass libertarian movement' (*The Economist*, 2013b: 30, quoting the Institute of Economic Affairs). This may be an overstatement but it is a sign of the hardening of views on collective values and social welfare that in turn may reinforce the popular foundation of neoliberal governmentality.

However, people's attitudes change and the future is still full of alternative possibilities! Furthermore, there are always tensions in the technologies of government. As Miller and Rose (1990: 23) suggest, although governmentality is characteristically optimistic, 'government is a congenitally failing operation'. Soon after its construction, cracks appear in the architecture of its technologies and render them unsuitable to the ideal mentalities of government. With regard to localism, one such crack is already surfacing. It stems from the assumption that liberated localities will behave responsibly and align their unified self-interests to that of government goals. Neighbourhood planning, localism's flagship policy, is a good example of such fallible assumptions, as it is yet to deliver the expected quantities of housing development irrespective of the introduction of financial incentives. Localities resist behaving homogeneously with one single aspiration, and the 'politics of place beyond place' (Massey, 2005) is proving more influential than is imagined. Tension remains high between the perceived moral and responsible individuals, communities and localities and their identification as rational economic actors whose decisions are solely motivated by the cost–benefit analysis of their self-interests; and finding ways of bridging the two remains a critical challenge for neoliberal governmentality.

Other cracks may appear from a sustained normative criticism of neoliberalism. One is based on the inherent social Darwinism of self-organisation and the constructed identity of individuals as self-reliant, resilient and skilled entrepreneurs of themselves. Given that not everybody fits this description and given the reduction of effective social security and public-sector support, inequalities may well be exacerbated and in turn challenge the liberal ideals of justice and fairness. Another is based on the anti-political tendencies of localism that invade and colonise politics by technocratic and calculative practices. This may lead to political foreclosure that, although it might help to achieve short-term consensus, in the long term may lead to social ruptures, challenging the liberal ideals of democracy and choice. Whether future technologies attempt to plaster over the cracks or reconstruct the entire architecture remains an open question.

Notes

1 Referring to David Cameron, the Conservative Prime Minister of Britain (elected in 2010).

2 However, the arguments against the state-centred conception of political authority do not imply that government has no centre; instead they suggest that 'centres of government are multiple' and depending on particular governmental rationalities, various locales are made to act as a centre (Rose and Miller, 1992: 185). For example, under the neoliberal rationality, communities and now localities are made to act as new centres of government.

3 These were based in Frieburg School and called Ordo-liberals after their close association with and writing in the journal *Ordo* (Lemke, 2010).

4 Named after the village in Switzerland where its headquarters is located.

5 Notably the Institute of Economic Affairs, founded by Fisher in 1955 in London.

References

Amin, A. (2005) Local community on trial, *Economy and Society*, 34(4): 612–633.

Baudrillard, J. (1983) *In the Shadow of Silent Majorities ... Or the End of the Social*, New York: Semiotext(e).

Beveridge, William. (1944) *Full Employment in a Free Society*, London: Allen & Unwin.

Blair, T. (1996) Battle for Britain, *The Guardian*, 29 January.

Bobbio, N. (1990) *Liberalism and Democracy*, London: Verso.

Brenner, N. and Theodore, N. (2002) Preface: From the new localism to the spaces of neo-liberalism, *Antipode*, 34(3): 341–347.

Burchell, G. (1993) Liberal government and techniques of the self, *Economy and Society*, 22(3): 267–282.

Cameron, D. (2010) *Prime Minister's Speech on Big Society*, Liverpool, 19 July.

Cameron, D. (2011) *Prime Minister's Speech on Big Society*, 14 February. Available at: www.number10.gov.uk/news/pms-speech-on-big-society (accessed 13 May 2014).

Clarke, N. and Cochrane, A. (2013) Geographies and politics of localism: The localism of the United Kingdom's coalition government, *Political Geography*, 34: 10–23.

Crick, B. (2002) Education for citizenship: The citizenship order, *Parliamentary Affairs*, 55(3): 488–504.

Cruikshank, B. (1999) *The Will to Empower: Democratic citizens and other subjects*, Ithaca, NY: Cornell University Press.

Davoudi, S. (2006) Evidence-based planning: Rhetoric and reality, *DisP*, 165(2): 14–25.

Davoudi, S. (2012a) The legacy of positivism and the emergence of interpretive tradition in spatial planning, *Regional Studies*, 46(4): 429–441.

Davoudi, S. (2012b) Resilience: A bridging concept or a dead end? *Planning Theory and Practice*, 13(2): 299–307.

Davoudi, S. (2014) Climate change, securitisation of nature and resilient urbanism, *Environment and Planning C*, 32(2): 360–375.

Davoudi, S. and Madanipour, A. (2013) Localism and neo-liberal governmentality, *Town Planning Review*, 84(5): 551–561.

Davoudi, S. and Strange, I. (eds) (2009) *Conceptions of Space and Place in Strategic Spatial Planning*, London: Routledge.

DCLG (Department of Communities and Local Government). (2011) *A Plain English Guide to the Localism Act*, London: DCLG.

Dean, M. (1999) *Governmentality: Power and rule in modern society*, London: Sage.

Deleuze, G. (1979) Introduction, in J. Donzelot, *The Policing of Families: Welfare versus the state*, London: Hutchinson.

Ely, J.W., Jr. (1992) *The Guardian of Every Other Right: A constitutional history of property rights*, New York: Oxford University Press.

Foucault, M. (1979a) *The History of Sexuality, Vol. 1: An introduction*, London: Allen Lane.

Foucault, M. (1979b) Governmentality, *Ideological Conscious*, 6: 5–21.

Foucault, M. (1982) The subject and power, in H. Dreyfus and P. Rabinow (eds), *Michel Foucault: Beyond structuralism and hermeneutics*, 2nd edn, Chicago: Chicago University Press, pp. 208–226.

Foucault, M. (1991a) On governmentality, in G. Burchell, C. Gordon and P. Miller (eds), *The Foucault Effect: Studies in governmental rationality*, Hemel Hempstead: Harvester-Wheatsheaf, pp. 87–104.

Foucault, M. (1991b) Questions of method, in G. Burchell, C. Gordon and P. Miller (eds), *The Foucault Effect: Studies in governmental rationality*, Hemel Hempstead: Harvester-Wheatsheaf, pp. 73–86.

Foucault, M. (1993) About the beginning of hermeneutics of the self (transcription of two lectures in Dartmouth, 17–24 November 1980), edited by M. Balsius, *Political Theory*, 21(2): 198–227.

Foucault, M. and Gordon, C. (1980) *Power/Knowledge: Selected interviews and other writings, 1972–1977*, New York: Harvester-Wheatsheaf.

Fraser, N. (2000) Rethinking recognition, *New Left Review*, 3 (May/June): 107–120.

Gaus, G. and Courtland, S.D. (2010) Liberalism, in Edward N. Zalta (ed.), *The Stanford Encyclopedia of Philosophy* (Spring 2011 edn). Available at: http://plato.stanford.edu/archives/spr2011/entries/liberalism (accessed 16 December 2013).

Gunderson, L.H. and Holling, C.S. (2002) *Panarchy: Understanding transformations in human and natural systems*, Washington, DC: Island Press.

Harvey, D. (2005) *A Brief History of Neo-liberalism*, Oxford: Oxford University Press.

Hayek, F.A. (1974) *The Pretence of Knowledge*, acceptance speech upon the award of the Sverige Rigsbank Prize in Economics in Memory of Alfred Nobel, Salzburg, 11 December. Available at: http://nobelprize.org/nobel_prizes/economics/laureates/1974/hayek-lecture.html (accessed 23 May 2014).

Hayek, F.A. (1976) *Law, Legislation and Liberty, Vol. 2: The mirage of social justice*, London: Routledge & Kegan Paul.

Hayek, F.A. (1978) Liberalism, in *New Studies in Philosophy, Politics, Economics and the History of Ideas*, London: Routledge & Kegan Paul.

Hayek, F.A. (1996 [1949]) *Individuals and Economic Order*, Chicago: University of Chicago Press.

Healey, P. (2007) *Urban Complexity and Spatial Strategies: Towards a relational planning for our times*, London: Routledge.

Hindess, B. (2004) Liberalism: What's in a name? In W. Larner and W. Walters (eds), *Global Governmentality: Governing international spaces*, London: Routledge, pp. 23–39.

HM Government. (2010a) *The Coalition: Our programme for government*, London: Cabinet Office.

HM Government. (2010b) *The Localism Bill*, London: Stationery Office.

HM Government. (2010c) *Decentralisation and the Localism Bill: An essential guide*, London: DCLG.

Holling, C.S. (1973) Resilience and stability of ecological systems, *Annual Review of Ecological Systems*, 4: 1–23.

Holling, C.S. (2001) Understanding the complexity of economic, ecological and social systems, *Ecosystems*, 4: 390–405.

Lemke, T. (2000) Foucault, governmentality, and critique, paper presented at the 'Rethinking Marxism Conference', University of Amherst, MA, 21–24 September.

Lemke, T. (2010) The birth of bio-politics: Michel Foucault's lecture at the College de France on neo-liberal governmentality, *Economy and Society*, 30(2): 190–207.

Maffesoli, M. (1991) The ethics of aesthetics, *Theory, Culture, Society*, 8: 7–20.

Marston, S. (2000) The social construction of scale, *Progress in Human Geography*, 24: 219–242.

Massey, D. (2005) *For Space*, London: Sage.

Milburn, A. (2004) *Active Citizenship: The ten year agenda*, speech to the Community Consultation Conference, London, 2 March.

Mill, J.S. (1963) *Collected Works of John Stuart Mill*, J.M. Robson (ed.), Toronto: University of Toronto Press.

Miller, D. (2003) *Political Philosophy: A very short introduction*, Oxford: Oxford University Press.
Miller, P. and Rose, N. (1990) Governing economic life, *Economy and Society*, 19: 1–31.
Mohan, G. and Stokke, K. (2000) Participatory development and empowerment: The dangers of localism, *Third World Quarterly*, 21(2): 247–268.
Nietzsche, F.W. (1969) *Thus Spoke Zarathustra*, London: Penguin.
Painter, J. (2010) Rethinking territory, *Antipode*, 42(5): 1090–1118.
Painter, J., Orton, A., Macleod, G., Dominelli, L. and Pande, R. (2011) *Connecting Localism and Community Empowerment: Research review and critical synthesis for the AHRC Connected Community Programme*, Project Report, Durham: Durham University, Department of Geography and School of Applied Social Sciences.
Paul, E.F., Miller, F. and Paul, J. (eds) (2007) *Liberalism: Old and new*, New York: Cambridge University Press.
Pickles, E. and Cable, V. (2010) Economy needs local remedies, not regional prescription, *The Financial Times*, 6 September.
Planning. (2013) Labour's localist, interview with Roberta Blackman-Woods, 28 June: 14–15.
Purcell, M. (2006) Urban democracy and the local trap, *Urban Studies*, 43(11): 1921–1941.
Rawls, J. (1971) *A Theory of Justice*, Cambridge, MA: Harvard University Press.
Robbins, L. (1961) *The Theory of Economic Policy in English Classical Political Economy*, London: Macmillan.
Rose, N. (1996) The death of the social? Re-figuring the territory of government, *Economy and Society*, 25(3): 327–356.
Rose, N. and Miller, P. (1992) Political power beyond the state: Problematics of government, *British Journal of Sociology*, 43(2): 173–205.
Rose, N., O'Malley, P. and Valverde, M. (2009) *Governmentality*, Legal Studies Research Paper No.09/94, Sydney Law School, University of Sydney.
RRAC (Risk & Regulation Advisory Council). (2009) *Building Resilient Communities, from Ideas to Sustainable Action*, London: RRAC.
Schedler, A. (ed.) (1997) *The End of Politics? Explorations into modern antipolitics*, Basingstoke: Macmillan.
Spencer, H. (1995 [1851]) *Social Statics*, New York: Robert Schalkenbach Foundation.
Stedman Jones, D. (2012) *Masters of the Universe: Hayek, Friedman, and the birth of neoliberal politics*, Princeton, NJ: Princeton University Press.
Stoker, G. (2004) New localism, progressive politics and democracy, *Political Quarterly*, 75 (Issue supplements 1): 117–129.
Swanstrom, T. (2008) Regional resilience: A critical examination of the ecological framework, *IURD Working Paper Series*, Berkeley, CA: Institute of Urban and Regional Development, UC Berkeley.
Thatcher, M. (1987) Interview, *Women's Own*, October, pp. 8–10.
Thatcher, M. (1993) *The Downing Street Years*, London: HarperCollins.
The Economist. (2009) The great giveaway, 31 October, pp. 39–40.
The Economist. (2012) The birth of neoliberalism, new brooms, 13 October, pp. 91–93.
The Economist. (2013a) Cities: The vacuum cleaners, in Special Report, Britain, 9 November, pp. 14–15.
The Economist. (2013b) Generation Boris, politics and the young, 1 June, pp. 29–30.

Tönnies, F. (1957 [1887]) *Community and Society [Gemeinschaft und Gesellschaft]*, Charles Loomis (trans. and ed.), New York: Harper & Row.

Walker, D. (2002) *In Praise of Centralism: A critique of new localism*, London: Catalyst Forum.

Walker, J. and Cooper, M. (2011) Genealogies of resilience: From systems ecology to the political economy of crisis adaptation, *Security Dialogue*, 42(2): 143–160.

PART II
LOCALISM AND DEMOCRACY

6

Civic Capacity, Place Governance and Progressive Localism[1]

Patsy Healey

This contribution to the discussion of the concept of 'localism' derives from my engagement with practices of local planning and neighbourhood regeneration in the UK, and my interest in place governance practices. I position the concept within the wider context of a search for more progressive approaches to place governance in complex, pluralistic and conflicted Western democracies. I centre the discussion on developing a civic capacity to promote integrated, richly informed and pluralistic conceptions of place qualities and connectivities, as these are evolving into the future. This requires recognition of the often deep conflicts that divide communities over current issues and future pathways, and the multi-scalar nature of many of the issues that need to be addressed. The challenge of place governance provides one of the key arenas within which the qualities of democratic systems are being tested at the present time. In this context, I discuss the hopes and dangers of the 'localist' agenda, and identify, amid the rhetorics and ideological abstractions, what the more progressive directions in this agenda might be, and how these translate into qualities to cultivate in the micro-practices through which place governance is actually done, at all kinds of levels and in all kinds of arenas.

The localist agenda arises in the UK, and England in particular, because of its particular history of centralised government. The arguments for greater decentralisation have been proceeding vigorously in recent decades, entwined with other reforming strands, focused on reducing heavy-handed bureaucratic regulation and concentrating the performance of public agencies on 'results', the mantra of the 'new public management'. But these strands are often in conflict with each other. Both nationally defined bureaucratic rules and centrally devised performance criteria distract practical action from attention to local particulars. Formal planning systems struggle to deliver to central demands and local considerations, leading to acute difficulties not only in England, but in countries such as Norway (Sager, 2012). So is there a different way to think about place governance that can move beyond placing the arenas of planning systems in the middle of a dualistic struggle between central control and local autonomy? Before addressing this question, I introduce the concept of place governance, and its relation to what I have elsewhere called 'the planning project' (Healey, 2010).

Place governance and the planning field

The planning 'field of endeavour' is called by all kinds of names – urban and regional planning, town planning, spatial planning, territorial planning, urbanism. For many, it is recognised by its institutional practices – the making of formal plans and the exercise of planning regulation under the aegis of a 'planning system', and/or by the work of people trained as planners. In this context, the 'localist' agenda is about which level of government and which social groups get to define the content of plans and the exercise of regulations. But in my view, we need to understand what the 'planning project' is about in a broader way. In my understanding, the focus of the planning idea is on places and their qualities. It is infused with the concern to shape place qualities to promote better trajectories than might otherwise occur. It involves the efforts of many people, not just those trained as 'planners'. And it can take place in many different arenas, not just in planning offices and planning committees. In this conception of the planning project, planning activity is located as part of the governance activity of a political community, meaning collective endeavours to manage spheres of activity in ways that would not otherwise occur if left to individual initiative. Formal planning systems provide arenas and resources for place governance, but do not encompass all of such governance activity. Nor do such systems always cultivate the values that the 'planning project' has promoted. Understood in this way, the idea of planning promotes a particular way of realising place governance.

Many people and many processes are involved in producing place qualities. These qualities are both material, in terms of the conjunction of built and natural forms into landscapes through which people and other life forms move as we go about in our lives. They are also mental constructs, 'imaginaries', created as we infuse particular places and their qualities with meaning and memory. In this way, we come to recognise places and realise why we care about them. The planning project contributes to these co-related processes of material and mental production through promoting qualities that a polity – a public, a political community, or a collective body of some sort – consider to be 'good', or at least better than what would otherwise occur.[2]

But what is 'good' about place qualities is inherently contestable, unless we assume that we all have the same meanings and memories, or are content to let someone else impose these on us. It is clear that, in the twenty-first century, political communities across the world make no such assumptions and are in no way content with imposition. Yet, there is deep concern about the qualities of places – as living environments and reservoirs of our memories and as resources for our futures. People are concerned about how such qualities can be improved and sustained for future generations. Conflicts

Table 6.1 Values promoted by the planning project

- An orientation to the future and a belief that action now can shape future potentialities.
- An emphasis on liveability and sustainability for the many, not the few.
- An emphasis on interdependencies and interconnectivities between one phenomenon and another, across time and space.
- An emphasis on expanding the knowledgeability of public action and the 'intelligence' of a polity.
- A commitment to open, transparent government processes, of reasoning in and about the public realm.

Source: Healey, 2010: 19.

over place qualities are therefore likely to be intense but yet unpredictable in focus and in how they play out. Every recognised 'place' has its own particular situation and its own accumulation of material relations and value-giving social processes. This makes place governance a particularly complex area of public policy.

In this context, a 'localist' agenda could be about ways in which places get 'recognised' and their 'qualities', strengths and threats appreciated and argued about, so that collective place-shaping in search of better futures can proceed intelligently and sensitively within this complexity. These ways of governance are as much about who gets involved and whose imaginaries get to count as they are about the processes involved. They are inherently, and intensely, political. This implies that those involved need to focus attention on situated particulars. Standardised prescriptions crowd out the necessary work of drawing together local particularities with wider knowledge and considerations. Collective place-shaping in search of better futures has to proceed with the grain of the contingencies of particular 'comings together' in time in specific locales. Yet this does not mean that such work should proceed in local bubbles, isolated from the rest of the world. There are very few places that are not threaded by all kinds of connections to other worlds, which provide resources as well as threats. A 'localist' agenda demands 'rights' to protection from the threats that may emanate from other worlds. But it needs to be accompanied by responsibilities too. The planning project, in its progressive form, has a clear message about these responsibilities. Place governance with a 'planning orientation' carries a particular set of values of its own (Healey, 2010; Rydin, 2011). My own attempt to summarise these is provided in Table 6.1.

So the planning project is not just about *any* place-focused collective action, but about collective place-shaping work with a particular emphasis or orientation. Its concern with the future means careful thought about how place qualities and relations evolve through time. Consideration of liveability and sustainability demands an integrated view of how lives are led in relation to the wider dynamics of our planetary environment and all the other species that co-habit this environment with us. This requires a multi-dimensional and multi-scalar perspective, connecting ecological relations, social relations and economic ones. It requires attention to multiple voices and perspectives, not just those of the most powerful or the loudest, to the exclusion of the many others. It involves a non-dualistic understanding of issues (not either/or but both/and) (Ansell, 2011; Hillier, 2011), and needs to develop a capacity for synthetic integration of multiple strands of ideas and analysis (Campbell, 2012; Davoudi and Pendlebury, 2010).

Much of formal planning practice in England these days does not live up to such demands (Allmendinger, 2011; Tewdwr-Jones, 2012). All too often we hear stories from elsewhere of how such a governance ambition has failed (Flyvbjerg, 1998; Meyerson and Banfield, 1955; Moore Milroy, 2009). Yet, if we were to look carefully at place governance stories in the UK today, I think we would find a good number where people, and not only those trained as planners, are struggling to realise such a way of shaping emergent place qualities in their areas. We would also find many people arguing that what has inhibited the emergence of a more effective place governance capacity has been the hyper-centralism of the English state. Somehow, our national governments over recent years have spoken of 'devolution' and 'localism', but keep acting in ways that continue to centralise.

From distant political control towers, the 'grasstops', as Briggs (2008) labels them, intelligence about what is happening on the 'ground' below may be limited, and the only 'place' really known about is the landscape of a control tower's own daily life-world. To those who challenge such central command, a heavy dose of 'localism' seems to be a good strategy. This could promote more informed understanding of place qualities and more sensitive ways of enhancing qualities that promote liveability and sustainability into the future. It could encourage more awareness of the multiplicity of 'stakes' that those near and far may have in a place and its qualities. It could promote more integrated ways of doing governance work in a locality, so that interdependencies and interconnectivities are better understood, resulting in more appropriate ideas about place qualities worth striving for and how to go about such efforts (Figure 6.1). But does a 'localist' momentum in governance processes always achieve this? What harm might one community do to other people and places and to succeeding generations if left completely unfettered of any demand for responsibility to wider publics? What kind of *governance capacity* should be encouraged to promote a localist agenda that accepted such wider responsibilities?

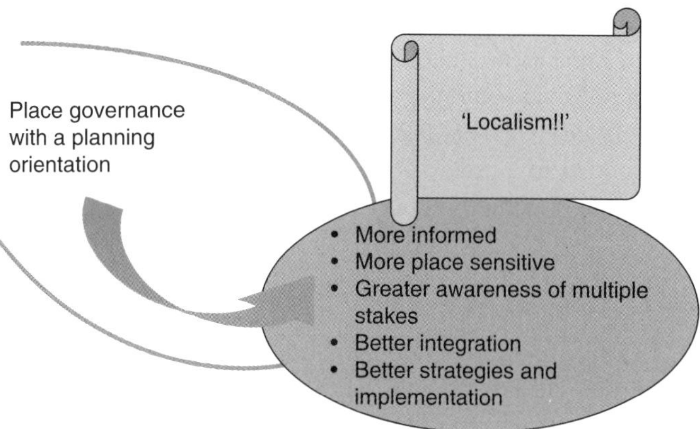

Figure 6.1 The planning project and 'localism'

Governance capacity and a localist agenda

The significance of capacities for collective action within political communities has been attracting much attention in recent years, as people come to recognise that how governance works has an impact not just on the delivery of specific policy programmes, but on people's quality of life, on the future of natural environments and on the health of economic relations. The analysis of politics, policy-making and governance has moved on from assessments of voting behaviour, party institutions, policy statements and the activity of politicians to the wider institutional nexuses through which collective action is defined and performed, both within the formal systems of government and in the wider governance environment (Hajer and Wagenaar, 2003; Hoppe, 2010; Peters, 1999). This allows a shift from a focus on formal administrative entities to the complex relations through which the nexus of formal public bodies and informal groups and networks come to bring a particular place and its qualities to policy attention – that is, to a focus on governance practices. This potential decoupling of administrative jurisdiction and place governance attention, for example through recognising 'sub-regions' or 'neighbourhoods', or groups of villages, has all kinds of advantages in our present context where economic and social geographies are no longer, if ever they were, co-terminous with our administrative units.

The resultant governance landscape is now often referred to by the concept of 'democratic network governance' (Sorensen and Torfing, 2007). But yet such a landscape creates potential dangers, if political communities are not strong enough to exercise adequate scrutiny over place governance activities or able to exercise multiple forms of accountability (Sirianni, 2009). Informal groupings of stakeholders may not be able to wield enough power to bring together the people, the ideas, the resources and the regulatory power to back up the strategies and projects they develop. This has led to an interest in governance 'capacity' – the capacity to define and deliver qualities deemed collectively important by a political community.[3]

So what kinds of governance capacity is it important to encourage if a localist rhetoric is to be grounded in a progressive governance practice and if the political and moral hazards of some practices of 'localism' are to be held in check? Some authorities have been promoting the idea of 'good governance', seeking universal principles to help governments, especially in the emerging economies.[4] But the danger here is that these become formulaic, rather than encouraging people to think about the issues they should address and the questions they should ask as they design and practise the work of place governance in specific contexts. The quality of governance lies in its situated practices, not its formal principles.

Others have been exploring the experiences of particular cities and localities, seeking to assess their 'civic capacity' to create governance forms and practices that release the energy of all kinds of initiatives, but which yet keep a watchful eye to limit the damaging impacts of one initiative on another, or the harmful social, environmental and economic consequences of the way initiatives build up through time. Especially interesting are those cases where the ambition and/or the outcome has been both an improvement in material place qualities, and a significant transformation in the culture and practices of the polity as a whole, not just of formal government and public-sector agencies. Such studies provide empirical support for analyses of the significance of 'evolutionary learning' (Ansell, 2011). These transformations involve more than a 'culture-change'. They are expressed in real shifts in formal organisation, in resource allocation, in political leadership, in the focus of policy attention and in the relation between citizens, businesses and their political institutions. In other words, they change structures, or, in Ansell's terms, the 'scaffolding' of social formations.

To see what such transformation looks like, we now have interesting narratives of experiences in various parts of the world that provide insights into what can be achieved and how. The Vancouver case, from Canada, is by now well known in the planning field for the way politicians, planners and neighbourhood residents, working together, learned to use a practice of 'neighbourhood design guidelines' to shape how the physical form of the city has evolved over the past 30 years. This has allowed for very substantial growth, through increasing densities while promoting a mix of activities and social groups within neighbourhoods, and enhancing the environmental sustainability of the city overall (Punter, 2003; Sandercock, 2005).

A similar story from Portland, Oregon was one of the inspirations behind the development of neighbourhood empowerment in Seattle on the US West Coast in the past two decades. Here all kinds of citizen groups, non-governmental organisations and some business groups came up with projects that offered volunteer labour and some sponsorship, which the City's Department of Neighbourhoods then match-funded with City resources. The result has been widespread investment in neighbourhood place qualities, through the provision of small parks and playspaces, landscape maintenance, all kinds of civic art and the provision of space for growing food.[5] The City had some problems linking this activity to the production of a citywide spatial plan, needed because of the introduction by Washington State of an 'urban growth boundary' (in the UK, we would call this a form of 'green belt'). But eventually, it was realised that such a plan had to be 'grown' through engagement with the various institutions that had emerged through the neighbourhood initiatives. Through much commitment and hard learning, a civic capacity has been developing in Seattle that combines citizen (and business) energy with the overview and facilitating work of City Council politicians and officials. Concern for social justice, economic opportunity and environmental sustainability are wrapped into this evolving work. These substantive concerns are closely linked to a broad project of building political community that understands the need for attention to its overall quality, while allowing its parts to experiment and explore ways of improving place qualities and the conditions of daily life (Sirianni, 2009: ch. 3).

Another example from Brazil has now become well known internationally. In Porto Alegre, citizen and workers' movements had long protested about the way in which conditions in poor neighbourhoods of the city had been neglected, while a nexus of elite politicians and property development interests promoted large investments in the city centre. Pushed along by political changes at national level as democracy became established as a political system in the past 25 years, emerging city leaders with strong political links to neighbourhood activism evolved a system for an inclusive, 'participatory' way of thinking about how the city's budget should be shaped and spent. What is interesting about what they invented is not just that large numbers of citizens did get involved in this budget-setting process. It was also designed organisationally in a flexible way, so that new voices could come in, and new neighbourhood groups could get involved, limiting the 'capture' of the process by people who become 'the usual suspects' (Abers, 1998; Baiocchi, 2003; Souza, 2001).

Cases such as these are richly inspiring, but it is important to delve into their details. Each is deeply embedded in a particular history and landscape of opportunity. City councils in all three cases had considerable legal and financial autonomy. They already had a history of struggles between citizens and their governments that led most parties to want to move on to something both more constructive as well as more sustainable and just. English governance landscapes are certainly very different. But yet some general lessons from these efforts in transforming governance practices and building new civic capacities can be learned.

First, they do not involve displacement of formal government. Sirianni (2009), in discussing the Seattle experience, underlines the importance of the co-evolution of governance capacities and practices among all sections of the political community, including formal government. What is needed is reasonable autonomy from external direction for such a political community, to enable 'horizontal' rather than 'vertical' capacity-building over time. Another important practice involves the reduction of sharp divides between public and private spheres, while building the capacity for monitoring of accountability and legitimacy within the political community as a whole.

Second, as Sirianni argues, the key to this capacity-building are the slow steps in creating trust across former divides, while not losing the critical but often creative 'grit' of all the conflict and contention that arises over so many issues about what should happen and where, which are the 'stuff' of local politics and of neighbourhood and spatial planning initiatives. In this way, 'public interest' principles are evolved and nurtured locally, rather than being imposed by external authorities. Such principles become a kind of 'common pool resource' (Ostrom, 1990).

Third, such capacity-building work needs to combine technical expertise, often of various kinds, with the experiential and craft knowledge of the many different people who 'inhabit' the place in question in one way or another. This has long been a key concern in the planning and environmental fields. The challenge is to develop a broadly based and shared 'intelligence' about issues and the complexities of sorting out and implementing what needs collective attention *across* a political community.

Fourth, some people and groups within a political community need to possess or develop the art of making relations across old divides – whether within formal government, between and among various agencies, between and among businesses and citizens, and between groups that share neighbourhood space but are fearful or hostile to each other. This skill involves working at boundary-crossing and boundary-spanning, creating a form of 'bridging capital' (Gilchrist, 2009). This may be just about connecting networks and groups to each other, but it is also about when to create a new node (forum, arena) in such networks, and when to turn such nodes into formal institutions. Such skill in network-building and attention to institutional design lies at the heart of any realisation of 'democratic network governance'.

Finally, the narratives of cases such as these demonstrate clearly that institutional space and time needs to be available to encourage experimentation and learning. Transformative change, especially in the culture of a polity, takes time as well as commitment and resources. There are no quick fixes or best-practice formulae that can produce these changes. They come about through

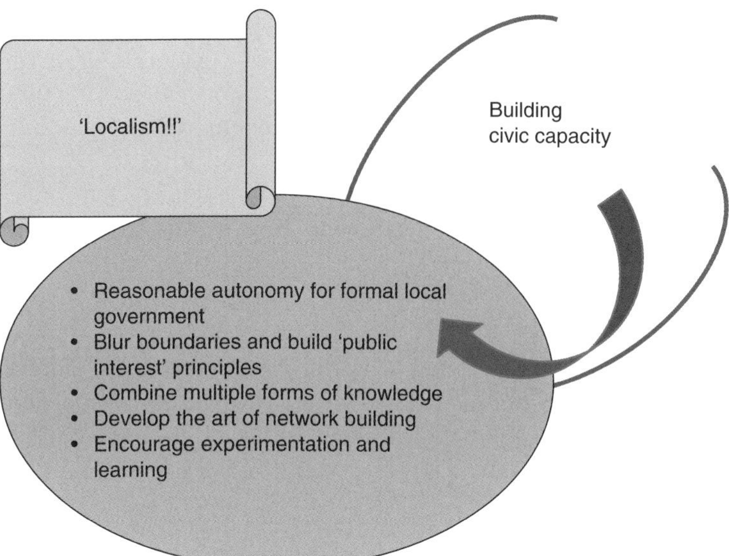

Figure 6.2 Building local governance capacity

building communities of practice and appreciative publics around the new governance practices. This involves hard institutional work. As recent English experience shows, governance capacities and competences are easy to undermine but difficult to build.

Building civic capacity in the ways outlined above meshes well with the promotion of place qualities in a 'planning way'. How far does a 'localist' agenda advance the building of this capacity? The cases were all in localities where local administrations had considerable autonomy. Within this context, they show the way politicians, agency staff and citizens took command of their city council, and moulded it in new ways. They did not replicate 'hierarchical thinking', nor were they continually oppressed by demands and rules imposed by higher tiers of government, although they were constrained by formal laws of the wider polities within which they were located. This experience underlines that a real localism, which decentralises resources and powers both to lower levels of government and to civil society initiatives (see Moulaert *et al.*, 2010), could be a great help in advancing the building of civic capacity for attention to place qualities, their liveability and sustainability (see Figure 6.2). At a local level, it is easier to see how strands of governance activity interrelate, and to identify positive synergies and counterproductive actions.

But such decentralisation does not mean passing on the work of formal government wholesale to civil society and businesses. Instead, what evolved in the cases cited was a blurring of old boundaries between the spheres of the state, economy and civil society, stronger flows of knowledge and ideas for initiatives between grass roots and Briggs's 'grasstops', and more coordinated working between the sections of formal government. The cases demonstrate democratic, multi-dimensional and multi-scalar 'network governance' in action, focused on place qualities. I try to capture what this implies for a 'localist' agenda in Figure 6.2.

Through these cases and others like them runs a key ambition to reconfigure the relationship between formal government – the worlds of formal law and politics, and of public administration and the associations and relations of civil society. There is of course a long history of the way formal government interlocks with economic activity, whether in the corporatist arrangements of some Western European states, or in the 'growth machines' familiar from US urban government. But many have argued that the way democratic practices evolved in the twentieth century has distanced citizens from formal government. Instead, an array of pressure groups and policy networks has grown up, which has privileged access to shaping government agendas. This, argues Skocpol (2003), has created a kind of 'diminished democracy'. Others talk anxiously of a 'democratic deficit' (Stoker, 2006). The concern here is not that there is no active civil society. Quite the opposite, in the UK at least. The problem is that citizens feel deeply distrustful and distanced from the arenas and processes of formal government and politics. In this context, a part of the 'localist' movement is infused with the mission of overcoming this deficit, and enriching the democratic experience. Cases such as those I have mentioned provide inspiring stories of how this could happen. But perhaps we should look more closely at what this enriching could involve. There are forms of 'localism' that could lead in quite different directions.

'Re-enchanting democracy' through forms of 'network governance'[6]

The search for ways of re-working democratic practices to overcome the distances, deficits and dysfunctions that so many have commented on has taken several directions, each with a different 'take' on what 'localism' could mean. I comment below on three 'caricatures' of such directions.

For the neo-liberals/neo-cons, the ideal is to cut down the size of the state, whether at national or local level. The ambition is to leave the field for market processes and civil society initiative. But, as long experience shows, markets need ground rules and a degree of stability, while citizens are very busy living other dimensions of their lives and have limited time to build up skills and knowledge in governance processes. Further, leaving the field to the economic and socio-politically energetic and powerful can have very regressive consequences – from oppression and exclusion to incompetence and ignorance. As

Sirianni argues forcefully, businesses and citizens need formal government to undertake a range of governance tasks that are better done by 'specialists' and by managers/administrators focused on advancing the well-being of a polity as a whole. It is not so much the degree of government that has been the problem all these years in the UK, but the *way* it has been done, and the way the various parts have pursued their separate agendas and practices. It is not regulation and bureaucracy as phenomena that should concern us, but the quality of our democratic practices. The challenge instead is to work out what kinds of regulation and what kinds of bureaucracy would work better, and how to combine both with all kinds of civic enabling work.

Similar arguments apply to the idea that individual locales, the small 'territories' celebrated by communitarians, should be allowed to operate autonomously. The assumption of this approach is that such territories can be treated as bounded, enclosed 'systems', which can, in separate bubbles, seal themselves from the influence of other systems, whether neighbouring places and territories or systems operating at quite different scales. But no place or social group is completely isolated from the rest of us. Just as rivers rise in mountains and flood valleys far away, so the tentacles of environmental, socio-cultural and economic sets of relations of all kinds may reach out into the fine-grain relations that constitute the lived reality of faraway places. This not only means that 'local communities' have to pay some attention to the outside world and need this outside world to acknowledge their rights to voice in matters that affect them. So too do they have responsibilities to these outside worlds and especially the wider polities of which they are a part. Without some encouragement to recognise responsibilities as well as rights, localised communitarianism can end up deeply regressive.

Between these two extremes, in the mid-twentieth century, the state-centred model focused on welfare delivery and support for a mixed economy evolved in various ways in Western democracies, with its hierarchies, bureaucracies and policy communities clustered around particular services. These days, many analysts look into the decomposing remains of these old welfare states and talk of fragmented government, or of 'voids' (Hajer, 2003). But what others see emerging in this 'in-between' space is a re-working of our welfare states through evolving new modes of governance, which recognise the multiplicity of ways that link citizens, business and state in the development of what become policy agendas, programmes and projects. Democracy, in this conception, is built through collective experiences of 'doing', 'deliberating', 'learning' and 'reflecting'. This does not mean that the machinery of 'representative democracy' is abandoned. It is merely recognised as an absolutely necessary but insufficient element of democratic polities that have to respond to the plurality of lives and values of contemporary political communities, and the complexity of the issues we need to face collectively. There are vigorous

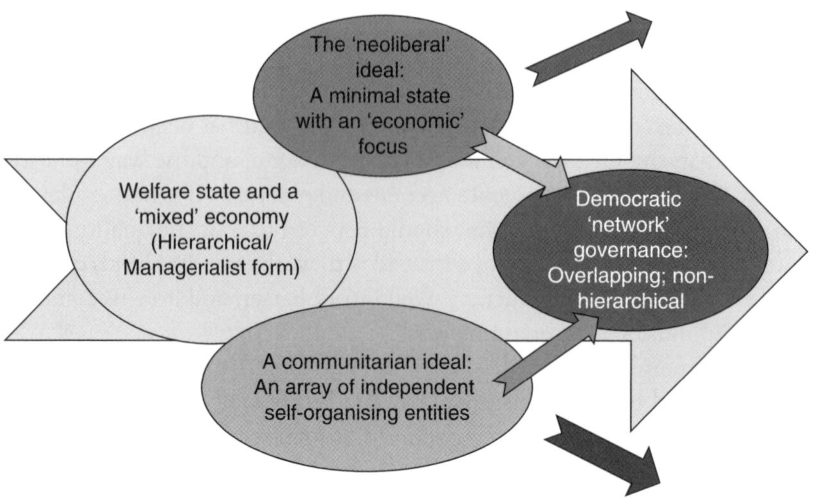

Figure 6.3 Alternative governance forms

discussions about what this 'democratic network governance' involves, how its institutional forms might develop and how to make it appropriately accountable to the polities within which such forms are emerging (Moulaert *et al.*, 2010; Sorensen and Torfing, 2007). Much depends on the way networks are interconnected and the development of nodal arenas in which wider 'wholes' get to be recognised and shaped in ways that give position and place to the many 'parts' of a polity and its concerns. But such democratic network governance seems to hold the potential to combine a democratic community sensitive to its diverse parts, while aware of the potentially several wider worlds in which the parts are located (see Figure 6.3).

Although it sometimes seems in England as if we are swaying unsteadily between the extremes of 'market liberalism' and 'idealised communitarianism', it is perhaps more appropriate to think of ourselves as in a period of experimentation, sometimes initially with a lot of public resources available and now with much less. Despite the often crude rhetoric, the experiments are not about reducing the state or about cutting out oppressive upper levels of formal government. They are about the institutional re-design of governance activity, and in particular, of the institutional sites, forms and practices of formal government. Within these experiments, some key elements of a progressive form of localism can be discerned (see Figure 6.4).

But the current experimentation with governance design should not be reduced to models. Models give us general ideas about potentials and dangers. They are useful thinking tools. But they do not and should not be used to provide a suite of possible replicable organisational forms. This would crowd out innovation. Innovators and experimenters are better helped by suggestions

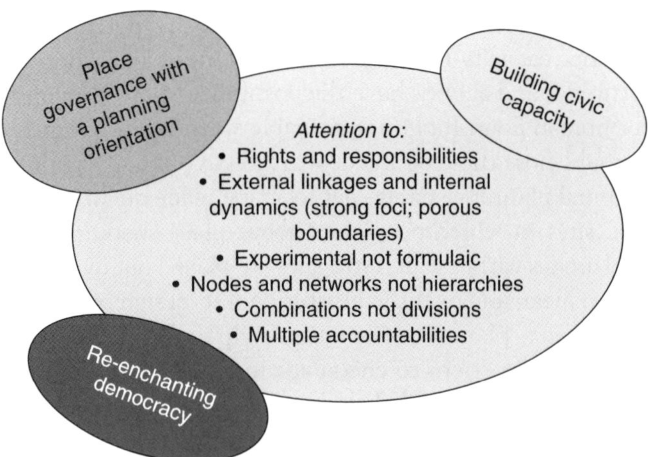

Figure 6.4 Towards a progressive 'localism'

about 'probes' or 'sensors' with which to explore and evaluate the ideas and practices they come up with in the flow of their experimenting, in the flow of action. Too strong an emphasis on 'models' inhibits imaginative learning ('does this new practice fit?'). Instead, it would be helpful to cultivate a political culture that engages in what Ansell (2011) calls 'evolutionary learning'. Probing inquiry cultivates open-minded exploration ('what might evolve from this action? What impacts might it have, where, when and how?') (Lindblom, 1990). In the final section of this chapter, I build on Figure 6.4 and provide some suggestions as to useful probing questions.

But how can we tell, as these experiments unfold, what may have progressive potential, and what to resist as leading to more regressive outcomes than might otherwise be achieved? Not all moves towards 'democratic network governance' are progressive, as many people concerned with issues of accountability and self-selecting partnerships have pointed out. I consider this first through a return to the values, knowledge and skills associated with a 'planning orientation', and then consider the practices that may characterise a 'progressive localism'.

The contribution of a 'planning orientation'

Through considering the 'planning project', I have tried to identify some reasons why enhancing the capacity of local political communities concerned with the qualities of the places of value to them to develop more locally relevant strategies, programmes and projects is an important ambition. I have reinforced this by considering important dimensions of such capacities and their relation to a much wider project of enriching our apparently decaying democratic polities. But I underlined that, in exploring the potential for enhanced local governance capacity-building, it is important to keep continuously in focus what attitudes and actions have the possibility of creating more progressive futures for human flourishing in sustainable ways, and what moral and political hazards could close these off in deeply regressive ways. The practices through which formal planning systems get to shape place qualities, and the other institutional sites in which people set about place-shaping work, provide key forums and arenas within which struggles are played out over what 'localist' initiatives get to mean and over the institutional re-design of governance arrangements. How can a 'planning orientation' help to distinguish what seem to be more progressive directions to encourage in a particular situation from those ideas and options that seem likely to be more regressive?

It is often said that the role of planners has been reduced to that of facilitator, or stage-setter, for debates about the relative merits of future possibilities and strategies. What is progressive or regressive is then the product of these debates. This is not an unimportant role, especially where a political community starts on a journey with little idea of what is at stake and what actions might have priority. Or an activity is already mired in conflict and conflicting positions about some issues so that taking any action at all is difficult to do. But the planning project as I have outlined it above is not just about assisting the emergence of 'problem-puzzling' practices (Ansell, 2011; Hoppe, 2010) and enabling 'probing' inquiry (Lindblom, 1990). It is also about understanding the dimensions of place qualities and how these relate to people, businesses and environmental relations in the flow of daily, yearly and intergenerational life. And it has a strong normative agenda too. The planning project demands attention to the multiple dimensions and scales through which we live our lives. It is for this reason that too strong a focus on economic growth without attention to the other dimensions of existence is resisted by many. A place-focus should recognise the complex interactions between economic, social, cultural and environmental relations as these play out in a particular place. It also requires consideration of the different times and scales of the various relations in play. It is the package of impacts that a strategy or development project might set in motion that needs attention, if regressive impacts that may evolve in the future, in the place in question or elsewhere, are to be guarded against, whether these be danger from floods, or traffic congestion, or destruction of valued heritage, or the many injustices produced by increasing social inequalities. It is the planning knowledge of interdependencies and interconnectivities that becomes of increasing importance.

This implies that those with skills in place governance with a planning orientation have an important substantive contribution to make, as well as providing skills in facilitating making network connections. This contribution centres on the expert understanding of the relational dynamics through which specific place qualities are evolving. The expertise involved is not just analytical. It also links to the capacity to connect issues together, and help political communities select which issues and actions are of greatest significance. This demands a synthetic imagination and an integrative skill. Such a capacity has been rather neglected in planning education and theory in recent years (Bertolini, 2010; Campbell, 2012; Davoudi and Pendlebury, 2010), but there are good exemplars in practice, both in local planning authorities and in the consultancy sector. To these areas of expertise, those experts in place governance with a planning orientation also know a good deal about the specifics of the particular institutional context in which planning work is done – the laws, regulations, tools, techniques and resources available and how they can be used. To do this work in a transparent way, it is important to develop the practice of giving explanations – not just of how a formal regulation works, but why it has evolved and what values it carries. In this way, other parties can get a better understanding of why their future imaginations about places they care about may need to be constrained by the regulations created by previous generations to safeguard or promote particular values (such as providing people with adequate housing and safeguarding wildlife havens) and limit harmful impacts (such as pollution, flooding, traffic hazards, etc.).

While integrative and synthetic capability and careful reasoning need more attention, the planning field is rich in case narratives of the 'dos and don'ts' of attempts to address, manage and move on from and through the complex place-focused conflicts that regularly erupt in place governance processes. These narratives highlight the importance of attention to governance micro-practices, replete as they are with 'devils' and 'details'. They also often show how outcomes and processes are inter-related. The accounts on which the cases cited earlier are based provide good examples of such narratives.

In contrast to abstract generalisations and 'best-practice' formulae and cameos, well-told case narratives provide valuable learning resources. They show how those involved navigated their way through challenge after challenge in an evolving landscape of political concern and governance capacity. And there are some great narratives around (several have been cited in this chapter). The key message of such accounts is that place governance needs to be understood as an evolving lived practice, in which inserting a progressive orientation, informed by many forms of knowledge including that of planners, needs continual attention. It is here that the probing questions suggested below could come in handy.

Towards a progressive localism with a 'planning orientation'

In contemporary public policy work, doing 'evaluations' has become a major area of technical work. But in the flow of shaping policies and programmes – the work of problem-puzzling, matching problems and solutions and turning

Table 6.2 Towards more progressive place-focused governance

Qualities to foster	*Qualities to resist*
Recognition of a shared, but diverse and often conflictual political community, in which distributional fairness matters	Dualistic conflict Factional stereotypes
Recognition and respect for multiple identities and ways of life, as well as commonalities	Divisions into exclusive groups and singular identities
Respect for different arguments, positions, feelings, etc. ('adversaries' not 'enemies')	Competitive persuasion Struggles between 'enemies' Destructively violent conflict
A practice of 'intelligent', multi-sided discussion of issues – learning and reasoning 'in public'	Polarised extremes Fixed positions and interests
Recognition of the complex relations in which 'parts' are connected to wider 'wholes' in open, often diffuse, ways	Concepts of closed, nested hierarchies Isolated 'bubble' communities
Critical respect for the role of formal government, while recognising the complexity of interactions between the spheres of state and society	'Us' vs. 'Them' polarities Sharp divisions between 'public' and 'private' spheres
Respect for those who do formal government work and perform 'public services'	Continual negative critique (of incompetent and unresponsive bureaucrats or public service staff)
Rich, responsive and respectful interactions between all levels and sectors of formal government	Hierarchical paternalism and struggles over 'organisational turf'

agreed solutions into practical outcomes – such formal assessments are only episodes in what are complex social interactions. They may provide points of reference and stimulate learning about what to encourage and what to avoid, but those actively involved in the process of doing place governance work make use of all kinds of knowledge, experience and insights as they work out what to do in specific situations.[7] Probing questions act as a kind of background 'alerting system' to keep in mind in the ongoing flow of practical action. In Table 6.2,[8] I suggest some such questions. I have organised them as qualities to foster and to resist, rather than directly as 'questions'. Turning them into questions 'in the flow of action', the first might become: 'Hang on! Are we remembering just how diverse we all are, and what conflicts might break out if we try to go ahead like this?'; or 'Watch out: here we go again, setting things up along these old battle lines!' Researchers and programme evaluators in their turn could try using the probes more systematically to explore a particular practice, proposal or project, to assess whether an initiative such as the pursuit of 'localism' was delivering on its progressive potential.

Such probing questions should allow more nuanced and effective distinctions to be made as the 'localist' agenda evolves in countries such as England. They take us beyond the kind of dualistic oppositions into which critique can so easily fall. They do not set citizens against formal government, innovative entrepreneurs against officialdom, small agencies against big corporations, the countryside against urban landscapes, economic issues against social and economic ones, although such fractures and conflicts may be roiling around in a particular political community. They demand instead a careful and respectful look at specific situations, at what is at stake and who the stakeholders are. They encourage careful learning about the fine-grain dynamics through which the qualities of particular places are evolving, and how these interconnect with wider systems. The 'probes' can be used in any institutional context, whether the micro-politics of shaping legislation, of realising a complex urban project, or of getting a rural land management strategy into the routines of farmers and water-system managers, or of administering necessary regulations about how people can use and develop their land and buildings. They do not imply reaching for and arriving at some kind of smooth enduring consensus about places and their qualities. Any effective place-focused polity needs plenty of 'grit' and argument about what issues are important to it,[9] to maintain attention to the multiplicity of webs of relations in play that weave within, around and across it. Yet some way of agreeing on what key actions to take at particular times and places is necessary governance work. As John Forester argues persistently (Forester, 2009), political communities, and people locked in conflict over an issue, do not have to agree on everything to be able to agree on some concrete actions now.

Some people will worry that the above hypotheses do not specify what outcomes to reach for. Should there not be a parallel localist agenda of specific material actions by which a progressive form of localism might distinguish itself? A progressive localism might show itself perhaps by an emphasis on providing more social housing integrated into well-designed neighbourhoods, or by the way a public transport network is designed and managed, or by multi-dimensional and integrated resource management practices aimed at reducing environmental stress, or a capacity to connect job creation and infrastructure provision to support for particular business sectors, or an emphasis on promoting environments that cultivate healthy and environmentally sustainable lifestyles. But a progressive localism has to recognise that what is a progressive trajectory in one place will not necessarily be so in another, and the adoption of well-publicised agendas from elsewhere without careful probing can lead to all kinds of regressive consequences. Local polities can learn from each other, but need to handle all 'solutions' proffered with care, to make sure that these address real problems that they experience, in ways that can work with the potentials and possibilities in their own situation. To repeat what should by now be well established in the planning literature, the process of governance proceeds interactively with the development of the content of governance programmes. Process and content co-evolve and co-produce each other. A progressive localism may therefore best be identified through the way people value and experience the place qualities of their daily life-worlds and the practices of the governance through which what is seen as collectively important is developed, delivered and maintained.

In England at present, many different hopes and fears are accumulating around 'localism' as this political idea moves into legislative form. The progressive opportunity is to enable the emergence of more clearly focused and integrated attention to places and their qualities, along with encouragement for more experimentation in governance forms. But it is also important to resist naive enthusiasm for local autonomy and initiative, and even more so for the idea that somehow our democracies can be enhanced by diminishing government.

As many studies show, experimentation with new forms of democratic engagement underlines the roles that formal government plays – in shaping, networking, providing resources and expertise, and crafting and shifting the regulatory background to both business and civil society initiative. Further, decentralisation initiatives that allow localities to cut themselves off from responsibilities to the wider polities of which they are a part need to be resisted. This is not just a matter of allowing some redistributive element into the way taxpayers' money flows across England and the UK. It means that some places have to accept responsibilities to accommodate development and infrastructure that is needed in the wider region or for the nation, and/or to recognise their role in safeguarding valuable assets for wider publics. This does not mean that wider polities should just impose their demands on resistant 'parts'. It means accepting and promoting vigorous multi-sided and multi-party debates 'across the scales' about these important issues before, during and after programmes, policies and projects are proposed. Institutionally, it is important to work out where, when and how such discussions and debates will move from broad public forums, to more specific institutional arenas as ways forward get to be resolved (Bryson and Crosby, 1992). Generally, and not just in the English political community, the challenge for those seeking to realise progressive values through planning work is to enhance the 'intelligence' of polities, as they deal with reconfiguring place-focused governance, and to revise and expand the repertoire through which place governance and the promotion of place qualities are enacted. In this way, there is the potential to move towards governance practices that embody a more people-centred, daily-life awareness of what makes for place quality for the multiple many of a political community.

Notes

1 This chapter is developed from a lecture given at UCL, London, on 6 October 2011 (RTPI Lichfield Memorial Lecture).
2 See Rhodes (1997) for the concept of 'political community' and Dewey (1991 [1927]) for the concept of 'publics'.
3 See Briggs (2008), Sirianni (2009), Stone (2001) on 'civic capacity' and Cars *et al.* (2002), Innes and Booher (2003), Healey (2006), Filion and Sanderson (2011), Barry (2012) for work on 'institutional capacity-building'.
4 Both the World Bank and UN-Habitat have promoted conceptions of 'good governance'.
5 Several cities have considered the provision of small parks and public spaces across a city as a key investment, with inspiration from programmes in places such as Barcelona, and in cities in Brazil and Turkey.
6 These ideas are taken from Healey (2012).
7 See John Forester's stream of research giving voice to how planners and others do their work.
8 This comes from Healey (2012). Here I have added an eighth quality – a place-focused 'probe'.
9 Here I make reference to the debates about agonism.

References

Abers, R. (1998) Learning democratic practice: Distributing government resources through popular participation in Porto Alegre, Brazil, in M. Douglass and J. Friedmann (eds), *Cities for Citizens*, London: Wiley, pp. 39–66.

Allmendinger, P. (2011) *New Labour and Planning: From new right to new left*, Abingdon: Taylor & Francis/Routledge.

Ansell, C.K. (2011) *Pragmatist Democracy: Evolutionary learning as public philosophy*, Oxford: Oxford University Press.

Baiocchi, G. (2003) Participation, activism and politics: The Porto Alegre experiment, in A. Fung and E.O. Wright (eds), *Deepening Democracy: Institutional innovation and empowered participatory governance*, London: Verso, pp. 45–76.

Barry, J. (2012) Indigenous-state planning as inter-institutional capacity development: The evolution of 'government to government' relations in Coastal British Columbia, *Planning Theory and Practice*, 13(2): 213–231.

Bertolini, L. (2010) Coping with the irreducible uncertainties of planning: An evolutionary approach, in J. Hillier and P. Healey (eds), *Conceptual Challenges in Spatial Planning: The Ashgate research companion to planning theory*, Aldershot: Ashgate, pp. 413–424.

Briggs, X. da S. (2008) *Democracy as Problem-solving*, Boston, MA: MIT Press.

Bryson, J. and Crosby, B. (1992) *Leadership in the Common Good: Tackling public problems in a shared power world*, San Francisco, CA: Jossey Bass.

Campbell, H. (2012) Planning to change the world: Between knowledge and action lies synthesis, *Journal of Planning Education and Research*, 32(2): 135–146.

Cars, G., Healey, P., Madanipour, A. and Magalhaes, C de. (eds) (2002) *Urban Governance, Institutional Capacity and Social Milieux*, Aldershot: Ashgate.

Corburn, J. (2005) *Street Science: Community knowledge and environmental health justice*, Cambridge, MA: MIT Press.

Davoudi, S. and Pendlebury, J. (2010) The evolution of planning as an academic discipline, *Town Planning Review*, 81(6): 613–645.

Dewey, J. (1991 [1927]) *The Public and Its Problems*, Athens, OH: Swallow Press/Ohio University Press.

Filion, P. and Sanderson, C. (2011) The impact of organizational crafting on planning, *Planning Theory and Practice*, 12(1): 77–94.

Flyvbjerg, B. (1998) *Rationality and Power*, Chicago: University of Chicago Press.

Forester, J. (2009) *Dealing with Differences: Dramas of mediating public disputes*, Oxford: Oxford University Press.

Gilchrist, A. (2009) *The Well-connected Community: A networking approach to community development*, Bristol: Polity Press.

Hajer, M. (2003) Policy without polity? Policy analysis and the institutional void, *Policy Sciences*, 36: 175–195.

Hajer, M. and Wagenaar, H. (eds) (2003) *Deliberative Policy Analysis: Understanding governance in the network society*, Cambridge: Cambridge University Press.

Healey, P. (2006) Transforming governance: challenges of institutional adaptation and a new politics of space, *European Planning Studies*, 14(3): 299–319.

Healey, P. (2010) *Making Better Places: The planning project in the twentyfirst century*, London: Palgrave Macmillan.

Healey, P. (2012) Re-enchanting democracy as a way of life, *Critical Policy Studies*, 6(1): 19–39.

Hillier, J. (2011) Strategic navigation across multiple planes: Towards Deleuzian-inspired methodology for strategic spatial planning, *Town Planning Review*, 82(5): 503–528.

Hoppe, R. (2010) *The Governance of Problems: Puzzling, powering and participation*, Bristol: Policy Press.

Innes, J. and Booher, D. (2003) Collaborative policy-making: Governance through dialogue, in M. Hajer and H. Wagenaar (eds), *Deliberative Policy Analysis: Understanding governance in the network society*, Cambridge: Cambridge University Press, pp. 33–59.

Lindblom, C.E. (1990) *Inquiry and Change: The troubled attempt to understand and shape society*, New Haven, CT: Yale University Press.

Meyerson, M. and Banfield, E. (1955) *Politics, Planning and the Public Interest*, New York: Free Press.

Moore Milroy, B. (2009) *Thinking Planning and Urbanism*, Vancouver, BC: UBC Press.

Moulaert, F., Martinelli, F., Swyngedouw, E. and Gonzalez, S. (eds) (2010) *Can Neighbourhoods Save the City? Community development and social innovation*, London: Routledge.

Ostrom, E. (1990) *Governing the Commons: The evolution of institutions for collective action*, Cambridge: Cambridge University Press.

Peters, G. (1999) *Institutional Theory in Political Science: The 'new institutionalism'*, London: Continuum.

Punter, J. (2003) *The Vancouver Achievement*, Vancouver, BC: UBC Press.

Rhodes, R.A.W. (1997) *Understanding Governance: Policy networks, governance, reflexivity and accountability*, Milton Keynes: Open University Press.

Rydin, Y. (2011) *The Purpose of Planning: Creating sustainable towns and cities*, Bristol: Policy Press.

Sager, T. (2012) *Reviving Critical Planning Theory: Dealing with pressure, neo-liberalism and responsibility in communicative planning*, London: Routledge.

Sandercock, L. (2005) An anatomy of civic ambition in Vancouver, *Harvard Design Magazine*, 22 (Spring/Summer): 36–43.

Sirianni, C. (2009) *Investing in Democracy: Engaging citizens in collaborative governance*, Washington, DC: Brookings Institution.

Skocpol, T. (2003) *Diminished Democracy: From membership to management in American civic life*, Norman: University of Oklahoma Press.

Sorensen, E. and Torfing, J. (eds) (2007) *Theories of Democratic Network Governance*, London: Palgrave Macmillan.

Souza, C. (2001) Participatory budgeting in Brazilian cities: Limits and possibilities in building democratic institutions, *Environment and Urbanization*, 13(1): 159–184.

Stoker, G. (2006) *Why Politics Matters: Making democracy work*, Basingstoke: Palgrave Macmillan.

Stone, C.N. (2001) Civic capacity and urban education, *Urban Affairs Review*, 36(5): 595–619.

Tewdwr-Jones, M. (2012) *Spatial Planning and Governance: Understanding UK planning*, London: Palgrave Macmillan.

7

The Promise of Democracy? Civic Enterprise, Localism and the Transformation of Democratic Capitalism

Hendrik Wagenaar and Jurgen van der Heijden

In this chapter we describe what we believe to be a new generation of social economy initiatives. We call them civic enterprises to distinguish them from the social economy as it has been practised, studied, made the object of government policies, and invested with hope by government officials and academic promoters for over two decades (Amin *et al.*, 2002). We will argue that civic enterprises contain considerable economic and democratic potential. Similar to the social economy this democratic potential rests on the close association of the economic and democratic benefits of civic enterprise. Social production and civic enterprise produce social goods (public services and products) in a democratic way (non-hierarchical, non-profit, democratic, sustainable, responsive to local and individual needs). Thus, they form an alternative to the traditional social production system of democratic capitalism in which large centralized firms, largely insulated from democratic control, provide mass-produced goods to consumers with little or no voice in the production system.[1] Moreover, as we will argue below, since the early 1970s the market economy has developed in a way that has eroded the quality of representative democracy in Western nations and threatens basic civic freedoms and social values. Social production and civic enterprise both operate on different democratic principles. In a nutshell these principles are associative democracy and informality. In this way the social economy and civic enterprise open up a perspective on economic, social and democratic governance that forms a real alternative to the inherent shortcomings of democratic capitalism.

For various reasons the democratic potential of the social economy, and as of yet civic enterprise, has not been sufficiently explicated. First, much of the recent literature on democratic innovation treats democracy as a phenomenon *sui generis*, detached from the world of multinational corporations, a rapacious financial sector, a policy elite that is in the grip of neoliberal ideology of governance, and huge economic and social upheavals. Democracy is reduced to the interplay of competitive parties and citizens who are more, or less, able and predisposed to participate in the democratic game, with a concern to enhance the quality of democracy through experiments with deliberation and citizen participation (Bohman, 1996; Verba *et al.*, 1995). But, as an earlier generation of democratic theorists was acutely aware (Dahl, 1989; Dryzek, 1996; Lindblom, 1977, 1982; Offe, 1984), liberal democracy cannot be seen apart from the capitalist system of production; it emerged as one coherent, more or less standard configuration,[2] in which democratic mechanisms simultaneously facilitate economic activity, while at the same time putting constraints on any deepening of democracy that threatens business interests. Without a more precise understanding of the many contradictions in the relationship between capitalism and liberal democracy, any project of democratic innovation is at worst misguided and at best naive. Contemporary democratic capitalism, particularly since the financial crisis of 2008 and the subsequent global economic recession, has created many anti-democratic constraints. As we will argue below, this is part of a longer trend in the transformation of democratic capitalism in which the large, multinational corporation became a dominant actor in the world-economic system, capital has extracted itself more and more from democratic oversight, while at the same time presenting more and more facilitative and financial demands to beleaguered states. The state plays a central role in this process, often operating against the very rules and spirit of liberal democracy that it purports to expedite. It is against the backdrop of this 'capitalism–state nexus' (Dryzek, 1996: 12) that any democratic innovation takes place, and that spaces must be found or created in which democratic experiments may succeed. This is certainly not impossible (Warren, 2002), but it will be obvious that it presents a considerable challenge to democratic advocates.[3]

The fate of the social economy, and this is our second point, provides an instructive example of the interpenetration of democracy, capitalism and the state. The social economy emerged against the background of the fiscal crisis and the ensuing retrenchments of the welfare state that affected most Western democracies in the late 1970s and the 1980s. As we will explain below, for various reasons the social economy did not, or rather could not, deliver on its, rather inflated, promises. Consequently, its democratic potential has been underdeveloped, for if one of the elements of the social production equation fails to materialize, the enterprise fails to be 'social and/or civic'. Because of its economic and democratic underperformance, social production turned out to be a mere footnote in the history of deregulation and the transformation of democratic capitalism that has characterized the liberal-representative democracies since the 1970s.

Third, the social economy and civic enterprise are responses to particular economic-social-democratic constellations. These responses are above all practical. Their specific form and nature emerges bottom up, in the very doing of it (Wagenaar and Specht, 2010), unreflexively, without 'an explicit theory of how and why to do so' (Hirst, 1994: 124). The purpose of this chapter is to provide such a theory. We do not know if in the end civic enterprise will also be a footnote in the ongoing transformation of democratic capitalism, or if instead it will live up to its economic and democratic potential and provide a real alternative or 'supplement' to it (Hirst, 1994: 96). By sketching its democratic potential and showing how that potential is embedded in its associative form of production, we hope at least to raise awareness of the economic and democratic promise of civic enterprise.

The social economy against the backdrop of the transformation of democratic capitalism

To understand the intricate relationship between democracy, politics and the economy, it is instructive to discuss the rise and decline of the social economy. In a general sense the concept of the social economy refers to 'not-for-profit activity geared towards meeting social needs'. It is 'economic activity with a social remit' (Amin *et al.*, 2002: 1). So, strictly speaking, civic enterprises should be considered as belonging to the social economy. One cannot dissociate the idea of a social economy from both its time and place of origin. The social economy emerged in the context of, and as reply to, the demise of a particular political-economic arrangement that had undergirded the post-war welfare state and liberal-representative democracies in the US and Western Europe. This is not the place to describe in detail the gradual unravelling, from the early 1970s onwards, of an economic system that combined mass production with full employment and universal welfare statism.[4] In brief, starting around 1970, the post-war social pact between capital and government in the Western world that had resulted in high growth levels, full employment and generous, universalist welfare state programmes, began to collapse under its own contradictions (Offe, 1984). After more than 20 years of uninterrupted economic growth, entrepreneurs began to fear that the ever-increasing expectations of the 'wage dependent' could no longer be met without severe declines in profitability. They were no longer willing to abide by their obligations in the post-war settlement and began to look for ways to desist their role in it. This resulted in an acute 'fiscal crisis of the state' (O'Connor, 1973) that set in motion an interlocking series of retrenchments and dismantling of key aspects of the post-war full-employment regimes. In the face of large-scale industrial restructuring, and the export of labour to low-wage countries, full, lifetime employment became untenable. Labour unions were actively resisted by governments and/or saw steep declines in membership; the practice of sector-wide wage agreements was abandoned. With the emergence of 'giant firms' (Crouch, 2011: 49) the balance between business and democratic politics shifted in favour of the firm and the economy began to liberate itself from political-bureaucratic or corporatist control (Streeck, 2013: 55). Cradle-to-grave, universalist welfare state arrangements were gradually abandoned, which put pressure on a model of citizenship that was based on collective rights, distributive justice and representative democracy (Amin *et al.*, 2002: 3). A powerful neoliberal narrative of an oversized, overbearing, inefficient state that obstructed 'natural' market efficiency led to the privatization of many state-provided services, the downsizing of the public sector and the introduction of corporate management techniques into public-sector agencies. This put even more pressure on the aforementioned model of citizenship.

It was against this background that the idea of a social economy as an alternative to the market economy and the disappearing welfare state became attractive. But for a full understanding of the emergence of the social economy as a solution to a generally acknowledged, 'self-evident' policy problem, one more element in the transformation of democratic capitalism needs to be introduced. Both Crouch and Streeck ask themselves why there was so little resistance against this erosion of the life chances of large parts of the population. Their surprising answer is that roughly from the late 1970s onwards, citizens were gradually transformed into consumers and thereby became implicated in the move away from a universalist Keynesian welfare state to a debt-fuelled, individualized, precarious employment system of 'privatized Keynesianism' (Crouch, 2011). With a combination of high government borrowing, the creation of state-supported schemes for individuals to borrow (such as government-backed mortgage schemes and easily available credit cards) and the commercialization of ever more reaches of social life through the art of marketing, a legitimation crisis was staved off and support of governments was secured by enabling large sections of the wage-dependent to become pseudo-capitalists who lived off, or rather believed themselves to live off, the appreciation of their assets (Streeck, 2013: 57–58).[5] Clearly this was an uneven process that left many people out, as is borne out by the rapidly increasing income inequality of the last 20 years (Mian & Sufi, 2014; Streeck, 2013: 59).

It is against this background that in the early 1980s the idea of a social economy became a focal point for a range of ideals and aspirations that were to replace the triple whammy of increasing structural unemployment, the flexibilization of the labour market and the shrinking welfare state. The transformation of post-war democratic capitalism created large groups of citizens who were excluded from both the welfare state as well as the newer forms of private capitalism. There was even a name for such groups: 'modernization losers'. The social economy was seen as the answer to these excluded groups. As Amin *et al.* put it: 'The premise is that the crisis of the welfare state potentially generates a huge market for the not-for-profit sector to deliver goods and services to help satisfy the largely under-met needs of excluded groups and communities' (2002: 6). In particular, the association of the social economy with the local became taken for granted in policy circles. Not only were the needs of excluded citizens better known by local organizations to transform them more effectively into active economic agents and better-equipped democratic citizens, the local was also the platform for bottom-up initiatives that would create employment, be financially independent, serve local markets and empower all those that were abandoned by the state and the mainstream economy (Amin *et al.*, 2002: 30; Wagenaar and Specht, 2010).

To better appreciate the possibilities and limits of civic enterprise, it is important to understand the central role of localism in the broader economic and governance context of the social economy. In broad brushstrokes, localism was a key element in the attempted reconciliation of the norms of a market economy with the ideal of a socially inclusive society, as articulated in the Third Way doctrine. As Amin *et al.* (2002) explain, the Third Way represented an amalgam of economic 'realism' and an ethic of responsibility. In many countries, Social Democrats accepted the neoliberal tenets of globalization, flexibilization of labour contracts, accelerating deindustrialization and the emergence of a service-based economy, with the cutting back and individualizing of universal welfare-state programmes. The moral underpinning of the Third Way was a shift from solidarity to individual responsibility as the basic ethical principle of the state's duty to provide a safety net for its citizens. The proven willingness to find and accept work became the main criterion for citizenship. Those who nevertheless found themselves without work were grouped together under the label of 'social exclusion'.

Two considerations came together to promote not only the policy category of social exclusion as the central problem of the beneficial state (CEC, 1993; Molloy *et al.*, 1999), but also localism as the solution of choice for those who lost their jobs or were unable to adapt quickly enough to the ongoing neoliberal transformation of post-war capitalism (Streeck, 2013). First, although the state, at least in its Social- and Christian-Democratic incarnation, carries a moral obligation to reduce social exclusion, it must do so in a way that makes minimal demands upon public expenditure (Amin *et al.*, 2002: 28; Offe, 1984; Streeck, 2013: 64). Second, social exclusion, as a catch-all term for a concentration of social pathology that allegedly resulted from unemployment, happened to be geographically concentrated in certain neighbourhoods or estates. What was in many ways geographically circumstantial, paradoxically became a central tenet of the Third Way's strategy of tackling social exclusion. As Amin *et al.* (2002: 26) put it:

> In the Third Way the harnessing of the local economy is central to the 'reinvention' of the nation, the creation of an inclusive society, and particularly to tackling social exclusion. The local community is both the site at which the phenomenon of social exclusion is manifest and is assumed

to be the most appropriate site of policy intervention. Under New Labour, social exclusion 'happens' at the level of the local community; the latter is therefore responsible for its alleviation.

In country after country the neighbourhood became the focus of intense policy attention, usually mixed in with lofty ideals of communitarianism and democratization (Lowndes and Sullivan, 2008; Specht, 2012; WRR, 2005).

In this way the social economy became inextricably linked to social exclusion. The neighbourhood social economy became both the preferred site and vehicle for local economic regeneration and job creation; a substitute for the relentlessly shrinking welfare state. Its take-up and enthusiastic promotion by the EU gave it official 'recognition' with European national governments. However, with hindsight, this confluence of social exclusion, localism and the social economy only resulted in 'buying time' in the ongoing dissociation of capitalism and democracy that characterizes the post-war advanced economies (Streeck, 2013). It goes without saying that this institutional interpretation of the social economy raised a number of serious problems. First, the social economy did not deliver as the poorest neighbourhoods simply did not have the resources to set up successful projects. Quite simply, the social economy was overstrained. It was asked to do too much, having to solve problems (structural unemployment, neighbourhood decline, youth crime, broken families, stagnating local development, the reduction of poverty) that neither the mainstream economy nor the state was willing or able to solve (Molloy *et al.*, 1999). Second, while the post-war universalist welfare state suffered from many implementation problems and perverse unintended consequences, localism in the context of social exclusion represents the abandoning of the principles of universalism and solidarity that were the foundation of a fair society and the accompanying notion of citizenship that both spawned and characterized the post-war welfare state. Third, the focus on localism means in practice the acceptance of the increasing, place-based inequality of income and life chances that is one of the characteristics of the global, neoliberal economic order.

The sudden emergence of civic enterprises

In the last two decades citizens in many European countries have begun to organize themselves, bottom-up, to produce energy, food and care. The impetus of these civic enterprises (CEs) is a mixture of idealism and pragmatism. Citizens want to create an alternative to the profit-oriented mass producers of energy, food and care, but they also produce goods and services that the state and large service corporations fail to provide. Energy and food are produced in a sustainable way; care is personalized. CEs are often local; they originate and work within and for neighbourhoods or small towns, although some, such as the Spanish energy cooperative, *SOM Energia*, work on a national scale. CEs do not seek to displace liberal democracy, but operate complementary to, and usually with the support of, private corporations, large-scale hierarchical government agencies and elected officials to provide more and better services with a higher level of control and agency by citizens. In fact, the relationship between CEs, the 'official' economy and the state is an important topic that we will explore later in this chapter. One aspect of this relationship is the relation between CEs and the nature of representative democracy. Although we must not exaggerate the impact of CEs, by introducing associative elements, civic enterprises have potentially important implications for the organization of representative democracy.

Although there is considerable continuity, CEs differ in some important respects from social production. While both are need-driven, citizen-controlled initiatives produce things in ways that differ from the 'official' economy. The social economy has different origins from the civic enterprise its aim is to tackle social problems; the production of goods or services is a means to alleviate the plight of the disadvantaged. And although some social enterprises make a profit, this is not their main purpose. Mission trumps profit in the social economy. CEs, on the other hand, aim at producing social goods in economically viable and democratic ways. They are for the most part founded by middle-class citizens in middle-class neighbourhoods. Although some emerge in disadvantaged neighbourhoods, CEs are not aimed at alleviating poverty and social pathology. In CEs the social exclusion aspect is primary. They are founded for idealistic reasons; from a strong conviction that things should, and can, be done differently. They are bottom-up, 'uninvited' initiatives by citizens; initially at least state and corporations are not involved, except as interested bystanders. Their aim is to provide an essential good or service that the state or the private sector is not able or willing to provide in an economically or socially acceptable way. And while both rely on government regulation and state subsidies, the aim of CEs is financial independence through profitability (Huygen, 2012: 14). It is probably for this reason that they do not shy away from forging productive links with businesses in their particular domain. As a result CEs are not burdened by the mix of excessive emancipatory and palliative expectations, on the one hand, and lack of resources, on the other, that was the undoing of social production. Finally, CEs, more than social enterprises, are democratic associations. They consist of people who organize themselves to decide in a democratic way how to improve their social or physical environment (Beunderman and van der Heijden, 2013).

For reasons of familiarity we take the Netherlands as an example of the sudden emergence of civic enterprise. What we have learned about CEs in other countries (Ahrensbach *et al.*, 2011; Boontje, 2013) has impressed upon us the importance of national and institutional specificity, but we have also observed the many similarities between different national civic enterprises. We are confident therefore that our generalizations about the Dutch case will by and large also apply to CEs in other countries.

As far as we know no survey of CEs has been done in any country.[6] Yet, van Ooijen has made an effort to systematically scan the landscape of CEs in the Netherlands (van Ooijen, 2013). Although he doesn't define CEs, he found 'thousands of citizen initiatives in all shapes and sizes' in the Netherlands. These occur in areas such as (long-term) care; renewable energy, sustainable food production; community improvement (these most resemble the original social production concept); family counselling to assist multi-problem families (through so-called Family Group Conferences); the communal management of libraries, swimming pools, sports facilities and local pubs and shops; transport; construction; development aid; cooperative banking (through credit unions and through crowd funding); mutual aid insurance for the self-employed; and social enterprises (for-profit firms with a strong social dimension).

This cataloguing of CEs does not do justice, however, to the sheer richness and diversity of the initiatives that have sprung up in the last few years. Let us, by way of example, look more closely at the area of social care. Van Ooijen observes, for example, that there are numerous apps, platforms and social media that facilitate self-care and self-management. New initiatives pop up every day, such as the platform for the elderly, *Dat Doen we Zelf* (We'll Do It Ourselves), which was launched on 4 April 2013, and the *Andromeda Society* that was set up by a group of seniors in the city of Eindhoven. In addition, he cites initiatives such as *Buurtzorg Nederland* (Community Care Netherlands), which was launched in 2006, with 550 local community care teams it April 2013. Another was *Thuishuizen*, small-scale residential care for elderly people who do not want to be on their own or are at risk of becoming isolated and lonely. The first such home was opened in the town of Deurne in 2011, while the feasibility of further homes in Eindhoven, Boxmeer and Amsterdam is currently being studied, and concrete initiatives for these kinds of homes are under way in ten cities. Further examples include *Buddy Rotterdam*, the *We Helpen* (We Help) website, the *Doordewijks Foundation* in Rotterdam for affordable help from within the community, the *Zorgvoorelkaar* website (launched on 17 October 2012), three crowd-funding platforms in the area of medical care (*Medstartr*, *MedCrowdFund*, *Farmafonds*), and there are already ten care cooperatives and a further 15 in the works. In some municipalities, such as Peel en Maas, elderly-care duties have been outsourced to local social cooperatives.

What explains the sudden emergence of the civic enterprise in Northwestern Europe? We argue that similar to the social economy, CEs are an answer to changes in the wider political-economic environment. If we restrict ourselves to the Netherlands, the emergence and the particular shape that civic enterprise takes are closely tied to the trajectory of the Dutch economy and democracy since the first fiscal crisis of the late 1970s. While the Netherlands has obviously not been immune to the large-scale transformation of democratic capitalism since the 1970s, it followed a particular trajectory that for many years mitigated its dislocating effects. This is not the place to describe in detail the organization and functioning of the Dutch political economy, but in broad brushstrokes, the following factors were important for the rearrangement of the relation between capital, labour and the state in the Netherlands. First, Dutch labour unions, while suffering from sharp declines in membership like in most developed economies, have retained their role in the corporatist structure of social-economic governance in the Netherlands. In exchange for wage reductions, employers were mostly, but not always, willing to abide by sector-wide wage agreements and benefits for part-time employees. Second, the coalition structure of Dutch government ensured that the effects of welfare-state retrenchment were abated. For example, the privatization of the health-care sector in 2006 was heavily regulated by the state, which guaranteed mandatory acceptance of patients by private health insurers, a generous guaranteed minimum 'package' of care for every insured citizen and tax benefits for lower-income groups who have trouble paying the minimum insurance premiums. A similar story of privatization, regulation and moderation applies to the housing corporations. Third, a powerful 'third sector' of care facilities, many of them managed by Christian-Democratic boards, have for a long time successfully resisted budget cuts and reforms. Fourth, building upon a tradition of elite deliberation in Dutch consociationalism, many municipal governments have extended this form of democratic participation to ordinary citizens. In the 1980s countless local experiments with 'interactive policy making', 'co-production' and 'citizen participation' attempted to draw citizens into the policy-making process. Although the effects are debatable, it can be argued that in some cities these experiments in effect functioned as a 'school for democracy', teaching citizens democratic skills and providing them with exemplars and ideals of democratic participation.

While these characteristics obscured the real changes that afflicted the organization of the social system of production in the Netherlands, the financial crisis of 2008 tore away the veil. The combined effects of interventions in the banking sector, subsequent loans to indebted Eurozone countries, the decline of GNP, higher social security outlays and declining fiscal returns have resulted in a rapid increase in Dutch government debt (Lukkezen and Suyker, 2013). Due to its relatively large banking sector the Dutch state became even more indebted than it already was. A sustained anti-Keynesian policy of austerity and a necessary but ill-timed restructuring of the generous mortgage programmes that had underpinned the Dutch housing market since the 1970s, ushered in a stagnating median household income, sharply declining housing prices and rapidly increasing unemployment.[7] In 2012, the government announced cuts of €18 billion in a range of programmes ranging from mortgage deductions to care. Public-sector salaries are frozen and the retirement age has been increased. In 2014 an additional €6 billion in cuts is expected.

Care is a good example of the shape and effect of the current budget cuts in the Netherlands. Long-term medical care, social care and care for the elderly all face large cutbacks in outlays. These are masqueraded as 'systems change', in the form of national decentralization operations. The largest one is the transfer of (parts of) the national Exceptional Medical Expenses Act (AWBZ) to the, locally administered, Social Support Act (WMO). Spending under the AWBZ will be cut from €27 billion to €12 billion; from 2015 onwards entitlement to several forms of (long-term) care will be curtailed and will have to be negotiated by citizens with their local government. Citizens will increasingly have to arrange care themselves or will have to ask family and neighbours for support. Citizens also face considerable co-payments. The current government aims to cut another €3.5 billion from the long-term care budget. Local government will have to cut €1.6 billion (on a total budget of €10 billion) on (long-term) care. In addition, the National Care Agreement that was signed on 24 April 2013 forces local governments to slash the domestic care budget by €600 million. This budget cut will lead to the loss of about 50,000 domestic care jobs. There is the suspicion that, to drive down costs, local governments and large privatized care providers collude in dismantling employee rights for workers in the care industry. Apart from the national government's cuts in spending, local governments also have to cut spending due to losses on the development of residential and industrial areas as a result of the slump in the office and housing markets. This will also lead to a reduction in public services. Against a demographic backdrop of a growing number of elderly people, the number of places available at nursing and care homes declined from 196,000 in 1980 to 158,000 in 2010; a further decline to 95,000 by 2020 has been predicted (van Ooijen, 2013). At the same time a number of spectacular bankruptcies of large privatized care corporations (with the usual auxiliaries of fraud, defective accounting and excessive CEO remuneration) have led to large declines in trust in political institutions and widespread political cynicism among citizens.

It is against this background of declining personal wealth, deep budget cuts in domains that affect everyday life, state retrenchment in the provision of key services and declining trust in political and corporate institutions that civic enterprises have sprung up. On the face of it, the middle classes who are most affected have taken the initiative in providing products and services that until recently had been exclusively provided by the state and privatized corporations. Their aim is not to displace public and private production of services, but to create an alternative that gives them more control over the provision of vital services. In the next section we will describe the organization and functioning of civic enterprises.

The organization and financing of civic enterprise

Key to CEs is that they are governed by the principle of *reciprocal delivery* in the aggregate social system of production (Rogers Hollingworth *et al.*, 2002). Energy production is a good illustration. Traditionally energy is produced by a small number of large (multinational) utilities that deliver, for example, electricity to households, businesses and public-sector organizations such as schools and offices. Individual users have no influence over the organization of the production system (sustainable or not), the price of the product and the fit of product and the needs of the user. Parallel to the centralized production mode, local actors produce energy in a decentralized way, directly through windmills or photovoltaic cells, and indirectly through various efficiency-enhancing, lifestyle-related measures that reduce the uptake of energy. The individual delivers energy to himself. He is both producer and consumer. Local production is thus rooted in and shaped by informality, the everyday practices of citizens (Wagenaar, 2014).

Between these two production sites, two additional forms of product delivery may occur. Local producers may give or sell their surplus to local consumers. Because of fiscal constraints this does not happen yet in the field of energy in the Netherlands, but in the domain of food and care this has become a common link in the social system of production. Small producers of food, for example, regularly sell their products to individual consumers, either at the production site or at farmers' markets. Finally, local producers may sell their surplus to central producers. Regulation requires large utilities to buy back, for market price, surplus energy that is produced by individuals or CEs. This can take the form of an exchange scheme (locally produced energy is subtracted from centrally produced energy) or, facilitated by smartly designed national regulation as in Germany, the locally produced surplus enters the national grid (Boontje, 2013: 8). Local–central delivery is less common in the domains of food and care.

How are CEs organized so that they can successfully engage in social production *and* retain their democratic potential? In legal terms, CEs in the Netherlands are either chartered as an association or a cooperative. These are the only two legal-organizational forms that allow full democratic transparency and in which decision-making power rests with the members/owners. The difference is that members do not own an association and do not share in the profits, as associations are legally prohibited from making profits according to Dutch civil law. Most CEs create a corporate entity, usually a Public Limited Company, to contain its commercial activities such as the production and sale of products or services to members and other clients. This way, the association or cooperative will be protected should the corporation encounter financial troubles. CEs, thus, have a public and a private part. The association

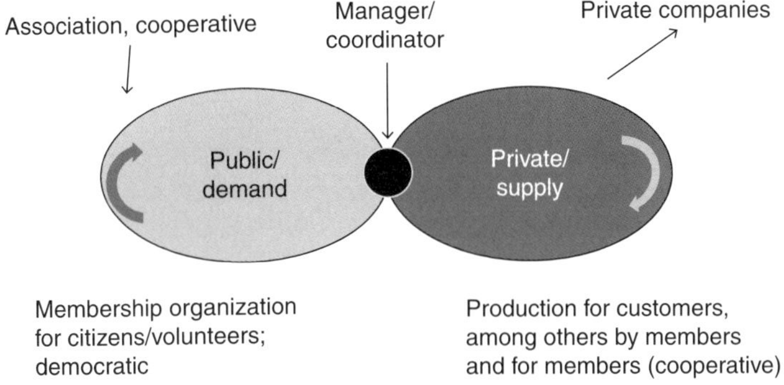

Figure 7.1 Organizationally, CEs can be said to be shaped as a lemniscate

or cooperative is the owner of the private corporation. Through contractual agreements the members' influence over the commercial decisions of the corporate arm is guaranteed. Many CEs appoint a coordinator or executive director who is in charge of the CE's commercial activities, manages its volunteers and facilitates innovation, such as branching out into different areas of social production. The public and private parts of the CE nourish each other. The corporate part engages in activities that both clients and members know contribute to the needs of the community or a sustainable environment. In addition, the democratic decision-making structure generates societal legitimacy in addition to individual democratic gains such as civic virtue. We will discuss this more extensively in the next section. Organizationally, CEs can be said to be shaped as a lemniscate (Figure 7.1).

Thus, CEs form a special type of associative production entity that produces social value, generates financial gain and brings about democratic legitimacy. Clearly, CEs are not an answer to the economic, social and environmental dislocations that are created by the current crisis of democratic capitalism. The most we can say at this stage is that civic enterprise expands the web of production and delivery sites and channels in the social system of production. At the moment this expansion is small and fragile, and could easily be reversed. But it contains a number of important innovations over and above traditional mass production and hierarchical administration. Civic enterprise is focused on local needs. This proves to be an engine of innovation; creative solutions arise out of struggling with local challenges and dilemmas. Whatever a CE produces, it does it in a sustainable and low-cost way. Costs are lower because the social bonds that are at the heart of the civic production system lower transaction costs. CEs also engage in multiple value creation. Many CEs expand their activities into adjacent areas. A care cooperation may add the provision of low-cost transport to its activities, or a neighbourhood energy cooperative expands into sustainable agriculture. Multiple value creation follows from the abandoning of the principle of maximizing shareholder value (Crouch, 2011: 103). In a profit-based firm, everything that distracts from the primary production process detracts from shareholder value. In a CE the aim is to be financially sustainable; all surplus value is ploughed back into the community. This allows the participants to engage in collective action, and for values such as environmental sustainability or social solidarity to be realized in practical enterprises.[8] In addition the associative, horizontal, self-governing structure of CEs has democratic effects such as generalized reciprocity, trust, mutual respect and conflict-resolution skills (Warren, 2001). CEs are schools of democracy.

The presence of a social economy that is based on principles of associative democracy in the middle of a market-based production system and liberal government raises the question of the relation of CEs to the state. Generally speaking CEs do not aim to displace centralized production. Instead, they are complementary to market-based production and hierarchical administration. Similar to the way that the state facilitates markets, in fiscal, financial and regulatory terms, so it can also facilitate CEs. Obvious areas for government involvement in the realm of social production are taxes (should civic production be taxed? Can the fiscal instrument be used to subsidize or stimulate social production?); the creation of a level playing field (CEs should not be discriminated against, as for example they are currently through the fiscal structure of energy production in the Netherlands); quality control (CEs should be subjected to quality control similar to for-profit enterprises); co-production of local ordinances of national laws (when citizens partly take over the production of energy, care, food production, safety or social services, it follows that they should have input in the formulation of laws and regulation in these domains; this is a simple extension of the principle of participatory governance) (Ansell, 2011; Bourgon, 2011).

Civic enterprise and the promise of democracy

What is the democratic promise that is inherent in civic enterprise – and, for that matter, in the social economy? Theoretically speaking, civic enterprise differs in two important ways from liberal democracy as the latter is implicated in the social system of market-based production. Or differently put, civic enterprise rests on two principles of democratic innovation. The first is associative democracy. The field of associative democracy is too large to discuss in any depth here,[9] but by way of summary the associative basis of civic enterprise amounts to the following. Associative democracy is founded on the idea of a decentralized economy based on the 'non-capitalistic principles of cooperation and mutuality' (Hirst, 1994: 15). Hirst contrasts these principles with both the 'centralized and sovereign state' (1994: 15) and market economies that fail to 'deliver substantive social outcomes like a healthy environment, an acceptable level of employment, [and] a desired composition of output' (Hirst, 1994: 78). The critique of the administrative state centres on the key role of a centralized and hierarchically organized administrative apparatus in liberal democracy and its pretension to be able to manage and regulate societal sectors. This ambition has been criticized extensively in the literature (Dryzek, 1990: ch. 6; Healey *et al.*, 2003; Wagenaar, 2007) and its obvious failures have led to periodic, although sometimes undemocratic,[10] manifestos for reform (Ansell, 2011; Bourgon, 2011; Moore, 1997; Osborne & Gaebler, 2000). Also, administrations themselves, particularly local administrations, have engaged in practical attempts to break through the proceduralism and rigid specialization of large-scale government agencies through the introduction of principles of corporate managerialism and/or invited democratic participation. But despite these attempts, the large, hierarchically organized administrative agency is still the cornerstone of liberal democracy, and it still has not been able to solve the problems of overload, coordination, responsiveness and effectiveness.

For a proper understanding of both the nature of civic enterprise and its democratic potential, it is important to enquire further into the conditions for the resilience of the hierarchical, centralized model of the administration of societal sectors. One obvious, and often overlooked, argument is that the administrative state functions quite well, in a taken-for-granted way, in delivering relatively simple, routinized services to the public. Think of roads and infrastructure, schools, parks, low-income housing, public transportation and an effective, non-corrupt police force. Even in more complex administrative tasks, such as managing a viable education or health-care system, tasks in which many governments are seen to fall short, the administrative state plays an important role in protecting the interests of low-income groups and balancing conflicting goals. Moreover, in advanced societies they do this under the guidance of an administrative ethos and legal-procedural regime that protects the individual from an arbitrary or overbearing state. So even where the administrative state is perceived as failing to deliver on its promises – in situations where the sheer complexity of the problem overwhelms the organizational capacity of the state, or in situations of self-inflicted impotence as a result of the privatization of public services, or situations in which the funds for effective administration are no longer available, situations that Warren (2014) labels as 'pluralized ungovernability' – most citizens are aware of the beneficial liberal-democratic functions of the administrative state.

There is a second and more insidious reason for the resilience of the administrative state, however: administrative hegemony. Hegemony denotes the radical exclusion of other possibilities and the self-evident legitimacy of the practices and language of public administration in addressing collective problems. In this sense it is an instance of the constitutive power of governing elites to naturalize the significance of state and market assumptions over the appeal of popular sovereignty. We use the concept of hegemony here in its Foucauldian sense of horizontal power, a form of power that is implicated in the taken-for-granted, internalized categories and practices that make up our everyday world. Hegemony implicates the subjected. The importance of administrative hegemony is, thus, its constitutive character; it operates simultaneously on the practical and the linguistic level, thereby (morally) demarcating particular groups and problems and naturalizing a particular administrative domain. Hegemony explains why, in liberal-representative democracies, hierarchical sectoral management is still the default option, although sometimes only rhetorically, for addressing collective problems, even in situations of 'pluralized ungovernability' where administrations sometimes spectacularly fail to deliver. For our argument a second implication of administrative hegemony is more important, however: namely the decoupling of administrative practice from the world and activities of ordinary citizens. It is to this aspect of the administrative state that we turn in the final section of this chapter.

The second pillar of the democratic potential of civic enterprise is informality. The concept of informality refers to 'informal modes of organizing space, livelihood and citizenship' (Roy, 2010). It is usually associated with hyper-urbanization in the global South, and it has been most extensively studied in these contexts (Chatterjee, 2006; Corbridge *et al.*, 2005; Holston, 2008; Roy, 2003; Simone and Abouhani, 2005). In the absence of state institutions that are sufficiently strong to provide essential services to the poor, the latter have to rely on their own practical skills to create such services. Although born out of different circumstances, that of corrupt and oppressing governments, we encounter a similar kind of decoupling of the informal lifeworld of citizens and the state in the developed economies of the West. But born of necessity, informality also contains hope. Informality becomes the expression of another kind of politics, a 'deep democracy', a 'countergovernmentality' (Chatterjee, 2006) that, informed by local knowledge of the conditions and experiences of the poor, allows them to construct an alternative 'insurgent' citizenship that destabilizes the entrenched hegemonic practices of state and market.

Our argument is that informality is a pervasive phenomenon that is not restricted to the global South, and should be considered an important analytical tool in understanding the different roles that ordinary citizens play in the constitution of local space, local production and local governance in general (Devlin, 2011; Lombard and Huxley, 2011: 121; Roy, 2010). First, as we have seen above, despite their highly developed public administrations and richly endowed policy programmes, citizens' distrust in local and national administrations is far from uncommon in the global North either. It is little wonder that in such an environment citizens take the initiative to manage pressing problems in their neighbourhoods and communities, often because residents feel abandoned by officials; in the process creating new 'space(s) of democratic possibilities' (Specht, 2012; Wagenaar and Specht, 2010; Warren, 2014: 1).

Second, the concept of informality contains an implicit normative contrast with the more 'desirable' formal procedures and institutions that are thought to constitute urbanization and urban governance. However, this normative contrast is misleading on two counts. First, informality is everywhere. Although it comes most clearly into view in situations of diversity and sharp inequality, informality is the fabric of everyday life. It is indeed the poor and ethnic minorities who, often ignored by the state and themselves distrustful of the state, have to rely on the more colourful and creative tactics of deception, evasion, subterfuge and 'playing the system' to make a living and secure shelter. But in a general sense these informal tactics are also spaces of freedom and possibility, alternatives to the official order, where alternative understandings and practices are hatched from which new, creative solutions to intractable urban problems may emerge. In effect, CEs are examples of the power of informality in addressing collective concerns that the state has given up on. Second, and more fundamentally, informality is not outside formal systems (Porter, 2011: 116). Instead, in an ontological sense formal structure and informal practices are always mutually implicated; with the formal depending upon the informal and vice versa. In this sense, as Hirst (1994) repeatedly emphasizes, informality and associative democracy are always supplemental to the administrative state.

As a set of claims about governance and citizenship, the concept of informality draws inspiration from Michel de Certeau's idea of the 'everyday tactics' of citizens (1984). These are the informal, ordinary activities and routines with which citizens lay claim to urban space and urban resources and literally create their own city, or, more precisely, a city that is adapted to their own needs, challenges and problems. Informality as informal citizenship contains both necessity and hope. That is, on the one hand, informality is about the imperative of obtaining the necessary means (money, information, connections, influence, space) to provide for an acceptable form of living in a situation in which such resources are scarce or unavailable. But it also safeguards the social ties, everyday practices and 'free spaces' (Boyte, 2004: 61) with which to articulate an identity that helps one to uphold and sustain oneself in the face of the hegemonic, disciplinary forces of the wider social environment (Roy, 2010: 96).[11] In his exposition of associative democracy, Hirst sees the virtues of cooperation, mutuality and voluntary self-governing as more or less self-explanatory, but we are now in a position to see that their value lies in the power of informality to provide practical, non-traditional answers to the hegemonic decoupling of state and economy, on the one hand, and the lifeworld of citizens, on the other. In the free space of informality citizens own the issues they choose to address and the solutions to them. They do not need to be told that sustainability is a good thing for the future of our planet because their energy- or food-production schemes are organized according to principles of sustainability that are embedded in everyday practices. They do not need to be admonished in a paternalistic, Christian-Democratic way to heed the needs of their elderly parents by a government that, strapped for cash, has de facto abandoned the elderly, because they live with their parents, understand their needs and find creative solutions to address these. They also do not need to be told that they must form well-integrated communities, because 'community' is a by-product of working on collective issues together; but in the case of informality it is a spontaneous, living, breathing community, not the abstract entities that populate the policy reports of neoliberal governments.

In civic enterprise informality and associative democracy come together to form a potentially powerful alternative to the currently toxic combination of the administrative state, production systems that are dominated by giant, transnational firms and precarious labour contracts, and the neoliberal discursive hegemony that pervades and sustains this arrangement. Civic enterprises can be regarded, in the words of the political philosopher James Tully, as a 'practice of freedom'. The aim of Tully's political philosophy is a 'redescription' of the system of liberal democracy so that the assumptions that guide the self-understandings of those who are part of it (both those who act as its functionaries as well as those who adapt and resist its working and outcomes), as well as those who study and theorize it, are revealed and can be subjected to critical reflection and action. The term 'redescription' is Tully's, and it will clarify our purpose to quote him more fully here:

> Rather, it [what Tully calls his public philosophy] seeks to characterize the conditions of possibility of the problematic form of governance in a redescription (often in a new vocabulary) that transforms the self-understandings of those subject to and struggling within it, enabling them to see its contingent conditions and the possibilities of governing themselves differently. (Tully, 2008: 16)

Tully suggests that being 'subject' to one particular form of government, no matter how oppressive or hegemonic, does not dictate 'the self-consciousness and self-formation of the governed down to every detail' (2008: 23). Rather, he identifies three general cases of practices of freedom that accompany practices of governance. Civic enterprise, we will argue, can fruitfully be seen as one of these practices: contesting 'existing rules of dominant practices, but do[ing] so with existing language games and institutional channels and procedures' (Tully, 2008: 23). It is in this sense that we envision civic enterprise's potential for democratic innovation. Not as a way to displace liberal democracy and the administrative state, but as an associative alternative that produces vital social goods, re-designs the social system of production and generates democratic values – an alternative that supplements, and partly supplants, large-scale, market-based production and its overwhelming negative externalities.

Notes

1 A social system of production consists of a society's norms, rules, habits, conventions, and values, which in turn influence the institutional arrangements (e.g. markets, the state, association, networks) that are dominant in a society. These in turn influence the structure and interaction of a society's business system with its institutional environment, which consists of financial markets, the industrial relations system, the educational and training system, and the state. The state has multiple roles in any social system of production. It both influences the rules of the system and is the ultimate enforcer of rules. Moreover, it can also be an owner of the means of production (Rogers Hollingworth, 2002). The concept of the social system of production emphasizes that in liberal democracies the business system is intimately tied into, and cannot be seen apart from, the principles and institutional and discursive organization of representative democracy.

2 As Dryzek (1996: 9) puts it: '(L)iberal democracy plus market capitalism seems to be the universal model of choice, and variation comes only in falling short of that model.'

3 Dryzek (1996: 10): '(M)y "realist" focus is intended to be creative and enabling, not just chastening and constraining. At a minimum it might tell friends of democracy when they are wasting their time, so that their energies might be better spent in other places. More important, it might show what kinds of innovations are possible and fruitful in particular kinds of times and places. The efforts of democratic theorists and advocates are likely to be productive to the extent they are directed toward the real opportunities for freedom in democratic innovation that exist amid a host of necessitarian constraints.'

4 For sublime analyses, see Crouch (2011) and Streeck (2013).

5 Crouch (2011: 116): 'Ordinary people played their part, not as workers seeking to improve their situation through trade unions, legislation protecting employment rights and publicly funded social insurance schemes, but as debt-holders, participants in credit markets. This fundamental political shift was more profound than anything that could be produced by alternations between nominally social democratic and neoliberal conservative parties in government as the result of elections … it has imparted a fundamental rightward shift to the whole political spectrum, as the collective and individual interests of everyone are tied to the financial markets, which in their own operations act highly unequally, producing extreme concentration of wealth.'

6 Boontje (2013: 14) counts 754 citizen renewable-energy cooperatives (RECs) in Germany at the end of 2012. He states that the expansion of these RECs took off in 2006 after a new energy law was introduced that made the feed-in of renewable energy into the grid possible at a price that is fixed for 20 years and that is higher for small than for large producers. This is a good example of the facilitation of civic enterprise by the state through smart legal design.

7 General government gross financial liabilities as a percentage of GDP increased from 51.5 in 2007 to 84.2 per cent in 2013 (OECD, 2013). Although this is well below the EU average of 106.4, the story of private debt is another one. Between 2002 and 2011 the gross debt-to-income ratio of households increased from 163.58 to 250.03, making

Dutch households the second most indebted in the EU. Much of that private debt went into mortgages. At the same time we see that median net household income has been flat since 2008 (2008: €20,156 – 2011: €20,310; source: Eurostat [http://appsso.eurostat.ec.europa.eu/nui/show.do?dataset=ilc_di04&lang=en; accessed 7 August 2013]) and housing prices have fallen by 18 per cent since the peak of 2008, with a quarter of mortgages now 'under water'. With nominal GDP declining because of EU and national austerity policies, private and public debt in the Netherlands is growing on a shrinking base.

8 We have observed examples where energy or care cooperatives branch out into low-cost transport enterprises. People who became acquainted in the original cooperative were willing to provide their car and their time to others who were in need of transportation.

9 See Hirst (1994) and Warren (2001) for accounts of associative democracy, its democratic effects, and its implications for contemporary economic and social governance.

10 As in the case of public choice (Osborne and Gaebler, 2000; Crouch, 2011: 62).

11 Boyte (2004: 61): 'Free spaces, rooted in everyday life settings, are places in which powerless people have a measure of autonomy for self-organization and engagement with alternative ideas.'

References

Ahrensbach, T., Beunderman, J. *et al.* (2011) *Compendium for the Civic Economy: What the Big Society should learn from 25 trailblazers*, London: 00:/.

Amin, A., Cameron, A. and Hudson, R. (2002) *Placing the Social Economy*, London: Routledge.

Ansell, C.K. (2011) *Pragmatist Democracy: Evolutionary learning as public philosophy*, Oxford: Oxford University Press.

Beunderman, J. and Van der Heijden, J. (2013) *De financiering van burgerproductie: Een verkenning van vraag en aanbod*, Zwolle: Provincie Overijssel.

Bohman, J. (1996) *Public Deliberation: Pluralism, complexity and democracy*, Cambridge, MA: The MIT Press.

Boontje, Ph.S. (2013) *Empowering the Next Generation: A German wind & solar energy cooperatives business model research*, master's thesis, Delft University.

Bourgon, J. (2011) *A New Synthesis of Public Administration: Serving in the 21st century*, Montreal: McGill-Queen's University Press.

Boyte, H.C. (2004) *Everyday Politics: Reconnecting citizens and public life*, Philadelphia, PA: University of Pennsylvania Press.

Chatterjee, P. (2006) *The Politics of the Governed: Reflections on popular politics in most of the world*, New York, NY: Columbia University Press.

Commission of the European Communities (CEC). (1993) *Growth, Competitiveness, Employment: The challenge and ways forward into the 21st century*, White Paper, Luxembourg: Office for the Official Publications of the European Communities (OOPEC).

Corbridge, S., Williams, G., Srivastava, M. and Véron, R. (2005) *Seeing the State: Governance and governmentality in India*, Cambridge: Cambridge University Press.

Crouch, C. (2011) *The Strange Non-Death of Neoliberalism*, Cambridge: Polity Press.

Dahl, R. (1989) *Democracy and Its Critics*, New Haven, CT: Yale University Press.

de Certeau, M. (1984) *The Practice of Everyday Life*, Berkeley, CA: University of California Press.

Devlin, R. (2011) Informal urbanism in the USA: New challenges for theory and practice, *Planning Theory and Praxis*, 12(1): 144–150.
Dryzek, J. (1990) *Discursive Democracy: Politics, policy and political science*, Cambridge: Cambridge University Press.
Dryzek, J. (1996) *Democracy in Capitalist Times: Ideals, limits and struggles*, Oxford: Oxford University Press.
Healey, P., de Magalhaes, C., Madanipour, A. and Pendlebury, J. (2003) Place, identity and local politics: Analysing initiatives in deliberative governance, in M. Hajer and H. Wagenaar (eds), *Deliberative Policy Analysis: Understanding governance in the network society*, Cambridge: Cambridge University Press.
Hirst, P. (1994) *Associative Democracy: New forms of economic and social governance*, Cambridge: Polity Press.
Holston, J. (2008) *Insurgent Citizenship: Disjunctions of democracy and modernity in Brazil*, Princeton, NJ: Princeton University Press.
Huygen, A. (2012) *Condities voor Zelforganisatie*, WMO Kenniscahier 18.
Lindblom, C. (1977) *Politics and Markets: The world's political-economic systems*, New York, NY: Basic Books.
Lindblom, C. (1982) The market as prison, *Journal of Politics*, 44: 324–336.
Lombard, M. and Huxley, M. (2011) Self-made cities: Ordinary informality?, *Planning Theory and Praxis*, 12(1): 120–125.
Lowndes, V. and Sullivan, H. (2008) How low can you go? Rationales and challenges for neighbourhood governance, *Public Administration*, 86(1): 53–74.
Lukkezen, J. and Suyker, W. (2013) *De naakte feiten over de Nederlandse overheidsschuld*, The Hague: Centraal Planbureau.
Mian, A. and Sufi, A. (2014) House of Debt. How they (and you) caused the great recession, and how we can prevent it from happening again, Chicago, IL: The University of Chicago Press.
Molloy, A., McFeely, C. and Connolly, E. (1999) *Building a Social Economy for the New Millennium*, Derry: Guildhall Press/NICDA.
Moore, M. (1997) *Creating Public Value: Strategic management in government*, Cambridge, MA: Harvard University Press.
O'Connor, J. (1973) *The Fiscal Crisis of the State*, New York, NY: St. Martin's.
OECD (2013) 'Government debt', in *Economics: Key Tables from OECD*, No. 21. doi: 10.1787/gov-debt-table-2013-1-en (accessed 4 August 2013).
Offe, C. (1984) *Contradictions of the Welfare State*, Cambridge, MA: MIT Press.
Ooijen, Dave van (2013) An overview of Dutch examples of citizen initiatives, paper presented at the TRP Seminar on Civic Enterprise, Department of Town and Regional Planning, University of Sheffield, 1 May.
Osborne, D. and Gaebler, T. (2000) *Reinventing Government: How the entrepreneurial spirit is transforming the public sector*, London: Longman.
Porter, L. (2011) Interface: Informality, the commons and the paradoxes for planning – Concepts and debates for informality and planning, *Planning Theory and Praxis*, 12(1): 115–120.
Rogers Hollingworth, J. and Müller, K.H. (2002) On social systems of production – and beyond, in J. Rogers Hollingworth, K.H. Müller, E.J. Hollingworth and D. Gear (eds), *Advancing Socio-Economics: An institutionalist perspective*, Lanham, MD: Rowman & Littlefield, pp. 235–239.
Roy, A. (2003) *City Requiem: Calcutta, gender and the politics of poverty*, Minneapolis, MN: University of Minnesota Press.

Roy, A. (2010) Informality and the politics of planning, in J. Hillier and P. Healey (eds), *The Ashgate Research Companion to Planning Theory: Conceptual challenges to spatial planning theory*, Farnham: Ashgate, pp. 87–109.

Simone, A. and Abouhani, A. (eds) (2005) *Urban Africa: Changing contours of survival in the city*, Dakar: Codesria Books.

Specht, M. (2012) *De Pragmatiek van Burgerparticipatie: Hoe burgers omgaan met complexe vraagstukken omtrent veiligheid, leefbaarheid en stedelijke ontwikkeling in drie Europese steden*, PhD thesis, Amsterdam, Free University.

Streeck, W. (2013) *Gekaufte Zeit: Die vertagte Krise des demokratischen Kapitalismus*, Berlin: Suhrkamp.

Tully, J. (2008) *Public Philosophy in a New Key, Vol. 1: Democracy and civic freedom*, Cambridge: Cambridge University Press.

Wagenaar, H. (2007) Governance, complexity and democratic participation: How citizens and public officials harness the complexities of neighbourhood decline, *American Review of Public Administration*, 37(1): 17–50.

Wagenaar, H. (2014) The agonistic experience: Informality, hegemony and transformative democracy, in A. Norval, S. Griggs and H. Wagenaar (eds), *Practices of Freedom: Democracy, conflict and participation in decentred governance*, Cambridge: Cambridge University Press.

Wagenaar, H. and Specht, M. (2010) *Geëngageerd Bewonerschap: Bewonersparticipatie in Drie Europese Steden [Engaged Residents: Citizen participation in three European cities]*, The Hague: Nicis Institute.

Warren, M. (2001) *Democracy and Association*, Princeton, NJ: Princeton University Press.

Warren, M. (2014) Governance-driven democratization, in A. Norval, S. Griggs and H. Wagenaar (eds), *Practices of Freedom: Democracy, conflict and participation in decentred governance*, Cambridge: Cambridge University Press.

Wetenschappelijke Raad voor het Regeringsbeleid (WRR). (2005) *Vertrouwen in de Buurt*, Amsterdam: Amsterdam University Press.

8

The Community's Capacity to Plan: The Disproportionate Requirements of the New English Neighbourhood Planning Initiative

Susannah Gunn, Elizabeth Brooks and Geoff Vigar

Recognising the importance of community engagement in plan-making is not new (Skeffington, 1969), nor is encouraging communities to participate in formal planning processes (Berkeley *et al.*, 1995), or responding to challenges when they do (Rydin, 2006). What may be 'new' in the Neighbourhood Planning Initiative (the latest initiative to open planning up to local stakeholders in England) is government encouragement to communities to initiate plan production and ultimately to produce statutory ratified plans with legal status, supported by local authorities. This appears to reflect a power shift in plan-making. In the familiar terms of Arnstein's (1969: 217) ladder of citizens' empowerment, it takes us to the very top rungs of 'delegated control' (rung 7) and 'citizen power' (rung 8).[1] Such empowerment, however, assumes a latent willingness and capacity within local communities to engage in plan-making and/or that these capacities can be developed.

This chapter reflects on the Coalition Government's new initiative in England of Neighbourhood Planning, in relation to its latent assumption that communities have the capacity to develop a plan that can gain statutory status. It does this by reviewing the trajectory of English planning's attempts to engage with communities, and reflects on whether increased opportunity for empowerment is accompanied by communities' capacity to take advantage of it. It then introduces the idea of community capacity as an analytical tool and uses it to reflect on a case study of one of the vanguard Neighbourhood Planning processes and the plan it produced.

This case study was observed over a period of more than two years, from when the initiative started in October 2010, up to the time of writing (July 2013). As part of this observation, key events and monthly meetings were attended, minutes collected and notes taken; plan documents and supporting documents were also obtained. Early interviews were conducted with local authority officers (mainly planners, but also a community worker), the Neighbourhood Plan Steering Group members (responsible for achieving the initiative), other Parish Council members, one or two significant figures in the setting up of the initiative, and the front-runners' central government representative; attending meetings allowed researchers to interact informally with Steering Group members. The case study has been anonymised to protect participants' identities, as agreed with participants at the outset of the research.

The chapter concludes that, in relation to the nature of the task to be achieved, the neighbourhood initiative requires a disproportionate level of community commitment, drawing from a deep well of community capacity in order to develop plans that can be ratified. It also concludes that in this particular instance the community was extremely well endowed in relation to its community assets, was operating in a relatively straightforward, well-protected planning context and had considerable help from the local planning authority. Even in such supportive conditions, the Plan Steering Group still found it expedient to use formalised processes to get tasks completed. Other communities with more limited assets, more complex and pressured development contexts and a less helpful local planning authority are likely to find it harder.

Community involvement in planning and the community's capacity to participate

Historically, commitment to include the community and other stakeholders in planning has ebbed and flowed, and even where such engagement has occurred, the genuineness of the intention has been challenged (Arnstein, 1969; Rydin, 2006). Over and over again, mainstream planning legislation has sought to incorporate the community into planning decision-making (Baker *et al.*, 2007; Berkeley *et al.*, 1995), into regeneration initiatives (Taylor, 2000) and into non-statutory plans on the margins of mainstream planning produced by citizens, such as parish plans. These initiatives have increasingly sought to include those who utilise planning into the planning processes they use (plan-making, development decision-making), shifting the emphasis from consultation to participation to engagement, and variously focusing on the public, stakeholders or communities to facilitate their particular say. Yet, again and again, there is a sense that planning has not succeeded in engaging with the public nor in truly ceding power to those it has tried to include (Doak and Parker, 2005; Mawson and Hall, 2000), except perhaps at the margins.

In this context, 'Neighbourhood Planning' can be seen as the latest attempt within England to include local stakeholders in mainstream planning processes, whereby local stakeholders become the producers of the plan they want (albeit in conformity with national policy and other Local Plans). This initiative has emerged primarily from the Conservatives' 'Big Society' and 'Localism' agendas, drawing on the relative success of citizen-led Parish Council plans and other voluntary initiatives. It sought to strengthen volunteerism in communities and to give participants the tools to have a greater say, and to act beyond the constraints of the existing modes of providing, operating and regulating – albeit at a very local level.[2]

The planning aspect of this new Localism agenda included a suite of new planning mechanisms (Neighbourhood Plans, neighbourhood development orders, Community Right to Build orders, etc.) through which local communities could gain statutory control of the planning and development of their local area. Neighbourhood Plans must be fronted by the Parish Council, or where no such body exists, at least 21 people may get together to form a Neighbourhood Forum to lead the process. The idea emerged in 2009; initial applicants for the initiative were selected in 2010. This set of pioneers ('front-runners') had their planning process up and running before the Localism Act was passed in 2011, while the relevant regulations were produced in December of that year. Each initial front-runner was given £20,000 to use in plan-producing activities; this was subsequently increased to £30,000, with benchmarks attached to ensure its expenditure on the production of a plan. Consequently much of the thinking in relation to Neighbourhood Planning emerged incrementally, as the initial front-runners progressed their plans.

While supposedly 'light touch', completing a Neighbourhood Plan with statutory planning status requires a number of uncertain, arduous and potentially contentious stages to achieve quite particular strategic outcomes. It is therefore not necessarily the easiest or most appropriate community planning activity in which communities might engage (Bridges, 2012). Nevertheless, its ultimate statutory status cedes a legal authority to communities that is lacking from other plans and strategies, such as a local Parish Plan.

Significantly, by contrast with processes where the local authority includes the community in plan-making, this initiative requires those communities that wish to be involved to initiate and produce their own plans with the local authority's cooperation. This represents a step 'up' Arnstein's ladder, as the responsibility for recognising the need for a plan, organising the production of the plan, actually producing the plan and getting it ratified has been delegated to the local citizens or their representatives (the Parish Council or Neighbourhood Forum). The citizens are in control, with the local authority relegated to a supporting role (to whatever degree it does so).

However, as many regeneration initiatives recognise, ceding power to people is not enough; there is also an issue about the community's capacity to engage. This is especially true in relation to the higher rungs of Arnstein's ladder, which demand more from the community than simply responding to consultation endeavours (see Table 8.1). Shifting the onus of the responsibility for producing these plans onto local communities also anticipates that

Table 8.1 Arnstein's higher rungs of citizen empowerment in relation to the community capacity dimensions

Arnstein's Ladder of Participation (taken from Arnstein, 1969: 217)	*Community capacity dimensions required to achieve this (taken from Norton et al., 2002: 206–207, and annotated)*
Rung 8: Citizen Control Citizens initiate the activity, proactively pursue it Other organisations accept the initiative, work with it	• Skills and resources o to identify the need for a plan, take control of the project and deliver • Nature of social relations o in relation to controlling the initiative, ensure it happens • Structure and mechanisms for community dialogue o to initiate and achieve the enterprise, shared ownership of delivery • Leadership o to initiate the enterprise, own it, deliver it • Civic participation o to include others in the enterprise, shared ownership delivery • Value system o in relation to particular enterprise, and more widely • Learning culture o reflecting on processes, including reflecting on citizen control
Rung 7: Delegated Power Citizens hold significant cards to ensure accountability of the programme to them Power-holders need to start the bargaining process rather than respond to pressure from the other end	• Skills and resources o to achieve the delegated remit • Nature of social relations o in relation to achieving remit • Structures and mechanisms for community dialogue o to achieve the delegated enterprise, share ownership of delivery • Leadership o to operate within delegated remit • Civic participation o to include others in the delegated enterprise, share ownership delivery • Value system o in relation to delegated enterprise, and more widely • Learning culture o reflecting on processes, including reflecting on delegated power

communities have a latent willingness and capacity within themselves to produce plans, or the wherewithal to gain this capacity.

Given Neighbourhood Planning's intention to delegate these powers to local communities (via Parish Councils and Neighbourhood Forums), it is reasonable to ask whether or not they have the community capacity they need to deliver these projects.

An analytical framework: dimensions of community capacity to achieve Neighbourhood Planning

Norton *et al.* (2002: 205) define community capacity as a 'set of dynamic community traits, resources and associational patterns that can be brought to bear for community building and community [initiatives]'.[3] According to Goodman *et al.* (1998), community capacity includes the notion of 'empowerment' to enable the community to achieve the intention set out by the community. However, it also includes a community's potential to address a situation, or optimise an opportunity – its 'capacity'; and the community's ability to apply this 'capacity' actively to a given situation – the community's 'competence'. All three ideas (empowerment, capacity, competence) are evident in the concept of community capacity, providing a more nuanced understanding of a community's propensity to engage in a particular opportunity, or to act effectively (or otherwise) against a particular threat.

Primarily qualitative in nature, the concept is value-laden, focusing as it does on the characteristics of individuals and social structures. Inevitably there is variability in the way these traits are characterised, connected and utilised within the community capacity literature, as well as in the way that community capacity is operationalised in actuality (Chaskin, 2001; Foster-Fishman *et al.*, 2001; Norton *et al.*, 2002).

Nevertheless, 'community capacity' as an idea does provide an analytical lens through which to view the potential and actual propensity for a community to engage in an initiative such as Neighbourhood Planning, and to investigate how this is happening in actuality.

The concept tends to subdivide community capacity into a range of traits, or dimensions (Beckley *et al.*, 2008; Chaskin, 2001; Foster-Fishman *et al.*, 2001; Goodman *et al.*, 1998; Norton *et al.*, 2002), but acknowledges the fuzzy interrelational quality and multi-dimensional nature of the components of community capacity (Goodman *et al.*, 1998; Norton *et al.*, 2002). Consequently, these dimensions and how they relate are at best limited expressions of multi-variable concepts, which are in turn inevitable simplifications of actual conditions (Beckley *et al.*, 2008; Chaskin, 2001; Goodman *et al.*, 1998).

Norton *et al.* (2002: 206) tabulate a range of different conceptual constructions of these dimensions and how they connect. In so doing, they identify seven different qualities as being important. These are: 'skills and resources', the 'nature of social relationships', 'structures and mechanisms for community dialogue', 'leadership', 'civic participation', 'value system' and 'learning culture'.

The following sections introduce these sub-dimensions and utilise them to explore whether one Neighbourhood Planning front-runner has the wherewithal to produce a Neighbourhood Plan, and how this is expressed. In many cases, aspects of the sub-dimensions overlap and some cross-referencing between sections addresses this. The analysis pays particular attention to evidence of Goodman *et al.*'s (1998) broad dimensions of empowerment, capacity and competence. It takes the opportunity to introduce the case through its description of the locality's and community's assets.

Skills and resources

This sub-dimension itemises a community's existing resources as capitals: economic/financial, social, natural, knowledge and human capital (Beckley *et al.*, 2008; Taylor, 2000), or as 'inventories of assets': for example, built infrastructure, financial assets, socially defined assets (Beckley *et al.*, 2008). For efficacy and social equality reasons, the diversity and distribution of these skills and resources and the willingness to share them are important (Beckley *et al.*, 2008; Chaskin, 2001; Goodman *et al.*, 1998). Other skills increase a community's potential capital by fostering competent use of resources, enabling participant training to increase the community's skill set and/or supporting access to resources beyond the community's own skill set, extending the community's resource base (Chaskin, 2001; Goodman *et al.*, 1998).

Many interpretations focus on transferable skills: communication skills (Foster-Fishman *et al.*, 2001), problem-solving skills (Chaskin, 2001) and others, which are useful for a whole range of tasks and activities. Other interpretations focus on more specialist/expert skills, such as having 'knowledge and skill in policy, politics, community change' or 'grant writing' (Foster-Fishman *et al.*, 2001: 244); and certainly for a task such as producing a Neighbourhood Plan, specialist planning-related skills (writing/planning policy, collating relevant evidence) are needed, as well as transferable ones.

Reviewing the case study's skills and resources collectively in relation to the community's capacity to engage and produce a Neighbourhood Plan, this analysis found an abundant potential, though much of it was not fully utilised for this initiative. The case is situated in a remote and beautiful rural locality, encompassing a small town and outlying hamlets. Its landscape, natural and heritage assets are well protected by national planning designations. While these designations place certain restrictions on what can be built, they also protect the traditional character of the built environment, so the community has been able to adopt a pro-development stance in the knowledge that their assets are already well safeguarded.

The population is around 2,000 people (ONS, 2012), with better health than the regional average, and a higher percentage of the population with specialist skills and further qualifications compared to the regional average, suggesting considerable community potential for activities such as producing a Neighbourhood Plan. It is also slightly older than the national and regional averages, mainly due to people moving into the locality in mid-life and remaining in the locality as they age, often living longer (85-plus) than those not in rural locations (Brooks, 2011; Champion and Shepherd, 2006). This raises substantive planning issues of housing affordability for locals, and concerns about retaining the younger generation in the locality to maintain its viability. In terms of process, this capable, older population provides a potentially skills-rich, time-rich population, able and available to contribute to plan-making activities. The community's particular skills set included a qualified statistician and others who worked or had worked in relevant planning-related organisations.

The community has managed to retain essential shops (general stores, pubs, chemist, post office) and tourism assets. Many residents are self-employed, working in the locality, providing local services, or engaging in often seasonal tourist or agricultural activities. Others commute to work in a nearby market town, or the nearest city (34 miles away).

However, the community's location on the periphery of most service provision means that some services do not exist at all, for example a gas supply. Equally, some services are part-time or mobile, while others are limited, such as the telecommunications network, and still others, notably the emergency services, are some distance away. A number of services are under threat: for example, a school closed during the production of the Neighbourhood Plan.

Given this marginality, the community is highly self-sufficient and resourceful, finding their own solutions, such as setting up an oil-buying cooperative to buy energy in bulk at a reduced cost, or becoming 'first responders' trained and relied on by the emergency services, while these travel in from more distant bases. This reflects a capacity within the community to identify new opportunities, such as the Neighbourhood Planning Initiative, and to capitalise on them; albeit, in the case of the Neighbourhood Plan, with some considerable reservations (discussed in more detail below).

These considerable social and human assets are further exemplified by the multitude of community groups (over 70) meeting informally around shared interests (keep-fit activities, amateur dramatics, cinema club, sports teams), shared needs (such as the parents and toddlers groups) and shared concerns (campaign-oriented activist groups). Potentially, these provided an immense opportunity for engaging with a rich and diverse social network about the Neighbourhood Plan – an opportunity that was not, however, taken full advantage of, as further discussed below.

More formally, the Parish Council is also a social asset, with its elected volunteer membership representing the community; attending meetings and making local decisions on others' behalf; and also using parish funds to help maintain some of the social and physical community assets (community halls, for example). The government's Neighbourhood Planning Initiative extends the remit of the Parish Council, where such exists, to include Neighbourhood Planning, empowering parishes to produce a plan. In this instance, an already actively engaged Parish Council, with a proven track record of completing projects, was in a positive position to engage in this initiative, had they wanted to do so. However, given the planning focus of the process, the council was not sure it would be an appropriate means to resolve their local issues, nor that it would provide the return on the time, energy and resources that would need to be expended on it. They were also cautious of the contentious nature of the substantive issues a Neighbourhood Plan is likely to cover, and how this might play out in practice.

However, having been induced to set up the case as a neighbourhood initiative front-runner, the Parish Council successfully negotiated assistance from the local authority, including a dedicated planner to ensure the project's progression to completion. This is discussed elsewhere, but reflects Chaskin's (2001) notion of the ability to access or acquire skills and resources when the community does not have them; and needless to say, it provided this case with 'free' specialist expertise not readily available to others in this initiative.

Nature of social relationships

This sub-dimension focuses on the quality of the relationships found within a community, with Foster-Fishman *et al.* (2001) highlighting that both individuals' and the community's/group's characters have an important part to play in determining the quality of these relationships, relating to individuals' mutual sense of reciprocity and trust (see Norton *et al.*, 2002); their sense of membership and belonging (Goodman *et al.*, 1998); and/or their sense of efficacy and confidence (see Norton *et al.*, 2002).

With regard to the case study, the Steering Committee for the Neighbourhood Plan was composed mainly of members drawn from the Parish Council, with the additional participation of an active community group. In terms of the sense of membership and belonging (Goodman *et al.*, 1998), most of the Parish Council members had a strong sense of belonging to the place, and also of belonging to and representing the community, and felt that their elected status legitimised their decision-making.

In terms of the sense of efficacy, the Parish Council members were not immediately committed to the Neighbourhood Plan project, and were unsure of the initiative overall, questioning what it would contribute, in terms of the time and resources it would take to achieve and the value of a completed plan for realising their wider intentions. They were initially very reticent about taking on the role of planner, and producing a plan for the locality that might not be approved by their friends and neighbours. However, in the course of the process, as consultation activities bore out the validity of their ideas, they came to gain confidence in the substance of their evidence and of the plan's intentions, although they continued to question its necessity.

Given their initial misgivings with regard to the project, the Steering Group members could feasibly have allowed the process to flounder; however, having accepted the challenge, the group and particularly the leader and vice-leader adopted a 'we've started so we'll finish' attitude and became fully committed to achieving it. In spite of lengthening timeframes, they were able to maintain trust in each other to see the task completed. Moreover, they also contributed considerably to the wider neighbourhood initiative, attending conferences, seminars and workshops, giving talks to interested groups and feeding back information to interested government representatives and others. This was greatly helped by the local authority planner, who negotiated the Steering Group set-up with a group of people unfamiliar to him, and who gained trust through his steadfast support with the Steering Group's efforts towards producing a plan.

The literature does acknowledge, albeit obliquely, that communities may be fractured or fragile through Chaskin's (2001) reflections on 'race/class dynamics', 'residential stability', 'patterns of migration' and 'safety', and Taylor (2000) recognises that while greater openness and diversity may be positive, they can also exacerbate existing tensions. However, these characteristics tend to be discussed positively and the space for dissent is downplayed, with a general perception that these disagreements can be overcome with stronger bonds of community friendship (Foster-Fishman *et al.*, 2001; Goodman *et al.*, 1998). This leaves open the question as to what happens if friendships fracture, and trust dissipates rather than compromises being found.

These are outcomes that are quite likely in Neighbourhood Planning exercises, where issues can be so contentious that agreement cannot be reached. The case study example could be said to be on a path towards diminishing tension, but this is only because its origins were highly fraught. Central government's initial lack of clarity over who could initiate the production of a Neighbourhood Plan allowed a community group to start the process, regardless of the Parish Council's initial reticence, creating tensions. The local authority negotiated a way forward with the council, widening the Steering Group membership to allow some non-Parish Councillor representatives onto it, and committed considerable local authority assets to facilitate the initiative. But inevitably, with something as contentious as a Local Plan, not everyone eventually felt able to come on board.

Structures and mechanisms for community dialogue

This sub-dimension focuses on the instrumental elements of community dialogue, rather than its general characteristics (discussed above). One aspect of this sub-dimension is the 'social and inter-organisational networks' that exist within communities (Goodman *et al.*, 1998). The Harwood Group (1996, cited in Norton *et al.*, 2002) lists five social arrangements that reflect increasing levels of commitment, responsibility and formality, probably reducing the number of participants as they are listed. They include: 'informal networks and links', 'abundance of social gatherings', 'organised space for interaction', 'catalytic organisations' and 'safe havens for decision-makers', and are a helpful typology for reviewing the networks of a community.

In this respect, producing a Neighbourhood Plan intended to become a statutory planning document, heeded by developers and local planners alike, needs a relatively high commitment from quite a small team of individuals, and perhaps some levels of formality in the carrying out of tasks and making of decisions in a 'safe haven', where the substance of the plans can be debated, questions can be asked and decisions can be taken. It would have been possible to develop a plan in a more networked way, perhaps drawing on the more than 70 community and activity groups existing in the locality, and some of the Steering Group were aware of more participatory community planning models that might have been utilised. However, in this case the production team was primarily the Steering Group, assisted by the local authority planner, with other experts on the planning side and the community side giving assistance at various points as required. Inevitably the writing process needs a relatively small and quite specialist team to draft and vet policy prose and this was completed within the Steering Group ahead of consulting with a wider audience.

Another aspect of these mechanisms for dialogue is how interaction occurs and what is discussed in relation to a particular initiative (such as a Neighbourhood Plan) or an event (such as a meeting). The literature identifies a range of mechanisms for 'participant interaction and decision-making', 'information sharing' and 'problem-solving' (see Norton *et al.*, 2002: 206), with some of these mechanisms and content allowing greater power-sharing than others. Much of the literature draws attention to the need for informal as well as formal processes, and for inclusive rather than exclusive mechanisms.

Goodman *et al.* (1998: 261) suggest that these networks should be characterised by 'reciprocal links throughout the network, [with] frequent supportive interactions, overlap[ping] with other networks within the community, an ability to form new associations, [and] co-operative decision-making processes'.

In this case the plan was primarily moved forward by the Steering Group, at a monthly evening meeting attended regularly by the local authority planner and other officers as required, and periodically by a London-based central government representative attached to the case. The meeting was minuted, and discussions were through the Chair. The meeting focused on the tasks of plan production – the need for particular evidence, consultation and examination, and how these might be achieved; the substance of the planning issues raised in issues papers, findings from the evidence and so on. As the plan progressed, drafts were circulated for comment. In an effort to be inclusive, part-way through the process two teenagers supported by a youth worker were included, as representatives of the future of the locality. The local authority planner usually completed the tasks required of him by the Steering Group's decisions once these had been made.

The Steering Group made genuine attempts to consult with the community, albeit in quite structured ways. They consulted on the plan three times ahead of a required final referendum.[4] The first time was the launch of the plan, to which all householders had been invited by postal invitation. This introduced the initiative to the community, and asked for their comments on their perceptions of the locality and what they would like the plan to tackle, albeit within the structuring categories from a recent existing Parish Plan. The second consultation was with representatives of the locality's societies and groups, local businesses and other interested parties, to read early drafts of the plan and comment on its intention and viability. This was held on three different evenings and was poorly attended, although the discussions were genuine. The third consultation was for the final draft of the plan, ahead of it being independently examined and going to a final referendum, and all householders were invited to comment on this once again. Throughout the process, information was also posted onto a dedicated website, and local school-children took part in a parish-wide infrastructure audit carried out by university students, prior to the school closing. The information gained from these events was considered at Steering Group meetings, and confirmed the Steering Group's own perceptions of the locality, the needs of the community and the policies that the plan should cover.

A third aspect of this dimension focuses on the more external or associative relations of the community and/or locality. In their 'spheres of social relations', Beckley *et al.* (2008) identify these as the 'market' and 'bureaucratic' spheres (which overlap with each other) and the 'communal' sphere. Each has distinct interests, values and modes of operation, and they may need to be negotiated with and accommodated on their own terms as well as on the community's if the initiative is to succeed.

In relation to these spheres of external or associative relations, the Steering Group was, as noted above, attended periodically by a national government representative, who had been assigned due to the area's 'front-runner' status. This civil servant could convey the government's intentions, interpret regulations and confirm courses of action in relation to the wider Neighbourhood Planning process; advice that the Steering Group did not necessarily always agree with, or adopt. At a local level, the Steering Group was also greatly assisted by the local authority officers – planners, community officers and others – who had a good understanding of the planning modes of operation and were familiar with negotiating with developers and land interests, on the one hand, and conservation and heritage interests, on the other. They were able to broker negotiations where necessary using these modes of operating and points of reference. This was an immense asset not afforded other Neighbourhood Planning groups.

Advised by the local planning officer, the Steering Group decided relatively early on that the plan would not designate particular sites for specific uses, as this was likely to be contentious and might also confer value to land and certainty of development to particular interests at the expense of others. It was also decided to try to avoid too much interaction with possible vested interests ahead of the consultation of the Draft Plan, to allow all to have the same level of influence. So, where possible, the Steering Group chose not to engage with these interests through negotiation, preferring instead to adopt more transparent methods of consultation, evident to all – and perhaps leaving the tricky negotiations to another occasion, when they might be guided by the plan.

Leadership

Leadership is frequently identified as important (see Norton *et al.*, 2002), but it is often only vaguely defined (Chaskin, 2001). Goodman *et al.* (1998: 262–263) discuss leadership with participation, and raise two key questions: 'who participates and leads?' and 'how do they participate and lead?'. They note that those who lead may not be representative of the demographics of the locality but may instead reflect the leader's or participants' sense of community, the costs and benefits associated with participation and their sense of engagement with the issue in hand. A key issue for Goodman *et al.* is the interplay between positional leaders (those who are elected and/or appointed; e.g. the Parish Council) and reputational leaders, who serve through informal leadership positions (community activists, opinion leaders; Neighbourhood Forums are more likely to be made up of these).

The regulations of the Neighbourhood Planning Initiative are preferential to local Parish Councils, requiring that where they exist a Parish Council should take the lead. Inevitably this means that those who are active elsewhere as positional leaders will tend to lead in Neighbourhood Planning Initiatives too. Elsewhere, where there is no existing Parish Council, recognised individuals (i.e. reputational leaders) may set up a 'Neighbourhood Forum' agreed by the local authority in relation to their representativeness of the community and their capacity to produce a plan. Ultimately, whether positional or reputational leaders take the helm, the likelihood is that the Neighbourhood Planning Initiative will replicate existing power dynamics and ways of working, rather than challenging them.

In the case study example, the leadership has been interesting, as the project was initiated externally to the Parish Council by a 'reputational leader' (Goodman *et al.*, 1998) or 'catalytic individual' (Harwood's catalytic organisation cited in Norton *et al.*, 2002), but the Parish Council, as elected/appointed leaders, then accepted the task, agreed to set up a Steering Group predominantly but not exclusively made up of Parish Councillors and enabled the project to move forward. The progress of the Steering Group and decisions taken would be regularly fed back to the Parish Council at the subsequent Parish Council meeting. This initiated the production of a plan, the purpose and value of which was questioned by many of those most involved in producing it, and which ceded power from the council itself that ultimately central government's Neighbourhood Planning regulations did not require it to cede, albeit in quite contained ways.

The literature's interest in 'how [leaders] lead' relates in part to their ability to organise: that is, their ability to administrate, use resources effectively, implement procedures and focus on both the task and process details (Foster-Fishman *et al.*, 2001; Goodman *et al.*, 1998). It also highlights the quality of their relational skills: that is, their skills in conflict resolution and external affairs (Foster-Fishman *et al.*, 2001), and their ability to include both formal and informal leaders in a responsive and accessible way, to encourage participation from a diverse community network, to encourage those participating to contribute in meetings and to share information (Goodman *et al.*, 1998); and reflects on their ability to inspire: to be visionary and to cultivate new leaders (Foster-Fishman *et al.*, 2001; Goodman *et al.*, 1998).

As already discussed, the group chose to use quite formal modes of operating at the point of decision-making and in their interactions with volunteers' offers of help, and their chosen methods of consultation. This was driven by, on the one hand, a perceived need to adhere to their legitimised role as elected, delegated representatives of the wider community in order to realise the initiative, and, on the other, a need to ensure equity of access to the decision-making processes, rather than allowing what were perceived to be potentially vested interests greater access through more participatory processes.

The Steering Group performed in a highly competent way, based on pre-existing strengths in effective resource management and project administration, but the local authority planning officer also provided project management skills directly related to plan-production processes, and in so doing took a lead through his advisory role. His advice was even-handed, and he sought to be steered by decisions from the Steering Group in relation to both substantive matters and procedural ones over what should be done and how. He worked with volunteers and/or with other officers to achieve the required tasks, as agreed by the Steering Group. His understanding of the plan-production process, policy writing, necessary consultation and evidence-gathering exercises and required ratification processes was invaluable to the initiative, and this was also instrumental in shaping the interactions relating to the plan and achieving a successful project. These contributions should not be underestimated, and similar assistance can be found behind most other Neighbourhood Plans that have been completed, suggesting that some planning knowledge and experience is essential to achieve these plans alongside more generic project management skills and leadership.

Civic participation

The concepts that relate to civic participation highlight the importance of the community being included in the process, and note a number of ways that they are included: through political participation (which would include Parish Councils in this case), faith-based engagement, civic engagement and engagement equally accessible across the community (see Norton *et al.*, 2002: 207). Goodman *et al.* (1998) suggest looking for these organisations and opportunities to see how the community participates.

Wider and more diverse participation is thought to be better than narrow participation, and accessibility to initiatives is encouraged for reasons of legitimacy, social equity and power-sharing (Goodman *et al.*, 1998; Taylor, 2000). That said, Taylor (2000) highlights the problem that widespread participation in community-led partnerships is needed to legitimise the initiative, but at the same time the core of the work (such as writing a Neighbourhood Plan) is likely to be confined to a few. Goodman *et al.* (1998) suggest that leaders may have to choose not to include some groups for efficacy reasons.

Aspects of civic participation have been discussed above in relation to other overlapping dimensions; however, as already noted, the neighbourhood initiative regulations favour political participation in the form of Parish Councils where they exist over other forms of participation, although the intention is that other forms of civic participation will also occur.

It would have been possible to adopt a different, arguably more participatory, model of engagement, drawing on the locality's wealth of social networks, but as this was not adopted or really suggested, how successful it would have been remains open to conjecture. All were invited to various events to give their views, and were given an opportunity to volunteer in the plan-production process at the initial consultation event, which enabled a few interested individuals, some of whom were embedded in civic groups and/or with vested interests, to discuss with the planner how they might participate; but apart from the youth representatives being invited onto the Steering Group, efforts were not specifically made to engage with other harder-to-reach groups, or those with particular relevant but vested interests (see Vigar *et al.*, 2012).

So, in actuality, much of the work has been achieved by the local authority planner, which has potentially reduced the need for greater civic engagement, although the planner himself has been keen to involve volunteers. Some attempts were made to be inclusive, such as inviting young people, as representatives of the future, onto the Steering Group. Where possible, volunteers' and others' offers of help from beyond the Steering Group were taken up in a number of tasks including the writing of a parish profile by a statistician living locally, and an infrastructure audit carried out by university students and local school-children. However, primarily for reasons of equity of access and efficacy of process, the Steering Group tended to choose methods of operating observed by Taylor (2000), whereby the tasks of producing a plan were limited to a few, legitimised and widely accessible (through relatively poorly attended) consultation processes. In this instance, these consultations have largely confirmed the Steering Group's intent.

Value system

Where these concepts address value systems, they focus on three aspects: one is the sense of giving – volunteering, philanthropy, sharing and caring (see Goodman *et al.*, 1998; Norton *et al.*, 2002: 207) – where those involved are giving to the wider community and beyond. A second aspect focuses on shared values and shared community norms, perhaps emerging out of a shared history (see Goodman *et al.*, 1998; Norton *et al.*, 2002: 207); and a third aspect focuses on community vision, shared purpose and civic pride (see Norton *et al.*, 2002: 207).

Although their interests and politics differ, the Steering Group collectively shared a concern for the locality and the community and sought to contribute to it as they could. In relation to the Neighbourhood Plan initiative, most of the group believed that the project was very resource-intensive for relatively little return, with one commenting that it was 'a huge waste of resources when the county was having to cut back elsewhere' (Steering Group member,

November 2011). However, the majority of the group believed that if a plan was being produced, the Parish Council should be the ones to have a major hand in its production, and collectively they committed considerable time to achieving a plan once it had been decided that they would go ahead with the initiative.

Moreover, a number of the Steering Group also attended promotional and facilitating/educating activities organised by government, and when asked, presented their views on the Neighbourhood Planning process to other interested communities at events arranged by those commissioned to help local authorities produce a Local Plan, as well as at county level. Events of such a kind took place on an almost monthly basis through 2011–2012 and were in addition to any activities connected to the production of the plan in the locality. Participation drew heavily on Steering Group members' time and goodwill, over and above their efforts in relation to plan-making activities.

In relation to the plan itself, there was also concern about further tensions that could be provoked through airing the issues, based on past history. Some members recognised the plan's potential for steering development, and the importance of being involved to influence where development might be directed, and what development that might be. However, such self-interest motivating involvement does not necessarily preclude cooperative action and community goals (Vigar *et al.*, submitted); in this case, potential acrimony was diverted relatively early on by agreeing that site-specific designations were not appropriate for this particular plan.

Moreover, as the plan progressed, the Steering Group drew encouragement from consultation events that largely confirmed the Steering Group's perceptions of what was most vital and relevant. As policies were written that challenged the previous received wisdom of planning officers and NGO representatives, and reflected the Steering Group's and community's intentions more nearly than the previous Local Plan policies, the Steering Group felt more confident about the plan's value.

Learning culture

This dimension focuses on a community's critical reflection and self-awareness at both an individual and group level. It includes an ability to challenge one's own individual and collective actions and assumptions, to live with paradox and contradiction and to accommodate alternative ways of thinking and new ideas in an attempt 'to generate alternative visions of the world' (Goodman *et al.*, 1998: 273).

It includes being self-aware and able to define situations clearly, being able to have conscious community discussion and to learn within a culture of ongoing learning (see Foster-Fishman *et al.*, 2001; Norton *et al.*, 2002).

As a 'front-runner' in a new national initiative, the context was a learning one and all parties had the opportunity to learn, including: central government, through their case representative (discussed earlier); the planning community of local authority planners; planning-related non-governmental organisations; representatives from two organisations commissioned to help other communities across England and Wales interested in Neighbourhood Planning; and interested academics. There was a sense of learning from each other about the initiative.

With regard to the national element of the initiative, in relation to this case, the learning was iterative, particularly at the start, with the front-runner experiences occurring ahead of legislation and regulations being written, and their experiences informing 'the experts' and feeding into the writing of the legislation through the national government's case representative. Concurrently, the Steering Group, and particularly the local authority planner, were also gaining interpretative messages from this same representative in person about government's intentions in relation to newly produced policy/process documents.

As noted in the last section, representatives from the Steering Group were asked to present their experiences at county events, organised by the county, and regional events, organised by commissioned organisations responsible for advising other communities interested in producing a Neighbourhood Plan. This gave these individuals time to reflect on their own process, and set them up as educators and advisors – a role they did not seek, but did accept.

However, the main focus of the Steering Group and the expectation placed upon them as a front-runner was the production of a plan (with no prototype to follow) within a reasonable project time. In this they relied heavily upon, and appreciated, the local planners' planning expertise to guide the process, and they made decisions in relation to the documents prepared by the planners. This approach focused learning onto the immediate issues at hand and the next tasks to be achieved, rather than encouraging the group to adopt state-of-the-art techniques that might have been more time-consuming, potentially more contentious and less certain in their outcomes.

While particular individuals were quite reflective, and the Steering Group as a whole was open to the substantive findings emerging from the various consultation events, this particular Steering Group was less reflective in relation to their processes. They tended to use the methods that they had used before to chair meetings and to consult on a plan, and accepted these as the way forward, with a limited amount of consideration for alternative ways of achieving these outcomes. In part this was due to their concerns about producing a plan that could be legitimised through their authorship as elected representatives, and in part it was due to time constraints and the level of commitment to the initiative overall, as no one wanted to spend longer on the production of the plan than was absolutely necessary or experiment with state-of-the-art methods of production that might be difficult/time-consuming to execute, contestable and possibly open up challenges.

Conclusion

Reflecting briefly on the idea of community capacity as an analytical tool, the discussion above shows its usefulness for analysing this particular case and in helping to identify dimensions of capacity and aspects of these dimensions that might otherwise have been overlooked. The literature around the concept highlights its limitations as a simplification of the actual conditions, and the definitional fuzziness of the dimensions due to the complexity of the multi-dimensional interplay of these traits (Beckley *et al.*, 2008; Chaskin, 2001; Goodman *et al.*, 1998), and in so doing presents this interplay as an important aspect of the concept. However, embedded in the concept is a notion that capacity might be quantified, to determine whether engaging in an initiative either increases or diminishes this capacity. Such an approach to applying the concept could easily lead to something of an auditing exercise. By contrast, in this instance the dimensions were used as a basis for reflection on how the dimensions analysed were expressed, and their quality, and to attempt to reflect critically and holistically across the complexity of a community's multi-dimensional, highly nuanced interactions in relation to the particular opportunity of Neighbourhood Planning, rather than analysing whether this opportunity increased or decreased this capacity.

Some of the literature implies that less than positive outcomes may result (e.g. Foster-Fishman *et al.*, 2001; Goodman *et al.*, 1998); with Beckley *et al.* (2008: 63–64) in particular providing a view that reflects more explicitly on some of the negative aspects of community engagement, highlighting that capacity may diminish through an activity as well as increase. However, the bulk of the literature frames the concept and its dimensions in a positive light, presenting them in an idealised way (e.g. Foster-Fishman *et al.*, 2001; Goodman *et al.*, 1998) and focusing on the growth potential for communities that engage in initiatives. Consequently, embedded in the community capacity concept is the notion that communities will almost inevitably become stronger by engaging in initiatives, and the initiatives themselves will gain, which may not be the case.

In relation to Neighbourhood Planning itself, the legislation has empowered communities, and more particularly Parish Councils, where they exist, to produce very localised statutory plans in conformity with national and local policy, that – when ratified – development will have to heed. Moreover, the programme has placed the responsibility for initiating this activity, and seeing it through to completion, in the hands of these community representatives.

To help with developing the capacity of those interested in producing a Neighbourhood Plan, central government helpfully provided a civil servant to each of the front-runner neighbourhoods, who could support them with interpreting emerging legislation and policy; it also commissioned organisations to advise and/or train communities. However, in the early days the emphasis was on the advisory organisations learning about the initiative from the front-runners, and it is only more latterly that the case study front-runner was able to gain from these organisations' planning and community engagement expertise.

This research shows that Neighbourhood Planning, in contrast to some other community plan activities, is time-, resource- and labour-intensive, and requires considerable commitment from a dependable core group for a considerable period of time.

This particular case is in a locality that is strongly protected by national and local planning policy, with an active Parish Council; a very high community capacity in terms of skills, resources, assets, time, social networks, ability to project manage, analyse datasets, make decisions and negotiate outcomes; and a highly supportive local authority providing a dedicated planner – an asset not available to other Neighbourhood Plans.[5] From this it would be possible to assume that this particular front-runner had the propensity to produce a statutory Neighbourhood Plan reflecting the policy intentions of those who produce it, ratified by the wider community through consultation activities and ultimately a referendum within reasonable timeframes.

However, although this particular front-runner is well on the way to having a statutory plan, it still has not quite achieved it, despite the Steering Group and planner meeting regularly, working diligently and choosing more formal, time-saving consultation and decision processes over more participatory methods of civic engagement. This raises fundamental questions about how replicable Neighbourhood Planning is countrywide, particularly in localities and communities that are less well endowed and more diverse than this one.

The government's Neighbourhood Planning Initiative, arguably positive in terms of delegated power and intended to be 'light touch' in design, has been impeded by the rapidly expanding processes that are required to achieve statutory status. This has resulted in huge issues of proportionality as those producing these plans have to engage in such processes for very localised and quite specialised documents, creating huge challenges even for relatively well-endowed communities. Meanwhile, the majority of the country is not engaged in these activities; and many, especially in more disenfranchised areas, may not have the capacity to engage even if they wanted to. This raises a question not only about the community's capacity but also about the overall social justice of this initiative.

Notes

1 While this chapter recognises that thinking in relation to community power has gone beyond Arnstein (e.g. Collins and Ison, 2009; Trittera and McCallumb, 2006), it accepts Arnstein's ladder as a helpful device for thinking about power in relation to this research. It also recognises that Arnstein is of its time and questionable in its assumption that it is always preferable for communities to have greater power. Indeed, this chapter focuses on whether or not communities have the capacity to utilise the remit being given them, and in so doing queries the assumption that more power is inevitably better.

2 This initiative also sought to encourage communities to provide essential services where large commercial enterprises determined they were not viable and left, e.g. a local village shop, a local post office, a small cooperative affordable housing scheme.

3 Norton *et al.* (2002) were discussing community capacity in relation to health theory, and health initiatives – so the actual quotation was 'community health improvement' but it is possible to highlight other policy initiatives here.

4 At the time of writing this referendum was still due to take place.

5 Some other groups producing Neighbourhood Plans, but not all, have also chosen to employ professional planners or others with relevant planning experience to facilitate the production of a plan, and most are having to pay for the planner's work.

References

Arnstein, S. (1969) A ladder of citizen participation, *American Institute of Planners Journal*, July: 216–224.

Baker, M., Coaffee, J. and Sherriff, G. (2007) Achieving successful participation in the new UK spatial planning system, *Planning Practice & Research*, 22(1): 79–93.

Beckley, T., Martz, D., Nadeau, S., Wall, E. and Reimer, B. (2008) Multiple capacities, multiple outcomes: Delving deeper into the meaning of community capacity, *Journal of Rural and Community Development*, 3(3): 56–75.

Berkeley, N., Goodall, B., Noon, D. and Collis, C. (1995) Involving the community in plan preparation, *Community Development Journal*, 30(2): 189–199.

Bridges, J. (2012) Oranges are not the only fruit: Beyond the neighbourhood plan, *Town and Country Planning*, 81(7–8): 330–333.

Brooks, E. (2011) *Are Country Towns and Villages Sustainable Environments for Older People?*, unpublished PhD thesis, Newcastle-upon-Tyne: School of Architecture, Planning and Landscape, Newcastle University.

Champion, T. and Shepherd, J. (2006) Demographic change in rural England, in P. Lowe and L. Speakman (eds), *The Ageing Countryside: The growing older population of rural England*, London: Age Concern.

Chaskin, R. (2001) Building community capacity: A definitional framework and case studies from a comprehensive community initiative, *Urban Affairs Review*, 36(3): 291–323.

Collins, K. and Ison, R. (2009) Jumping off Arnstein's ladder: Social learning as a new policy paradigm for climate change adaptation, *Environmental Policy and Governance*, 19(6): 358–373.

Doak, J. and Parker, G. (2005) Networked space? The challenge of meaningful participation and the new spatial planning in England, *Planning Practice & Research*, 20(1): 23–40.

Foster-Fishman, P.G., Berkowitz, S.L., Lounsbury, D.W., Jacobson, S. and Allen, N.A. (2001) Building collaborative capacity in community coalitions: A review and integrative framework, *American Journal of Community Psychology*, 29(2): 241–261.

Goodman, R., Speers, M., McLeroy, K., Fawcett, S., Kegler, M., Parker, E., Smith, S., Sterling, T. and Wallerstein, N. (1998) Identifying and defining the dimensions of community capacity to provide a basis for measurement, *Health Education and Behavior*, 25(3): 258–278.

Mawson, J. and Hall, S. (2000) Joining it up locally? Area regeneration and holistic government in England, *Regional Studies*, 34(1): 67–74.

Norton, B.L., LeRoy, K.R., Burdine, J.N., Felix, M.R.J. and Dorsey, A.M. (2002) Community capacity: Concept theory and methods, in R. DiClemente, R. Crosby and M. Kegler (eds), *Emerging Theories in Health Promotion Practice and Research*, San Francisco, CA: Jossey-Bass, pp. 194–227.

ONS (Office for National Statistics). (2012) *2011 Census, Population and Household Estimates for Wards and Output Areas in England and Wales*. Available at: www.ons.gov.uk/ons/rel/census/2011-census/population-and-household-estimates-for-england-and-wales/index.html (accessed June 2013).

Rydin, Y. (2006) Popular planning: Coin Street London, in T. Brindley, Y. Rydin and G. Stoker (eds), *Remaking Planning: The politics of planning change*, London: Routledge.

Skeffington, A. (1969) *People and Planning: Report of the Committee on Public Participation in Planning*, London: HMSO.

Taylor, M. (2000) Communities in the lead: Power, organisational capacity and social capital, *Urban Studies*, 37(5–6): 1019–1035.

Trittera, J. and McCallumb, A. (2006) The snakes and ladders of user involvement: Moving beyond Arnstein, *Health Policy*, 76(2): 156–168.

Vigar, G., Brooks, E. and Gunn, S. (2012) The innovative potential of neighbourhood plan-making, *Town and Country Planning*, 81(7–8).

——(submitted) Institutional design for neighbourhood plan-making: The possibilities of agonism, deliberation and collaboration, submitted to *Planning Theory and Practice*.

9

Is Small Really Beautiful? The Legitimacy of Neighbourhood Planning

Paul Cowie and Simin Davoudi

A key justification for the localism agenda in the UK is democratization of decision-making. Decentralization of power to local communities and neighbourhoods is premised on shortening the distance between those making the decisions and those affected by them (Gallent, 2013). In the face of an increasing transfer of decision-making away from citizens and towards corporations (Keating, 1991), the idea of reversing the process is particularly seductive. This coupled with oppositions to globalization have led to the view that devolving power to the local level produces more democratic processes and better outcomes (Green and Haynes, 2001). Decentralization is uncritically equated with democratization and the local scale is considered as the site of empowerment. The critique of this 'local trap' is growing with a focus primarily on the portrayal of the local as a bounded spatial unit that contains a unified and homogeneous community (Purcell, 2006).

In this chapter we aim to complement this critique by questioning the democratic legitimacy of neighbourhood planning, which is currently the most visible manifestation of localism in England. It was introduced, by the Localism Act 2011, as a key mechanism for reforming the English planning system in 'favour of local communities' and for giving local people 'genuine opportunities to influence the future of the places where they live' (DCLG, 2011: 15). Particular emphasis is put on 'Reform to ensure that decisions about housing are taken locally' (DCLG, 2011: 9). Thus, localities are now given a new right to draw up Neighbourhood Plans. The authority to do so is assigned to two different bodies: Town/Parish Councils and Neighbourhood Forums (NFs). While the former have long been part of the lowest tier of the elected government system engaged in planning, the latter are entirely new planning institutions.[1] NFs can be established by a minimum of 21 non-elected local 'stakeholders' in places where no Town or Parish Council exists. On the one hand, the rhetoric of localism portrays the 2011 reform of the planning system and particularly the introduction of neighbourhood planning as a way of making planning 'more democratic and more effective' (DCLG, 2011: 6). On the other hand, the creation of NFs can be regarded as a departure from democratic planning processes because unlike the established planning authorities, decisions in NFs are taken by non-elected members.

As with localism, neighbourhood planning has attracted growing criticism related to issues such as: the gap between the rhetoric and reality of community empowerment, the administrative inconsistencies in its implementations and the underlying neoliberal motivations for the reform of the planning system (see, for example, the special issue of *Planning Practice and Research*, 2013; Clarke and Cochrane, 2013; Davoudi and Madanipour, 2013). Our aim is to propose a framework for examining the democratic legitimacy of NFs and apply part of it to an illustrative example of neighbourhood planning. After this introduction, the following section will discuss the concept of legitimacy and its multiple interpretations. The third section will provide an overview of the sources of legitimacy. This will be drawn upon in the fourth section to develop a conceptual framework which is partly used, in section five, to examine the legitimacy of neighbourhood forums. Throughout, we will draw on the evidence provided by the existing literature on neighbourhood planning as well as a case study of the North Shields Fish Quay (NSFQ) Neighbourhood Forum in the North East of England, where we followed the process of plan-making and undertook interviews with key actors during 2013.[2] We acknowledge that a fuller assessment of NFs' legitimacy requires a more detailed empirical investigation and as such our analysis and conclusions, presented in the final section, remain tentative and preliminary.

Legitimacy

The discussion on legitimacy is tightly connected to the concepts of political authority (i.e. the use of political power by a political entity) and political obligation (i.e. the moral duty of a political community to obey its commands). The debate about why we need political authority has a long history with influential contributions notably from Thomas Hobbes, John Locke and Jean-Jacques Rousseau, with those rejecting the need for political authority often being seen as anarchists who advocate that social relations can be coordinated through either face-to-face community or market transactions. In developing a framework to examine legitimacy, we concur with neither and, following Miller (2003: 23), believe that societies need political authority with power to compel, because such authority creates a climate of security within which people can trust one another, and it is these relations of trust that enable them to cooperate with one another and produce societal benefits. Contrary to the anarchists' views, 'neither communities nor markets – important as these are in many areas of human life – can replace political authority and its modern embodiment, the state'. So, 'the real choice is not whether to have political authority or not, but what kind of authority to have, and what its limits should be' (Miller, 2003: 29, 31). Opinions on these questions are spread across a spectrum where on the one side lies Hobbes' Leviathan and his idea of absolute government, which, if not obeyed unconditionally, would lead to 'every man becoming the ENEMY of every man' (Hobbes, 1968 [1651]: 62); and on the other side Rousseau's idea of people's self-government based on continuous participation in all decisions (1988 [1762]). At the heart of the debate about political authority is the concept of legitimacy. However, what legitimacy means and when a political authority is considered as legitimate have remained open questions.

Descriptive and normative legitimacy

Depending on how these questions are answered, a distinction can be made between normative and descriptive interpretations of legitimacy. The *descriptive* perspective, according to Max Weber's (1964) influential account, considers a political authority as legitimate if its participants have belief or faith in it based on: tradition (the established norms and customs), charisma (the status and reputation of the rulers) or legality (the trust in rationality and legality of the rules). This implies that people's preferences and demands have no place in the Weberian interpretation of legitimacy. His is based on the argument that people obey rules because they believe in the 'appropriateness' of their origin, which could be the divine ordain of kings or enlightened upbringing of aristocrats. The *normative* interpretation considers legitimacy as the moral justification for political authority and obligation. Legitimacy in the normative sense justifies the function of political authority and the moral duty to obey the laws and rules that are made by it. A notable advocate of the normative interpretation is John Rawls (1993), who considers legitimacy as an underlying principle of political authority but maintains that it is a less demanding moral value than justice. His point is that political institutions and their decisions may be legitimate but not just.

Both descriptive and normative perspectives have been subject to a number of criticisms. With regard to descriptive legitimacy, Beetham (1991: 11; original emphasis) argues that 'a power relationship is not legitimate because people believe in its legitimacy, but because it can be *justified in terms* of their beliefs' by, for example, an appeal to the sources of legitimacy as discussed below. John Simmons (2001) states that what distinguishes *de facto* authority (which is based on capacity to maintain order and secure obedience) from *legitimate* authority depends on whether or not the authority is accepted, and not on whether it ought to be accepted because of some a priori beliefs in its superiority. A purely normative account of legitimacy is also criticized for neglecting the historical formation and the social and cultural specificity of legitimation processes. Habermas (1979: 205), for example, argues that 'Every general theory of justification remains peculiarly abstract in relation to the historical forms of legitimate domination'. He, along with other scholars such as Beetham (1991), argues for a concept of legitimacy that combines elements of both descriptive and normative legitimacy. Such a hybrid position is captured in Mark Suchman's definition, suggesting that legitimacy is 'a generalized perception or assumption that the actions of an entity are desirable, proper, or appropriate within some socially constructed system of norms, values, beliefs, and definitions' (Suchman, 1995: 574).

We concur with Suchman's contextualized and relational definition of legitimacy and consider it as a means of social order and control. Legitimacy endows power with authority to rule and to enforce the rules without recourse to means of coercion. Indeed, as Hannah Arendt (1989: 92) suggests, where force is used, authority fails. Legitimacy demands compliance on the basis of an internal sense of moral obligation rather than coercion. It is a product of internalization of rules. Drawing on Emile Durkheim, Hechter (1987: 3) argues that 'the maintenance of social order depends on the existence of a set of overarching rules of the game; rules that are to some degree internalized, or considered to be legitimate'. These overarching rules set the goals and preferences for the society and specify the way in which they can be pursued. In this sense, legitimacy is subjective and relational between the ruler and the ruled.

Sources of legitimacy

While the contextualized and relational interpretation helps moving beyond the descriptive versus normative legitimacy, there remain other critical questions about the sources of legitimacy. Why do actors perceive a given authority as legitimate? Is it because of: the voters' initial consent to it; the quality of ongoing procedures through which authority is exercised; the substantive quality of the outcome of its actions; or a combination of all three? We elaborate on these in turn.

Consent-based legitimacy

The *consent* of the governed as the main source of political legitimacy has been debated since the seventeenth century when John Locke placed it at the centre of his 'social contract' theory. He argued that 'no one can be put out of this estate and subjected to the political power of another without his own consent' (Locke, 1980 [1689]: 52). The 'social contract' refers to the transfer of political authority from 'free and equal' individuals to the state. According to Locke (1980 [1689]: 52), if the transfer takes place in a proper way and is based on the individual's consent, then the state and its political authority is legitimate. Locke's consent theory has been criticized on several grounds, such as the infeasibility or wishful thinking of being able to gain everyone's consent (Wellman, 1996). Pateman (1988) goes further to suggest that the consent theory masquerades structures of subordination. There is a broad agreement that although consent is necessary for political legitimacy, it is by no means sufficient; that consent may legitimize political authority (the right to rule), but it does not legitimize political obligation (the duty to obey the rule) unless other conditions are met (Edmundson, 1998; Miller, 2003: 33). Among such conditions, two are at the centre of debate about legitimacy: procedural inputs and substantive outcomes,[3] as discussed below.

Procedural legitimacy

Referring to Locke's consent theory, Rawls (2007: 124) argues that the institutionalization of a political authority through an initial 'organising consent' is not enough and has to be complemented by an ongoing 'joining consent' based on continuous assessment of the authorities' performance through democratic procedures. This procedural view of legitimacy implies that people 'will accept a democratic decision even if they disagree substantively with it' (Peter, 2014: 16). In other words, if the procedure through which an outcome is chosen is democratic, the outcome itself is deemed legitimate, and those who disagree are obliged to go along with it. Otherwise, they would be treating others unfairly because 'they are assuming for themselves a right to determine how things should go that overrides the equal rights of all the others' (Christiano, 2012: 31); they are assuming the positions of dictators in relation to the others (Singer, 1973). Fair procedures, based on equality, lie at the heart of democratic legitimacy. Equality is regarded as both equal *respect* for the opinion of others (Singer, 1973) and equal *concern* for the interests of others (Christiano, 1996). A democratic assembly, as Christiano (2012: 31) puts it, 'has the right to rule and to the obedience of its members'. One way of forming a democratic assembly is through representation, but representation itself can be achieved in multiple ways, as Hanna Pitkin demonstrated in her influential work in 1967. She identifies four different ways in which the concept of representation is invoked and argues that they should be assessed by different approaches. These include: formalistic, descriptive, symbolic and substantive representations, as summarized in Table 9.1.

Formalistic representation refers to conventional accounts of representation and is about formal procedures of authorization and accountability. It conceptualizes representation as primarily a principal–agent relationship whereby the principals elect agents to speak and act on their behalf. This is the basis of all representative democracies in which the most critical relations are those of authorization and accountability. Attempts to assess formal representation are therefore focused on the mechanisms by which representatives have obtained

Table 9.1 Multiple forms of representations

Forms of representations
Formalistic: Do they *speak* for the represented?
Symbolic: Do they *stand* for the represented?
Descriptive: Do they *resemble* the represented?
Substantive: Do they *act for* represented?

Source: Davoudi (2013: 5), drawing on Pitkin (1967).

their position and are held responsive to their constituents. *Symbolic* representation relates to the meaning that representatives have for the represented. It is about the extent to which representatives are accepted by the represented. *Descriptive* representation is about the degree to which representatives resemble those being represented by sharing common interests and experiences with them. The accuracy of such resemblance is the focus of evaluation. *Substantive* representation refers to the outcome and is about the actions of representatives, so the focus of assessment is on the extent to which the representatives serve the interests and preferences of the represented. Pitkin's main argument is that in order to understand the meaning of representation we should know the context in which representation is situated. We will further elaborate on and use these multiple forms of representation in the fifth section when we examine the legitimacy of NFs. Next, we turn our attention to substantive legitimacy.

Substantive legitimacy

The argument for substantive legitimacy can be traced back to David Hume's objection to Locke's consent theory. He suggested that we should look for 'beneficial consequences' as a source of political legitimacy and argued that what made political institutions legitimate is the quality of their outcomes irrespective of the procedures by which they are generated. If the outcomes are beneficial, institutions are justified to rule and their rules ought to be obeyed. But, how do we judge what is beneficial and for whom? The answer to these questions differs depending on one's philosophical position. From a utilitarian perspective, a beneficial outcome is that which contributes to the 'greatest happiness of the greatest number of people', as Jeremy Bentham (1987 [1843]) famously put it. His view was rejected by liberal thinkers, notably John Stuart Mill (1998), on the ground that an outcome-driven view of legitimacy restricts individuals' rights and liberties, which are of such great value that they should not be interfered with by even the best constituted governments. In addressing the dilemma of reconciling individual liberty with public interests, Rousseau (1988 [1762]) has offered an interesting solution. He distinguishes between citizens' *private* will (personal liberty), *their* general will (their interpretation of the common good) and *the* general will (the common good). He then argues that we can only talk about a democratic decision when it concerns the common good; that democratic decision-making is a process through which citizens compare their interpretations of what constitutes the common good, and if the process is properly conducted the common good will be revealed and the decision will be legitimate. This means that 'individuals are only bound by their own will, but everyone is bound by a democratic decision' that concerns the common good (Peter, 2014: 17).

An alternative, and widely acknowledged, perspective on what constitutes a beneficial outcome is that which appeals to social justice. Thus, political authority is legitimate if the outcomes of action and decisions are just. This is reflected in Wellman's (1996: 213; original emphasis) critique of the utilitarian view of beneficial outcome, suggesting that 'what ultimately legitimizes a state's imposition upon *your* liberty is not merely the services it provides *you*, but the benefits it provides *others*'. The pursuit of justice is particularly significant in the justification of political obligation because authorities seek to achieve 'fair play' in social relations and ensure that the cost and benefits of societal activities are shared fairly among the individual participants (Miller, 2003: 35). However, what constitutes fair raises a new set of philosophical and political debates that goes beyond the scope of this chapter (for a review, see Davoudi and Brooks, 2014).

Mixed conception of legitimacy

Implicit in substantive legitimacy is the belief in the existence of an 'ideal outcome' that can be defined independently of the process. However, like 'pure' proceduralism, this 'pure' substantivism has its limitations. Indeed, it is difficult to draw a sharp line between the quality of outcome and the quality of process (Davoudi, 2013). That is why scholars, who are sometimes classed as 'rational proceduralists' (such as Peter, 2008), advocate a mixed conception of legitimacy, suggesting that legitimacy depends on both procedural and substantive qualities and the link between the two is deliberation. According to Habermas (1996: 304), 'deliberative politics acquires its legitimating force from the discursive structure of an opinion- and will-formation that can fulfil its socially integrative function only because citizens expect its results to have a reasonable quality'. By suggesting that deliberative processes are uniquely positioned to reach an 'ideal outcome' – that is, an outcome that is rationally justified and everyone has reasons to endorse it – Habermas provides a link between procedural and substantive democracy as the basis for a mixed conception of legitimacy. However, much has been written about the 'discursive dilemma' that can undermine the rationality of the outcome of deliberation

(List, 2006). For example, Rawls (1971: 175f.) and Waldron (1987: 143f.) argue that deliberation alone will not necessarily carry with it everyone's consensus and will 'ultimately only convince those who stand to benefit from felicific calculus' and not those who stand to lose (Peter, 2014: 13). To address this dilemma, Peter (2008) suggests that we should focus not so much on the rationality of the outcomes, but on the premises upon which the decisions are made and considered as beneficial. These include, for example, referenda, expert judgements, market mechanisms or judicial processes. Furthermore, he advocates the need to pay attention to 'epistemic democracy' as an important component of deliberation, one that emphasizes the role of cognitive and social learning processes. This implies that the knowledge created through deliberations is in itself an important outcome.

Legitimacy: a conceptual framework

The above discussions show that to judge the democratic legitimacy of a given political authority (such as neighbourhood forums) we need to move beyond not only normative-descriptive dualism but also procedural-substantive dualism and consider a broader framework that allows for a situated and contextualized assessment. Such a framework seeks to understand the relationship and interplay between these binary definitions of democratic legitimacy. The framework considers both procedural/democratic and substantive/outcome sources of legitimacy. As regards the former, it broadens the concept of representation to include its multiple forms. As regards the latter, it focuses on the processes through which the outcome can be judged a success. In the following section, we draw on part of this framework to provide some tentative and preliminary examination of the democratic legitimacy of NFs while acknowledging that a more robust assessment requires more detailed empirical investigation.

Are neighbourhood forums democratically legitimate?

If we draw on 'consent theory' as the main source of legitimacy, we need to assess whether the Coalition Government had the initial consent of all citizens to take office. This is clearly not the case and in fact for the first time in 60 years in British politics, none of the main political parties achieved a majority vote and a coalition had to be built based on a relatively small majority. Furthermore, even if the government had taken office with a landslide majority and hence a strong legitimate base, such initial consent would not have been enough to oblige citizens to obey every single planning rule legislated by the government unless other conditions were met. As mentioned above, at

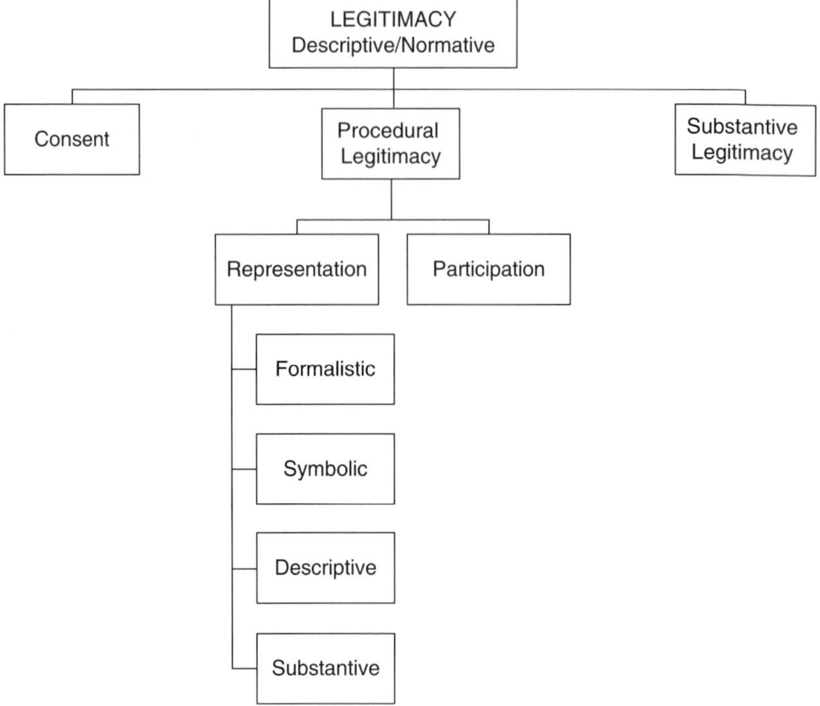

Figure 9.1 Framework of legitimacy (source: authors)

the heart of such conditions are the qualities of procedural inputs and substantive outcomes. It is, therefore, more useful to examine NFs against the mixed (procedural-substantive) conception of legitimacy. In this chapter, however, we have limited our attention to the democratic/procedural legitimacy of NFs judged against Pitkin's four types of representation (Figure 9.1).

Neighbourhood forums and formalistic representation

As mentioned above formalistic representation is the basis of all representative democracies whereby citizens elect other citizens to speak and act on their behalf. The critical question is the way in which representatives have obtained their position and how they are held responsive to their constituents. From a *formalistic* perspective the representativeness of NFs appears to be highly questionable because NFs do not formally represent their constituency; their members secure their position not through a formal election process, but through volunteering and self-selection. They even define who is to be represented *by* them, because they have the power to delineate the boundary of the area for which they plan. By doing so, they essentially define their own constituency and determine who should be included in the political community that is to be engaged in the planning process. Similarly, there is no formal direct mechanism of accountability to hold NFs responsive to their constituents. Neither is there a clear indirect line of accountability through the local council apart from the need for their initial joining approval by the council, the criteria for which have remained opaque. The obligatory referendum, which is often seen as the height of democracy, is related to the substance of the plan and not the procedures by which those who produce the plan are selected. It is an *output* rather than *input* legitimacy (Backstrand, 2006) and, as discussed below, has its limitations with regard to neighbourhood planning processes.

All this indicates that NFs can hardly be seen as democratically legitimate from a formalistic perspective. However, representation is not limited to people's periodic capacity to vote. Indeed, the formalistic perspective offers a limited view that casts political representation primarily as a principal–agent relationship (Urbinati and Warren, 2008). Problems of such relationships are widely recognized, ranging from information deficit to corruption (Urbinati and Warren, 2008). Furthermore, a focus on formal procedures of authorization and accountability is no longer sufficient in the current political reality in which myriad international, local and non-governmental actors who are not necessarily elected by their constituents play an increasingly significant role in polity. Contemporary associational life that is manifested in, for example, interest groups, civic associations and neighbourhood action groups is critical for the survival of democracy. In short, in today's complex and broadly democratic societies representation is the subject of competing claims. Citizens increasingly represent themselves and serve in 'informal' representative capacity with the power to influence 'formal' public policy-making (Warren, 2008). Therefore, given the fluidity of the relationship between represented and representative, it is naive to think about democratic representation as a monolithic concept based on formal relations of authorization and accountability. As Mansbridge (2003) argues, our understanding of political representation is contingent, to a large extent, on the political practices of representation that do not always match its normative understanding. Thus, if we consider NFs as an example of citizens representing themselves, it is more appropriate to assess their democratic legitimacy against Pitkin's three *informal* forms of representation.

Neighbourhood forums and symbolic representation

Symbolic representation is about the extent to which representatives are accepted by the represented. According to the *symbolic* form of representation, the key assessment criterion is the extent to which NFs are accepted among local communities and trusted by them to draw up neighbourhood plans. One way to examine this is to use the level of turnout in the referenda

Table 9.2 Turnout for Neighbourhood Plan referendum as at 13 June 2014

Neighbourhood Forum	*Turnout (%)*	*Parish/town council*	*Turnout (%)*
Norland	25.0	Lynton and Lynmouth	16.9
Exeter St James	20.8	Tattenhall	52.0
		Upper Eden	33.7
		Ascot, Sunninghill and Sunningdale	23.6
		Astley	38.3
		Cringleford	30
		Kidford	44
		Woburn Sands	42
		Sprowston	16
		Much Wenlock	42
		Edith Weston	22
		Woodcote	59
		Arundel	27
		Strumpshaw	59
		Thame	39.8
Average turnout NF	22.9	Average turnout Parish	36.35

Source: www.DCLG.gov.uk and the individual neighbourhood plan websites.

on neighbourhood plans as a proxy for citizens' acceptance of the NF as the legitimate authority to draw up a plan for their neighbourhood. Early results shows low level of participation that in turn may indicate that NFs have not been widely accepted by even their own self-defined local constituencies. For example, the turnout in the referendum for Exeter St James (Devon) Neighbourhood Plan, which was the first to be drawn up by an NF (as opposed to a Parish Council) in an urban area, was 20.8 per cent. The turnout for the third such plan to reach the referendum stage (Thame in Oxfordshire, drawn up by Parish Councils) was 39.8 per cent (*Planning*, 2013b: 8).[4] As Table 9.2 shows, with two exceptions, the turnout is consistently higher in Parish/Town Council referenda than in NFs. This may suggest that people in areas with NFs feel less well represented by those preparing the plans than they do in areas with democratically accountable governance institutions. However, to substantiate this possibility more data is needed. As more neighbourhood plans reach the referendum stage, a clearer picture will emerge for examining this relationship in more detail. It should also be noted that in practice, there is not always a popular vote in Parish Council elections and often members are appointed unopposed and some are co-opted with little scrutiny.

What is also striking about the data in Table 9.2 is the degree to which the process is being dominated by Town/Parish Councils who are responsible for 15 of the 17 neighbourhood plans that have been completed and successfully passed the referendum vote. This may also be indicative of a struggle by NFs' representatives to be accepted as the legitimate representatives of their community.

A deeper understanding of the nature of symbolic legitimacy in NFs requires complementing the use of the turnout in referenda with detailed qualitative research. The findings from our case study of NSFQ NF shows the NF's members' own attitude to the issue of representation and how that changed as the process unfolded.

The NSFQ NF was built on an existing sub-committee of the Fish Quay Heritage Partnership (see the subsection on descriptive representation for further details) and was later expanded by the local council, which identified and invited other 'stakeholders' to join the forum. These included individuals who were seen as representing the fishing industry, other business interests and residents. As a result, each stakeholder felt they were invited to participate in the NF to 'represent' and fight for the particular interest group that they were perceived to be symbolically representing. This created a fragmented form of symbolic legitimacy with limited legitimacy for the NF as a whole. The forum and particularly its facilitators (a planner seconded from a local charitable body) were conscious of this limitation and attempted to gain a greater degree of acceptance within the community.

> There was no great optimism at the outset … but never mind it was worth it because it distilled down into what was, or certainly tried to be, a constructive group, that tried to forge a holistic approach given the diversity that is the fish quay. (Interviewee, 2012)

It appears that NSFQ NF members' perception of their symbolic legitimacy changed over time from considering themselves as representative of particular interests or groups to seeing the group as representing the neighbourhood. However, the most relevant question of whether 'the neighbourhood' accepted them as their symbolic representative remains open to further research. One tentative indication is the response rate to a household survey that was conducted by them to gain the views of those not able to attend their regular meetings. The response rate was 25 per cent, which, although higher than the usual rate for local planning consultation, was seen by members of the NF as disappointing. The feeling was that a plan that involved only a quarter of the population of a relatively small plan area could not be said to be representative; as one member put it:

> The idea of reaching out, the idea that a questionnaire was suitable and [name removed] reassuring people that 25% was a fantastic percentage back, well it the council never achieve that … but that's the Council, we're not the Council and we are the neighbourhood. It's not acceptable to say 25% is OK. (Interviewee, 2012)

For them there was a risk that the neighbourhood plan would be perceived as being produced by 'the usual local worthies' (Interviewee, 2012).

Neighbourhood forums and substantive representation

Substantive representation, which to some extent overlaps with substantive legitimacy, refers to the outcomes, so the focus of assessment is on the extent to which the representatives produce an outcome that serves the interests and aspirations of the represented.

The focus is on the quality of outcome, but how do we judge the outcome of neighbourhood planning; how do we know whether the neighbourhood plan (which is the main outcome of the NF) is effective and fair; how do we find out who benefits from it? These are pertinent questions, yet are difficult to judge on the basis of some ideal notion of effectiveness or fairness; and certainly beyond the scope of this chapter. However, as Peter (2008) suggests, it is possible to focus on the premises upon which the quality of the outcome is assessed. The neighbourhood plan, which is the core outcome of the NFs, is subject to three quality assessments: a direct referendum, a technical-professional examination and a judicial process.

As regards the referendum, of those who turned out in neighbourhood planning referenda a decisive majority has so far voted in favour of the plans. This could arguably be considered as a sign of voters' satisfaction with the outcome, i.e. the neighbourhood plan's policies and proposals. What is less clear and needs further investigation is the extent to which the plan satisfies the interests and values of the wider community, including those who did not vote on the basis of what was discussed above and those who were excluded from the referendum because they lived outside the self-delineated boundaries of the neighbourhood plan area. The contentious nature of the substantive legitimacy of NFs was clearly visible in the discussion about whether or not to carry out a referendum in the NSFQ case.

In NSFQ, because the process started before the statutory rules and procedures for neighbourhood plans were set out by central government, the decision was made to make the plan a Supplementary Planning Document (SPD).

This is only advisory and carries less weight in the local planning process than a neighbourhood plan. Once the rules and procedures were set out, the NSFQ forum considered the possibility of switching to produce a neighbourhood plan but eventually decided against it for two main reasons. The first related to time. The process had been under way for about six months when the option arose. To produce a neighbourhood plan would have meant starting all over again and the NF members were not prepared to do this. The second reason was the referendum. It was not clear, during the development of the NSFQ neighbourhood plan, who would be entitled to take part in the referendum. The local authority thought that it would be the residents of the wider district, in which case two politically contentious issues could have arisen. On the one hand, the referendum could exclude those who have businesses in the area but do not live there; and on the other hand, it could include a large number of people voting in the referendum (and forming a majority) who live outside the boundary of the planned area. While there was an argument that these people had an indirect interest in the area, it was decided that there was too high a risk to include them in a referendum because they thought that all their hard work would have been undone if the majority of voters outside the area decided to vote against the plan. The likelihood of this happening was great because the neighbourhood plan initiative was promoted by the Conservative mayor, while the balance of political power in the wider district was subsequently shifted away from the Conservatives to other political parties. Although it has now become clear that only those who live in the neighbourhood plan area are eligible to vote in the referendum (save in exceptional circumstances), by then the decision was made not to switch to neighbourhood plan and instead produce an SPD.

As regards the technical examination of the outcome, neighbourhood plans, like other plans, are subject to scrutiny by an independent inspector. Those who are not satisfied with the plan can present formal objections to it. The validity of such objections is then judged by a planning expert, i.e. the inspector. Finally, the inspector's decision and perhaps the referendum itself is open to challenge in the courts if any interested party feels the process has not been carried out correctly. This may be a judicial review of the planning inspector's decision or else a challenge to the validity of the plan during a particular planning application. Given the cost involved, only those with resources and know-how (i.e. major developers or organized environmental groups) make use of this process. Both the inspection and the judicial process enable a degree of checks and balances on the outcome against criteria that are pre-determined by the government. They do not necessarily assess the outcome against the value and interest of the represented. Hirschl (2006) calls this the 'Judicialization' of politics that enables powerful interests to use the judicial process to overturn unpalatable decisions. He argues that this will become more pronounced as the economy recovers and development pressures increase and come into conflict with the provisions of neighbourhood plans that tend to be against perceived excessive development. In the case of NSFQ, the decision to produce an SPD instead of a neighbourhood plan exempts the process from the inspector's scrutiny.

As mentioned above, one intangible yet substantive outcome of neighbourhood planning is social learning and development of greater social capital. While in some areas the process has led to a negative impact on community relationships, where 'many people were very hurt, offended and ashamed. People stopped talking to their neighbours' (Winter, 2012: 14), in others it has led to cooperation and learning. In NSFQ, which officially started in June 2011, a number of distinct phases were followed, of which the first was essentially a *capacity-building phase* when members of the NF were identified and officers and members of the Neighbourhood Plan Committee were organized with an elected chair and deputy chair and an appointed secretary. This was followed by a *learning phase*, during which the NF began to acquire the necessary knowledge and technical skills for producing a highly technical neighbourhood plan. It was a process of 'turning fishermen to planners'. It was also a process of transferring local knowledge to professional planners. During the process it became clear that contrary to the common perception about the declining state of the fishing industry in the area and the need for planning for a post-fishing neighbourhood, it became clear that North Shields has actually benefited from the decline of other ports and is expanding. While not comparable to the boom time, it became clear that it is none the less thriving and continuing to develop. Through the neighbourhood planning process the local residents began to appreciate this and accepted that the North Shields Fish Quay does have a future in the fishing industry that should be protected.

A significant issue with regard to capacity building is the lack of continuity. Although neighbourhood plans are designed to be living documents that are used by the community to manage their environment, once they are completed the NF disbands. This means that the social capital that may be developed during the planning process is almost lost, and if, for example, the plan is challenged in the future or requires updating, a new governance body will need to be mobilized and the process of building capacity will need to start over again. This issue is being looked at by the Coalition Government, which has recently consulted on a proposal to provide a fast-track process to allow NFs to become Parish Councils without the need to reconsult (DCLG, 2014).

Neighbourhood forums and descriptive representation

Descriptive representation is about the extent to which representatives 'resemble' those who are being represented, by sharing with them common interests and experiences. Here, it is the accuracy of such resemblance that should be the focus of assessment. The procedure for the establishment of NFs requires an initial self-nomination followed by the approval of the local councils, which is based on the degree of their so-called 'representativeness'. At face value, this presents elements of *descriptive* representation and shows that attention is paid to shared interests and experiences with those who are being represented in the neighbourhoods. However, the test of representativeness seems to be based on group types, such as: businesses, residents, students, developers, fishermen and so on. Such broad categories fail to recognize the diversities within groups and as such often end up with the 'usual suspects', undermining the potential benefits of descriptive representations. This raises a number of critical questions: does the 'resident' represent marginalized voices as well as the vocal residents; does the 'business person' represent small businesses as well as large corporations; and does the 'developer' represent the tenants as well as the landowners?

These questions matter if NFs' claim of legitimacy is to be based on descriptive representation of their neighbourhoods. For an NF to be officially designated, both the area proposed and the nature of the group making the proposal have to be ratified by the local planning authority. To date there has only been one reported instance of a proposed NF being rejected by the local authority on the grounds that it is not representative of the community it seeks to represent (*Planning Resource*, 2014). In this case the councillors rejected the application on the basis of insufficient community consultation and the small number of people putting forward the proposal. This does raise an interesting question about the interplay with substantive representation, as reflected in the following statement by the nominal chair of the proposed NF: 'You can't get people interested in these activities until you put something on the table. Very few people understand the implications until you start and it gathers pace' (*Hartlepool Mail*, 2014).

While there is limited empirical evidence to support a robust assessment, evidence from the formation of existing NFs show that several are established around pre-existing groups. For example, a conservation group formed the basis of the Norland NF in Kensington, London, which has now completed the process and adopted its plan. Aireborough NF was formed out of a pre-existing pressure group called WARD (Wharfedale & Airedale Review Development). This tendency to utilize existing community groups challenges claims of legitimacy as these pre-existing groups may not be descriptively representative of their neighbourhood. This was certainly the case in NSFQ, where the NF was initially an official sub-committee of the Fish Quay Heritage Partnership. The Partnership was formed between the local authority and a resident pressure group called FISH (Folk Interested in Shields Harbour) in 2005. They led the production of a conservation area character appraisal statement, named 'FISHcast', to guide future development of the area. Thus, FISH was central to the formation of the NF and the group's FISHcast was a key input into the plan (turned into an SPD) itself. Its emphasis on the redevelopment of the redundant buildings to attract tourism and other investment to the area was an indication of its limited descriptive representation and hence lack of knowledge about the continuing significance of the fishing industry. Later, conscious efforts were made by the group, the facilitator and the local authority to include other stakeholders, notably the fishing industry, which led to a change of attitude and statement in the plan (SPD) that 'The Fish Quay and related fishing industry area will essentially continue to be available for economic activity on a 24 hour, 365 days a year basis' (NSFQ NPG, 2012: 15). Despite these efforts, some key interests were not represented, such as that of the tourism sector and visitors to the area. While their involvement was initially recognized as important for the future development of the neighbourhood, it was found to be too difficult and costly to engage meaningfully with them. On the other hand, there was a strong presence on the NF from the business community. These had a clear and pre-defined understanding of their interests and objectives, which contrasted with the often unfocused and slightly fuzzy understanding demonstrated by the resident representatives. This asymmetric level of clarity played into the power relations in the process.

In summary, the NF formation can be seen as the institutionalization of *descriptive representation* in the planning processes. This has the potential to enhance democracy if it fulfils at least four functions in four different contexts. These include:

> (1) adequate communication in contexts of mistrust, (2) innovative thinking in contexts of uncrystallized, not fully articulated, interests, (3) creating a social meaning of 'ability to rule' for members of groups in historical contexts where the ability has been seriously questioned and (4) increasing the polity's de facto legitimacy in contexts of past discrimination. (Mansbridge, 1999: 628)

In planning polity, it is widely acknowledged that there exists a degree of mistrust, poorly articulated interests, feelings of disempowerment and historical, structural discrimination in favour of private property rights, market freedom and free trade (Harvey, 2005). In these contexts, marginalized and disadvantaged groups can benefit by being represented by those who share their interest and experiences in the planning decisions that affect their lives. But, is this case? Do NFs truly reflect the diverse range of values and interests even *within* the planned neighbourhoods? Broad categories such as residents, ethnic groups, businesses, etc. are a poor substitute for diverse values and interests among them. These categorizations can lead to further marginalization by suppressing *differences*. As Iris Marion Young argues, rather than seeing descriptive representation as a 'relationship of identity', we should see it as 'differentiated relationship' (Young, 1986: 357). This implies that in order to make democratic politics more inclusive, the emphasis should be on not just how to incorporate marginalized groups, but also how to limit the influence of privileged groups who are often over-represented (Dovi, 2009).

Descriptive representation of NFs becomes more problematic when we examine their legitimacy in the context of the city, the region or the national level. The asymmetric take-up of neighbourhood planning powers at the national level reveals potentially undemocratic trends. The self-selective nature of NF formation has created an uneven geography of representation in favour of the more affluent, better-educated and more vocal social groups who often have time, resources and know-how at their disposal. A 2013 survey, undertaken by the *Planning* journal, showed that 'town halls in England's most deprived areas are least likely to have received applications from local groups to take up neighbourhood planning powers'. Only a tenth of 433 applications were from the 20 per cent most deprived local authorities (*Planning*, 2013b: 4), of which less than half were designated (20 out of 45). By contrast, from the top 20 per cent least deprived authorities, 92 applications were received of which 60 were designated. Drawing on these, we have argued elsewhere (Davoudi and Cowie, 2013: 565) that neighbourhood forums 'have, until early 2013, failed to expand the diversity of political representation in the planning processes by engaging with those who do not have the time, the capacity, the knowhow, or the political resources to participate'.

As highlighted by an experienced planning practitioner, 'neighbourhood planning is quite an expensive process … If you are in a very wealthy parish, you can employ people to assist you in drawing up a neighbourhood plan', but 'people in more deprived areas tend to have greater pressures on their lives' (*Planning*, 2013a: 5). NFs are supply-driven rather than demand-driven (Andonova and Levy, 2003), in the sense that they are created by those with capacity rather than the need to participate. At the national level, this uneven process can undermine the democratic legitimacy of the NFs. The NFs' descriptive representation (which may be their only legitimacy claim) falls short of resembling the diversity of the social groups in England and risks reinforcing existing power relations in planning polity in favour of those with a stronger presence and voice.

Conclusions

> Democracy … is not an all-or-nothing matter, but a continuing struggle to give the people as a whole the final authority over the affairs of the state. (Miller, 2003: 48)

Localism and neighbourhood planning claim to be a step in this direction. However, there are a number of critical questions that have yet to be addressed if neighbourhood planning is to live up to its ambitions. In this chapter, we argued that to examine the legitimacy claims of the NFs, we need to use a broader framework that combines descriptive with normative legitimacy and incorporate both procedural and substantive sources of legitimacy. Using existing literature and the example of NSFQ neighbourhood planning, we have attempted to demonstrate that legitimacy is not a given within localism. We put a particular emphasis on the nature of representation (drawing on our previous work on this subject) to show that even when we broaden the notion of representation beyond the conventional ballot-box representative democracy, there remain several open questions with regards to the legitimacy of NFs. If these are not addressed, governance institutions that are set up under the localism agenda may reinforce rather than reduce the asymmetry of power relations and inequality in local communities. While recognizing the potential of neighbourhood planning for progressive localism and for leading production of 'self-build neighbourhoods and cities' (Farnsworth, 2013: 481), the varying capacity of communities to engage with neighbourhood planning and the potential for asymmetric coverage of neighbourhood planning across England remains a major concern, because 'not all communities will be able to find the 100,000+ that the Thame Neighbourhood Plan (a Frontrunner) cost, and the level of support made available to communities from proactive councils' (Brownill and Downing, 2013: 374). The same could be said about NSFQ, which had the support of a full-time officer over its lifetime. This implies that under- and over-representation may become a more pronounced feature of planning processes because, in the absence of the abstract equality of one person one vote for electing representatives, other privileges, such as better education, higher income and capacity, can more easily creep in and lead to marginalization of certain groups and localities.

Acknowledgement

This chapter draws on and expands the authors' previous work, which includes: S. Davoudi (2013) On democracy: Representation beyond the ballot box, *DiSP: The Planning Review*, 49(3): 4–5; and S. Davoudi and P. Cowie (2013) Are English neighbourhood forums democratically legitimate? *Planning Theory and Practice*, 14(4): 562–566.

Notes

1 Parish Councils have their origin in the old system of church parishes and are the lowest (after national and local) tier of elected government in England. However, there

is rarely a popular vote in Parish Council elections and most members are appointed unopposed, with some co-opted members, with little scrutiny.

2 This study was undertaken as part of a European project, *ESPON TANGO, Territorial Approaches for New Governance, 2011–2013*. The complete project report is available at: www.espon.eu.

3 A simplified version of these two sources of legitimacy is used in Scharpf's (1997) assessment of the European Union's decision-making where he introduces the terms input and output legitimacy. These terms are also used in a growing number of legitimacy assessments, particularly in the field of global environmental governance (see, for example, Backstrand, 2006).

4 We acknowledge that non-participation does not necessarily mean unacceptability of the plan.

References

Andonova, L. and Levy, M. (2003) Franchising global governance: Making sense of the Johannesburg type II partnerships, in O.S. Stocke and O.B. Thomessen (eds), *Yearbook of International Cooperation on Environment and Development 2003/2004*, London: Earthscan.

Arendt, H. (1989) *Lectures on Kant's Political Philosophy*, Chicago: University of Chicago Press.

Backstrand, K. (2006) Multi-stakeholder partnerships for sustainable development: Rethinking legitimacy, accountability and effectiveness, *European Environment*, 16: 290–306.

Beetham, D. (1991) *The Legitimation Power*, Basingstoke: Palgrave.

Bentham, J. (1987 [1843]) Anarchical fallacies, in J. Waldron (ed.), *Nonsense upon Stilts*, London: Taylor & Francis, pp. 46–69.

Brownill, S. and Downing, L. (2013) Neighbourhood planning: Is an infrastructure of localism emerging? *Town and Country Planning*, 82(9): 372–376.

Christiano, T. (1996) *The Rule of the Many*, Boulder, CO: Westview Press.

Christiano, T. (2012) Authority, in E.N. Zalta (ed.), *The Stanford Encyclopedia of Philosophy*. Available at: http://plato.stanford.edu/archives/spr2013/entries/authority.

Clarke, N. and Cochrane, A. (2013) Geographies and politics of localism: The localism of the United Kingdom's coalition government, *Political Geography*, 34: 10–23.

Davoudi, S. (2013) On democracy: Representation beyond the ballot box, *DiSP: The Planning Review*, 49(3): 4–5.

Davoudi, S. and Brooks, E. (2014) When does unequal become unfair? Judging environmental justice claims, *Environment and Planning A*, forthcoming.

Davoudi, S. and Cowie, P. (2013) Are English neighbourhood forums democratically legitimate? *Planning Theory and Practice*, 14(4): 562–566.

Davoudi S, Cowie P, Madanipour A, Vigar G. (2013) ESPON TANGO – Territorial Approaches for New Governance. Final Report. Luxembourg: ESPON Coordination Unit.

Davoudi, S. and Madanipour, A. (2013) Localism and neo-liberal governmentality, *Town Planning Review*, 84(5): 551–561.

DCLG (Department of Communities and Local Government). (2011) *A Plain English Guide to the Localism Act*, London: DCLG.

DCLG. (2014) *Consultation on a Proposal to Use a Legislative Reform Order for Making It Easier to Set up a Town and Parish Council*, London: DCLG.

Dovi, S. (2009) In praise of exclusion, *Journal of Politics*, 71(3): 1172–1186.

Edmundson, W. (1998) *Three Anarchical Fallacies*, Cambridge: Cambridge University Press.

Farnsworth, D. (2013) Incremental plans and self-build cities, *Town and Country Planning*, 82(11): 481–484.

Gallent, N. (2013) Re-connecting 'people and planning': Parish plans and the English localism agenda, *Town Planning Review*, 84(3): 371–396.

Green, G. and Haynes, A. (2001) *Asset Building and Community Development*, Thousand Oaks, CA: Sage.

Habermas, J. (1979) *Communication and the Evolution of Society*, trans. and with an introduction by Thomas McCarthy, Boston: Beacon Press.

Habermas, J. (1996) *Between Facts and Norms*, trans. William Rehg, Cambridge, MA: MIT Press.

Hartlepool Mail. (2014) Councilors reject residents' plans for Park area of Hartlepool, *Hartlepool Mail*, 21 February. Available at: www.hartlepoolmail.co.uk/news/local/councillors-reject-residents-plans-for-park-area-of-hartlepool-1-6452719.

Harvey, D. (2005) *A Brief History of Neo-liberalism*, Oxford: Oxford University Press.

Hechter, M. (1987) *Principles of Group Solidarity*, 4th edn, Berkeley: University of California Press.

Hirschl, R. (2006) The new constitutionalism and the judicialization of pure politics worldwide. *Fordham Law Review*, 75(2): 721–753.

Hobbes, T. (1968 [1651]) *Leviathan*, ed. C.B. MacPherson, Harmondsworth: Penguin.

Keating, M. (1991) Local development politics in Britain and France, *Journal of Urban Affairs*, 13: 443–459.

List, C. (2006) The discursive dilemma and public reason, *Ethics*, 116(2): 362–402.

Locke, J. (1980 [1689]) *Second Treatise of Civil Government*, ed. C.B. MacPherson, Indianapolis, IN: Hackett.

Mansbridge, J. (1999) Should Blacks represent Blacks and women represent women? A contingent 'yes', *Journal of Politics*, 61 (August): 628–657.

Mansbridge, J. (2003) Rethinking representation, *American Political Science Review*, 97: 515–528.

Mill, J.S. (1998) *On Liberty and Other Essays*, ed. John Gray, Oxford: Oxford University Press.

Miller, D. (2003) *Political Philosophy: A very short introduction*, Oxford: Oxford University Press.

NSFQ NPG (North Shields Fish Quay Neighbourhood Plan Group). (2012) *North Shields Fish Quay Neighbourhood Plan 2012: Draft supplementary planning document*.

Pateman, C. (1988) *The Sexual Contract*, Cambridge: Polity Press.

Peter, F. (2008) *Democratic Legitimacy*, New York: Routledge.

Peter, F. (2014) Political legitimacy, in E.N. Zalta (ed.), *The Stanford Encyclopedia of Philosophy*. Available at: http://plato.stanford.edu/archives/spr2014/entries/legitimacy.

Pitkin, H.F. (1967) *The Concept of Representation*, Berkeley: University of California Press.

Planning. (2013a) Poorer areas see few local plan applications, 25 March, pp. 4–5.

Planning. (2013b) Referenda back neighbourhood plans, 17 May, pp. 8–9.

Planning Practice and Research. (2013) Special issue on Spatial Planning and the New Localism, 28(1).

Planning Resource. (2014) Hartlepool neighbourhood plan area designation blocked over consultation concerns. Available at: www.planningresource.co.uk/article/1282051/hartlepool-neighbourhood-plan-area-designation-blocked-consultation-concerns.

Purcell, M. (2006) Urban democracy and the local trap, *Urban Studies*, 43(11): 1921–1941.
Rawls, J. (1971) *A Theory of Justice*, Cambridge, MA: Harvard University Press.
Rawls, J. (1993) *Political Liberalism*, New York: Colombia University Press.
Rawls, J. (2007) *Lectures on the History of Political Philosophy*, Cambridge, MA: Harvard University Press.
Rousseau, J.J. (1988 [1762]) *On the Social Contract*, Indianapolis, IN: Hackett.
Scharpf, F.W. (1997) Economic integration, democracy and the welfare state, *Journal of European Public Policy*, 4(1): 18–36.
Simmons, A.J. (2001) *Justification and Legitimacy: Essays on rights and obligations*, Cambridge: Cambridge University Press.
Singer, P. (1973) *Democracy and Disobedience*, Oxford: Oxford University Press.
Suchman, M.C. (1995) Managing legitimacy, strategic and institutional approaches, *Academy of Management Review*, 20(3): 571–610.
Urbinati, N. and Warren, M. (2008) The concept of representation in contemporary democratic theory, *Annual Review of Political Science*, 11: 387–412.
Waldron, J. (1987) Theoretical foundations of liberalism, *The Philosophical Quarterly*, 37(147): 127–150.
Warren, M.E. (2008) Citizen representativeness, in M.E. Warren and H. Pearse (eds), *Designing Deliberative Democracy: The British Colombia Citizens' Assembly*, Cambridge: Cambridge University Press, pp. 50–69.
Weber, M. (1964) *The Theory of Social and Economic Organization*, ed. Talcott Parson, New York: Free Press.
Wellman, C. (1996) Liberalism, Samaritanism and political legitimacy, *Philosophy and Public Affairs*, 25(3): 211–237.
Winter, M. (2012) Localism up close was not a pretty sight, *Planning*, 24 August, pp. 13–14.
Young, I. M. (1986) *Justice and the Politics of Difference*, Princeton, NJ: Princeton University Press.

PART III
LOCALISM AND SUSTAINABILITY

10

Avoiding Collapse: An Agenda for De-growth and Re-localisation

William E. Rees

Introduction and rationale

The overarching premise of this chapter is that global change represents a new context for local planning that cannot safely be ignored. Both ecological and socio-economic trends at the global scale should now be a major consideration in reframing local development policy.

Support for these assertions is compelling. While denialists have managed to befuddle popular understanding, there is solid scientific consensus that the world is in ecological overshoot. Environmental and earth scientists have shown that human demands on the ecosphere exceed its regenerative capacity and that global waste sinks are over-flowing. The accumulation of anthropogenic greenhouse gases, particularly carbon dioxide, is perhaps the best-known example, but is just one symptom of humanity's frontal assault on the ecosphere – climate is changing, the oceans are acidifying, fresh waters are toxifying, the seas are over-fished, soils are eroding, deserts are expanding, tropical forests are shrinking, biodiversity is declining. The growth of the human enterprise continues only at the expense of depleting self-producing natural capital and polluting life-support systems (Rees, 2013a; Rockström *et al.*, 2009).

Moreover, for the first time since the beginning of the Industrial Revolution, the world economy is facing shortages of essential *non*-renewables. Global extraction of conventional petroleum had peaked by 2006 (IEA, 2010) and current consumption can be maintained only by exploiting ever-more-difficult-to-extract and expensive crude oil from the seabed, or 'tight' oil from ancient shale and tar-sands deposits (and it is questionable how long even this can last) (Heinberg, 2013). By 2008, 63 of the 89 depletable mineral resources that sustain modern industrial economies had become globally scarce, as revealed by diminishing returns to exploration and dramatically rising prices (Clugson, 2012; World Bank, 2013a). As the impacts of resource exploitation and excess consumption exceed safe planetary boundaries (Rockström *et al.*, 2009), *Homo sapiens*' remarkable evolutionary success morphs into ecological dysfunction that threatens the survival of global civilization.

There is also an attendant social problem. The litany of ecological damage and resource scarcity is largely the result of production and consumption to satisfy just the wealthiest 20 per cent of the world's population. At purchasing power parity exchange rates, this privileged elite enjoys more than 70 per cent of global income (i.e. consumption) while the poorest 20 per cent survive on a paltry 2 per cent, less than $1.25 per person per day. And if these data are not sufficient to underscore chronic gross inequity, consider that the wealthiest 61 million individuals – less than 1 per cent of the population – enjoy the same income as the poorest 3.5 billion (or 56 per cent of the human population) (Ortiz and Cummins, 2011; Shah, 2013). While recent decades have seen a decline in the proportion of people in abject poverty, mostly in China, progress is glacial. Ortiz and Cummins (2011) estimate that it would take more than 800 years for the bottom billion to reach ten per cent of global income at current rates of improvement. Meanwhile, the absolute numbers of impoverished have never been greater. In 2005, 40 per cent of the human family – 2.6 billion people – lived on less than $2 daily. This is more than the entire global population in the early 1950s. Chronic poverty and egregious inequality are the roots of social upheaval and arguably as much barriers to sustainability as is ecological decay.

The mainstream 'solution' to this double-barrelled conundrum is for everyone to become rich (Beckerman, 1992). Prompted mainly by corporate interests (through lobbying and election campaign financing), politicians of every stripe assert that only an expanding GDP can eliminate poverty and provide the wealth needed to address ecological concerns. This 'solution' ignores ecological overshoot and conveniently obviates any discussion of the means to ensure a more equitable sharing of Earth's bounty. The world community has therefore expended much effort in recent decades restructuring the global economy to facilitate growth. The accompanying rhetoric extols deregulation, globalization, expanding trade, competition and freer markets; nagging environmental concerns are dismissed with the promise of greater economic efficiency, ecologically benign technologies and enhanced factor productivity (essentially producing more from less). A deluded public generally cheers approvingly from the bleachers.

Arguably, this business-as-usual (BAU) panacea is doomed, even on its own terms. BAU ignores the 'rebound effect' and discounts the ecological impacts of increased inter-regional connectivity. The past half-century of efficiency-driven global market integration has been accompanied by unprecedented gains in material productivity and technological innovation. Yet the world has witnessed an equally unprecedented explosion in the consumptive throughput of just about everything (e.g. half the fossil fuel ever burned has been consumed in just the past 35 years; see Steffen *et al.*, 2007). Meanwhile, the material effect of globalization is to expose the world's remaining pockets of resources to growing numbers of expectant and increasingly affluent consumers. Global restructuring extends the formal economy spatially, while enhanced efficiency lowers prices and increases wages. As more people with more money chase cheaper goods and services, demand rises, the world economy expands and resource depletion/pollution accelerates. Various 'resources' from honey-bees through petroleum to songbirds slip down the scale from abundance to scarcity.

The overarching problem is one that the mainstream has yet to acknowledge: on a planet already in overshoot, there is no possibility of raising even the *present* world population to, say, Western European material standards sustainably with known technologies and available resources. By 2008, the world population had already reached 6.7 billion with an average eco-footprint of approximately 2.7 global average hectares (gha) per capita.[1] However, there were only about 12 billion productive hectares on Earth or just 1.8 average hectares per capita – *humanity has already overshot long-term carrying capacity by at least 50 per cent* (WWF, 2012).[2]

We can refer to '1.8 average hectares per capita' as one's equitable or fair 'Earth-share'. It represents the biocapacity available to support each person if the world's productive ecosystems were distributed equally (Rees, 2010). In this light, consider that average Europeans require the productive and carbon assimilative capacities of four or more gha per capita to support current levels of consumption. Thus, if everyone on Earth reached European material standards, aggregate demand would exceed 30 billion gha on a planet with a total of only 12 billion hectares of productive land and water. We would have a biocapacity shortfall of almost two Earth-like planets. The North American eco-footprint is seven gha/capita; to achieve North American levels of consumption and carbon emissions for everyone would demand at least *three* additional Earths (and we would still have to accommodate the material demands of the additional two billion people expected by 2050). This already precarious situation is deteriorating because the fair Earth-share is a moving target, one that shrinks annually with increasing population and accelerating ecosystem degradation. Even the arithmetically challenged should recognize that trying to grow our way out of poverty is ecologically naive and potentially disastrous for everyone.[3]

Moreover, should we not be concerned that demand in most densely populated high-income countries has long since exceeded domestic biocapacity? The United Kingdom, for example, uses at least three times as much extra-territorial biocapacity to maintain its consumer lifestyles as is contained within its national boundaries. The world's 'haves' live, in part, on biocapacity imported from the global commons and poorer countries half a planet away (Kissinger and Rees, 2009, 2010; Rees, 2002, 2013b).[4] By contrast, the chronically impoverished survive on 0.5 gha or less and leave almost no footprint beyond their local environs. The world's poor simply do not have the money needed to access even their equitable allocation of the world's bounty.

Indeed, if current trends continue, it is unlikely they will ever achieve 'fair-share' levels of consumption, let alone eco-equity. Even as climate change and ecosystem degradation take their toll on productivity, remaining 'surpluses' of local biocapacity are being appropriated by the rich through trade and, most recently, the phenomenon of 'land-grabbing'. Richer countries and local and transnational corporate interests are leasing or buying outright millions of the most productive hectares of land in poorer countries in Africa, Latin America and elsewhere, denying access to, and sometimes forcibly evicting, local people from their traditional lands.[5] Oxfam (2011, 2012) reports that as many as 227 million hectares of land – an area the size of Western Europe – had been sold or leased in developing countries since 2001 (enough to feed a billion people, roughly the number of currently calorically undernourished people on the planet). This latest expression of egregious inequality in an increasingly fractious resource-poor world is likely to foster civil unrest and exacerbate geo-political instability in coming years.

Against this background, the goal of the present chapter is to advance a precautionary, transformational approach to sustainability planning. This framework recognizes that despite a half-century of alarm over the 'environmental crisis' and 20 years of political rhetoric on 'paradigm-shifting' and 'sustainable development', action to date has been mere reform-at-the-margin, not fundamental transformation (Rees, 1995). Arguably, no real progress is possible while the beliefs, values and assumptions of growth-oriented market capitalism remain intact (Rees, 2008). I therefore develop the rationale for re-writing global society's dominant economic narrative to reflect limits to growth. Then, drawing on various disciplines from cognitive psychology through environmental science, sociology, economic history and development planning, I outline some of the broad framing necessary at the global level and specific policies needed at the national and (bio)regional scales to achieve a planned descent to a sustainable steady-state.

Framing an action plan: are we up to the task?

> We, like Ahab and his crew, rationalize madness. All calls for prudence, for halting the march toward environmental catastrophe, for sane limits on carbon emissions, are ignored or ridiculed. Even with the flashing red lights before us, the increased droughts, rapid melting of glaciers and Arctic ice, monster tornadoes, vast hurricanes, crop failures, floods, raging wildfires and soaring temperatures, we bow slavishly before hedonism and greed and the enticing illusion of limitless power, intelligence and prowess. (Hedges, 2013)

Chris Hedges' (2013) analogy between the world community and the crew of the *Pequod* in Melville's *Moby Dick* describes a world in deep denial. Is this an inevitable response to crisis or is there another way? How might a more mindfully conscious world address the (un)sustainability conundrum? This section provides the rationale and major elements for a transformational approach to sustainability planning.

The proposed strategy will seem impossibly extreme to so-called 'practical people'. However, unlike mainstream 'solutions', it is consistent with the dire implications of growth-induced global change.[6] In particular, it recognizes that global-scale ecological turmoil and social turmoil usher in a unique phase in human history. Climate change has already disrupted the lives of millions and, eventually, everyone will suffer the consequences of systemic collapse. No individual can implement the policies necessary (e.g. carbon taxes, resource quotas) to significantly reduce his/her ecological footprint or revamp the social programmes needed for social stability. No country, however virtuous, can be sustainable on its own or remain insulated from global turmoil. *Unsustainability is a collective problem that demands collective solutions*. Thus, a world steeped in the rhetoric of competitive individualism must now grapple with the notion that individual and national interests have all but converged with humanity's common interests. Arguably, civilization will not survive without recognition that we are all on the same fragile spaceship whose safe passage depends on unprecedented inter-institutional cooperation at all spatial scales.

Working cooperatively for the common good will require the ardent exercise of several intellectual and behavioural qualities that are unique (or nearly so) to our species:

1 high intelligence, the capacity to reason logically from available facts and data;
2 the ability to plan ahead, to direct the course of events towards desired ends;
3 an unequalled array of behavioural means and social mechanisms for cooperation;
4 the capacity for moral judgement, the ability to distinguish right from wrong; and
5 the ability to empathize with other people and even non-human species and to exercise compassion towards 'the other'.

It is worth noting that certain of these capacities have been repressed in the socio-political discourse of recent decades.

Arguably, the starting point for any survival strategy should be to embrace a possibility that mainstream governments and international agencies have thus far been loath to contemplate (at least in the public arena): in coming decades, *the human enterprise will likely be forced to contract.* Two basic scenarios bookend the narrow range of possible contraction possibilities:

1 *Business as usual* – any sustained effort to maintain the growth-based status quo risks triggering systemic collapse in the form of widespread ecological destruction, the loss of essential life-support functions, general resource shortages and increasing social disparity (Barnosky *et al.*, 2012) that, in turn, may terminate in civil insurrection, geopolitical turmoil and resource wars (Klare, 2001, 2012);
2 A *cooperative, well-planned orderly descent* – deliberately planning and executing a 'prosperous way down' (Odum and Odum, 2001) would restore and maintain the ecosphere while ensuring reasonable economic security and social order for all (Victor, 2008). However, it would also require a complete transformation of national and global development paradigms (e.g. Greer, 2008).

Can there be any doubt about which end of the spectrum an objective member of an intelligent, forward-thinking, plan-capable, morally astute and (mostly) cooperative species would choose? An orderly contraction is the only viable means to a just sustainability and this, in turn, implies nothing less than a deliberate re-write of contemporary society's grand cultural narrative. In particular, the world would have to abandon its core myths of perpetual technological progress and material growth and focus instead on de-growth towards a sustainable steady-state with greater equity.

Socially constructing a no-growth alternative

> It seems implausible that humanity will not alter its energy course as consequences of burning all fossil fuels become clearer. Yet strong evidence about the dangers of human-made climate change have so far had little effect. (Hansen *et al.*, 2012)

Those who track the state of the ecosphere should be excused for being discouraged. A complex of inter-related behavioural tendencies combine to stifle the political will for decisive action. For example: (1) people are not wholly rational in dealing with threats to their socio-economic status or political power; (2) privileged elites with the greatest stake in the status quo increasingly control the political process; (3) humans have difficulty processing information that conflicts with what they already 'know'.

This last is perhaps most important at the 'whole society' level. Here we encounter a unique quality of *Homo sapiens* – much of what we assume to be true, much of what masquerades as 'reality' in our conscious minds, is to some degree *socially constructed* (Berger and Luckmann, 1966). Other sentient organisms respond to the world as they find it, their reactions dictated by instinct, predictable stimulus-response mechanisms and simple trial-and-error learning. By contrast, human groups collectively create complex abstract frames of understanding through which they filter subsequent sensory and emotional inputs. Different framings will produce different responses to the same stimuli with correspondingly different impacts on the well-being of the individual or group involved.

As post-modernists like to remind us, there are no theoretical limits to the diversity and form of alternative perceptions. Every religious doctrine, political ideology, academic paradigm, worldview and cultural narrative – indeed, all cultural norms – are socially constructed. It is particularly important to recognize that, despite such potentially flimsy foundations, social constructs profoundly influence how people 'act out' in the world and dramatically affect people's lives.[7] Indeed, the evidence shows that social constructs carry sufficient weight in the face of evident reality *to determine the fates of entire societies* (see Diamond, 2005; Tainter, 1988).

With these facts in mind, consider the words of Neil Postman (1999: 76): 'You may say, if you wish, that all "reality" is a social construction, but you cannot deny that some constructions are "truer" than others. They are not "truer" because they are privileged, they [become] privileged because they are "truer."' Postman is arguing that 'truer' constructs correspond more closely to reality than do competing versions.[8] While many social constructs are pure products of mind and subsequent social negotiation (e.g. civil rights), countless real-world entities exist whose properties and behaviour are unaffected by whether or how humans perceive them (e.g. gravitational force, climate change). More accurate perceptions of such phenomena will be substantiated by repeated application over time; devices, behaviours and activities based upon better constructs will produce predictable results; better constructs will not jeopardize the health and safety of agents who act as if they were true.

Now let's consider key elements of the world's presently dominant cultural narrative: 'competitive individualism', 'growth-based neo-liberal economics', 'techno-optimism', 'globalization theory' and the 'free' flow of goods and capital. These elaborate constructs powerfully influence the nature and scale of human interaction with the real finite ecosphere, yet contain no reference to the physical laws governing energy and material transformations, biophysical limits to growth, or the chaotic behaviour of biophysical systems under stress. Our growth-oriented economic models simply do not 'map' to the biophysical reality with which the economy interacts. Nor do they accurately portray the complexity of individual behaviour, social dynamics (including loyalty to persons and place) or the distorting influence of power politics. We need look no further than these fundamental flaws in society's prevailing paradigm for the proximal cause of the (un)sustainability crisis. Clearly, to achieve sustainability will require a new, much 'truer' cultural narrative.

Grappling with the elephant in the room

> Anyone who believes in indefinite growth in anything physical, on a physically finite planet, is either mad or an economist. (attributed to Boulding, 1973)

The idea that the economy would eventually stop growing dates from at least the mid-eighteenth century and Adam Smith, who (incorrectly) predicted that a surplus of labour and resource scarcity would impose a limit on growth after just 200 years (Smith, 1776). Almost a century later, John Stuart Mill also argued that society would reach a 'stationary state' but he hoped for a *deliberate* transition. Society would eventually reach a point of universal enoughness in which virtually everyone would be able to enjoy 'sufficient leisure ... to cultivate freely the graces of life'. Mill saw no virtue in becoming richer than one need be and advocated instead for a just distribution of property 'attained, by the joint effect of the prudence and frugality of individuals, and of a system of legislation favouring equality of fortunes'. Thoroughly modern, Mill even made an ecological connection. He lamented that the 'unlimited increase of wealth and population' would cause the Earth to lose 'that great portion of its pleasantness which it owes to [nature], for the mere purpose of enabling it to support a larger, but not a better or a happier population'. He therefore hoped that people would come to 'be content to be stationary, long before necessity compels them to it' (all quotations from Mill, 1848: Book IV, ch. iv).

It took yet another century to reawaken interest in Mill's 'stationary state' (though he would regret that 'necessity compels [us] to it'). Beginning in the 1960s, the work of Nicholas Georgescu-Roegen (1971), his acolyte Herman Daly (1973, 1991) and others culminated in a new discipline, Ecological Economics, which has debated the notion of a 'steady-state' economy for the past 25 years.[9] Also with intellectual roots in Georgescu-Roegen, the first decades of the twenty-first century have spawned an increasingly global 'degrowth' (*décroissance*) movement. Proponents advocate a gradual downscaling of production and consumption towards a more equitable and cooperative society that would ensure both ecological stability and human well-being (Gheorghică, 2012; Kerschner, 2010).

Thoughtful people contemplating steady-state sustainability with justice (the essence of scenario 2) usually draw on the following arguments:

1 Continuous growth of anything in a finite space is anomalous and ultimately self-correcting. For 99.9 per cent of human history, local

populations rarely grew for extended periods but rather fluctuated near carrying capacity as a function of food supplies, disease, etc. The recent 200 years of more or less continuous growth that we consider normal is actually the single most *abnormal* period in human history. Indeed, the present (socially constructed) policy fixation on growth dates only from the 1950s.

2 Economic *production* is actually mostly a *consumptive* process. The economy irreversibly transforms large quantities of useful energy and material into an equivalent mass of useless waste. (Even the small portion that is embodied in useful produces eventually joins the waste stream.) Economic activity inexorably dissipates resources and increases the entropy (randomness, disorder) of the ecosphere.

3 Beyond a certain income level (long past in high-income countries) there is no further correlation between GDP/capita and either objective indicators of population health or felt well-being (Lane, 2000; Victor, 2008). Once basic material needs are met, it is not rich countries but rather countries with greater income equality that perform better on standard quality-of-life indicators. Greater social equity is 'better for everyone' (Wilkinson and Pickett, 2010).

4 An increasing proportion of the income gain from GDP growth accrues to the already wealthy who do not tangibly benefit. Meanwhile, real incomes of the middle and lower classes stagnate or fall.[10] The income gap increases as excess energy and resource consumption depletes 'natural capital' and undermines life-support systems. The chronically impoverished are hit the hardest but such trends ultimately threaten everyone.

5 With integrated fiscal, tax, employment, population, etc., policies, it should be possible to create a more equitable, economically stable, no-growth economy with minimal unemployment and poverty (Jackson, 2009; Victor, 2008).

Even the climate-change literature provides explicit support for an orderly economic contraction. Unless the world can reconcile economic growth with an unprecedented 6 per cent per year decarbonization rate, avoiding a potentially catastrophic 4 C° increase in mean global temperature may well require a 'planned economic recession' (Anderson and Bows, 2008). Mill was clearly a century-and-a-half ahead of his time.

Action on the global scale: catching up with Mill

> It is only in the backward countries of the world that increased production is still an important object: in those most advanced, what is economically needed is a better distribution, of which one indispensable means is a stricter restraint on population. (Mill, 1848: Book IV, ch. vi)

Let's assume that the rising costs of global change or some major catastrophe precipitates a great awakening, that world leaders are shocked into agreeing that the science of climate change is basically correct and demands a decisive collective response. They are on a war footing and, with unprecedented unity, launch a World Assembly for Mutual Survival.

The first thing this high-level forum might acknowledge is that the crisis is the inevitable result of an ill-conceived economic paradigm that assumes poverty and most other human problems can be resolved by technology and growth alone. The question then becomes, 'what alternative beliefs, values and assumptions might provide the foundation for a new global narrative that better maps to reality?'

Certainly recognition of biophysical limits to growth would be near the top of the list. The World Assembly might therefore adopt as its overall goal: *to engineer the creation of a dynamic, more equitable 'steady-state' economy that can satisfy the basic needs of the entire human family within the means of nature*. Fair enough. However, our best science tells us that for the human enterprise to operate compatibly 'within the means of nature', merely *curtaining* growth would not be enough. This is a world in overshoot – a sustainable steady-state economy will be a materially smaller economy. The world needs to achieve a 50 per cent overall reduction in fossil energy use, material consumption and pollution.

Moreover, to address egregious inequality, wealthy countries would have to reduce their energy/material throughput by up to 80 per cent. The additional commitment is necessary to free up the 'ecological space' needed for consumption growth in developing countries where, in Mill's words, 'increased production is still an important object'. If growth is no longer available as a poverty-reduction tool, 'a better distribution' (Mill again) emerges as the only viable policy option.

Needless to say, contraction is not an idea that resonates with contemporary economic thinking. If an orderly transition requires the consent and involvement of a majority of citizens, it also demands a dramatic shift in social-cultural norms. Specifically, the new narrative must de-emphasize competitive individualism, greed and short-term self-interest and trumpet instead the adaptive strengths of cooperation, community and people's common interest in survival. It must also discard the shrivelled representation of the human character portrayed in current economic models. *Homo oeconomicus* is an atomistic, self-interested, insatiable utility maximizer devoid of family, community, place or any meaningful relationship with nature; this creature defines 'rational' strictly in terms of utility maximization. Real people are vastly more complex, capable of expressing a full spectrum of attitudes, behaviours and relationships to the world. We can all be greedy and self-serving on one occasion, generous and selfless on another; anyone can enjoy the thrill of competition but is just as capable of joyful cooperation; for most people, money is a means to live not an end in itself. The key insight is that, while human nature displays a spectral palate of attributes and behaviours, cultural nurture helps determine which of these 'colours' shines most brightly. *We socially construct the cultural norms that shape our interactions with each other, with other species and with the ecosystems that sustain us.*

This is good news. As part of a survival plan, the world community will agree to a world-wide social marketing programme designed both to bring the majority of citizens on board and to counter the inevitable 'push-back' from those with the greatest stake in the status quo. Public re-education is necessary to inform ordinary citizens of the severity of the crisis and to instil values and behaviours compatible with the steady-state. The programme must advance a positively attractive vision of the future that ensures economic security, social cohesion and ecological stability. It must also graphically contrast this vision with the future of resource wars, geopolitical turmoil and climate chaos likely to unfold if we maintain our BAU trajectory.

There will undoubtedly be objections to any such global social learning exercise. However, let's remember that the denizens of today's self-destructive consumer society are *already* the most thoroughly socially engineered generation of humans ever to walk the planet; that the current programme is destroying their future prospects; and that billions are spent every year in public relations, advertising and deliberate misinformation campaigns to ensure that they remain tuned to the status quo.

Basic policies for global/local sustainability

The cult of consumerism is not only spiritually empty but also ecologically destructive. To repair the failing ecosystems and life-support functions upon which we all depend, steady-state thinking emphasizes investment and conservation over spending and consumption. It also must work to restore trust in government as needed to mend our social safety nets and cultivate mutually supportive relationships among social groups.

Fixing broken markets

Ecological and social sustainability both require that we abandon capitalism's unbridled confidence in markets as the sole wellspring and arbiter of social values. Climate change, fisheries collapses, ecosystems degradation and illegal sweatshops are all examples of gross market failure. The emergency assembly must re-legitimize government intervention in markets to protect the common good; the world needs sound planning, selective re-regulation and comprehensive extra-market adaptation strategies for global change.

A major goal is to ensure that prices reflect the full costs of production and use. True-cost economics recognizes the need to:

- end perverse subsidies to the private sector (e.g. to the fossil fuel sector, fishing fleets, the corn ethanol industry and private banks 'too big to fail');
- re-regulate the private sector as necessary to protect the public interest;
- introduce scheduled ecological fiscal reforms – tax the bads (depletion and pollution) as well as the goods (labour and capital). This might require a combination of pollution charges/taxes on domestic produce and import tariffs on underpriced trade goods;
- tie development policy to the 'strong sustainability' criterion (i.e. maintain constant, adequate per capita stocks of critical natural, manufactured and human capital assets in separate accounts). This requires that we learn to:
- live on sustainable natural income, not natural capital liquidation. Society must therefore:
- implement 'cap-auction-trade' systems for critical resources such as fossil fuels – i.e. place sustainable limits on rates of resource exploitation (or waste discharges); auction off the exploitation rights to available capacity; and use the rents thus captured to address subsequent equity issues;
- revise systems of national accounts to include biophysical estimates of essential natural capital stocks and sinks in support of the previous measure;
- enforce an adequate minimum wage;
- replace or supplement GDP with more comprehensive/realistic measures of human well-being such as the Genuine Progress Indicator.

Re-writing the social contract

Trotsky is alleged to have commented that 'society is only three square meals away from revolution' (Gingles, 2006: 127). He recognized that civilization is a thin veneer – for social order people must feel adequately provisioned, economically secure, trusting of their neighbours and supported by family and friends. If BAU leads to trade disruption, supply shortages, economic upheaval and job loss, then civil unrest, riots and general chaos are inevitable, particularly if food and other essential resources run out and people are left to fend for themselves.[11]

Consistent with the principles of community, cooperation and people's common interest in an orderly transition, the World Assembly would charge individual nations with renewing the social contract and repairing social safety nets. National plans would include programmatic tax reform based on the recognition that taxation is society's means of pooling resources in service of the common good, particularly in times of widespread threat. Specific elements of the programme might include:

- a return to more progressive taxation policies encompassing income, capital gains, estate and corporate taxes;
- using taxes and positive incentives to promote a shift from private capital accumulation to investment in public infrastructure (e.g. transit, community facilities) and human development;
- recognition that a negative income tax may be necessary to assist low-income families through the transition and to guarantee access to the basics for life;
- investment in job training and job placement. Obsolete, unsustainable 'sunset' industries must be phased out (e.g. coal-based electricity generation) and workers will need new skills for employment in emerging sunrise industries (e.g. solar energy technologies);
- capitalizing on the advantages of a shorter work week and job sharing to improve people's work–life balance (self-actualization);
- implementing state-assisted family planning programmes everywhere to stabilize/reduce human populations.

Rethinking globalization, restoring locality

The global survival plan would also partially unravel today's increasingly unsustainable eco-economic entanglement of nations. The rationale is clear: first, the human mind is incapable of adequately understanding let alone safely controlling the behaviour of complex global-scale systems under stress.[12] By contrast, local/regional human communities and ecosystems are more manageable and any negative 'surprises' will be confined to the affected region. Second, unfettered trade: (a) allows trading regions to exceed local carrying capacities with short-term impunity; (b) both depletes remaining reserves of natural capital and accelerates global pollution, increasing the risk to all. Global 'overshoot' would be eliminated if each region were sustainably managed. Third, the economic restructuring (e.g. national/regional economic specialization) required for global market efficiency reduces economic diversity and resilience, destroys livelihoods and sometimes whole communities, and de-skills local populations. Moreover, because specialization makes people dependent on trade for everything no longer produced locally, it increases their vulnerability to global change – crop failures, energy bottlenecks, geopolitical instability and even changes in market conditions (Kissinger and Rees, 2009, 2010; Rees, 2002, 2013b). What will China do when it can no longer feed itself because global surpluses are inaccessible or have disappeared? Fourth, global economic integration is partially a product of abundant cheap energy. With the approaching end of the fossil fuel bonanza, the re-localization of production in heavy-goods sectors affected by rising transportation costs is already occurring and, as energy supplies shrink, the rest of the economy will *necessarily* follow. Fifth, unlike capital most people are loyal to their home communities (and are not fluidly mobile in any case).

To rebalance the tension between the global and local economies, the world community should revise WTO rules and similar regional trade treaties (e.g. NAFTA, the European Union). Nations and regions will be able to adapt creatively to emerging conditions only if they are free to:

- develop de-globalization plans to reduce dependence on foreign sources and sinks (i.e. reduce national ecological footprint on the others' ecosystems and global commons);
- generally increase national self-reliance in food, energy and other essential resources as a buffer against climate change, rising scarcity costs and global strife;
- simultaneously re-localize; re-skill domestic populations and diversify local economies through import displacement. Every nation/region should be able to produce the basic goods to feed, clothe and house itself, for example;
- encourage development of local currencies and local exchange trading systems to facilitate intra-regional trade and buffer local economies from external market fluctuations;
- strengthen local and national domestic markets to reduce exporters' dependence on global sales;
- insist on terms of international trade that provide the producer surpluses needed to maintain essential natural capital stocks (e.g. soils, fish stocks) (capital-depleting trade should be prohibited);
- invest in rebuilding local/regional natural capital stocks (e.g. fisheries, forests, soils, biodiversity reserves, etc.) that have been traded away using revenues collected from carbon taxes or resource quota auctions.

Let's be clear that rebalancing does not mean abandoning international trade. Trade does provide an important buffer in the event of domestic shortages caused by drought or disaster; it is necessary to acquire vital goods that cannot be produced locally. In any event, some countries and regions with large ecological deficits will remain highly trade-dependent at least until their populations fall to more sustainable levels. The rule for resilient local economies should be: export only true ecological surpluses (no net loss of productive natural capital) and import only important commodities that cannot reasonably be sourced at home. 'Trade if necessary, but not necessarily trade' serves as a convenient shorthand.

Bringing it all back home: re-localization

> Those people ... living in relatively self-reliant, organic, village-scale settlements should be able to ride the change with minimal difficulty and will emerge into the post-civilization phase intact. (Mare, 2000)

The uncertainties associated with global change also have important implications for urban form and function (Register, 2006). Urban designers and planners should begin now to rethink cities – or rather urban regions – so they function as complete quasi-independent human ecosystems. This is the ultimate form of functional bio-mimicry (Rees, 2012).

The city-as-ecosystem requires the re-localization of many ecological functions. Contemporary urbanization, combined with globalization has transformed local, integrated, cyclical human ecological production systems into global, horizontally disintegrated, unidirectional, throughput systems (Rees, 1997, 2012). Rather than being recycled on the land, essential nutrients contained in grain from the Russian steppes or Canadian prairies wind up in distant oceans, irreversibly discharged from urban sewage outfalls all over the world. The soils of some of the world's most important bread-baskets have lost half or more of their natural nutrients in just a century of mechanized agriculture.

The least vulnerable and most resilient urban system might be a new form of urban-centred bioregion (or eco-city state) in which a densely built-up core is surrounded by essential supportive ecosystems. The goal is to consolidate as much as possible of the human community's productive hinterland in close proximity to its consumptive centre. Organic 'wastes' and nutrients could then be economically recycled back to farms and forests.

Such a bioregionalized city would reconnect its human population to 'the land'. Citizens would see themselves to be directly dependent on local ecosystems and thus have a strong incentive to manage them sustainably. Less dependent on imports for the necessities of life, bioregionally focused populations would be partially insulated from external climate vagaries, resource shortages and distant conflicts.

Ideally, regional eco-cities would develop economic and social planning policies to facilitate reducing their residents' ecological footprints to a globally equitable 1.8 gha per capita. This is technically possible and the implicit greater equity could actually improve individual and community well-being (Wilkinson and Pickett, 2010). In any case, footprint contraction (particularly in rich countries) is essential to protect the regenerative capacity of nature and, where possible, to maintain populations within regional carrying capacity.

Clearly, the bioregional vision would require new governance structures that devolve to eco-city states significant control over their extended territories and resource hinterlands. These mechanisms would function to manage land, ecosystems and other resources vital to sustaining human life in the long-term collective interests of the entire community. This, in turn, may require stinting some customary private property rights. On a planet in overshoot, it is unacceptable for landowners to destroy through 'development' life-support functions required by everyone.

Localism, UK style

Contrast the foregoing prescription for re-localization with the Localism agenda in the UK. This agenda is actually consistent with the subsidiarity argument for re-localization: 'The Government is committed to passing new powers and freedoms to town halls. We think that power should be exercised at the lowest practical level – close to the people who are affected by decisions, rather than distant from them.' Accordingly, the Localism Act gives authorities 'the legal capacity to do anything that an individual can do that is not specifically prohibited'. That said, it is clear that the real intent is to deregulate local land development and stimulate economic growth: 'Localism is about liberating the natural desire of local communities to become more prosperous … Evidence from the UK and overseas shows that local communities need the right mixture of powers, incentives and accountability to maximise their prosperity.' In short, the UK Localism agenda is a model of business-as-usual, only more so. There is no mention of climate change, overshoot or anything else that might advise a cautionary approach to growth: On the contrary, 'The notion that communities choose decline and reject prosperity [read "material growth"] is perverse, wrong-headed and not based on evidence' (all quotations from DCLG, 2011). This could hardly be more at odds with the thesis advanced in this chapter.

Epilogue: mired in denial?

> The bad news is that evidently things still have to get much worse before we will muster the courage and clarity to try to make them better. The 'good news' is that things are indeed getting worse … (Daly, 2013)

This chapter started from the premise that the human enterprise has already overshot carrying capacity and that accelerating global change will, in coming decades, force the world community to contemplate the end of material growth. Indeed, if our best climate and environmental science is basically correct then humanity faces a choice between maintaining business-as-usual, in which case nature is likely to impose a chaotic implosion, or planning an orderly equitable descent. In short, to achieve sustainability with justice we will have to deliberately scale back the global economy (or at least reduce the throughput of energy and material) and consider means to redistribute wealth. This would require the world community to collaborate in the 'social construction' of a new economic narrative founded on stationary or 'steady-state' thinking. We must also reconsider the role of globalization and trade and begin the re-localization of much economic activity at the community and regional levels.

Contemplating wholesale re-localization after decades of rhetoric on the inevitability of global integration makes it appear the most daunting of tasks. However, there is nothing ordained or sacred about contemporary globalization. It is a pure social construct, the product of many human minds, extensive debate and laboriously negotiated global and regional agreements, designed mostly to serve the interests of capital and the corporate sector. It can therefore be deconstructed and replaced. A global network of largely self-reliant bioregional subsystems based on the principles described above would ensure a more economically secure, ecologically stable and socially equitable future for the majority of the world's people. If each such interlinked bioregion managed to stabilize its domestic population and conserve adequate per capita stocks of natural capital, the aggregate effect would be global sustainability.

It theory, opting for this alternative should not be a difficult choice for *Homo sapiens*. Would an ostensibly intelligent, forward-thinking, morally conscious, compassionate species continue to defend an economic system that wrecks its planetary home, exacerbates inequality, undermines social cohesion, generates greater net costs than benefits and ultimately threatens systemic collapse?

Remarkably, the answer so far seems to be 'yes'. There are simply no strong voices for caution among contemporary leaders and certainly no political constituencies for de-growth. There is no nascent plan for a World Assembly for Mutual Survival. Humanity's unique capacities for collective intelligence, rational analysis and planning ahead for the common good play no major role in the political arena, particularly when they challenge conventional myths and accepted norms, corporate values and monied elites. In short, there is virtually no possibility that anything like the proposals outlined above will actually be implemented. Daly (2013) was right: 'evidently, things still have to get much worse before we will muster the courage and clarity to try to make them better'.

Indeed, we are our own worst enemy. People are naturally both short-sighted and optimistic and thus discount the future; we generally react emotionally/instinctively to things that threaten our social status or political/economic power; those most vested in the status quo therefore resist significant change; corruption and greed (all but sanctioned by contemporary morality) overshadow the public interest.

As powerful as any other factor is mindless dedication to entrenched beliefs that blind us to otherwise obvious truths. History shows that such

> Woodenheadedness ... plays a remarkably large role in government. It consists in assessing a situation in terms of preconceived fixed notions [i.e. ideology] while ignoring any contrary signs. It is acting according to wish while not allowing oneself to be deflected by the facts. (Tuchman, 1984: 7)

Neuroscientists have long recognized the general phenomenon, but the means by which people become so deeply committed to particular concepts has only recently been revealed. In the course of individual development, repeated social, cultural and sensory inputs actually trace a semi-permanent record in the individual's synaptic circuitry – cultural norms, beliefs and values can acquire a physical presence in the brain! Once engraved, these neural structures alter the individual's perception of subsequent experiences and sensory inputs. People tend to seek out situations, people and data that reinforce their neural 'presets'. Conversely, 'when faced with information that does not agree with their internal structures, they deny, discredit, reinterpret, or forget that information' (Wexler, 2006).

Such learned or 'soft-wired' cognitive barriers can be broken down, but this requires acknowledgement of the problem and significant effort on the part of the individual, or an external shock powerful enough to shatter the treasured illusion. Many citizens of market democracies are burdened by a socially constructed bias towards capitalist values and market ideology that combines with innate behavioural conservatism to form a formidable barrier to societal transformation. The fate of global civilization may therefore rest on humanity's penchant for self-delusion in the face of harsh reality.

So where does this leave us? The pace of global change is quickening, but it may well be that the mainstream world community is too fractious in outlook, too belligerent in defence of political status and tribal territory and too wedded to conventional myths to rise to the sustainability challenge. Despite considerable grass-roots activity and the proliferation of sustainability-oriented NGOs, preferred lies and shared illusions may hold sway over discomforting facts until it is too late to engineer a 'prosperous way down' (Odum and Odum, 2001).

Should this be our fate, it wouldn't be the first time human society risked tripping into the abyss. As Tainter observes, the most intriguing thing about the evolution of human societies is 'the regularity with which the pattern of increasing complexity is interrupted by collapse' (Tainter, 1995).[13] What would be unprecedented is the sheer scale of the implosion. Previous ill-fated societies were merely regional but if *global* civilization goes down, it could mean the end of the entire human experiment. *Homo sapiens* will have been selected out by ecological and social environments in turmoil. We will have failed to adapt, despite exquisite documentation of the changing reality destined to do us in.

Suggested epitaph: 'Too clever by half but not nearly smart enough'.

Notes

1 A population's eco-footprint is the area of productive land and water ecosystems required, on a continuous basis, to produce the renewable resources that the population consumes and to assimilate its carbon wastes (Rees, 1996, 2013a; Wackernagel and Rees, 1996). A 'global average hectare' (gha) is a hectare of world average productivity. We convert population eco-footprints into standard ghas to enable fair comparisons among regions or countries with differing ecosystem productivities.

2 This means that it would currently take about 1.5 years for the ecosphere to regenerate the renewable resources people use, and to assimilate the carbon their economies emit, each year (WWF, 2012). Alarming enough perhaps, but note that eco-footprint data are generally under-estimates because, in the absence of adequate data, they do not account for local over-exploitation (e.g. soil erosion or declining fish stocks) and include only carbon wastes (Rees, 2013a).

3 Including for other species – biocapacity appropriated for human use is irreversibly unavailable for non-human organisms. Continuous growth of the human enterprise therefore necessarily diminishes nature.

4 Regrettably, globalization and trade separate high-end consumers spatially and psychologically from the ecosystems that support them. Wealthy consumers thus remain blissfully unaware of their increasingly precarious dependence on distant 'elsewheres' for their very existence, even as excess consumption depletes the faraway supportive ecosystems.

5 The 2007–2008 boom in food prices, and subsequent high and volatile prices, reminded many import-dependent countries of their food insecurity, prompting them to seek secure supplies overseas. Together with the reduced attractiveness of other assets, this led to a 'rediscovery of the agricultural sector by different types of investors and a wave of interest in land acquisitions in developing countries' (Deininger and Byerlee, 2011: xxv).

6 The mainstream is showing signs of awakening. Even the World Bank has acknowledged the folly of BAU: 'The science is unequivocal that humans are the cause of global warming', that 'we are on a path to a 4°C (7.2°F) warmer world', with potentially 'devastating impacts on agriculture, water resources, ecosystems, and human health'. Bottom line? Four degrees of warming 'must be avoided'; '*bold, … immediate global action is needed to slow the growth in greenhouse gas emissions this decade*' (World Bank, 2013b [emphasis added]: 2012). Other conservative assessments of the human prospect agree that 'We are at a critical juncture in human history, which could lead to widely contrasting futures' and that 'the future is not set in stone, but is malleable, the result of an interplay among megatrends, game-changers and, above all, human agency' (Kojm, 2012).

7 Consider the extraordinary impacts of such constructs as communism and capitalism, civil rights and women's liberation, conservatism and liberalism, Islam, Judaism and Christianity.

8 In effect, a given social construct is a hypothesis to be tested against reality; when we act as if it were 'true', we are performing an uncontrolled experiment.
9 An economic steady-state implies a more or less constant rate of energy and material throughput, compatible with the regenerative and assimilative capacities of the ecosphere. The steady-state is not to be confused with a stagnant state. A steady-state economy can be dynamic, constantly changing with the rise of new and the decline of 'sunset' industries. It is an economy dedicated to qualitative improvement in well-being, not merely quantitative accretion.
10 In 1980 the richest countries with 10 per cent of the world's population enjoyed a gross national income 60 times that of the poorest countries with 10 per cent of the world's population. By 2005 the ratio stood at 122:1. Meanwhile, the poorest quintile of the population within many countries has suffered a declining share of national consumption over the last 15 years (WHO, 2013). In the US, the top 1 per cent of income earners have captured 95 per cent of total income gains since 2009 and now enjoy 10 per cent of total household income. The richest 10 per cent of households take home half the nation's income (Saez, 2013).
11 Signs are that this is already beginning, evident in everything from the relatively benign 'occupy Wall Street' movement through food riots (increasingly common in various countries) to civil war in Egypt, Ethiopia and Syria.
12 This is perhaps the most powerful argument against attempts to 'geo-engineer' solutions to climate change. Unintended systems responses are inevitable, unpredictable and most likely to be negative.
13 There are occasional exceptions – societies that reject core values and beliefs that have become problematic and replace them with more adaptive cultural narratives (Diamond, 2005).

References

Anderson, K. and Bows, A. (2008) Reframing the climate change challenge in light of post-2000 emission trends, *Phil. Trans. R. Soc. A*, doi:10.1098/rsta.2008.0138. Available at: http://rsta.royalsocietypublishing.org/content/366/1882/3863.full.

Barnosky, A.D. *et al.* (2012) Approaching a state shift in Earth's biosphere, *Nature*, 486: 52–58. doi:10.1038/nature11018.

Beckerman, W. (1992) Economic growth and the environment: Whose growth? Whose environment? *World Development*, 20: 481–496.

Berger, P.L. and Luckmann, T. (1966) *The Social Construction of Reality*, Garden City, NY: Doubleday.

Boulding, K. (1973) *Energy reorganization act of 1973: Hearings, Ninety-third Congress, first session, on H.R. 11510*, Washington, DC: United States Congress, p. 248.

Clugson, C.O. (2012) *Scarcity: Humanity's final chapter?* Port Charlotte, FL: Booklocker.com, Inc.

Daly. H.E. (ed.) (1973) *Toward a Steady-State Economy*, San Francisco, CA: W.H. Freeman.

Daly, H.E. (1991) *Steady-State Economics: Second edition with new essays*, Washington, DC: Island Press [originally published 1977].

Daly, H.E. (2013) The fracking of 'the limits to growth', *The Daly News*, Center for the Advancement of the Steady State Economy. Available at: http://steadystate.org/the-fracking-of-the-limits-to-growth.

DCLG. (2011) *A Plain English Guide to the Localism Bill (Update)*, London: Department for Communities and Local Government. Available at: www.gov.uk/government/uploads/system/uploads/attachment_data/file/5958/1923416.pdf.

Deininger, K. and Byerlee, D. (2011) *Rising Global Interest in Farmland: Can it yield sustainable and equitable benefits?* Washington, DC: World Bank. Available at: http://siteresources.worldbank.org/INTARD/Resources/ESW_Sept7_final_final.pdf.

Diamond, J. (2005) *Collapse: How societies choose to fail or succeed*, New York: Viking Press.

Georgescu-Roegan, N. (1971) *The Entropy Law and the Economic Process*, Cambridge, MA: Harvard University Press.

Gheorghică, A.E. (2012) *The Emergence of La Décroissance*, CES Working Papers, IV (1), Centre for European Studies, Alexandru Ioan Cuza University of Iași, Romania.

Gingles, W.J. (2006) *A Journey on the Trans-Siberian Railway*, Bloomington, IN: Author House.

Greer, J.M. (2008) *The Long Descent*, Gabriola, BC: New Society Publishers.

Hansen, J., Sato, M., Russell, G. and Kharecha, P. (2012) *Climate Sensitivity, Sea Level, and Atmospheric CO2*, New York: NASA Goddard Institute for Space Studies and Columbia University Earth Institute. Available at: http://arxiv.org/ftp/arxiv/papers/1211/1211.4846.pdf.

Hedges, C. (2013) We are all aboard the Pequod, *Nation of Change – Human Rights*, 9 July 2013. Available at: www.nationofchange.org/we-are-all-aboard-pequod-1373377109.

Heinberg, R. (2013) *Snake Oil: How fracking's false promise of plenty imperils our future*, Santa Rosa, CA: Post Carbon Institute.

IEA. (2010) *World Energy Outlook 2010: Executive summary*, Paris: International Energy Agency. Available at: www.worldenergyoutlook.org/media/weowebsite/2010/WEO2010_es_english.pdf.

Jackson, T. (2009) *Prosperity without Growth: Economics for a finite planet*, London: Earthscan.

Kerschner, C. (2010) Economic de-growth vs. steady-state economy, *Journal of Cleaner Production*, 18: 544–551.

Kissinger, M. and Rees, W.E. (2009) Footprints on the prairies: Degradation and sustainability of Canadian agriculture in a globalizing world, *Ecological Economics*, 68: 2309–2315.

Kissinger, M. and Rees, W.E. (2010) Importing terrestrial biocapacity: The U.S. case and global implications, *Land Use Policy*, 27: 589–599.

Klare, M. (2001) *Resource Wars: The new landscape of global conflict*, New York: Owl Books (Henry Holt).

Klare, M. (2012) *The Race for What's Left: The global scramble for the world's last resources*, New York: Metropolitan Books (Henry Holt).

Kojm, C. (2012) Chairman's preface letter in *Global Trends 2030: Alternative Worlds*, Washington, DC: National Intelligence Council. Available at: www.dni.gov/index.php/about/organization/national-intelligence-council-global-trends and http://globaltrends2030.files.wordpress.com/2012/11/global-trends-2030-november2012.pdf.

Lane, R. (2000) *The Loss of Happiness in Market Democracies*, New Haven, CT: Yale University Press.

Mare, E.C. (2000) *Sustainable Cities: An oxymoron?* Seattle, WA: Village Design Institute.

Mill, J.S. (1848) *Principles of Political Economy With Some of Their Applications to Social Philosophy* (7th edition [1909], ed. by W.J. Ashley), London: Longmans Green and Co. Available at: www.econlib.org/library/Mill/mlP.html.

Odum, H. and Odum, E. (2001) *A Prosperous Way Down: Principles and policies*, Boulder: University Press of Colorado.

Ortiz, I. and Cummins, M. (2011) *Global Inequality: Beyond the bottom billion*, UNICEF Social and Economic Policy Working Paper, New York: United Nations Children's Fund (UNICEF), April. Available at: www.unicef.org/socialpolicy/files/Global_Inequality.pdf.

Oxfam. (2011) *Land and Power: The growing scandal surrounding the new wave of investments in land*, Oxford: Oxfam International. Available at: http://policy-practice.oxfam.org.uk/publications/land-and-power-the-growing-scandal-surrounding-the-new-wave-of-investments-in-l-142858.

Oxfam. (2012) *Our Land, Our Lives*, Oxfam Briefing Note, Oxford: Oxfam International. Available at: www.oxfam.org/sites/www.oxfam.org/files/bn-land-lives-freeze-041012-en_1.pdf.

Postman, N. (1999) *Building a Bridge to the 18th Century*, New York: Alfred Knopf.

Rees, W.E. (1995) Achieving sustainability: Reform or transformation? *Journal of Planning Literature*, 9(4): 343–361.

Rees, W.E. (1996) Revisiting carrying capacity: Area-based indicators of sustainability, *Population and Environment: A Journal of Interdisciplinary Studies*, 17(3): 195–215.

Rees, W.E. (1997) Is 'sustainable city' an oxymoron? *Local Environment*, 2: 303–310.

Rees, W.E. (2002) Globalization and sustainability: Conflict or convergence? *Bulletin of Science, Technology and Society*, 22(4): 249–268. Available at: www.terry.ubc.ca/files/rees.pdf.

Rees, W.E. (2008) Human nature, eco-footprints and environmental injustice. *Local Environment*, 13(8): 685–701. Available at: www.tandfonline.com/doi/abs/10.1080/13549830802475609#.UgV2sNLVCSo.

Rees, W.E. (2010) What's blocking sustainability? Human nature, cognition and denial, *Sustainability: Science, Practice & Policy*, 6(2): 13–25. Available at: http://sspp.proquest.com/archives/vol6iss2/1001-012.rees.html.

Rees, W.E. (2012) Cities as dissipative structures: Global change and the vulnerability of urban civilization, in M.P. Weinstein and R.E. Turner (eds), *Sustainability Science: The emerging paradigm and the urban environment*, New York: Springer.

Rees, W.E. (2013a) Ecological footprint, concept of, in Simon Levin (ed.), *Encyclopedia of Biodiversity*, 2nd edn, Salt Lake City, UT: Academic Press/Elsevier.

Rees, W.E. (2013b) Carrying capacity, globalisation, and the unsustainable entanglement of nations, in P. Lawn (ed.), *Globalisation, Economic Transition and the Environment: Forging a path to sustainable development*, London: Edward Elgar.

Register, R. (2006) *EcoCities: Rebuilding cities in balance with nature*, rev. edn, Gabriola Island, BC: New Society Publishers.

Rockström, J., Steffen, W., Noone, K., Persson, Å., Chapin, F.S., *et al.* (2009) A safe operating space for humanity, *Nature*, 461: 472–475.

Saez, E. (2013) *Striking It Richer: The evolution of top incomes in the United States (updated with 2012 preliminary estimates)*, Berkeley: University of California at Berkeley, Department of Economics.

Shah, A. (2013) Poverty facts and stats, *Global Issues: Social, Political, Economic and Environmental Issues that Affect Us All*. Available at: www.globalissues.org/article/26/poverty-facts-and-stats.

Smith, A. (1776) *An Inquiry into the Nature and Causes of the Wealth of Nations*, London: W. Strahan.

Steffen, W., Crutzen, P.J. and McNeill, J.R. (2007) The Anthropocene: Are humans now overwhelming the great forces of nature? *Ambio*, 36(8): 614–621. Available at: http://mfs.uchicago.edu/public/institutes/2013/climate/prereadings/steffen_et_al--the_anthropocene.pdf and www.pik-potsdam.de/news/public-events/archiv/alter-net/former-ss/2007/05-09.2007/steffen/literature/ambi-36-08-06_614_621.pdf.

Tainter, J. (1988) *The Collapse of Complex Societies*, New York: Cambridge University Press.

Tainter, J. (1995) Sustainability of complex societies, *Futures*, 27(4): 397–407.

Tuchman, B.W. (1984) *The March of Folly, from Troy to Vietnam*, New York: Alfred Knopf.

Victor, P. (2008) *Managing Without Growth*, Cheltenham: Edward Elgar.

Wackernagel, M. and Rees, W.E. (1996) *Our Ecological Footprint*, Gabriola, BC: New Society Publishers.

Wexler, B.E. (2006) *Brain and Culture: Neurobiology, ideology and social change*, Cambridge, MA: MIT Press.

WHO. (2013) *The Social Determinants of Health*, Geneva: World Health Organization. Available at: www.who.int/social_determinants/thecommission/finalreport/key_concepts/en/index.html.

Wilkinson, R. and Pickett, K. (2010) *The Spirit Level: Why equality is better for everyone*, London: Penguin Books.

World Bank. (2012) *Turn Down the Heat: Why a 4°C warmer world must be avoided*, report for the World Bank by the Potsdam Institute for Climate Impact Research and Climate Analytics, Washington, DC: World Bank. Available at: http://documents.worldbank.org/curated/en/2012/11/17097815/turn-down-heat-4%C2%B0c-warmer-world-must-avoided.

World Bank. (2013a) *Commodity Markets Outlook: Global economic prospects*, Vol. 2, July 2013, Washington, DC: World Bank. Available at: http://siteresources.worldbank.org/INTPROSPECTS/Resources/334934-1304428586133/CommodityMarketsOutlook_July2013.pdf.

World Bank. (2013b) *Climate Change Overview*, Washington, DC: World Bank. Available at: www.worldbank.org/en/topic/climatechange/overview.

WWF. (2012) *Living Planet Report 2012*, Gland, Switzerland: Worldwide Fund for Nature.

11

'Localism' and the Environment: Effective Re-scaling for Sustainability Transition?

Richard Cowell

Appeals to the merits of 'local action' feature prominently among the ideologies of twentieth-century environmentalism. Key texts in the birth of radical environmentalism, such as *Small Is Beautiful* (Schumacher, 1973), have extolled the desirability – and often the necessity – of moves towards smaller-scale social organisation if ecological crisis is to be averted. From the 1990s, localist threads have come to permeate debates about institutional structures for promoting sustainable development, from the exhortations of Local Agenda 21, to initiatives like Cities for Climate Protection (Bulkeley *et al.*, 2011) and the Transitions Towns movement (Whitehead, 2012). On first glance then, the 'localism' agenda of the Coalition Government that took power in the UK in May 2010 – in which 'localism is constructed as a univocally positive phenomenon' (Featherstone *et al.*, 2012: 177) – resonates with decades of eco-political thinking.

There might be elements of continuity, but one should not confuse discourse continuities around local environmental action with analytical simplicity or with significant efficacy. The emphasis given to localism in eco-political thinking has attracted an equally large and diverse set of critiques, challenging the logic, adequacy and desirability of downscaling the locus of power as a means of promoting greater environmental sustainability. In particular, questions have been raised about the power of localised social and political formations to change the ecological metabolism of the modern, globalised, predominantly urban worlds that we inhabit (for example, Marvin and Guy, 1997). If the Coalition's localism agenda attracts a slight green glow from history, so it might equally be subject to the cumulative force of years of critique.

This chapter takes the form of a critical review and proceeds as follows. First, I review the principal lines of criticism that have been mounted against localist agendas within eco-political thinking. From this I establish my main concern as the potential role of localist strategies in promoting more environmentally sustainable development trajectories at the wider scale – the issue of transition. Second, I identify ways in which local arenas may possess positive qualities for transitions to sustainability: in providing contexts for the creation of more diverse, contextually embedded solutions to environment and development problems; and in mobilising resistance to unsustainable business-as-usual. I identify each as potential qualities (contingent on other relations), rather than necessary qualities. Important observations arise from this discussion: that the effects of local environmental action need to be viewed in relation to the wider governance arrangements surrounding a particular sector; and that rather than viewing localities as arenas for 'promoting environmental sustainability', they are more fruitfully viewed as one set of arenas in which struggles about the reconciliation of economy and environment are played out.

Third, this framework is used to assess how the Coalition Government's localism agenda intersects with these qualities of local environmental action, focusing on renewable energy policy and land use planning in the UK, and particularly England. For each policy sector, the analysis considers how government actions might be seen as re-scaling power to local arenas, and the consequences for environmental sustainability. This perspective shows that, in practice, localism is scarcely seen by the Coalition as a motor for environmental protection; there is more concern to discipline local action, to ensure that local environmental actions do not unduly restrict economic growth.

Localism and environmental sustainability: a critique

There are rich veins of eco-political thinking that claim that decentralisation of political and economic power is integral to the creation of a more sustainable society (Eckersley, 1992). In Murray Bookchin's social ecology, for example, the source of ecological crisis lies in the social sphere, in the domination exerted by social hierarchies (Bookchin, 1982), which need therefore to be removed. Deep green thinkers such as Arne Naess (1973) promote the re-embedding of humans in the natural world, which requires small-scale, decentralised communities and, in their train, the adoption of technologies that are more democratically manageable and locally appropriate. The equation between ecological sustainability and decentralised political and social structures is also made by an array of 'eco-communalist' theories, variously promoting community-based and cooperative modes of living and working (such as Goldsmith's *Blueprint for Survival* (1972)), and arguing for the creation of relatively self-sufficient and stable economies from small-scale communities (Roszak's *Person/Planet* (1979)).

Localist thinking in environmental politics was re-energised and reformulated from the early 1990s with the emergence of global sustainability agendas, as exemplified by Local Agenda 21. The politics were generally less overtly radical than the earlier eco-anarchists and deep ecologists but, as Marvin and Guy (1997: 312) observed, ideologies often asserted the 'importance of the locality ... as being pivotal and self-evident in the shift to a more environmentally sustainable future'. Such localist thinking regularly claimed that 'environmental policy initiatives at the local level will effectively deal with the ecological chaos of today' (Marvin and Guy, 1997: 311), not least by helping to cultivate a sense of environmental responsibility among the citizenry. The scalar logics of Local Agenda 21 retained a strong emphasis on grass-roots action, but gave a bigger role to local government leading the development of more sustainable communities and lifestyles. Indeed, many localist sustainability formulations have been as much about fostering the environmental potential of existing, smaller-scale political communities as about actively re-scaling society towards new, smaller units.

Such connections between localisms – i.e. more decentralised social, economic and political arrangements – and environmentally sustainable patterns of development are, as many have observed, subject to a number of problems.

Logic and necessity

The first problem is whether there is necessarily a strong relationship between specific scalar structures of governance and particular material outcomes. Such claims are widely questioned. Certainly, one can point to higher levels of environmental sustainability achieved by small-scale social communities, from the Centre for Alternative Technology in mid-Wales that emerged in the 1970s to more recent expressions like the Transition Towns movement (Seyfang and Haxeltine, 2012). However, one can equally see instances where local political communities have used any autonomy they possess to pursue very exploitative agendas. Whitehead (2012) points to the US community of Mesa, Arizona, forging a development strategy built around new airport runways and based heavily on air travel – a 'hyper-liberal urbanism' in which communities do anything to compete. Harvey's account of the US 'wise-use movement' notes how discourses of local autonomy are used to legitimise the intensive exploitation of 'local' resources, free from externally imposed environmental constraints (Harvey, 1996).

Trying to forge a necessary connection between localism and environmental sustainability is a subset of a much wider difficulty – that it is far from clear that any particular social arrangements are necessarily ecologically benign. As Fox puts it: 'the relationships between the internal organization of human societies and their treatment of the nonhuman world can be as many and varied as the outcome of any other evolutionary process' (1989). Analysts have shown that the relationship between democracy and sustainability is similarly complex (Jacobs, 1997; Lafferty, 2004), with much depending on the dominant actors in particular arenas. The same applies to connections between civil society and sustainability transition (Smith, 2012). Further muddying the waters is the multiplicity of pathways towards environmental sustainability, embracing an array of potential socio-technological relationships. One cannot simply see localism as functional for environmental sustainability without asking for what conception of sustainability are particular localisms functional?

We can begin to see that the extent to which local action supports environmental sustainability is highly contingent on other factors. This concern with wider relations is also relevant to the next problem – leverage for transition.

Leverage for transition

As noted above, it is not difficult to point to examples of local initiatives that support greater sustainability, from experimental communities, to communes, to exemplar local government-led strategies. There is also wider consensus that a more environmentally sustainable world will be one in which *more localised* social relations play a bigger role. This world is likely to entail less long-distance, high-energy personal mobility (like flying or driving), more diverse and modularised energy supplies, and securing a greater proportion of food resources from within the immediate region (Whitehead, 2012). Resilience thinkers argue that societies that are better able to withstand the risks of disruptive environmental events and resource depletion are those where the supply chains of key goods and services are shorter, which in turn helps economic sustainability in terms of the local circulation of value (see, for example, Hopkins, 2008; Simms, 2008).

Clearly then, localised, sustainable visions of the future are thinkable, and to varying degrees realised in particular cases. However, this thinkability may tell us very little about how more sustainable forms of production, consumption and mobility might be promoted more widely. Eco-communalist agendas have often emphasised withdrawal from industrialism as a means for its renewal, but such visionary and utopian strategies have uncertain relevance for fostering social and ecological change at wider scales, in the modern, urban world (Eckersley, 1992). Even within their 'boundaries', it is often the case that initiatives are bigger on rhetorics of local commitment to environmental causes than they are on significant, demonstrable changes in local consumption and production practices. Whitehead (2012), for example, notes how cities that formally claim to be committed to sustainability rarely achieve so much in practice (see also Bulkeley and Broto, 2013).

Overall it is far from clear how decentralised solutions exercise agency, to foster change at a wider scale, to get us from infinitely various 'heres' to much more sustainable 'theres'. There are a number of modes by which local actions could generate wider change (after Seyfang and Haxeltine, 2012: 383–384): *replication* (a growth in the number of localities adopting certain practices); *up-scaling* (a growth in the size and impact of local initiatives); and *jumping scale* (where local ideas influence mainstream practices or major actors, or are mobilised to challenge or destabilise business as usual [see also Cox, 1998]). But multiplicity of modes does not equate to efficacy. As Rootes (2013: 96) suggests, although local environmental campaigns may be ubiquitous, 'few produce sustained mobilisation, fewer succeed in mobilising at a level beyond the local, and fewer still are effectively translated into national issues'. Adapting Rootes's ideas, we can see that whether local environmental actions exert wider leverage depends on key intermediary or networking actors, such as environmental NGOs, and whether the issues raised by local actions attain salience in national policy agendas and become implemented.

Far from being a simple alternative arena for change, whether local actions exert wider leverage depends on their relationship to wider frameworks of government and governance. For Eckersley (1992: 154), addressing ecological crisis requires that we:

> 'march through' and reform the existing institutions of liberal parliamentary democracy (where they are available and despite their many limitations) and employ the resources (legal, financial and diplomatic) of the State to promote national and international action, curb ecological degradation, and foster the redistribution of resources between the rich and poor nations of the world.

Issues of international injustice are difficult to address through wholly local movements, requiring actions by and across multiple scales of government. Indeed, promoting more localised social and economic relations also requires reflexive engagement with state action. For example, fuel taxation by the state has an important role in raising the cost of long-distance vehicular travel. Another illustration would be the effects of tightening EU restrictions on landfilling waste in underpinning (local) recycling activities.

The question, then, is whether localist agendas increase the agency available to transform unsustainable development trajectories. This issue is bound up with the third problem, the coherence of 'the local' as a sphere for action.

The coherence of 'the local' and 'local action'

Sociologists and geographers have long problematised the social coherence of geographical communities (Glass, 1948), and Marvin and Guy (1997) apply such insights to early 1990s 'localist' ideologies of sustainability transition. They criticised the misplaced assumptions about the spatial and cultural coherence of 'localities', as bounded places,[1] such that they can be a straightforward basis for social mobilisation, and steered by local government towards improved environmental performance. Localities and communities can be contested constructs, where debates about class, identity and ethnicity may be caught up with contrasting views about how environment and economy should be reconciled. Moreover, the 'local' is clearly far from a taken-for-granted category; it potentially embraces anything from very small, face-to-face groupings to being a synonym for 'local government' that, in some countries, can be responsible for communities of many thousands of people.

For Marvin and Guy, localist thinking also rested on an incomplete analysis of what shapes cities (1997: 311) – too inward-looking and constricting – that ignores the significance of the nation state and global processes that shape social relations, and the ways in which 'individuals are embedded in consumption and production cycles that transcend local boundaries and local institutions' (p. 316). The idealism of localist agendas frequently neglects the ways in which the changing social organisation of resource flows (such as privatisation of the utilities or contracting out of service provision (Raco, 2013) has reallocated levers of control away from local spaces and often away from the public sphere altogether.

What one can take from these critiques is that acting on environmental conditions in localities, and reducing the environmental impacts of local actions, is not always effectively achieved wholly through local action.

A reconstruction

These criticisms of localist eco-political theories need taking seriously, but perhaps there is something to be rescued about the local sphere as an arena for progressing sustainability provided we are more modest and less essentialist in our claims. In the discussion below I discuss two sets of capacities of local arenas that could be functional for promoting environmental sustainability, in certain conditions. In so doing, I rely less on the normative claims of political theory, and more on social science research about local action and change.

Local as laboratory

There is widespread support for the view that capacity for change and adaptation in human–environment relations depends on the maintenance of diversity: of technologies, practices and forms of social organisation. Numerous theorists from a range of different perspectives thus give special attention to local spaces in fostering this diversity (e.g. Bulkeley and Broto, 2013; Roszak, 1979). We might label this 'local as laboratory'.

To focus on one example, analysts of technological transitions typically identify the importance of 'niches' that, because they 'are protected or insulated from "normal" market selection', 'act as "incubation rooms" for radical novelties' (Geels, 2002, drawing upon Schot, 1998). Niches are the context for variation, providing 'locations for learning processes' (Geels, 2002: 1261), which help new technological practices to emerge and teething problems to be resolved, before being unleashed on a wider audience. We could readily extrapolate from technology to policy and social innovations: for example, the banning of plastic carrier bags in Modbury, Devon, car-free days in city centres, or the Merton Rule for low carbon development. In Merton, London, in 2003, the local authority instigated new planning policies requiring developers of larger schemes to supply at least 10 per cent of energy demands from renewable energy sources, which went on to become more widely adopted (Owens and Cowell, 2010).

It has also long been argued that smaller-scale communities, whose daily lives are more embedded in particular environments, can be more responsive to that context and alert to the fine-grained opportunities for environmentally sensitive development (Norgaard, 1994). One does not have to believe there are innate ecological dimensions to 'local knowledge' to recognise that more abstract scientific expertise and standardised state practices can be blind to nuances of ecological–societal relations in specific territories: Scott's work on the problems of high modernist development schemes is a classic exposition (1998); Wynne's work (1996) on scientists' failure to grasp the effects of radiocaesium in upland sheep farms is another example.

If local arenas can be functional for innovation and environmental adaptation that does not imply that such propensities are ubiquitous. There are systematic inequalities in the resources and social capital available to localities that affect their scope to innovate (Park, 2012). Moreover, as noted above, whether local practices achieve any wider influence depends on processes that transcend the locality, in the market, governmental and technological systems that shape the provision of resources and services. In the language of transitions theories, these 'select' but also 'retain' and adopt these novelties: aggregating and extending their effect to a systemic level (Geels, 2002: 1270).[2] Government policy and regulation is one component of such systems, and state action can also help to co-produce niche innovations. One can see this in the Merton Rule example. In constructing the new policy, the borough of Merton wove together both local and non-local components, drawing initial legitimacy for its actions from increasingly ambitious national greenhouse gas reduction targets. The further spread of Merton Rule policies was based both on other local authorities adopting Merton's ideas (replication) but also lobbying for them to be included in national planning standards for building performance, to give them wider reach (i.e. jumping scale; Owens and Cowell, 2010).

Locality, mobilisation and resistance

Marvin and Guy (1997) are correct to suggest that 'localities' are far from homogeneous, contained spaces around which mobilisation for sustainability can focus. However, one can still adopt a complex, fragmentary and relational conception of localities, while also recognising that place – as an assemblage of social, environmental and economic qualities – is a significant mobiliser of public action.

Sociologists and environmental psychologists have shown repeatedly that the public are more readily engaged in environmental issues that connect to the places in which they live and work rather than in issues that seem detached and abstract, like climate change (Burningham and Thrush, 2001; Lorenzoni *et al.*, 2007). As Szerszynski (2006) puts it, people show a greater propensity to connect with environmental threats as denizens (of particular places) than according to the more abstracted ideals of environmental citizens. Rydin and Pennington (2001) use rational choice theory to explain why the public tend to feel more incentivised to act around local place defence, where the social and material benefits can be more obvious, than more dispersed and complex environmental threats like water pollution and air quality. From a range of theoretical perspectives then, we can see how concern for local environments mobilises public action. This does not mean that places speak with one voice: those concerned about the environment can also face place-based concerns prioritising the jobs that environmentally damaging development can bring.

The role of place in wider sustainability transitions has been relatively under-theorised, however. This may be partly due to the emphasis of much transitions thinking on technological innovation rather than social movements and resistance (Seyfang and Haxeltine, 2012; Smith, 2012). However, as Shove and Walker (2007) point out, sustainability transitions entail more than the emergence of new technologies: there is also a need to understand how *un*sustainable technologies became destabilised and replaced. In practice, one can point to a number of areas where environmental concerns have led place-based groups to question the desirability of infrastructure that underpins modern, mass-consumption societies. Resistance to new roads, mineral extraction sites and landfills, for example, have not only problematised specific projects, but also contributed to pressure on the policy regimes that underpin such projects and to the articulation of alternatives (Featherstone *et al.*, 2012: 180; Owens and Cowell, 2010; Rootes, 2013). In the language of transitions theory, Geels (2002) notes how openings for innovations arise when there is pressure on existing regimes, which loosen up previously firmly established socio-technical configurations.

The empowerment of resistance to unwanted development is one of the more predictable consequences of any move towards political decentralisation. However, suggesting that place is a significant driver of local resistance to development is not to imply that place-defensive actions necessarily put pressure on wider, unsustainable growth trajectories. Place-based resistance organisations do not always train their arguments and sights on overarching policies or pursue socially progressive agendas. Griggs and Howarth (2008; also Rootes, 2013) have analysed how some anti-airport expansion processes have become engaged in wider debates about the sustainability of flying (as at Heathrow airport), but others have remained Nimbyist in their goals (as at Stansted airport).[3] However, even place-based action that is essentially defensive in its goals can have the effect of making unsustainable business-as-usual more difficult. More complex dilemmas around governance re-scaling, local resistance and sustainability begin to arise when certain pathways *towards* sustainability are seen to entail large-scale infrastructure, as I discuss below in the context of renewable energy.

What then might we take from the above review? Clearly, if we are to grasp the relationship between local actions and sustainability we need to look not just at the conditions operating within the localities themselves, but also at the processes by which such actions extend their reach to challenge or supplant dominant development trajectories. This requires some understanding of the governance architecture of the state. One dimension of this is the opportunity structures available for connecting localised environmental concerns to policy cores (Kitschelt, 1986), and their openness to wider input or local variation in practice. A second dimension, intersecting with this, is the extent to which the state seeks to orchestrate the relationship between environment and economy, which may vary between sectors and policy 'objects'. For some objects, the state may be content to allow local actions to reformulate environment–economy relations, but in others local action may be positioned firmly within governance arrangements seeking to ensure that very particular balances are struck (Cowell and Murdoch, 1999). These wider governance dimensions become clear when we turn to examine the localisms being promoted in the UK in the second decade of the twenty-first century.

Localism and the environment in the UK: energy provision and planning

Tracing relationships between the localism agenda of the May 2010 Coalition Government and the environment is not easy. It is difficult in part because, as other commentators have noted, the Coalition's localism agenda is far from coherent. It is also difficult because such agendas were not driven by environmental concern; procedural concerns featured more strongly, especially a desire to reform the centralising national–local governance arrangements developed by preceding Labour governments. As we shall see below, the Coalition has been much less exercised by whether localism would deliver better environmental outcomes than that environmental protection should not undermine economic growth.

The main area of explicit connection – but not one discussed in depth here – is in the sphere of local environmental services: street cleaning, park management and waste policy. Here, the short-lived rhetoric of the 'Big Society' was rolled into 'The Big Green Society', as an agenda for 'nudging' and 'enabling' communities to 'help themselves' deliver environmental outcomes (Rustecki, 2011: 4). This could be seen as a reformulation of localist sustainability ideologies of the mid-1990s, with their emphasis on grass-roots action. In the context of fiscal austerity, the 'Big Society', green or otherwise, was widely seen as a way of using civic action to supplant slashed government spending (Sullivan, 2012). Yet, one should acknowledge that there may be practical reasons for engaging publics in co-producing environmental outcomes – not readily dismissed as co-option or a fig leaf for austerity – especially those in which consumption processes are a major factor (for example, reducing food waste).

Beyond the sphere of local environmental services one is left inferring the implications for localism, the environment and the connections between them from the array of government policy statements and initiatives that have emerged in different policy sectors. This too makes it tricky to pronounce on 'localism and the environment' in any generalised way. However, something of the character of what is happening can be conveyed by looking at two sectors – energy provision and planning. In each case, I consider the extent to which localisms are emerging, the forms they are taking, and how localist practices are positioned within wider governance arrangements for environment and development.

Energy provision

Successive UK governments have signalled their support for more sustainable systems of energy provision, in which dependence on fossil fuels is substantially replaced by low carbon sources. If this broad transition commands almost universal support, the pathways by which it is to be achieved are much more contested. There are advocates of conventional 'hard energy paths', dominated by large-scale, centralised forms of electricity generation, supplying power over long distances through grid systems, and those who see it as preferable to promote 'softer' energy paths, in which energy production is smaller in scale, often using simpler technology, and more decentralised: geographically, and in terms of ownership and control (Lovins, 1977).

This distinction has long been recognised as an over-simplification of the myriad potential pathways for future energy development (Verbong and Loorbach, 2012), but localist agendas for sustainable energy would seem to share many qualities with the softer path: more diverse technologies, lower and more dispersed impacts, lower energy losses from long-distance transmission, more dispersed ownership and greater resilience. Indeed, the experience of wind-power expansion in Denmark and Germany indicates further advantages to a localist strategy, insofar as the much greater presence of community and cooperative ownership facilitated widespread social support for the initial take-off, with public resistance much less prominent than it has been in Britain (Toke, 2005). This example also shows the interconnections between actions at different levels. National financial support systems for renewable energy in Germany and Denmark have been based on feed-in tariffs (FITs), a guaranteed price policy that provides a predictable system of support against which smaller-scale actors can more readily gain credit. Reciprocally, the broad basis of social engagement in renewable energy in Germany has helped maintain political and financial support for renewable energy, and FITs, in the face of opposition from incumbent energy businesses (Lauber, 2012).

To what extent have UK governments promoted localist paths to sustainable energy provision? It is not hard to find statements supportive of community-owned and -developed renewable energy (DECC, 2011, 2013; DTI, 2003), and the Coalition Government have been especially vocal supporters. Before he became prime minister, David Cameron expressed his support for widening engagement in energy production (Jones, 2008); in the Coalition Agreement, the government states that '[w]e will encourage community-owned renewable energy schemes where local people benefit from the power produced' (HM Government, 2010: 17). In practice, however, community-led electricity generation remains something of a Cinderella (see discussion in Strachan *et al.*, 2014). Most new renewable energy capacity in the UK has come from major, international companies in larger facilities (Stenzel and Frenzel, 2008; Szarka, 2007), a situation perpetuated in part by key facets of the regulatory and market regime. Historically, the UK has not followed Denmark and Germany in using generalised FITs, but has adopted tradable certificate mechanisms that – although not wholly inaccessible to smaller producers – are most easily exploited by larger players with ready supplies of capital (Lauber, 2012). Local renewable energy initiatives have been held back by limited access to credit, difficulties with grid access and the highly uneven availability of skills and social capital across communities (Park, 2012). Although there is a growing number of energy initiatives around the country with strong community credentials (Harnmeijer *et al.*, 2012; Turcu and Rydin, 2012), their overall contribution to energy supply has been small.

Arguably, the prospects for local engagement in energy production were significantly recast by the creation of a system of FITs to support small-scale renewable energy schemes. This was put in place in the final years of the 2005–2010 Labour government,[4] and prompted a surge in interest, with over 1 GW of installed capacity by March 2012 (OFGEM, 2012). The stable income flows created by FITs, and the levels of payment initially available, made engaging in the sector very attractive. In broad terms, the Coalition have maintained the FIT support arrangements; however, the passing of time enables us to see exactly what kinds of energy localism are being created. The vast bulk of new renewable energy generating capacity has come from individuals – typically installing solar photovoltaics on their own property – along with businesses such as farms. Intermediary bodies have been very important, including Housing Associations and local authorities, who see financial benefits – to their organisational budget, and the situation of their tenants – by installing micro-renewables in housing schemes (Mendonça, 2011; see also Bulkeley and Broto, 2013). Community groups – in the sense of collective bodies or social enterprises – remain a small proportion of the take-up of FIT.

It is difficult to foresee local, communitarian energy initiatives expanding quickly in the UK in the foreseeable future, for a number of reasons. Community groups wishing to develop local energy initiatives are often dependent on grant or loan funding for the development costs, which tend to be over-subscribed and time-limited (see the review by Park, 2012). The Coalition have created new grant schemes for such initiatives – notably the proposed £15 million Rural Community Energy Fund[5] – but this does little more than replace previous schemes that have been wound up. Much of what has been achieved has been concentrated in particular, propitious local circumstances, where energy/environment enthusiasts connect with organised social groups and willing landowners. A further, related issue is the political marginality of community renewables actors. Few bodies exist to represent the sector collectively. Most community renewables enthusiasts are focused on delivering local schemes (replication or modest up-scaling), rather than acting politically (jumping scale) to challenge the direction of energy policy (Seyfang and Haxeltine, 2012), while the trade associations for the sector are dominated by the big electricity producers.

The prospects for moves towards localism in the energy sector thus illustrate a number of the points made earlier about the intersection between localism and sustainability. Localities can be important sites for environmental action and innovation, but the capacity to act in this way is not ubiquitous, and the reach of such initiatives depends also on the positioning of local actions within wider institutional contexts: particularly socio-technical regimes of energy provision and their responsiveness to local inputs. If Coalition politicians have made positive noises about locally owned energy, the generality of their approach to energy policy has not significantly expanded the space for it. Indeed, the Energy Market Reform agenda is widely regarded as designed to facilitate investment in the most centralising of energy technologies, nuclear power, and the proposed system of financial support – contracts for difference – will more generally favour large, incumbent energy businesses, and be even harder for new entrants to access (Harvey, 2012). For the Coalition, the idea of community ownership of energy provision is just one strand in a much more pervasive discourse that 'communities should benefit' from energy investment, as exemplified by community benefit funds from wind energy and fracking, moves to allow greater retention of local business rates from on-shore wind, and channelling more of the royalties from exploiting offshore renewable towards coastal communities (Cowell *et al.*, 2012). Such discourses extol a fairer distribution of benefits between resource exploitation and people that live near the facilities, but leave the overall energy development pathway dominated by major, international corporations. In other respects, too, the Coalition is keen to maintain an emphasis on decidedly centralised modes of infrastructure provision, and to contain the 'objects' that local arenas are allowed to govern. This is clear when we consider the reach of localism in planning.

Planning

Planning has been more directly and explicitly subjected to the Coalition's localist agenda than energy, but the implications for the environment are no less ambivalent. In certain respects, localism for planning could be read as advancing 'negative freedom' (Berlin, 1969), with the removal of mechanisms for central steering of local decision-making. National targets and indicators have been cut back, including housing targets and minimum housing densities; regional planning bodies – which worked in part to reconcile those targets with local planning objectives – have been abolished. The Coalition has also taken steps to reduce the volume of central government planning policy guidance (see below). At the same time, a host of new powers have been rolled out for lower scales of governance. These include giving local authorities a power of general competence, making provision for local referendums, giving neighbours a bigger say in planning decisions and allowing neighbourhoods to prepare their own development plans.

Such steps might allow more scope for innovative and locally tailored planning solutions, insofar as local arenas are less trammelled by the need to accommodate national goals. Indeed, while Marvin and Guy argued that the 1990s localism of Local Agenda 21 over-egged the powers and capacities of British local government as an agent of change, this might become a less persuasive criticism if the Coalition's localism agenda genuinely extends the power of local authorities to drive environmental goals. However, to go any further in predicting a dividend for environmental sustainability runs into the criticisms of localism outlined above.

On the issue of necessity, it is far from clear that local authorities will use their new-found power to promote environmental agendas, especially in the context of economic austerity, unless there are economic and political advantages.

Local energy-generation or energy-conservation initiatives fit with this convergence of environmentalism and budget pressure, but not so all environmental issues. For example, research conducted in 2011 found two-thirds of local authorities deprioritising or narrowing their work on climate change, and focusing more on actions that would simultaneously cut costs, with the authors noting that the new freedoms for councils had not been backed by any new environmental responsibilities (Green Alliance, 2011). Freeing local authorities from higher-level impositions does not automatically make them more responsive to environmental problems that operate at larger scales, or slide across their boundaries (such as issues of water supply and flood risk), or better empower them to engage with issues of production and consumption shaped by wider infrastructural systems or major international companies. One corrective measure for this potential insularity has been the government's introduction of a duty on public bodies to cooperate on planning issues that cross administrative boundaries (CLG, 2012: para 178), though how diligently this is undertaken is as yet unclear.

Initial reflections on the consequences of localism in planning for the environment might thus be characterised as uncertainty – new opportunities, yes, but also uncertainty as to how new local freedoms would be exercised and to what aggregate effect. However, gradually the reality of localism has become clearer. Initial agnosticism, even positivity, from the government towards a flowering of local actions has become increasingly disciplined by measures deemed necessary to secure economic recovery. One example is that provision for local referendums on council tax changes can only veto increases, not reductions or freezes (Sullivan, 2012). A second example is that the provision for neighbourhood planning is conditional on such plans providing for more development than the statutory local development plan, not less, with uncertain scope to pursue more ambitious environmental standards (Green Alliance, 2011). A third example – and the one discussed in more detail here – is the way in which new national planning policy guidance re-regulates local autonomy.

The replacement of reams of national planning policy guidance by a shorter, simpler National Planning Policy Framework (NPPF; CLG, 2012) has been badged as a move to make the planning system more responsive to local needs and accessible to non-experts. However, the NPPF has not simply condensed and simplified previous guidance; it has also reallocated policy resources between different interests (Cowell, 2013). Key goals for planning are that 'significant weight should be placed on the need to support economic growth through the planning system' (CLG, 2012: para 19), it should be responsive to 'market signals', and that business should not be 'overburdened'. Meanwhile, environmental principles have been cut, or qualified by the need to consider implications for economic viability. A much-publicised feature of the NPPF is its presumption in favour of sustainable development, but this mobilises a conception of sustainability that gives much importance to economic growth. Environmental concerns are not absent – traditional presumptions in favour of protecting designated landscapes and habitats still apply – but there is precious little in the NPPF to encourage local planning authorities to use planning to help promote ambitious environmental agendas, or to exert leverage over unsustainable patterns of development.

The importance of this is that the one environmental outcome from decentralising power within planning that many would have predicted is that it would have empowered those seeking to resist what they perceive to be environmentally damaging development. After all, local opposition to development in the countryside was one factor driving support for the Conservative Party's opposition to housing targets and regional planning. Yet this capacity of local arenas to mobilise resistance is precisely what is being curtailed by the planning reforms. The resulting economic emphasis of the NPPF would appear to advantage developers, as they seek to exploit sites previously seen as environmentally constrained. The burden of proof weighs heaviest on those seeking to challenge growth: thus, in general, 'development needs' should be met, and development proposals be approved, unless 'any adverse impacts of doing so would significantly and demonstrably outweigh the benefits' (CLG, 2012: para 14).[6] By their very nature, environmental impacts are not always easily demonstrable, thus making it difficult for local planning authorities to take a precautionary stance.

So, when it comes to the relationship between development and the environment, the government is decidedly disinclined to allow local authorities to use their planning powers to strike greener agendas than national norms. To this extent, the Framework specifies the environment parameters *within which* localism is to unfold. Not only does the NPPF remove policy resources from 'resistance localism' (Featherstone *et al.*, 2012), it is scarcely a conducive context for local innovation. Perpetual debates about whether local authorities should be allowed to set environmental standards for development that go beyond national norms seem to have been won, for now, by the development interests declaiming the efficiencies of standardisation. So, for example, planning authorities seeking to follow Merton, by driving forward local improvements to the environmental performance of buildings, must now 'do so in a way consistent with the Government's zero carbon buildings policy and adopt nationally described standards' (CLG, 2012: para 95).

As in the energy field, it is clear that any moves towards decentralised governance excludes certain objects, notably 'nationally important infrastructure'. On this there is significant continuity with the preceding Labour government. In 2008 Labour enacted legislation designed to streamline the consenting regime for major infrastructure – electricity generation and major grids, ports, etc. – by replacing traditional public inquiries with new procedures, presided over by specialist units of inspectors, working to strict timetables for running cross-examinations and issuing reports. These procedures did make provision for more pre-application consultation with local publics and stakeholders, but the overall need for such infrastructure has been specified in National Policy statements, and cannot legitimately be questioned once individual projects come forward. The Coalition Government only tweaked these arrangements, such as returning the making of final decisions to ministers from Labour's independent Infrastructure Planning Commission, but it has also presided over their extension: to major hazardous waste facilities, waste-water treatment and transport networks, as well as to proponents of any major application in poorly performing planning authorities, by giving developers the option of applying for planning permission directly to the Planning Inspectorate (under the Growth and Infrastructure Act 2013).[7]

Rationalising such moves is a localising discourse – also inherited by the Coalition from its Labour predecessors (Cowell and Owens, 2006) – that represents the public as interested primarily in localised issues of visual amenity. Thus, through planning, 'local people come together and agree, "this is what we want our area to look like"' (Clark, 2010: 6); or decentralising planning will 'give neighbourhoods far more ability to influence the shape of the places in which their inhabitants live' (Cabinet Office, 2010). By such discourses, local planning arenas can be firmly marginalised in debates about the direction and implementation of 'national' infrastructural development.

Although major energy development is intended to benefit from these centralising reforms to planning, certain types of energy infrastructure also show the complex entanglements between governance re-scaling and particular objects. From its arrival in office, the Coalition Government has come under sustained political pressure from local groups, local councillors and members of parliament (MPs) in swathes of rural England, concerned about the expansion of on-shore wind across the landscape.[8] Within its broadly pro-growth thrust, the NPPF had already made initial policy shifts to legitimise more restrictive, spatial planning controls over wind power but, in the summer of 2013, the government announced yet more revisions of planning guidance, presented in parts of the press as giving communities a 'veto' over on-shore wind proposals.[9] The reality may amount to nothing like a veto (Early, 2013), but it illustrates how local environmental protests can exert more leverage where there is a high degree of networking between local conflicts, where the issue concerned achieved high electoral salience and where there are national policies on which opposition can be focused (Rootes, 2013). On-shore wind also illustrates why there can never be a straightforward equation between localism and environmental sustainability: across and within local areas there can still be contrasting views of whether particular developmental pathways – no matter that they might be regarded as low-carbon – are socially and environmentally desirable.

Conclusions

This chapter has critically examined the relationship between localism and the environment, focusing on the extent to which decentralising power towards smaller units might be functional for environmental sustainability. It was concluded that while calls for 'local action' may be a popular rallying cry for environmentalists, any claims that the pursuit of localism is inherently functional for sustainability transition must confront the necessity issue (to what extent is any scalar structure of governance inherently functional for sustainable development?) and the leverage/agency issue (the disposition of some localised social communities to pursue strong conceptions of sustainability does not tell us much about their capacity to promote change). We need to be more modest and nuanced about the connections.

To understand whether locally based actions exert leverage at wider spatial scales, to affect development trajectories, we must also understand how they expand in scope and reach (Seyfang and Haxeltine, 2012). In this regard, successful local environmental actions – be they innovations or place-based protest movements – are likely to depend on local conditions, but also the wider governance and infrastructural systems in which 'local action' is embedded; including political factors, such as the salience of local issues to NGOs and government (Rootes, 2013). Thus we can see how well-connected local opposition to wind power has arguably achieved greater influence on Coalition policy than the community renewables agenda. Acting successfully on environmental conditions within a given locality often means assembling resources – policies, finance, networks of supporters – from an array of different arenas and localities.

This leads to three final concluding remarks. First, and more methodological, when we shift the analytical focus from explicit discourses of localism to the policies and practices that govern particular sectors, one can identify more continuity between the Coalition Government and its predecessors in the scalar structuring of governance. Although the Coalition has removed key structures of national-to-local coordination, it has been no more keen to allow local 'resistance localism' to deflect growth objectives than its Labour predecessors. There is little difference between the main parties on their desire to facilitate large-scale energy infrastructure, for which an excess of local environmental democracy is considered a risk to delivery; though the electoral vulnerability of Coalition MPs to wind-power protests has made that technology more problematic.

Second – and following from this – rather than seeing the relationship between environment and development as something shaped *by* any programme of localism, strong government desires to configure the relationship between development and environmental protection can powerfully delimit the scope for local agency (Cowell and Murdoch, 1999). In planning especially, for all the rhetoric of freeing local actors from the restrictions of national policy, where there are risks that locally driven environmental arguments might be used to disrupt favoured growth objectives, then the scope of localism has been readily curtailed (see also Sullivan, 2012).

Third, and more speculatively, while all governance re-scalings seek to construct a new scalar fix for development they are rarely stable and, indeed, the environment may become a key battleground shaping the evolution of the Coalition Government's formulation of localism. On the one hand, the 'Big Green Society' discourse would appear precisely to be an appeal to affluent, organised communities to take responsibility for delivering environmental improvements in their locality. However, such social groupings are also very often the basis of development resistance in planning, which the Coalition is seeking to contain. Whether this constituency will show electoral support for the Conservatives in the next general election remains to be seen.

Notes

1 I leave aside the more disruptive implications of ontological perspectives that would eschew any foundational, hierarchical conception of scales in favour of seeing a world composed of assemblages (see Leitner and Miller, 2007). Nevertheless, one can see how such perspectives might capture the way in which 'local environmental action' connects components from assemblages at a diversity of 'levels', and that corporate boardrooms are localities, too.

2 The levels of Geels's multi-level framework are not literal scales, but heuristic devices that capture the need for reinforcing processes at wider scales if localised practices are to effect more systemic change.

3 NIMBY: 'not in my back yard'.

4 Initially using powers under the 2008 Energy Act.

5 Press Release: 'Onshore wind: communities to have a greater say and increased benefits'. Available online: www.gov.uk/government/news/onshore-wind-communities-to-have-a-greater-say-and-increased-benefits (accessed 6 June 2013).

6 When assessed against the policies in the NPPF as a whole which, inter alia, does include protection for nationally and internationally designated sites.

7 This only applies to local councils failing to determine at least 30 per cent of major applications within 13 weeks, but 'major applications' is a much wider category of development than 'nationally important infrastructure'.

8 Electricity power stations over 50 MW capacity have long been subjected to special centralised consenting procedures (Owens, 1985), so the Labour and Coalition reforms

are to some extent a refinement of this position. However, few on-shore wind farms in England exceed this size (because the sites available tend to be small), meaning that most are determined by local planning authorities.

9 *The Telegraph*, 6 June 2013, 'Locals to get veto power over wind farms'.

References

Berlin, I. (1969) Two concepts of liberty, in *Four Essays on Liberty*, Oxford: Oxford University Press.

Bookchin, M. (1982) *The Ecology of Freedom: The emergence and dissolution of hierarchy*, Palo Alto, CA: Cheshire.

Bulkeley, H. and Broto, V.C. (2013) Governing by experiment? Global cities and the governing of climate change, *Transactions of the Institute of British Geographers*, 38(3): 361–375.

Bulkeley, H., Broto, V.C., Hodson, M. and Marvin, S. (2011) *Cities and Low Carbon Transitions*, London: Routledge.

Burningham, K. and Thrush, D. (2001) *Rainforests Are a Long Way from Here*, York: Joseph Rowntree Foundation.

Cabinet Office. (2010) *Coalition Agreement: Our Programme for Government*. Available at: www.gov.uk/government/uploads/system/uploads/attachment_data/file/78977/coalition_programme_for_government.pdf (accessed 10 November 2014).

Clark, G. (2010) *Better Planning: From principle, to practice*, speech given to Localis, London, 18 November. Available at: www.localis.org.uk/article/769/Greg-Clark-reveals-details-of-planning-reform-at-speech-hosted-by-Localis.htm (accessed 20 December 2010).

CLG (Communities and Local Government). (2012) *National Planning Policy Framework*, London: CLG.

Cowell, R. (2013) Greenest government ever? Planning and sustainability after the May 2010 coalition government, *Planning Practice and Research*, 28(1): 27–44.

Cowell, R. and Murdoch, J. (1999) Land use and the limits to (regional) governance: Some lessons from planning for housing and minerals in England, *International Journal of Urban and Regional Research*, 23(4): 654–669.

Cowell, R. and Owens, S. (2006) Governing space: Planning reform and the politics of sustainability, *Environment and Planning C: Government and Policy*, 24(3): 403–421.

Cowell, R., Bristow, G. and Munday, M. (2012) *Wind Energy and Justice for Disadvantaged Communities*, viewpoint produced for the Joseph Rowntree Foundation, York: JRF, p. 44.

Cox, K. (1998) Spaces of dependence, spaces of engagement and the politics of scale, or: Looking for local politics, *Political Geography*, 17: 1–23.

DECC (Department of Energy and Climate Change). (2011) *UK Renewable Energy Roadmap*, July, London: DECC.

DECC. (2013) *Community Energy: Call for evidence*, 6 June, London: DECC.

DTI (Department of Trade and Industry). (2003) *Our Energy Future*. Available at: http://webarchive.nationalarchives.gov.uk/+/http://www.berr.gov.uk/files/file10719.pdf (accessed 12 September 2012).

Early, C. (2013) 'No veto' for wind farm plans, *Planning*, 14 June: 6–7.

Eckersley, R. (1992) *Environmentalism and Political Theory: Toward an ecocentric approach*, London: UCL Press.

Featherstone, D., Ince, A., Mackinnon, D., Strauss, K. and Cumbers, A. (2012) Progressive localism and the construction of political alternatives, *Transactions of the Institute of British Geographers*, 37: 177–182.

Fox, W. (1989) The deep ecology-ecofeminism debate and its parallels, *Environmental Ethics*, 11: 5–25.
Geels, F.W. (2002) Technological transitions as evolutionary reconfiguration processes: A multi-level perspective and case-study, *Research Policy*, 31: 1257–1274.
Glass, R. (ed.) (1948) *The Social Background of a Plan*, London: Routledge & Kegan Paul.
Goldsmith, E. (1972) Blueprint for survival, *The Ecologist*, 2(1).
Green Alliance (2011) *Is Localism Delivering for Climate Change?* London: Green Alliance.
Griggs, S. and Howarth, D. (2008) Populism, localism and environmental politics: The logic and rhetoric of the Stop Stansted Expansion Campaign, *Planning Theory*, 7(2): 123–144.
Harnmeijer, A., Harnmeijer, J., McEwen, N. and Bhopal, V. (2012) *A Report on Community Renewable Energy in Scotland*, May, Edinburgh: SCENE Connect.
Harvey, D. (1996) *Justice, Nature and the Geography of Difference*, Oxford: Basil Blackwell.
Harvey, F. (2012) Plans to reform electricity markets 'unworkable', says green businesses, *The Guardian*, 15 May. Available at: www.guardian.co.uk/environment/2012/may/15/reform (accessed 16 May 2012).
HM Government (2010) *The Coalition: Our programme for government*, London: Cabinet Office.
Hopkins, R. (2008) *The Transition Handbook: From oil dependency to local resilience*, Totnes: Green Books.
Jacobs, M. (1997) Environmental valuation, deliberative democracy and public decision-making institutions, in J. Foster (ed.), *Valuing Nature: Economics, ethics and environment*, London: Routledge, pp. 211–231.
Jones, D. (2008) *Cameron on Cameron: Conversations with Dylan Jones*, London: HarperCollins.
Kitschelt, H. (1986) Political opportunity structures and political protest: Anti-nuclear movements in four democracies, *British Journal of Political Science*, 16: 58–95.
Lafferty, W.M. (ed.) (2004) *Governance for Sustainable Development: The challenging of adapting form to function*, Cheltenham: Edward Elgar.
Lauber, V. (2012) Wind power policy in Germany and the UK: Different choices leading to divergent outcomes, in J. Szarka, R. Cowell, G. Ellis, P.A. Strachan and C. Warren (eds), *Learning from Wind Power. Governance, societal and policy perspectives on sustainable energy*, Basingstoke: Palgrave Macmillan, pp. 38–60.
Leitner, H. and Miller, B. (2007) Scale and the limitations of ontological debate: A commentary on Marston, Jones and Woodward, *Transactions of the Institute of British Geographers*, 32(1): 116–125.
Lorenzoni, I., Nicholson-Cole, S. and Whitmarsh, L. (2007) Barriers perceived to engaging with climate change among the UK public and their policy implications, *Global Environmental Change*, 17: 445–459.
Lovins, A.B. (1977) *Soft Energy Paths: Toward a durable peace*, Harmondsworth: Penguin.
Marvin, S. and Guy, S. (1997) Creating myths rather than sustainability: The transition fallacies of the new localism, *Local Environment*, 2(3): 311–318.
Mendonça, M. (2011) *The UK Feed-in Tariff: A User Survey*, Working Paper, Birkbeck Institute of Environment, Birkbeck College, University of London.
Naess, A. (1973) The shallow and the deep, long-range ecology movement, *Inquiry*, 16: 95–100.
Norgaard, R. (1994) *Development Betrayed: The end of progress and a co-evolutionary revisioning of the future*, London: Routledge.
OFGEM (2012) *Feed-in Tariff (FIT): Annual report 2011–2012*, London: OFGEM.

Owens, S. (1985) Energy, participation and planning: The case of electricity generation in the United Kingdom, in F. Calzonetti and B. Soloman (eds), *Geographical Dimensions of Energy*, Dordrecht: Reidel, pp. 225–253.

Owens, S. and Cowell, R. (2010) *Land and Limits: Interpreting sustainability in the planning process*, 2nd edn, London: Routledge.

Park, J. (2012) Fostering community energy and equal opportunities between communities, *Local Environment*, 17: 387–408.

Raco, M. (2013) The new contractualism, the privatization of the welfare state, and the barriers to open source planning, *Planning Practice and Research*, 28(1): 45–64.

Rootes, C. (2013) From local conflict to national issue: When and how environmental campaigns succeed in transcending the local, *Environmental Politics*, 22(1): 95–114.

Roszak, T. (1979) *Person/Planet: The creative disintegration of industrial society*, Garden City, NY: Doubleday and Co.

Rustecki, D. (2011) *The Big Green Society: Empowering communities to create cleaner, greener neighbourhoods*, London: Localis and City of Westminster. Available at: www.localis.org.uk (accessed 31 January 2012).

Rydin, Y. and Pennington, M. (2001) Discourses of the Prisoners Dilemma: The role of the local press in environmental policy, *Environmental Politics*, 10(3): 48–71.

Schot, J.W. (1998) The usefulness of evolutionary models for explaining innovation: The case of The Netherlands in the nineteenth century, *History of Technology*, 14: 173–200.

Schumacher, E.F. (1973) *Small is Beautiful: Economics as if people mattered*, London: Blond and Briggs.

Scott, J.C. (1998) *Seeing Like a State: How certain schemes to improve the human condition have failed*, New Haven, CT: Yale University Press.

Seyfang, G. and Haxeltine, A. (2012) Growing grassroots innovations: Exploring the role of community-based initiatives in governing sustainable energy transitions, *Environment and Planning C: Government and Policy*, 30: 381–400.

Shove, E. and Walker, G. (2007) Caution! Transitions ahead: Politics, practice, and sustainable transition management, *Environment and Planning A*, 39(4): 763–770.

Simms, A. (2008) *Nine Meals from Anarchy: Oil dependence, climate change and the transition to resilience*, New Economics Foundation in association with Schumacher North, London: NEF.

Smith, A. (2012) Civil society in sustainable energy transitions, in G. Verbong and D. Loorbach (eds), *Governing the Energy Transition: Reality, illusion or necessity?* London: Routledge, pp. 180–202.

Stenzel, T. and Frenzel, A. (2008) Regulating technological change: The strategic reactions of utility companies towards subsidy policies in German, Spanish and UK electricity markets, *Energy Policy*, 36: 2645–2657.

Strachan P, Cowell R, Ellis G, Sherry-Brennan F and Toke D (2014) *Promoting Community Renewable Energy in a Corporate Energy World: Policy Developments in the UK and the Impacts of Devolution*, Papers in Environmental Planning Research 32, Cardiff School of Planning and Geography.

Sullivan, H. (2012) Debate: A Big Society needs an active state, *Policy and Politics*, 40(1): 145–148.

Szarka, J. (2007) *Wind Power in Europe: Politics, business and society*, Basingstoke: Palgrave Macmillan.

Szerszynski, B. (2006) Local landscapes and global belonging: Toward a situated citizenship of the environment, in A. Dobson and D. Bell (eds), *Environmental Citizenship*, Cambridge, MA: MIT Press.

Toke, D. (2005) Explaining wind power planning outcomes: Some findings from a study in England and Wales, *Energy Policy*, 33: 1527–1539.
Turcu, C. and Rydin, Y. (2012) Planning for change in urban energy systems, *Town and Country Planning*, May: 227–232.
Verbong, G. and Loorbach, D. (eds) (2012) *Governing the Energy Transition: Reality, illusion or necessity?* London: Routledge.
Whitehead, M. (2012) The sustainable city: an obituary? On the future form and prospects of sustainable urbanism, in J. Flint and M. Raco (eds), *The Future of Sustainable Cities: Critical reflections*, Bristol: Policy Press, pp. 29–46.
Wynne, B. (1996) May the sheep safely graze? A reflexive view of the expert–lay knowledge divide, in S. Lash, B. Szerszynski and B. Wynne (eds), *Risk, Environment and Modernity*, Thousand Oaks, CA: Sage Publications, pp. 44–83.

12

Localism, Scale and Place in Claims for Sustainable Urbanism: Moving beyond the Idealist and Materialist

Andrew Hoolachan and Mark Tewdwr-Jones

In this chapter, we discuss the relationship between urban planning, place and localism. We are interested in how places and localities manifest themselves through planning processes, and contextualise our contribution by deconstructing the meaning and contestation over the word local. We also make reference to observations and discussions of contemporary events that have been occurring in localities in England. We identify elements of local activism in place contention and sustainability and planning disputes, as part of a wider shift in localism and participatory processes as they are unfolding, divergently, uniquely, in different localities, often centred on different issues. According to the Coalition Government's view implemented since the passing of the Localism Act 2011, localism offers communities an opportunity to take decisions for themselves, often in place of elected local government, and meets an increasing appetite on the part of neighbourhood to become more involved in governing and shaping their destinies (DCLG, 2011). Localism and new neighbourhood planning exercises will refocus mindsets on the importance of what is local, what is distinctive, and how change may assist or threaten that. As the legislative form of localism and neighbourhood planning unfolds, we may therefore witness an increasing fuzziness between how communities see the locale and local places, with contention over what counts for important and relevant.

It is possible to suggest that localism is precipitating new neighbourhood interests in both place concern and sustainable urbanism, but those interests often create new forms of local civic entrepreneurialism that have both intended and unintended consequences. The Coalition Government has sponsored a particular form of localism, a top-down imposed version. It is a form that is often, or at least expected to be, bounded. But, in reality, localism on the ground will lead to shifting plates of governance, and shifting coalitions of localism actors. David Cameron, the Prime Minister, has claimed that 'entrepreneurialism is going to make [localism] work' (Wintour, 2012). That entrepreneurial spirit will not only involve co-opting individuals into the process of governing places. Localism constructs can still be shaped and in some senses regulated from below. The locale can be reanimated into potential sites of resistance to the expected in order to achieve something different, not only for the sake of opposition, but rather to reflect and celebrate place distinctiveness and differentiation.

Two trends could serve to reinforce the reanimation of the locale: citizens' declining trust and interest in elected local government and boundaried local politics (Frandsen, 2002); and central government's own mistrust of elected local government as managers and agents of local change, which, in turn, is mirrored by the electorate's own apathy towards elected national government (Hay, 2007). This political and institutional mistrust, coupled with the reduction in public-sector budgets under the guise of austerity post-depression, could create a desire for more creative solutions to meet localities' expressed needs. Those citizens positioning themselves to shape these new forms of localism, who in some but not all cases may be labelled 'activists', may attempt *pushing* localism to see how far elected government will permit alternative forms of localism in the interests of sustainability and ecology. This could take many forms and stem from commitments, for example, to: counter-democracy in more radical terms; alternative proactive policies that are not centred on the market; outright hostility towards globalisation; a belief in authentic place-based governance, however one defines that; or a commitment to sustainability urbanism and green interests. These become proactive possibilities for some; a chance to promote untold stories and forge new scalar associations – possibly within neighbourhoods, between communities and other communities, between communities and the private sector, or between local communities and national political movements. These associations have the potential to give rise to dynamic and active urban relations.

In contrast to new ways of looking at the local, the question of place has also been revived under a new guise. In some parts of England, the scale of the local is now explicitly becoming the focus for 'saving the High Street', community cohesion and sustainable urbanism. These concerns have not replaced the traditional sustainable development tripartite concern with economy, society and environment that in policy terms are still relevant. To what extent, then, is a 'sense of place', being masked by vague catch-all language of holistic thinking such as 'sustainable urbanism'? Will we see a genuine engagement in the planning process by local people, business and institutions, which will create a sense of ownership, involvement and distinct local identities?

Urban planning has often, throughout the twentieth century, concerned itself with viewing society and space as either closed systems requiring management to preserve a natural social, political and environmental order, or open systems that are more complex and dynamic. The language currently employed by localism presents a danger of pandering to socially conservative and exclusive place-making alongside environmentally deterministic notions of our relationship with 'nature'. This chapter, by focusing debate through the lens of scale and sustainable urbanism, seeks to challenge what it sees as a romantic, nostalgic, pre-industrial, exclusive vision of place under the guise of community empowerment and localism.

Forging the local

Urban planning as a practice is laden with historically powerful assertions of what it is to be local. Beginning with the birth of modern town planning at the end of the nineteenth century, Howard's Garden City idea (1902) began to heavily influence the British government's designs planning after the Great War and for New Towns after the Second World War. At the legislative ascendency of the twentieth-century planning system, the 1947 Town and Country Planning Act, the mass urban planning of British cities began. It was here was that the idea of community, rooted firmly in a social-democratic state, was physically dug into the ground and built from the earth (Hall, 2002). As was fashionable at the time, the idea of a city based on a hierarchy of functions and networks dominated urban planning. Life was spatially conceived into realms of work, shopping, leisure and family and these were to be connected through a system of roads and paths that may not have been connected to each other but all were connected to a central zone of high-order services. This zone was the main shopping area, the town hall, the civic and leisure centres. Outside the town centres lay the 'neighbourhoods' with their lower-tier services such as schools and clinics (Wilson, 1991). The assumption was that a rational resident would not have any need to visit the neighbouring community, so why plan for an irrational need? Such a form of planning has gone on to be hugely influential and has gained much criticism from the likes of Christopher Alexander and Jane Jacobs. But planning for the 'local' has not only been in a functional form. This functional planning, however, is not the only way in which planners have tried to create a sense of the local.

Since the 1980s, the local has also been delineated along cultural lines, whereby the exact definition of place is ambiguous, and boundaries are more porous and open than those of the functional period. Much of this can be attributed to city branding through polities who both influenced and were altered by the 'creative class' discourse espoused by Richard Florida (Atkinson, 2003; Colomb, 2007; Florida, 2002). Cities engaged in branding, tourism or heritage, often using artistic or ethnic labels, and defined them over an area of the city to sell the idea of the uniqueness of place. In London, the area at the southern end of Brick Lane was branded 'Bangla-town' and offered a 'unique' experience of some form of authentic Bangladeshi–British culture, usually reflected by food. This, too, is common in the emergence of Chinatowns. Again, using a London example, Chinatown on the surface seems independent, with its own language, restaurants, hairdressers, supermarkets and networks. But it is spatially defined by the street decorations to signify that you are 'in' China Town. In terms of the arts, by contrast, many cities outside London have invented 'Cultural Quarters'. The clue to localness here is in the word 'quarter', which reflects an older, segmented understanding of the city. In most cases, flagship or iconic buildings were built, around which more informal sites of commerce and interaction garnered association to a local identity. We see this strongly in Manchester's Northern Quarter, Belfast's Cathedral Quarter and Glasgow's Merchant City. In such cases, the physical element of the planning comes with deliberate landscape architecture, public art and signage to remind the citizen that they are again within the boundaries of a 'cultural' area.

In addition to functional and cultural, eco-localism inherently defines a local. Italy is perhaps the most famed example where it has pioneered *Cittaslow* initiative that adopts the Slow Food movement. Generally speaking, a town of fewer than 50,000 people is required to gain all of its food produce from the surrounding hinterland for sale in the city. Within the city, globalised chains are heavily regulated and often completely excluded from town centres, adding a diverse economy to an issue underpinned by environmental concerns of unsustainable food production. Many towns and cities in the UK in recent years have also adopted 'farmers markets', again where the emphasis is on 'local' food but also the market itself acts a local social space. Totnes in the south-west of the UK is a small town known for its 'Bohemian' lifestyles. It is a transition town and is trying to make the town completely free from oil so that it can be self-reliant economically and environmentally. The town has introduced its own currency, the Totnes Pound, in order to encourage people to keep businesses in the area. A recent cause célèbre in Totnes involved the Costa coffee chain who wished to set up an outlet in the town, which boasts that it has over 40 independent coffee shops (Kelly, 2012). Due to pressure from the local community, Costa backed down from opening a branch there, as the locals said that they would try to boycott it. So it is possible to see the local as an environmental–economic system as well.

Urban planning – which is not just about functionalism, but rather about 'design', 'community' and policies – has grown since the introduction of the Town and Country Planning Acts of the 1940s. A drift into spatial planning in the 2000s (Haughton *et al.*, 2010; Morphet, 2010; Tewdwr-Jones, 2012) is perhaps the most recent attempt to balance the social, economic and environmental, and functionally delivered through good urban design and master planning. However, the Localism Act 2011 introduced by the Coalition Government, despite it being billed as a way of removing some elements of urban planning, is also a consolidation of the social, environmental, economic and political processes, albeit at the local scale. This more recent change rests on the notion that the planning system in itself is the problem. It aims to give more power to citizens and bring decision-making back to communities, in the realm of housing provision, infrastructure, flood defences, local schools and community events. It is an arm of the much lauded and much criticised 'Big Society', an idea in which citizens should become more active in their communities to revive a sense of local spirit and conviviality. This is hoped to further curb the powers of a perceived authoritarian, inflexible and wasteful state.

The discussion above shows the various ways 'the local' has manifest itself in physical masterplanning, cultural planning, ecological economics, and governance. But these examples are end results of underlying initiatives. These are also highly problematic policies, whereby in many cases 'the local' is internally inconsistent or incoherent. It would be difficult in each case to isolate a location from having any interaction with neighbouring locations, or higher-level processes, such as the nation.

What, then, is the local? It might be very simple for a citizen to suggest they know what it is, but of course from their perspective it would surely only include them and their associations. Does the local have to be named by a common power such as a local government, and then become mapped, known and formalised, or are there hidden everyday practices that can never become visible but ontologically take the form of the local whether we know it or not? And where is the local located? Is it in a hierarchy of scales, the next level being the city, then the region and finally the nation? And where does it end? Does the local have boundaries, edges, and how hard or porous are these? And is a community always defined by two-dimensional material space? Can we describe a network of localities across the global local? In order to understand 'the local', we need to understand scale.

Scaling the local

Scale has been articulated in all sorts of ways. Notwithstanding its use in policy terms such as localism, it is used to describe the physical world in terms of boundaries, entities, vertical or horizontal hierarchy and relations between these components. Herod (2011) provides an account of how scale has been conceived. This is not simply a case of understanding common scalar measurements but asking precisely how we think about scale as a concept. Herod views scale in three ways: idealist, materialist and discursive. Often these categories influence each other, or overlap. The idealist and the materialist concepts of scale can be discussed together, as they fall along the same philosophical axis. At one end, idealism posits that scalar categories and measurements such as 'regional', 'national', 'global' would exist a priori, whether or not human perceptions had the tools to measure and recognise them. On the other side of this line, materialist understandings of scale are those that claim that we can perceive and measure scale through their material expressions in the 'real world'. For example, 'regional', 'national' and 'global' exist because we can take something like population, the flow of goods, or the construction of cities that demonstrate scalar differentials. Clearly, though, we can see that both are using the same language; materialist understandings of scale rely upon the same categories that idealists claim exist a priori (Herod, 2011). The interplay between creating the idea of 'region' and its empirical measurement in, for example, Travel To Work Areas, serves to reveal that both types of scalar concepts are likely to mutually reinforce each other. Given this mutual reinforcement, we can see how much politics can be generated over tensions, reconfigurations and constant reworkings between, for example, the region as an idea and the region as something more substantive.

It is these tensions through which there has been debate over our understandings of scale. Marxist geographers, whom Herod (2011) considers part of the materialist camp, have argued strongly about the 'realness' of scale and have shown its quantifiable truth. Smith (1984) argues that there are fundamental geographical tensions at play within the very structure of capitalism itself, which leads to the production of various – measurable – geographic scales; capitalists must constantly negotiate the tension between the need to be in a fixed place so that accumulation can occur, and the need to be flexible in order to find more profit. But this has been supplemented by various critiques of scale that may be underpinned by a sense of the ideal, and that cannot be measured (Herod, 2011). Delany and Leitner (1997), for example, countered Smith, by looking at the construction of scale from bottom-up and 'non-capital-centric' perspectives. In addition, Swyngedouw's notion of the glocal implies that global and local processes co-evolve or are co-dependent: one cannot exist without the other. In fact, it is hard to say that anything is uniquely 'global' or 'local', but that 'local actions shape global flows, whilst global processes affect local actions'. He also argued that we should not be primarily concerned with 'form' of scales, but the processes through which scales become 'reconstituted'; scale should not be the starting point for analysis, but we should look at process, and therefore the politics of scale: 'the area of struggle where conflict is mediated and regulated and compromises settled' (Swyngedouw, 1997 in Herod, 2011: 19).

Massey has contributed to the debate throughout her work on localities studies throughout the 1980s and as part of the ESRC project, the 'Changing Urban Regional Systems' programme (CURS). Based on her 'global sense of place' (Massey, 1991), she argued that materialist-minded writers were conflating the 'specific-general' with the 'concrete-abstract', and that research could validly be grounded in the locality and at the same time say something about both the general/abstract economic geographies. Thus her assertion of a 'global sense of place' was a way of viewing the locale as containing global processes on very local scales. In so doing Massey's work brought concepts such as mobility, openness and flows to the forefront of thinking about place.

The debate surrounding the ideal and the material lead us on to thinking about the quality of the scale. We often think of scale in terms of vertical or horizontal hierarchies, heavily derived from both idealist-materialist thinkers. It is natural, as planners often suggest, for the city to follow region to follow nation, in a vertical hierarchy. In other words, there is a pre-determined notion of scales that aggregate. However, the verticality of scale has been challenged: Fine (2010) argues that local communities are able to establish rules among themselves that enable them to mediate between their local neighbourhoods while simultaneously engaging with general issues outside their locale. Cox (1998) refer to these as 'spaces of dependence' and 'spaces of engagement'; the former are connections in our community that we depend upon to realise essential interests that we cannot find elsewhere. At the same time, in spaces of engagement we find broader sets of relationships, with other locales, with the nation and with the polity, which constantly undermine the former. Therefore the local is always a process of negotiation and is not simply a passive position at the bottom of an established hierarchy. Howitt (1998), for example, rejects the idea that scale is a nested hierarchy in which the sum of all the small scales 'produces the large scale total'. He argues that relations between scales should be considered in a dialectical fashion in multi-dimensional and simultaneous processes (Howitt, 1998). The local is not distinct from other scales but contains elements of other geographic scales so that we achieve a more complex understanding of place as 'inter-penetration of the global and local'. Indeed, Massey notes:

> Local places are not simply always the victim of the global; nor are they always politically defensible redoubts against the global. For places are also the moments through which the global is constituted, invented, co-ordinated, produced. They are 'agents' in globalisation. (Massey, 2004, cited in Marston *et al.*, 2005: 419)

Therefore, we have seen that through acknowledging the idealist and materialist conceptions of scale, an explanation as to how differences in its conception could arise: an idealist notion that scalar categories *should* exist, a materialist notion that scalar categories *do* exist, and that within the latter, there are multiple disagreements about what we *ought* to measure, mixed up and bounded with some of the underlying stable categories of 'ideal' scales. In addition, the hierarchical ordering of scale has been challenged wherein local actors may bypass the next scalar level, for example bypassing metropolitan or regional levels and engaging directly with global issues.

Following on from this understanding we can begin to discuss scale as a productive discourse. Perhaps the most radical approach to scale comes from Marston *et al.* (2005). In suggesting that places are interconnected and that the general and the particular can no longer be so strongly distinguished, Marston *et al.* question whether we are not simply abstracting space and detaching ourselves from the uneasy politics on the ground: 'It is the stabilizing and delimiting effects of hierarchical thinking – naming something "national", for example – that calls for another version of the "politics of scale": the need to expose and denaturalize scale's discursive power' (Marston *et al.*, 2005: 420). They claim that Massey relies too heavily on oppositional binaries of scale in her conceptualisation of the local (Marston *et al.*, 2005). They argue that such thought is so pervasive that many binary oppositions have latched onto or conflated themselves with a local–global binary. It can be seen in conjunction with structure and agency; agency is viewed as a local process, which lends itself to broader, higher, more general and structural. This is also true, they argue, in research where abstract/concrete is also conflated with global/local. An understanding of 'networks' and 'flows' will not be disturbed by a particularly hardened hierarchical ontology. They provide the example of the favoured academic discourse since the 1980s of 'macro-ism', or, favouring global processes in analysis of place, and unquestioning the narratives of globalisation. Localities researchers, too, often look 'up' and not 'sideways', and when they are trying to show how 'the global is in the local' they are too often making broad generalisations about the totalising effects of so-called globalisation. They argue that some thinkers have placed too much emphasis on 'globe talk'. Despite phrases such as 'unique manifestations' and the 'everyday sphere of the local', they argue that in fact very little agency is actually given to basic everyday situations that are instead closed off in a scalar metaphor of smallness (Marston *et al.*, 2005).

This view has been criticised from various positions (see Herod, 2011, for a summary). Some have suggested that it merely mirrors actor network theory, that Marston *et al.* have misinterpreted the distinction between epistemology and ontology, or that it is repackaged Kantian idealism (Herod, 2011). One of the main critiques here that has been levelled at Foucault is that one can never escape discourse even if one wishes to critique it; one is always active in discursive practice. In writing that the local is the 'only place where social things happen', Marston *et al.* (2005) open themselves up to the critique that they are not at all abandoning scale, but reifying the local, and in doing so privilege a site-based epistemology. Kaiser and Nikiforova (2008) argue that 'writing scale out … will help to hide the social constructedness of scales and the way they are used to naturalise a set of socio-spatial practices' (cited in Herod, 2011). Without an active acknowledgement of scalar practices, there can be no language of spatial politics.

Localism, therefore, is very much a process of scaling by central government; an attempt is being made to imagine an ideal level at which the planning issues should be realised; we can see localism as a form of imposition. Conversely, the same arguments apply here as can be levelled at the nation: it does not matter whether the nation 'exists' as a reality or not; the fact is that the 'idea' of the nation is far more powerful than assuming it exists as a physical entity. The idea of the nation as an ontological reality physically shapes the actions of its government and people. For example, the notion of Britishness has real effects on how people act in certain situations, at elections and in speech, act and thought.

Implicitly, planning for a defined locale could therefore be seen to be oppressive: when one group attempts to claim a space for themselves, it can have an immediately present meaning that may exclude or oppress the opportunities for multiple and transcendent identities (Young, 1986). The local is not only a question of a physical space, but for whom and who is not included in that place by those who have the power to name it as such. In the UK, there have been arguments along these lines towards the most recent articulation of top-down localism through the Localism Act 2011. The legislation allows the establishment of neighbourhood forums or Parish Councils in communities to shape new development; forums have been designated by the local authority and comprise 21 individuals but the criteria for establishing the forums have been kept as simple a possible to encourage new and existing residents' organisations and voluntary and community groups to put themselves forward. In giving power to communities, existing Parish Councils in rural areas have become the new neighbourhood forums, but some have questioned how this would work in Britain's multicultural and diverse inner cities. London, Manchester, Leicester, Birmingham, Bradford and Leeds all have vastly greater proportions of minorities than smaller cities and swathes of the countryside. In the latter, where there is wealth and some form of homogeneity, then a revolutionary populism may work in the interest of these communities; perhaps it is little wonder that when the Coalition Government announced the policy initiative, the launch was accompanied by photographs of England's rural villages.

Emerging evidence from urban experiences of localism suggests increased tensions between competing neighbourhood and community groups as to who takes the lead and who represents the community interest. In Stoke Newington, in North London, tension has mounted between two rival organisations – the Stamford Hill Neighbourhood Forum and the Hackney Planning Watch Group – with intense campaigns through the media, via social media and out on the street, to be designated the official neighbourhood forum by the London Borough of Hackney, with minority and ethnic interests being used in arguments both for and against (Booth, 2013). The furore locally was so intense that it led Hackney Council to reject both candidate forums and designate its own 'neighbourhood area' (Mitchell, 2013).

Parvin (2011) argues that, on the whole, evidence has shown that people do not want more democracy, as evidenced by declining rates of political participation. More importantly, he argues, the wealthier and most educated will monopolise local power structures, thus excluding smaller, less visible groups, entrenching further an already unequal society. Mohan (2001) suggests that the consensus over local participation is 'fraught with dangers' as it can be used for different purposes for very different ideological stakeholders. So rather than serve to meet place needs and allow community desires to be voiced, a constructed form of localism may only serve to highlight and exacerbate tensions within the same neighbourhood. Given this, how appropriate is it for the nation to undermine both regional and local planning power by transferring decisions and procedures to myriad geographically differentiated places and unequal groups? In essence, it provides different places with unequal planning power at a time when the UK faces a number of wider structural challenges (for example, the worst housing crisis since 1945); a solution to these problems must surely involve a more coherent and joined-up vision of how cities and regions function.

Changing track: reconfiguring the local for popular sustainable urbanism

With a new wave of so-called Garden Cities in the pipeline (Murray, 2014), which are being portrayed as a sustainable solution to the housing shortage while protecting the environment, we must turn our attention to the scaling of these new sustainable communities. The question is, therefore, does urban sustainability require deployment at a specific scale and, if so, what scale is appropriate for wider structural needs such as infrastructure, energy, housing and waste? Do we adopt the 'slow city' ideas from Italy; what boundaries do we impose on the city? Do we intervene with district heating systems and how far should these extend and what unit of housing should they serve? Do we provide urban greenways and should they connect a few neighbourhoods, the entire city, or a vast region of many urban centres?

The ways in which scale is deployed in thinking about sustainable urbanism has similar ontological problems to how we think about ecology. Namely, whether we think that Nature is something that exists a priori, reflecting Man's desire for an opposed subject to both fear and control; or that humanity is inherently part of nature and, as such, in preserving our future survival, we are also preserving Nature. On the surface these may seem like simplistic divisions, but the former has had enormous influence on urban planning and ecology and has also destroyed the very thing it seeks to protect.

There is a schism in the way we think about ecology, derived from how we value nature (Carter, 2007). On the one hand, there has been a strand of thought going back to Romanticism and, some argue, to the Renaissance; this is the idea that Nature has an essence, that Man has disturbed some natural order in which he was placed (biblical motifs are highly prevalent). We should strive to live within our natural capacities or 'get back to Nature' if we are to achieve balance with nature (Carter, 2007; Scott, 1998). By the nineteenth century, Malthus's notions of population had been proved wrong through developments in technology, despite Romantic-inspired artists such as William Morris calling for a return to medievalism that, in turn, influenced the early writings of the Garden City movement (Cosgrove and Daniels, 1989). The problem with this line of thinking, however, is that, in assuming Man and Nature are separate ontological categories, it fails to consider how humans and nature have co-evolved, since, essentially, humans *are* nature. Writers such as Žižek have considered modern ecology as an atheist version of the 'Fall of Man', and geographers such as Swyngedouw have claimed ecology to be an 'Opiate for the Masses' (Swyngedouw, 2010). In considering Man and Nature as separate realms, much damage has been caused to our environment. Ebenezer Howard's Garden Cities, for example, came right out of the Romantic tradition and, in many ways, their return to the courtyards-within-gardens typology of housing was highly symbolic of medieval cloistered life. But the Garden City invariably had a factor in producing the vast suburban sprawls we see today (Wilson, 1991). Think of how much extra carbon, how much road material and maintenance and how many longer journeys need to be applied to maintain this form of urbanism. And yet it was partly a desire for everyone to own a patch of outdoor space, or 'Nature' (among other factors), which contributed to the Garden City and to this unsustainable suburban typology. We see this desire for a suburban form articulated by Ebenezer Howard:

> Human society and the beauty of nature were meant to be enjoyed together … As man and woman by their varied gifts and faculties supplement each other, so should town and country. The town is the symbol of society … of science, art, culture, religion … The country is the symbol of God's love for and care for man … We are fed by it, clothed by it, and by it we are warmed and sheltered. On its bosom we rest … Town and country must be married. (Howard, 1946, cited in Wilson, 1991: 102)

By the time we reach the actual planning of cities in the early twentieth century, it was culturally taken-for-granted that not only should everyone have the right to some form of *private* green space (as in the ground-breaking

Hampstead Garden Suburb), but that the city itself should be built within a large green area, with de facto green spaces between every building and road. Of course, a crisis over public health and social equality did motivate the Fabians of Hampstead-Letchworth-Welwyn plans, but their unproven notion that 'green-ness' was the cure of all social ills was never actualised. When the US government liberalised the housing market and subsided the construction of highways during the Great Depression's New Deal, it paved the way for America to take the lead in the growth of the garden suburb, a process that remains enduring.

Therefore, Romanticism and the valorisation of Nature as an object of aesthetic desire could be shown to lead the destruction of the very thing it has tried to protect – the environment itself. One of the greatest challenges of current sustainable urbanism is the fight against the mistakes of the twentieth-century car-dependent, carbon-intensive lifestyles of suburban sprawl. This cannot be achieved if a large population in England and the US believes suburbia to be a natural liberty, which historically they often have (Wilson, 1991).

The opposing view of ecology, which takes into account technological development and the co-evolution of humans as a species with their environment, suggests urban forms that promote development and urbanity without increasing the need for carbon use. By decoupling the concepts of 'the natural' and 'sustainability', it articulates solutions to our environmental crisis through evidence, empiricism and best practice, rather than through Romanticism, aesthetics and wishful thinking. Coming closer to an urban form that can handle both population growth and development and maintain low carbon footprints has been strongly articulated in Richard Rogers' Compact City perspective, which was and continues to be heavily influential: densifying cities around transport nodes, while allowing some in-fill spaces for low-density family homes seems to have taken off in some places in the UK, such as at North Greenwich, and typifies plans for the housing in the Olympic Legacy Development Corporation area in Stratford (despite the entire development being in a 'park').

If we are to leave behind the Garden City as a hallmark of twentieth-century planning, what could work for the twenty-first century? Some of the most practical ideas come from anecdotal evidence from 1950s New York in Jane Jacobs' *The Death and Life of Great American Cities* (1961), which provides highly specific guidance for the planning of parks and green spaces. Jacobs argues that, like the rest of the city, parks cannot rely on one function alone, and therefore only succeed when there are mixed functions at its edges. A park must be fully integrated into the workings of the city if the negative effects of open space are to be avoided. Such methods would be allowing people or traffic to move through the park, connecting different parts of the city, and providing an everyday use for the park and maintaining activity within it. Structures in parks are also useful, as small shops or cafes, or just providing shelter from the rain or sun.

Pathways in the city can also provide both a practical and aesthetic use of green space in the form of 'green ways'. In many cities, there have been attempts to reclaim the former lines of transport or infrastructure such as old railway paths, and turn them into both functional pathways and green spaces in which to enjoy nature (the combining of both inherent and instrumental value; see Carter, 2007). Rogers' Compact City could work well if it embraces notions of green spaces that are not just there to be looked at as an aesthetic quality, driven by an inherent value, but also that it could be used in both practical and aesthetic ways, such as the High Line in New York City or Tschumi's Parc de Villette in Paris.

A way of conceptualising the local, which accepts the political construction of scale and exposes the varying value placed on nature, opens us up to two implications in practice. First, there are more nuanced ways to think about infrastructure. We can look to writers such as Donna Haraway, who argues strongly at the socially constructed and produced form of nature and how the sharp boundaries often presented are often produced through semantics (Haraway, 1990). Like the notions of smooth and striated space, we can think of the actually existing phenomena of nature as the nomad, and the means to define it as the state (Deleuze and Guattari, 1988). In practical terms of the planning of cities for sustainability, Birkenholtz argues for a 'network political ecology' as an approach to fill in the gap between the politics of scale and the politics of networks (Birkenholtz, 2012). This allows us to understand political ecology as a hybrid system that is responsive to resource use, socio-ecologies and governance. For example, in a research case study of Indian irrigation farmers, the researchers note the importance of the individual agents, and their relationship to the regional resource-use system, in order to better inform debates about adaptation and resilience to climate change. Throughout their research on infrastructure, Gandy (2005) and Graham and Marvin (2001) have sought to highlight the political implications and its often-overlooked role in practices of everyday situations. Such a contribution should be considered when discussing the governance of sustainability that involves both planning for infrastructure and the spaces of governance.

Bulkeley (2005) follows a similar framework by arguing that we can overcome the debate between scalar and non-scalar perspectives by making sense of scalar and networked politics. This would be achieved through a revision of the concepts of hierarchy and territory. There are many examples across Europe whereby local governments do not follow the traditional hierarchy of bureaucracy, but instead work across scales based on themes such as health, sustainability, or even regional issues. Scalar and networked readings of spatiality are not opposed, but can be co-dependent and mutually beneficial and constituted. This would develop a hybrid governance arrangement and multi-level environmental governance, of which there are many examples to draw on (see Bulkeley, 2005). These are often a 'coalition of cities, states, governments and corporations committed to collaboration to cutting greenhouse gas emissions'. This new 'spatial grammar' can make 'such modes of governing central to our understandings of the politics of environmental issues' (Bulkeley, 2005) and could develop an approach to infrastructure as seen in examples of the High Line and in the work of Gandy (2005), less rooted in idealism, Romanticism and pseudo-science, and might prevent the past problems of fetishising parks and nature from being repeated. It would allow for an open and inclusive idea of place that is not limited by governance structures, imposed institutionalism, or pre-conceived notions of localism.

Given the central role that sustainability will play in the future planning of communities, it has been useful for us here to interrogate the relationship between localism, scale and sustainability and how the two are socially constructed. It is not uncommon in current times in the popular imagination and discourses to present an idealised size and quality of a locality as being synonymous with some natural state of our relationship to the natural world; an idea whose roots span several centuries, and have been shown to have already contributed to carbon-dependent sprawl. And, it is very common to find contestation over who belongs and who doesn't in these various localisms.

Conclusion

Garden Cities were a strong articulation of scale; Ebenezer Howard explicitly called for ideal-sized towns. We know that defining the local on ecological grounds combines the twin discussions in this text of scale and ecology. Indeed, 'sustainable' implies ecology, and 'urbanism' implies a scale of intervention. Let us then consider how a localism of 'sustainable urbanism' might look in the future.

The Big Society has been argued to be a strong form of populism, and we must consider localism a part of this. Localism under its current governmental understanding speaks to an imagined 'we', an imagined 'people' centred on an imagined locale, who, despondent with big government working at a scale too distant from local needs and understanding, must be unleashed to enable communities to claim back their democratic right, rooted in the direct representation of those communities. But this rhetorical stance resonates strongly with common forms of populism: 'The belief that the majority of the people is checked by an elitist minority' and that 'Populism proclaims that the will of the people as such is supreme over every other standard' (Laclau, 2007). Populist parties give back to the 'people', but at the same time are symptomatic of the problem of reducing politics to hollow discourse. And it is these traits that we can see in localism rhetoric today.

There are two main problems, therefore, with a localism agenda seeking to work alongside sustainable urbanism. First, sustainability cannot function in isolation at the scale of the community, the high street, or the neighbourhood alone. Notwithstanding how we can or should even define these urban ideals, and not to discredit the role of 'organic' or bottom-up approaches, the governance of sustainability should still acknowledge working in partnerships at a varying set of scales from a direct link to national objectives, to going next door and sharing common environmental services with a neighbouring borough. With more fragmented localism rooted in celebrating place, this could become more problematic. As Cowell (2013: 33) argues:

> it is unclear how local experiments in sustainability might 'jump scale' … to bring pressure to bear on wider systems of production and consumption that govern resources flows, and which are not readily steered by local actors … One might also ask 'how can we reproduce success and mitigate failure in a localist system.'

Second, there is the question of who is being represented in the local. Under a populist notion of localism, an appearance of consensus may be achieved but a reality of political dissent behind the scenes may be seen. Indeed, in places of multi-ethnic and transient populations, for example in inner-cities, it may be a case of 'whoever shouts the loudest gets representation'; or the largest minority wins out over the expense of the majority-yet-cosmopolitan population.

There are striking similarities between a sustainable localism of today and the late-nineteenth-century Garden Cities the Fabians advocated: the moral conscience of 'deserving and undeserving' poor (which was upturned by the post-1945 welfare state), the deep concern with environmental problems and a wish to return to a past simplicity. What we should remember as we go forward then is that great mistakes were made by planning 'for nature'; the thinking in which everyone has the right to a garden only created resource and sprawl problems for the second half of the twentieth century. What we need is a reference that does not separate humanity and nature, but integrates them in technically functional ways as one and the same, in which aesthetics (which is different to urban design) are secondary. We need to stop patronising communities with a collective forced conviviality. We need to move away from the idea that a community can only be measured by its vitality. We must focus our planning efforts on evidence, on process and on technological skills that will address the real challenges of climate change and social justice; and above all, we should stop romanticising a pre-industrial past. Credible localism may occur where discretion is combined with arbitration and incentivisation, with the emergence of new opportunities for neighbourhoods to see places as unique local assets.

References

Atkinson, R. (2003) Domestication by cappuccino or a revenge on urban space? Control and empowerment in the management of public spaces, *Urban Studies*, 40(9): 1829–1843.

Birkenholtz, T. (2012) Progress in Human Geography Network political ecology: Adaptation research, *Progress in Human Geography*, 36(3): 295–315.

Booth, R. (2013) Hackney planning row exposes faultlines in orthodox Jewish area, *The Guardian*, 8 March 2013. Available at: www.theguardian.com/society/2013/mar/08/hackney-planning-row-orthdox-jewish (accessed 3 October 2013).

Bulkeley, H. (2005) Reconfiguring environmental governance: Towards a politics of scales and networks, *Political Geography*, 24(8): 875–902. Available at: http://linkinghub.elsevier.com/retrieve/pii/S0962629805000880 (accessed 31 January 2013).

Carter, N. (2007) *The Politics of the Environment: Ideas, activism, policy*, 2nd edn, Cambridge: Cambridge University Press.

Colomb, C. (2007) Unpacking New Labour's Renaissance Agenda: Towards a socially sustainable re-urbanisation of British cities? *Planning Practice and Research*, 22(1): 1–24.

Cosgrove, D. and Daniels, S. (1989) Introduction, in D. Cosgrove and S. Daniels (eds), *The Iconography of Landscape: Essays on the symbolic representation, design, and use of past environments*, Cambridge: Cambridge University Press.

Cowell, R. (2013) The greenest government ever? Planning and sustainability in England after the May 2010 elections, *Planning Practice and Research*, 28(1): 27–44.

Cox, K. (1998) Spaces of dependence and spaces of engagement, or: Looking for local politics, *Political Geography*, 17: 1–23.

DCLG. (2011) *The Plain English Guide to the Localism Act*, London: DCLG.

Delaney, D. and Leitner, H. (1997) The political construction of scale, *Political Geography*, 16(2): 93–97.

Deleuze, G. and Guattari, F. (1988) *A Thousand Plateaus: Capitalism and schizophrenia*, London: The Athlone Press.

Fine, G. (2010) The sociology of the local: Action and its publics, *Sociological Theory*, 28(4): 355–376.

Florida, R. (2002) *The Rise of the Creative Class*, New York: Basic Books.

Frandsen, A.G. (2002) Size and electorial participation in local elections, *Environment and Planning C: Government and Policy*, 20(6): 853–869.

Gandy, M. (2005) Cyborg urbanisation: Complexity and monstrosity in the contemporary city, *International Journal of Urban and Regional Research*, 29: 26–49.

Graham, S. and Marvin, S. (2001) *Splintering Urbanism: Networked infrastructures, technological mobilities, and the urban condition*, New York: Routledge.

Hall, P. (2002) *Cities of Tomorrow: An intellectual history of urban planning and design in the twentieth century*, Oxford: Wiley-Blackwell.

Haraway, D. (1990) *Simians, Cyborgs and Women: The reinvention of nature*, London: Free Association.

Haughton, G., Allmendinger, P., Counsell, D. and Vigar, G. (2010) *The New Spatial Planning: Territorial management with soft spaces and fuzzy boundaries*, London: Routledge.

Hay, C. (2007) *Why We Hate Politics*, Cambridge: Polity Press.

Herod, A. (2011) *Scale*, Abington: Routledge.

Howard, E. (1902) Garden Cities of To-Morrow. London: S. Sonnenschein & Co., Ltd.

Howitt, R. (1998) Scale as relation: Musical metaphors of geographical scale, *Area*, 30: 49–58.

Jacobs, J. (1961) *The Death and Life of Great American Cities*, New York: Random House.

Kaiser, R. and Nikiforova, E. (2008) The performativity of scale: The social construction of scale effects in Narva, Estonia, *Environment and Planning D: Society and Space*, 26(3): 537–562.

Kelly, J. (2012) The independent coffee republic of Totnes, BBC News Magazine. Available at: www.bbc.co.uk/news/science-environment-19146445 (accessed 9 May 2013).

Laclau, E. (2007) *On Populist Reason*, London: Verso.

Marston, S.A., Jones, J.P., III and Woodward, K. (2005) Human geography without scale, *Transactions of the Institute of British Geographers*, 30(4): 416–432.

Massey, D. (1991) A global sense of place, *Marxism Today*, pp. 24–29.

Mitchell, J. (2013) Hackney rejects Stamford Hill Neighbourhood Forum, *East London Lines*. Available at: www.eastlondonlines.co.uk/2013/07/hackney-council-rejects-stamford-hill-neighbourhood-forum-in-favour-of-new-neighbourhood-area (accessed 3 October 2013).

Mohan, G. (2001) The convergence around local civil society and the dangers of localism, *Social Scientist*, 29(11): 3–24.

Morphet, J. (2010) *Effective Spatial Planning in Practice*, London: Routledge.

Murray, W. (2014) Garden cities: David Cameron accused of stifling plan for new communities, *The Guardian*, 11 January 2014. Available at: www.theguardian.com/politics/2014/jan/11/garden-city-david-cameron-stifling-plans (accessed 21 January 2014).

Parvin, P. (2011) Localism and the left: The need for strong central government, *Renewal*, 19(2): 37–49.

Rogers, R. (1997) *Cities for a Small Planet*, London: Faber & Faber.

Scott, J. (1998) *Seeing Like a State: How certain schemes to improve the human condition have failed*, New Haven, CT: Yale University Press.

Smith, N. (1984) *Uneven Development: Nature, capital and the production of space*, Oxford: Blackwell.

Swyngedouw, E. (1997) "Neither Global Nor Local: 'Glocalization' and the Politics of Scale." In *Spaces of Globalization: Reasserting the Power of the Local*, ed. Cox, K, 137–166. New York/London: Guilford/Longman.

Swyngedouw, E. (2010) The trouble with nature: Ecology as the new opiate for the masses, in J. Hillier and P. Healey (eds), *The Ashgate Research Companion to Planning Theory: Conceptual challenges for spatial planning*, Farnham: Ashgate.

Tewdwr-Jones, M. (2012) *Spatial Planning and Governance*, Basingstoke: Palgrave.

Wilson, E. (1991) *The Sphinx in the City*, London: Virago Press.

Wintour, P. (2012), 'David Cameron to unveil year-long relaxation of planning laws', The Guardian, 6 September 2012 http://www.theguardian.com/politics/2012/sep/06/david-cameron-planning-laws-growth-plan (accessed 10 November 2014).

Young, I.M. (1986) The ideal of community and the politics of difference, *Social Theory and Practice*, 12(1): 1–26.

13
Localism and Rural Development

Mark Shucksmith and Hilary Talbot

In terms of spatial and social readings of localism conjuring up community and neighbourhood, rural areas might be thought to exemplify localism. Indeed, sociological studies of rural areas often report just such social constructions among inhabitants. When it comes to political readings of localism, however, things could not be more different. As one respondent in rural Scotland told researchers, 'I don't know where decisions are made about this area. Inverness, Edinburgh, London, Brussels – it doesn't matter. They're all away ...' (Shucksmith, 2000a: 12).

Notwithstanding this, the policy and practice of rural development has embraced ideas of localism for many years, with policy being given practical expression through the OECD's 'New Rural Paradigm', the EU LEADER programme, the EU's community-led local development (CLLD) initiative, and numerous national policy initiatives across Europe and beyond. These developments speak implicitly to agendas of social and economic sustainability, although this is rarely explicit. In contrast, such dimensions are generally absent from the predominantly environmental discourses that characterise reference to 'sustainability' in agricultural and rural policies. This neglect of the social and economic dimensions of sustainability in agricultural and rural policy may be seen as a deployment of discursive power (Shucksmith, 2009; Sturzaker and Shucksmith, 2011) in favour of agricultural and environmental (as opposed to rural or local) interests.

This chapter introduces the main conceptualisations, policies and practices of rural development in the UK that resonate with a 'localism' agenda, including not only those initiated by the state but also those of local people working collectively to address local needs and problems. It goes on to discuss, in particular, how these depart from many mainstream themes in the localism literature. Finally it outlines how rural localism is being damaged by government austerity measures, and how even fully resourced localism is not sufficient to address all rural problems in the UK: some can only be addressed by larger-scale structural adjustments at national or supranational scales.

Localisation of rural development

New conceptualisations

The classic formulation of rural development, prevalent in post-war Europe, was an *exogenous* model ('driven from outside', or '*top-down*'), based on industrialisation, economies of scale and concentration. Urban centres were regarded as growth poles for the economic development of regions and countries. Rural localities were thought of as distant technically, economically and culturally from the main (urban) centres of activity. In all of these respects rural areas were perceived as 'backward' and marginal. From this perspective, appropriate policy might subsidise the improvement of agricultural production, while encouraging labour and capital to leave. Most European countries adopted an exogenous approach to their rural areas but it was particularly strongly pursued in France, Ireland, the UK and Scandinavia, and became the dominant approach of the EU's Common Agricultural Policy (CAP). But by the late 1970s there was growing evidence that the model had not worked (and indeed had been to the detriment of many rural areas). Exogenous development was criticised as 'dependent development', reliant on continued subsidies and the policy decisions of distant agencies or boardrooms. It was seen as 'distorted development', which boosted single sectors, selected settlements and certain types of business (e.g. progressive farmers) but left others behind and neglected the non-economic aspects of rural life. It was cast as 'destructive development', which erased the cultural and environmental differences of rural areas and was unresponsive to the local knowledge held within these localities, and 'dictated development' devised by experts and planners from outside local rural areas (Lowe *et al.*, 1995).

Instead, by the 1990s, many advocated an *endogenous* approach to rural development ('driven from within', or '*bottom-up*') based on the assumption that the specific resources of an area – natural, human and cultural – hold the key to its development. This was the rationale also for Local Agenda 21. Whereas exogenous rural development saw its main challenge as overcoming rural differences and distinctiveness through the promotion of universal technical skills and the modernisation of physical infrastructure, endogenous development saw the primary challenge as valorising difference through the nurturing of locally distinctive human and environmental capacities (Bryden and Hart, 2004; van der Ploeg and Long, 1994; Shucksmith, 2000b). The endogenous model mainly concerns the mobilisation of local resources and assets by those living in the place itself. The EU Commission (1988: 62) argued that this incorporation of local knowledge would avoid 'errors of diagnosis' and also would create a network of rural development agents that could 'play a stimulating, mobilising and coordinating role'. The Scottish government offered a more principled rationale, insisting that 'rural people should be the subjects and not the objects of development' (Scottish Office, 1998). In practice, though, local interests complained of a 'top-down' approach in which central government set the parameters too tightly and exercised control (Ward and McNicholas, 1998).

The spread of endogenous (bottom-up) development ideas elicited a further critique from researchers at Newcastle University, proposing instead the notion of *neo-endogenous* development (Lowe *et al.*, 1995; Ray, 2001), or what we might call *networked development*. They argued that social and economic development processes in any locality inevitably include a mix of endogenous (bottom-up) and exogenous (top-down) forces. The local level necessarily interacts with the extra-local. The critical issues are the balance of internal and external control of development processes and how to enhance the capacity of local actors to steer these larger processes to their benefit. Critical to the socio-economic development process are those institutions, actors and networks that have the capacity to link businesses, communities and institutions involved in governance at a variety of scales. Networked development therefore also advocates an emphasis on local capacity-building. From this perspective, development should be re-oriented so as to use local territorial resources (physical or human, tangible or intangible, within or outside) with the objective of retaining as much as possible of the resultant benefit within the area concerned. It agrees that local territorial partnerships should assume responsibility for the design and implementation of development initiatives so long as they make full use of both internal and external markets, institutions and networks. In this way, rural areas are no longer seen as playing a passive, dependent role in the global economy but are able to generate innovative processes and shape future development (Shucksmith, 2010). Regions and localities become involved in 'place shaping' using communication between actors and institutions to identify and exploit territorial potential (CEC, 2009). Moreover, the lessons learned from place-based action may help to inform, and indeed transform, policies and processes that operate more broadly.

The focus of *networked* development is therefore not only on the dynamic interactions within local areas but also on those between local areas and the wider political, institutional, trading and natural environments. Dense local networks are important for building social and economic capital but strategic extra-local connections are vital in positioning the territory to its best advantage. Such connections may be created and maintained by a variety of actors and institutions.

These ideas were reflected in the OECD's influential *New Rural Paradigm* report (2006). This highlighted an international transition whereby the relative economic importance of agriculture in rural areas is declining, so creating development opportunities for the growth of new businesses and the adaptation

Table 13.1 The new rural paradigm

	Old approach	*New approach*
Objectives	Equalisation, farm income, farm competitiveness	Competitiveness of rural areas, valorisation of local assets, exploitation of unused resources
Key target sector	Agriculture	Various sectors or rural economies (e.g. rural tourism, manufacturing, ICT industry, etc.)
Main tools	Subsidies	Investments
Key actors	National governments, farmers	All levels of governments (supra-national, national, regional and local), various local stakeholders (public, private, NGOs)

Source: OECD (2006).

of the production-based sectors. The OECD saw this as accompanied by shifts in approaches to rural policy and governance, with rural policy increasingly based on territorial or 'place-based' approaches to rural development across a range of sectors, focusing especially on local specificities as a means of generating new competitive advantages, such as amenities (environmental or cultural) or local products. It also advocated coordination of sectoral policies, decentralisation and increased use of partnerships between public, private and voluntary sectors in the development and implementation of policies. This approach underpins all of the OECD's rural policy reviews, including those of Scotland (2008) and England (2011).

Both the bottom-up (endogenous) and networked development perspectives emphasise the mobilisation of local assets. In the UK, the Carnegie UK Trust (2007) has promoted and developed Asset-Based Community Development (ABCD), defined as 'an approach that is driven by the community for their own local development', focusing on their own strengths and assets. It seeks to build inclusive and resilient communities again through capacity-building, rejecting portrayals of areas as weak and instead emphasising strengths. Of relevance here is the '7 Capitals Framework', which draws on work on community development in the US to suggest that the asset base consists of seven basic types of 'capital' – financial capital; built capital; social capital; human capital; natural capital; cultural capital; and political capital. It must be emphasised that this is a practice-based framework, not theory-based. Asset-based approaches are complementary to ideas of networked rural development, having a basis in similar philosophies of the capacities and capabilities of rural communities and institutions. But networked rural development challenges us to think about the ways in which assets and resources *external* to the territory can be used creatively to enhance rural development, so extending understanding of the asset base and of how assets can be mobilised and enhanced. It also highlights the important role of governance institutions in enabling the local and extra-local to come together to mobilise and extend the asset base.

One further strand of academic work of direct relevance to rural development practice derives from urban planning theory and practice, where the concepts of 'collaborative planning' and 'deliberative place-shaping' (Healey, 2004) have proved highly influential in urban areas. At its heart, place-shaping is about 'self-conscious collective efforts to re-imagine a city, urban region or wider territory and to translate the result into priorities for area investment, conservation measures, strategic infrastructure investments and principles of land use regulation' (p. 46). It highlights the connection between the past and the future, continuity and change. In the context of new modes of governance, Healey argues this activity must more than ever be reorganised around deliberative processes and collective action – involving stakeholders and citizens in thinking together about what future they seek for their place and how to achieve this. Deliberative place-shaping can therefore be seen to be closely related to ideas both of networked development and of asset-based development, emphasising the imperative to mobilise actors and communities in pursuit of their development objectives, with support from the state and other social actors. Indeed, while the concept of deliberative place-shaping has its intellectual roots in urban regeneration initiatives, the mobilisation of local actors around place-based identities and symbolic constructions of community has been the basis of recent practice in rural development (Shucksmith, 2000b), as noted above.

These approaches place emphasis on the capacity of people themselves to ensure the future prosperity of their places, drawing both on local and extra-local assets and networks. This raises important questions regarding the autonomy of local actors, the distribution of local power, and inequality more generally.

Localisation of rural policies

The last section has described a shift in thinking to a new paradigm: networked rural development. This section explores how this shift has been implemented as policy by the EU, a key determinant of rural policy at the UK level. However, it must be noted that EU rural policy remains dominated by older thinking and by sectoral rather than place-based approaches: the overwhelming majority of expenditure of the CAP is still market support to farmers mainly through direct payments related to past production or to area farmed (known as 'Pillar 1' of the CAP). The descriptions below, then, of new rural policies must be viewed in the context of the dominant old model of exogenous rural development: CAP's Pillar 1.

During the mid-1980s, interest grew among EU policy-makers in the idea of rural development as a new justification for agricultural support as agricultural surpluses and growing environmental concerns challenged the identity of the rural with the agricultural (EU Commission, 1988). In direct opposition to the agriculture-sectoral basis of existing rural policy, 'rural development' was presented as essentially territorial and 'became fashionable in the early 1980s in European countries such as the UK as part of the struggles to reform discredited support policies' (Ward, 2002: 2). Accordingly, a second pillar of the CAP was conceived, the so-called 'Rural Development Regulation' (RDR). This was introduced by a Council Regulation in 1999 (European Council, 1999). Since that time, Member States have drawn up six-year rural development plans 'at the most appropriate geographical level', either as a single plan for the entire state or as a set of regional programmes. In the UK, the 2000–2006 plan was far more regionally determined than the 2007–2013 plan.

The EU provides a menu of measures that are available for Member States to utilise under the RDR, framed in 2007–2013 under four higher level 'axes' to be addressed (European Council, 2006):

- improving the competitiveness of the agricultural and forestry sector;
- improving the environment and the countryside;
- improving the quality of life in rural areas and encouraging diversification of the rural economy;
- building local capacity for employment and diversification.

Each Member State then devises its own plan that summarises the situation of the territory it covers, justifies the priorities to be pursued and sets out the measures included. Within the confines of the EU prescriptions, each plan is able to reflect the different needs of different rural territories.

Axis 4 of the RDR 2007–2013 introduces into the CAP a significant strand of policy that emanates from the networked rural development model. This axis is known as the Leader Approach, an approach to be adopted in implementing some or all of the other axes of the RDR. Although new to the CAP in 2007, the Leader Approach has its origins in the LEADER community initiative of the Structural Funds under the EU's Cohesion Policy, dating back to 1991. That initiative supported innovative rural development in small, distinct rural areas, initially within the Structural Fund's Objective 1 and 5(b) regions; subsequent programmes altered the eligible geographic coverage of the programme, but adhered to three underlying principles of the LEADER philosophy:

- inclusive participation of the whole local community;
- leadership and facilitation through the formation of 'Local Action Groups': cross-sectoral partnerships involving the public, private and voluntary sectors;
- learning from international example through sharing experience via the LEADER Observatory in Brussels (until 2006).

This approach became mainstreamed within EU rural policy as Axis 4 of the RDR in 2007, and most of the original LEADER philosophy remains (European Council, 2005). For the 2007–2013 planning period, Member States were required to spend at least 5 per cent of their RDR funds on this approach, with the aim that the RDR programme would increasingly be delivered through Local Action Groups based on cross-sectoral partnerships with a high degree of community participation.

Local initiative

Rural areas in the UK have long been applauded as places where local communitarian approaches to problem resolution are common. There are many examples of such places: where local transport groups have formed to provide travel arrangements for those without a car where there is little or no public transport service available; where people from the community are the local providers of broadband; or where rural community organisations now own the local shop or the pub. Such locally initiated activity is triggered in a multitude of ways, including by the efforts of a particularly effective local activist, by the threat of withdrawal of a local service, or as an outcome of community-led planning.

All of these types of trigger apply also in urban areas of the UK, but perhaps community-led planning as a long-standing rural endeavour needs further elaboration. Examples of people in rural communities coming together to deliberate over the development of some form of local plan go back at least 50 years. The generic term 'community-led planning' in rural areas embraces Village Appraisals, Parish Maps, Village Design Statements, Parish/Town Plans and more. Some community-led planning has been promoted, and financially supported, by government or its quangos, but through the use of community-sector organisations such as Rural Community Councils as agents to administer the scheme. The most recent rural specific government-sponsored scheme was Parish/Town Plans, with over 4,500 being produced, all led by local communities.

In some places, the development of a Plan was seen by the local group as an end in its own right, or as a tool that should influence the priorities of the local authority. In others, though, the production of the Plan was a stage in the process of local people identifying the priority needs of their neighbourhood and of subsequently taking action to meet these needs, directly or indirectly. At this point such 'community planning groups' typically become formalised organisations such as Development Trusts, Industrial and Provident Societies, or Companies Limited by Guarantee (CLG).

An example of rural community-led planning that led to a Development Trust that has successfully addressed a number of priorities identified from its Plan comes from Glendale in the north of Northumberland. With stimulation from the Community Council of Northumberland, a local group formed and undertook a Village Appraisal in the early 1990s. A high priority within this was a major proposal to develop a new building as a community hub that would provide a community centre facility, a tourist information centre, the library and more. In order to take this proposal forward, the Glendale Gateway Trust was formed in 1996, according to their website as 'an independent, charitable, community development trust set up to support the community of Glendale'. The Cheviot Centre, complete with its library, tourist information centre and small business facilities, now provides a vibrant community hub. The Trust currently also owns or manages commercial properties on the town's high street, the youth hostel and a number of affordable housing units, as well as undertaking many other activities for the benefit of people in the local area. In order to take forward its proposals, the Trust seeks out support from numerous organisations well beyond its locality; however, it is clear that any such support is to further its own priorities: the word 'independent' in its self-description on the website is purposeful.

This section has provided a description of shifts in thinking from an exogenous model of rural development to a model of networked development that has a clear localising tendency; it has charted the development of rural policies with a more territorial focus; and it has highlighted examples of how rural people have taken the initiative in bringing about much-needed local change. The rubric of localism would appear to embrace them all.

Localism in rural UK: discussion

This section aims to investigate further the aspects of rural localism described above, and to draw out insights these provide into 'localism' more generally. Specifically it asks whether the rural experiences noted above suggest a more nuanced elaboration of localism, or alternatively a divergence of rural experience from mainstream conceptualisations of localism. For the time being they are referred to as 'variations'.

There is a substantial literature on localism that has been addressed elsewhere in this book. We wish to highlight one paper, though, which synthesises much of this literature and develops it into a useful analytic framework of localism in Britain since 1997: Hildreth's article in *Local Economy* (2011) in which he develops three models of localism. His three models are of:

- conditional localism
- representative localism
- community localism.

Conditional localism is where, in the process of decentralisation, the 'centre' puts conditions on the local authority/community, such that they should accept the centre's policy objectives, priorities, standards, etc. Increasingly this has been accompanied by a set of managerial technologies such as targeting, audit and financial control, which are deployed to ensure that local institutions are accountable to, and do the bidding of, (central) government (MacKinnon, 2002).

Representative localism is where:

> local authorities are placed at the heart of local government in a democratic system and are seen to have an essential role to connect with and enable citizens to achieve their basic democratic right to participate in the conduct of public affairs. (Hildreth, 2011: 708)

Devolution should be to the 'lowest tier commensurate with their efficient and accountable delivery' (Hildreth, 2011: 708). For Hildreth, the emphasis in this model is on local representative leadership, which he sees as prevalent in most of Western Europe (but not the UK).

Community localism is the least well-specified model in Hildreth's paper. He discusses this as a process of decentralisation from the centre to individual citizens and local communities that could manifest themselves in a range of mainly unspecified ways. He provides two elaborations of this: the *commissioning option*, and the *community asset option*. The first reflects the growing tendency for government to commission other organisations to deliver 'public services'. The second is characterised by the local community taking over responsibility from the centre for the running of a service or a physical asset (e.g. a school or a bus route).

These models are regularly referred to in the discussion that follows. The text, though, is structured around three key areas where rural localism provides further elaboration of, or divergence from, mainstream conceptualisations.

Central/local relations

Academic commentary on UK central/local relations typically casts 'central' as central government and 'local' as local authorities. For the last 30 years, the long-term trend has been centralisation even though the prominent rhetoric from central government has been of decentralisation (Lodge and Muir, 2010). Notions of local participation and democracy associated with decentralisation are conceptualised as in tension with a set of managerial technologies such as targeting, audit and financial control which ensure central control, as noted above. This model of the relationship with central government exerting at-a-distance power over local government is aligned with Hildreth's conditional localism, while local democracy and participation are more aligned with his representative localism.

Conditional localism is broadly apparent in rural policies of the UK, while the extent of representative localism varies significantly between the jurisdictions of the devolved governments. So while Hildreth's assessment of local representative leadership being underdeveloped in the UK may reflect the reality in rural England, the Scottish model would appear much more predicated on representative localism where National Outcome and Single Outcome Agreements are agreed with each local authority. This has been enabled by the integration of all policy domains into a single national institution, and a focus on agreed outcomes. The approach is predicated on

> a hierarchy of shared outcome-based objectives which stimulate approaches that cut across conventional functional boundaries … the focus on outcomes and the negotiation of a set of National Outcomes has provided a framework for a different relationship between central and local government. (Elvidge, 2012: 43)

Thus national government agreed that local authorities would over time have increasing discretion to pursue the priority outcomes each had specified in a Single Outcome Agreement while in return local authorities agreed to incorporate aspects of the national priorities into their Agreements.

While conditional and representative localism and the tensions of central–local government relations highlighted in the literature can be evidenced in the rural UK, the rest of this section focuses on the 'variations' to the common narratives that rural policy and practice highlight. The first variation is that the 'central' actor that governs the local from a distance is not only the nation state but also the EU. Decisions are taken at the EU level on such aspects as the scope of the LEADER programme/approach, how much budget is allocated and the menu of measures available for use by member states. Within these parameters, each Member State's Plan for CAP Pillar 2 spending, subject to approval from Brussels, identifies which measures will be used, identifies the LEADER areas, can choose to enhance the budget from EU Pillar 1 and national sources, and so on. In the LEADER areas, their Local Action Groups (LAGs) make decisions over funding allocations, but this is severely limited by both the EU and central government's funding rules, and again each local strategy has to be approved centrally. In the UK, a major concern about the measures available under CAP Pillar 2 at the EU level is that so many can only benefit farmers and not other rural beneficiaries. Jacques Chirac, the French President at the time of the Pillar 2 inception, is reputed to have queried rhetorically whether the CAP was 'pour l'agriculture ou pour les coiffures' (for farmers or for hairdressers). For rural areas of the UK, the conditions imposed by the EU as a supranational power are highly significant and constraining.

The second 'variation' is that the local is so often conceived in the localism literature to be local authorities, in line with Hildreth's conditional localism. However, in UK rural (and urban) development the relationship is more often between the centre (EU or nation state) and a local governance structure, with 'governing styles in which boundaries between and within public and private sectors have become blurred' (Stoker, 1996: 2). Here, the predominant view is that the state acting on its own can no longer achieve its goals, and that for policies to meet diverse needs and circumstances there has to be a mobilisation of local actors, supported by partnership structures and arrangements (Furmankiewicz *et al.*, 2010; Goodwin, 1998). According to Goodwin (2003: 2), the increasing use of the term governance 'indicates a significant change in the processes by which rural society is governed and rural policy is delivered'. The LEADER LAGs are an example of such governance structures and changing processes. Each of these is a cross-sectoral partnership involving the public, private and voluntary sectors charged with developing inclusive participation of the whole community within their LEADER area.

While the EU's CAP conditionally empowers governance through LAGs at the local level, the government in England is furthering central/local relationships with organisations other than local authorities in rural areas, providing the third 'variation'. The Localism Act 2011 had an aim of transferring some powers to local communities (Lowndes and Pratchett, 2012) in urban and rural areas alike; however, in areas where they exist, the right to prepare Neighbourhood Development Plans, Neighbourhood Development Orders and Community Right to Build Orders (referred to here as Neighbourhood Planning) is given specifically to Parish Councils (PCs). These organisations cover almost all neighbourhoods and their hinterlands in rural areas but rarely exist in urban areas. So the latest manifestation of community-led planning in rural areas (but with many more conditions from central government than previous schemes) is a significant new power for PCs in England.

PCs, where they exist, add a neighbourhood tier to local government below the local authority tier. For example, Northumberland County Council (a unitary local authority) has more than 150 PCs within its boundaries. PCs hold elections alongside those for local authorities and have the right to raise a precept from the electorate via the local authority council tax. In terms of representative localism, although not named by Hildreth, PCs in theory meet his requirement of formal democratic mandate, while the LAGs do not. However, PCs 'in general inadequately represent their communities to meet the challenge of change because of their lack of power and resources. There is little local interest by the large majority of rural residents in most parish or community [Scotland] councils' (Carnegie UK Trust, 2007: 34–35) and most include co-opted members as much as elected representatives. LAGs, by contrast, have no formal democratic mandate but must build partnerships between representatives of the various sectors and encourage participation from the wider community. Such 'participative democracy' in rural areas can be argued to be at least as legitimate as the 'representative' leadership provided by many PCs.

The fourth variation on central/local relations from a rural development perspective is to reconceptualise the power of the state. The discussion so far has exposed the need for Hildreth's conditional localism to be extended so that local governance institutions are seen as recipients of the centre's conditions as well as local government. But within this conditional localism, rural development commentators identify not only the state exerting 'power over' the local, but also the state providing 'power to' do something in line with Stone's statement that 'what is at issue is not so much domination and subordination, as a capacity to act and accomplish goals' (1989: 229) and how that capacity might be built. Essentially, in networked rural development local actors are cast as the catalysts for change through collective, networked development. Rural communities gain support, and exchange information, through a multitude of internal and external *networks* – indeed these constitute one of the principal assets for community action and in building community capacity (Miller and Wallace, 2012; Shucksmith, 2012). In a practical sense, the state provides not only the financial resources and the associated conditions of use, but also becomes part of the wider network for local rural development and a key player in enabling the local action.

Within LEADER, each LAG is empowered to mobilise local resources and actors to undertake deliberative place-shaping. In this way, these new partnerships gain a greater capacity to act and so exhibit agency, reflexivity and resistance. Typically, there will be local authority representatives and personnel from agencies of the state within the membership of the LAG who bring their own expertise but also wider networks of resources and act to stimulate action and innovation rather than being the directing force in the partnership.

The central government department with responsibility for rural affairs in England (DEFRA) provides networking opportunities to the LAGs (and others) through its RDPE Network, and LAGs are encouraged and supported by the EU to visit LAGs in other parts of Europe. The 'central' state, then, provides conditional financial support to the LAGs, which in itself gives power to the LAGs to undertake appropriate local rural development, at least in spaces chosen and limited by the central state (McAreavey and Swindal, 2012); it provides for the local state to support (not direct) the actions of the partnership; and it also provides wider networking opportunities through information and visits across Europe to the LAGs, so extending their extra-local networks and their capacity to act.

This discussion of the role of the state in giving power to the local partnership to undertake local rural development has already hinted at the fifth 'variation' to be discussed here: to conceptualise the relationship in networked rural development as being the local with the extra-local as much as the central with the local. The 'extra-local' includes the wider political, institutional, trading and natural environments at many different scales from the global to the local, and extra-local institutional actors will emanate from all three sectors, not simply the public sector. So in addition to the state's role in empowering the LAGS, these are also empowered by the range of extra-local networks that they enjoy with non-state partners. For example, those Scottish communities that have purchased the landed estates on which they live, bringing them into community ownership, have drawn not only on their assets *in-place* but also on HIE's Community Land Unit, a network of sister organisations in Community Land Scotland, the expertise of supportive lawyers, academics and activists and an enlightened and supportive Scottish government's land reform legislation.

Community-led localism

Hildreth's model of community localism, although not fully developed, involves a decentralisation from the central and local state to citizens and local communities. This shift of responsibility supposes that the state has power to accomplish this, and initiates the change through legislation, policy schemes and so on. This type of model of community localism would seem to fit with some of the analysis above, which discusses networked rural development, and especially the example of LEADER, as an extended model of central/local relations. However, there is much evidence of networked rural development in the UK where the initiative comes from local people or where the state plays only an indirect or minor role in stimulating the action, which substantially extends Hildreth's model of community localism to include localism that is more 'community-led' rather than state-initiated. Attention in this section is hence turned to initiatives in local rural areas that aim to bring about development.

As described above in the section on 'Local initiative', there are myriad ways in which local people in rural areas have come together to bring about improvements in their local area. Our focus here is on positive action rather than resistance by local people. In some cases local people are triggered to action because of something that is missing or withdrawn from their local community (broadband, the village shop, public transport, for example). Such activity usually starts out with a single-issue focus, but in some cases will later mutate to take on a wider local agenda. For example, members of Bay Broadband, a local collective action in North Yorkshire to provide Robin Hood's Bay premises with broadband, claimed that if there ceased to be a need for community-run broadband services in the future they would find another local issue to resolve (Talbot, 2011).

The example elaborated in 'Local initiative' is of a more planned and comprehensive approach to community-led action, with its basis in an assessment of local need. Many of the schemes to encourage local plan-making have been initiated by government, although non-governmental organisations have often been employed to activate and administer the schemes locally. However, until the advent of Neighbourhood Planning in the Localism Act 2011, the government made no commitment to deliver on the priorities set out in community-led plans. This has frustrated some local groups such that the publication of the Plan has been the only direct outcome of the process (Gallent *et al.*, 2008), but others, like the Glendale Gateway Trust, are committed to taking responsibility for the delivery of the Plan (Moseley, 1997). Such local delivery organisations are set up and constituted by local people, very much independent of government, and this type of action may also be seen as a rejection of neoliberalism, i.e. promoting instead a much more communitarian approach to local rural development. These community-led organisations allow a more varied and radical approach than those designed by governments.

Such organisations are initiated and determined by local people, but in line with the networked rural development approach they need resources beyond the purely local. These organisations network with the extra-local, the boards of many will include local councillors, and resources from outside the locality are usually welcomed. In such cases, though, the local organisation typically asserts its independence, but will accept support from the public sector and/or grant-giving organisations that help meet its objectives. Some have also found means of financing themselves in ways that greatly reduce their dependency on the state (central or local) for funding: investment in local buildings or community share options, for example.

A key problem with community-led planning is that it is typically the 'more affluent and already active communities' (BDOR Limited, 2011: 12) that have the greater institutional capacity to act, with poorer communities lacking the knowledge, networks and ability to mobilise without external support. And such inequalities become self-reinforcing: 'areas where established partnerships have successfully encouraged communities to become proactively involved in regeneration tend to generate more applications to funding programmes, and have the advantage of experience and stable structures in bidding for new sources of funding' (Shucksmith, 2000a). There is therefore strong consensus among researchers and professionals that there is a need for capacity-building by the state in two respects. First, this is necessary to enable the most marginalised individuals to gain the confidence, competencies and skills they need to participate as active citizens in local civil societies. Second, this is necessary to allow new institutions and groups to emerge in less active places, enabling them to articulate a collective view on the form and content of regeneration for their locality and on how best to realise this vision. Without the state engaging in such an active, enabling role, inequalities between rural communities will widen and only some voices within communities will be heard.

Policy territorialisation

Although the introduction of Pillar 2, the Rural Development Regulation, was outlined earlier as a territorialisation of the CAP, it has hardly featured in the discussion of localism thus far. Our key question here is whether the second Pillar of the CAP (beyond the LEADER approach component) is only masquerading as localism, or indeed as policy territorialisation, and by extension whether theories of localism need to address this. From the perspective of those who advocate a territorial approach to rural development, whether conceived as networked rural development or place-shaping,

> the profound weakness of the new Rural Development Regulation becomes immediately apparent when the scope of its menu of eligible measures is compared with what needs to be addressed if failing rural areas are to be turned around economically and demographically. (Bryden and Hart, 2004: 342)

Instead it is dominated by agri-environment payments to farmers that are presented self-evidently as *sustainable* policy, even though they are recurrent (revenue) payments over a finite funding period rather than *investments*, in the terms of the OECD's new rural paradigm, and not addressed towards territorial rural development at all. The second Pillar of the CAP has effectively been captured by environmental and farming interests through the exercise of discursive power (Lowe and Ward, 2007; Shucksmith, 2009).

Some point also to the exercise of discursive power through the concept of 'multi-functionality' as pivotal in enabling the capture of the term 'rural development' by environmentalists and farming interests, so frustrating any shift from sectoral to territorial policies (e.g. Saraceno, 2009). The concept of multi-functionality was developed in the late 1990s to encapsulate the re-orientation of the agricultural sector towards the provision of environmental and other public goods (now termed ecosystem services). The inclusion of agricultural policies within WTO negotiations threatened the dismantling of agricultural protectionism, so stimulating farming lobbies and many governments to seek new justifications for remunerating farmers, in terms of agriculture's multi-functionality. Powerful interests within the bureaucracies, farmers unions and elsewhere therefore became engaged in the social and political construction of a discourse of multi-functionality and deployed this in pursuit of their own interests (Bryden, 2007), capturing the second Pillar of the CAP and frustrating attempts to shift the CAP from a sectoral policy towards more territorial rural development approaches, informed by evidence of the effectiveness of networked rural development and place-shaping. Naturally, this was also cloaked in claims of sustainability.

Conclusion

This chapter has examined localism through the lens of local rural development in the UK, which is commonly conceptualised and practised as networked rural development. In discussing networked rural development using common themes in the mainstream localism literature, and particularly using Hildreth's models, we have identified a number of distinctive features.

Commentators on rural localism and policy ask the question 'who leads?', rather than taking domination from the central state as their starting point. And for networked rural development the agency and leadership of local actors is emphasised, with the state (central and local) cast in an enabling role. If the agent of local development was set up by the central state, such as with LEADER, then the state's support might be conditional, but it should also be enabling and empowering. Where a group of local people take the initiative, in a Development Trust for example, then there may be a role for the state, central or local, but this should be on terms set by the local organisation. The state's (central and local) enabling role is in enhancing the local organisation's ability to act, ensuring that all local voices are heard and helping to build its capacity when necessary.

A further vital role for the state, of course, is to support and enable local rural development in places that have less capacity to act: in other words, to help build the capacity of those places that have not historically taken the initiative, and to ensure against inequality between places. In addition, the state plays the crucial role of ensuring non-local interests are represented, where appropriate – for example, in relation to global warming, national parks and so on. This raises the important question of who should pay for such regulation in the broader interest.

Networked rural development as a form of localism is about local people having greater control over local development. It is not, however, about them only drawing on local resources to do this. It is predicated on the need for local control but drawing on the resources of extra-local networks, with the state having an important role to play in places where local activity is already under way and where it is not. This form of localism would be significantly damaged by a reduced capacity in central and local government and in the voluntary and community sector as appears inevitable given the current and planned budget cuts. These circumstances raise the spectre of localism as reversion to 'self-help': in other words a bottom-up development model, in which rural communities are increasingly left to themselves without support from cash-strapped central or local government – with other external institutions and networks also under pressure from reduced resources. Some would say that this is the essence of the UK Coalition Government's 'Big Society' idea. This is a recipe for growing inequality and a 'two-speed countryside' (Shucksmith, 2012).

The central theme of recent thinking about rural development, and of the preceding sections, has been place-based, networked development actions. As we have seen, these employ concepts of assets, networks, capacity and local empowerment. But is networked localism and place-shaping enough? The recent EDORA study of processes of differentiation among rural areas of Europe (Copus and Hörnström, 2012) reveals the multi-scalar processes that influence rural change. The EDORA analysis presents authoritative evidence that at the macro scale there are clear and persistent patterns of structural differentiation, closely associated with disparities in economic performance between core and periphery; between the consumption countryside and agricultural and ex-industrial rural areas; and between Western and Eastern Europe, for example. At the micro scale, the authors find that the key issues do indeed relate to 'territorial capital' – tangible and intangible assets, institutional capacity, etc., as indicated above – which 'points to neo-endogenous forms of intervention, termed "local development" by the Fifth Cohesion Report', notably LEADER. 'However, EU policies such as those mentioned above can never be sufficient.' (p. 128). In sum, the authors conclude:

> there is still clear evidence that some aspects of rural change exhibit large scale systematic variation across the EU space. This suggests that there is still a strong argument for macro-scale diagnosis, strategic planning and intervention. Localised, place-based policy processes will not be sufficient. A two-tier structure is more appropriate. (Copus and Hörnström, 2012: 133)

Nor can networked localism be effective in the face of national and EU policies that are blind to the territorially differentiated impact they have. Most EU sector policies have been found to run counter to the objectives of territorial cohesion, including most notably the territorial impacts of the CAP (Shucksmith *et al.*, 2005). Within the UK, economic policy, social policy, housing policy and even science policy embody, if only implicitly, certain principles of spatial organisation and ordering, and these have too rarely been given explicit consideration. Instances of a new attention being paid to these issues include the requirement for all English policies to be 'rural-proofed', and the Welsh Assembly's study of the spatial dimensions of sectoral policy (Harris and Hooper, 2004). This issue was also identified in the OECD's review of rural policy in England (OECD, 2011), which scrutinised the policy and practice of rural-proofing across government and its agencies.

References

BDOR Limited. (2011) *Communities, Planning and Localism*, Gloucestershire: CPRE.

Bryden, J. (2007) Changes in rural policy and governance: The broader context, in A.K. Copus (ed.), *Continuity or Transformation? Perspectives on rural development in the Nordic countries*, Nordregio Report 2007.4, Stockholm.

Bryden, J. and Hart, K. (2004) *A New Approach to Rural Development*, Lewiston, NY: Edwin Mellen Press.

Carnegie UK Trust. (2007) *A Charter for Rural Communities*, Dunfermline: Carnegie UK Trust.

CEC. (2009) *Territorial Cohesion: Unleashing the territorial potential*, background document, Kiruna, December 2009.

Copus, A. and Hörnström, L. (eds) (2012) *The New Rural Europe: Towards a rural cohesion policy*, Stockholm: Nordregio.

EDORA. (2010) *European Development Opportunities for Rural Areas (EDORA) Draft Final Report*. Available at: www.espon.eu/main/Menu_Projects/Menu_AppliedResearch/edora.html.

Elvidge, J. (2012) *The Enabling State: A discussion paper*, Dunfermline: Carnegie UK Trust.

EU Commission. (1988) *The Future of Rural Society: Commission Communication, 29 July COM (88) 501*, Luxembourg: Office for Official Publication of the European Communities.

European Council. (1999) Council Regulation (EC) No 1257/1999 on Support for Rural Development from the European Agricultural Guidance and Guarantee Fund (EAGGF). Available at: http://defra.gov.uk/erd/docs/council.htm.

European Council. (2005) Council Regulation (EC) No 1698/2005 of 20 September 2005 on Support for Rural Development by the European Agricultural Fund for Rural Development (EAFRD). *Official Journal of the European Union L277*.

European Council. (2006) Council Decision of 20 February 2006 on Community Strategic Guidelines for Rural Development (Programming Period 2007 to 2013) (2006/144/EC). *Official Journal of the European Union L55*.

Furmankiewicz, M., Thompson, N. and Zielinska, M. (2010) Area based partnerships in rural Poland: The post accession experience, *Journal of Rural Studies*, 26: 52–62.

Gallent, N., Morphet, J. and Tewdwr-Jones, M. (2008) Parish plans and the spatial planning approach in England, *Town Planning Review*, 79(1): 1–29.

Goodwin, M. (1998) The governance of rural areas: Some emerging research issues and agendas, *Journal of Rural Studies*, 14(1): 5–12.

Goodwin, M. (2003) *Rural Governance: A review of relevant literature*, prepared for DEFRA, ESRC and Countryside Agency, Aberystwyth: University of Wales.

Harris, N. and Hooper, A. (2004) Rediscovering the 'spatial' in public policy and planning: An examination of the spatial content of sectoral policy documents, *Planning Theory and Practice*, 5(2): 147–169.

Healey, P. (2004) The treatment of space and place in the new strategic spatial planning of Europe, *International Journal of Urban and Regional Research*, 28(1): 45–67.

Hildreth, P. (2011) What is localism, and what implications do different models have for managing the local economy? *Local Economy*, 26: 702–714.

Lodge, G. and Muir, R. (2010) Localism under New Labour, *The Political Quarterly*, 81: S96–S107.

Lowe, P. and Ward, N. (2007) Sustainable rural economies, *Sustainable Development*, 15: 307–317.

Lowe, P., Murdoch, J. and Ward, N. (1995) Networks in rural development: Beyond exogenous and endogenous models, in J.D. van der Ploeg, and C. van Dijk (eds), *Beyond Modernisation*, Assen, the Netherlands: Van Gorcum, pp. 87–105.

Lowndes, V. and Pratchett, L. (2012) Local governance under the Coalition Government: Austerity, localism and the 'Big Society', *Local Government Studies*, 38: 21–40.

McAreavey, R. and Swindal, M. (2012) Rural governance: Participation, power and possibilities for action, in M. Shucksmith, D.L. Brown, S. Shortall, J. Vergunst and M.E. Warner (eds), *Rural Transformations and Rural Policies in the US and UK*, New York: Routledge.

MacKinnon, D. (2002) Rural governance and local involvement: Assessing state–community relations in the Scottish Highlands, *Journal of Rural Studies*, 18(3): 304–327.

Miller, M. and Wallace, J. (2012) *Rural Development Networks: A mapping exercise*, Dunfermline: Carnegie UK Trust.

Moseley, M. (1997) Parish appraisals as a tool of rural community development: An assessment of the British experience, *Planning Practice and Research*, 12(3): 197–212.

OECD. (2006) *The New Rural Paradigm: Policies and governance*, Paris: OECD.

OECD. (2008) *OECD Rural Policy Reviews: Scotland, UK 2008*. Available at: www.oecd-bookshop.org/oecd/display.asp?lang=EN&sf1=identifiers&st1=9789264041639.

OECD. (2011) *OECD Rural Policy Reviews: England, United Kingdom*. Available at: www.oecd.org/gov/regional-policy/oecdruralpolicyreviewsenglandunitedkingdom.htm.

Ploeg, J.D. van der and Long, A. (eds) (1994) *Born from Within: Practice and perspectives of endogenous rural development*, Assen, the Netherlands: Van Gorcum.

Ray, C. (2001) *Culture Economies*, Newcastle: Centre for Rural Economy, Newcastle University. Available at: www.ncl.ac.uk/cre/publish/Books/CultureEconfinal.pdf.

Saraceno, E. (2009) Pluriactivity and multifunctionality, paper presented at Brydenfest, Tarland.

Scottish Office. (1998) *Towards a Development Strategy for Rural Scotland*, London: HMSO.

Shucksmith, M. (2000a) *Exclusive Countryside? Social inclusion and regeneration in rural areas*, York: Joseph Rowntree Foundation.

Shucksmith, M. (2000b) Endogenous development, social capital and social inclusion: Perspectives from LEADER in the UK, *Sociologia Ruralis*, 40(2): 208–218.

Shucksmith, M. (2009) Are rural policies across Europe supporting sustainable ruralities? Invited plenary paper to XXIII European Society of Rural Sociology Congress, Vaasa, Finland.

Shucksmith, M. (2010) Dis-integrated rural development: Neo-endogenous rural development, planning and place-shaping in diffused power contexts, *Sociologia Ruralis*, 50: 1–15.

Shucksmith, M. (2012) *Future Directions in Rural Development?* Dunfermline: Carnegie UK Trust.

Shucksmith, M., Thomson, K. and Roberts, D. (2005) *The CAP and the Regions: The territorial impact of the Common Agricultural Policy*, Wallingford: CABI.

Stoker, G. (1996) Public–private partnerships and urban governance, in G. Stoker (ed.), *Partners in Urban Governance: European and American experience*, London: Macmillan.

Stone, C. (1989) *Regime Politics: Governing Atlanta 1946–1988*, Lawrence: University of Kansas Press.

Sturzaker, J. and Shucksmith, M. (2011) Planning for housing in rural England: Discursive power and social exclusion, *Town Planning Review*, 82(2): 169–193.

Talbot, H. (2011) *Rural Broadband: Local interventions to enhance delivery to rural areas*. Available at: www.northernruralnetwork.co.uk/archive/rural-broadband-local-interventions-to-enhance-delivery-to-rural-areas.

Ward, N. (2002) *Integrated Rural Development: A review of the literature*, Centre for Rural Research, University of Trondheim.

Ward, N. and McNicholas, K. (1998) Reconfiguring rural development in the UK: Objective 5b and the new rural governance, *Journal of Rural Studies*, 14: 27–39.

14
Epilogue: Promises and Pitfalls of Localism

Ali Madanipour and Simin Davoudi

The contributions in this book have explored the ambiguous character of the local and localism largely through the framework of political and ecological controversies. The aim of this final note is to chart some of the promises and pitfalls of the local and localism that have emerged from the discussions and in relation to two central themes of the book: democracy and sustainability.

Localism and the local

The ideas and practices of localism, understood as 'favouring the local', can lead to both progressive and regressive paths. On the one hand, localism can enable local democratic capacity-building and the opening up of possibilities for more sustainable practices. On the other hand, it can encourage parochialism and, paradoxically, further centralisation of power. Localism is interpreted in different ways, from a re-ordering and liberalisation of political spaces to a site of empowerment and a framework for social integration and community-building, and from a locus of knowledge-generation to the localisation of economic activities and a platform for resistance and environmental activism. One important theme that has emerged from the preceding chapters is the acknowledgement of the ontological, contextual and perspectival plurality of the local and localism. We elaborate on these in turn.

First, localism is not a single phenomenon but rather a complex and multidimensional process that can be directed towards diverging and even conflicting paths by diverse forces. This implies that the ambivalence of localism is partly due to its inherent ontological multiplicity. Second, localism is a situated process that unfolds in specific contexts. It can take different characters and lead to varying outcomes depending on factors such as: the context in which it takes place, the actors who initiate the process, the level of inclusion and exclusion of other actors, the nature of what is upgraded to the centre and what is downgraded to the margin, the nature and influence of extra-local forces and the framework of interactions between different power relations. This means that the ambivalence of localism is also due to its social and historical context, its political and economic makeup and its conditions of possibility. Third, various interpretations of localism depend on the perspectives through which it is analysed. It reflects the analysts' ideological positions, disciplinary backgrounds, methodological tools, personal experiences and life trajectories. What is interpreted as a welcoming development by one analyst may be seen as a threatening future by another, reflecting as much the complexity of the phenomena being described as the diversity of the analysts' dispositions. In other words, the ambivalence of localism may also lie in the diversity of the perspectives that seek to understand it.

Furthermore, the scale and scope of what is 'local' is wide-ranging, so any attempt to define it with a degree of precision is fraught with difficulty if not impossibility. The geography of 'the local' spans from a single street to an entire country. Under the conditions of intensified global interconnections, the local can never be confined to any particular spatial limits. However, while the local can be simultaneously part of a series of processes stretching far beyond the local, individuals in everyday life continue to have a sense of what the local means to them. The question emerging from the discussions in the book is whether a distinction should be made between a phenomenological conception of locality and its analytical conception. The former refers to people's sense of a sphere of locality around them. The latter refers to the multiplicity and relationality of the local. The analytical conception of the local emphasises that its meanings differ according to the point of reference, the subject of interest and the context of analysis. It challenges the imagined fixity of the phenomenological understanding of the local.

Localism and democracy

Several contributions in this book have approached localism in its political sense engaging in particular with the debate about decentralisation, which is often defined as: a change in the balance of power in favour of the local, a shift in governance towards a focus on places, and the extent of autonomy that the institutions of a locality can claim. They have problematised the idea that localism is the answer to democratisation and demonstrated the complexity of political relations and implications that arise from localism. Frequently, decentralisation and autonomy are expected to be the twin elements of an institutional transformation in favour of the localities. However, the form and impact of decentralisation varies in different governance traditions depending on the extent to which favouring the local is embedded in political institutions and cultures and shared by different shades of political opinions. Another controversy centres on the question of capacity. As a number of chapters in this volume have shown, the capacity for local autonomy is asymmetric. A peaceful, prosperous, confident and well-connected locality is well-placed to benefit from a process that favours the local. Localism in this context may lead to the reconfirmation of the status quo and furthering of the existing privileges. In such circumstances, active networks and civic enterprises are more likely to be able to fill the gaps left by the withdrawal of the state institutions and support. However, if a locality is riddled with conflict, unable to mobilise resources, exposed to the dominance of larger players and located unfavourably in the broader political and economic processes, localism is likely to find a different meaning. It may well become a trapdoor leading to the abandoning of people and places in the face of potentially unsurmountable challenges. Moreover, if support for localism is formulated as technical rather than political concerns, and if localist institutions and processes are not democratically legitimate, localism can further entrench inequalities and fail to be the solution that its advocates promise.

The pressure for decentralisation is closely associated with the structural changes in the political economy of Western countries in the last 30 years, in which the globalisation of the relations between capital and labour have transformed the intra-national relationships between the state and the market and between the employers and employees. These changes have intensified as a result of the global economic crisis of 2007–2008, further encouraging the state to transfer some of its roles to the market and civil society. The implications of such decentralisation may be presented as democratisation, enhancement of local identities and development of local capacities to take control of their future, but they can also be seen as a process of deregulation, extending marketised relations to new places that, given the nature of globalised markets, can contradict these ambitions. The local becomes a player in the global marketplace, forced to embrace the concepts and methods of competition, from branding, networking and product differentiation to the suppression and neglect of the weaker elements of a locality.

An inherent assumption about localism is the positive values that are associated with the local. However, as the cases of conflicting cities show, the local can also become a contested site of the politics of identity. In contexts such as these, the formulas used to address local politics of, for example, planning and regeneration activities that are formulated for the more peaceful or cosmopolitan places, may in fact exacerbate adversities and divisions. As the cases of local planning in England show, local actors may follow and replicate the models used by higher tiers of authority and thus fail to enhance active participation of local civil society groups. From a distance, the local appears to be a unified political entity, but from close up the local is a world of complex social relations, power struggles and exclusionary processes.

Having said that, it is important to note that the local is also the sphere of everyday life, habits and familiarity, personal attachments and face-to-face interactions. It is concrete, here and now, rather than abstract, distant and alien. This does not mean that the local is always a force for good, but it perhaps explains why so much hope and aspiration is invested in the local, however defined. While the local does not cover every aspect of life or indeed collectivity, it offers a sphere of action that deserves careful consideration. Such attention is imbued with many potential promises for the improvement of the quality of life in places, made possible through resistance, activism, deliberation, collaboration, mobilisation and collective action.

Localism and sustainability

William Rees starts the third part of the book by providing the evidence for the growing global ecological crises. For him, the intelligent solution is one that centres on the reduction of humanity's ecological footprint through a global coordination of 'an orderly contraction'. This means creating an economy that uses much less natural resources and is contained within its ecological carrying capacities. Such an economy, he argues, is a de-globalising and re-localising economy. Here, the local is defined in terms of ecosystems and localities are those that function as 'complete quasi-independent human ecosystems'. They are bioregions in which a dense human settlement is surrounded by and lived within the limits of the essential supportive ecosystems.

Advocating re-localisation as a path to sustainability is an early and important line of argument in environmental debates. The idea of a locality in which production and consumption of goods and services are largely localised has been envisaged as a model for a sustainable future. However, as other contributions to this book have shown, local action on its own may not be sufficient for addressing the global ecological crisis. Equating localism with environmental sustainability risks a 'localist trap' similar to equating localism with democracy. Decisions made by autonomous local communities are not necessarily based on environmental considerations. The path to sustainability requires action at all levels, and in a highly interdependent world it is difficult to envisage how global environmental/developmental problems can be effectively addressed without some form of global coordination and action. This, however, is not to suggest that the local, however defined, does not matter. On the contrary, the local may offer a place of experimentation, innovation and inspiration. Resisting unsustainable practices that threaten a locality may raise questions on wider environmental concerns. Favouring the local does not de-politicise the tensions between the dynamics of economic growth, democratic governance and ecological sustainability.

The contributions to this book acknowledge both the pitfalls and the promises of favouring the local. The latter, however, needs to be qualified by three key considerations: localities are not similar to each other, they are not internally homogeneous and they are not detached from the rest of the world. Treating them as unified, homogeneous and isolated entities would lead to misguided understanding and action.

Index

Note: page numbers in italic type refer to Figures; those in bold type refer to Tables.